Troubleshooting and Maintaining Cisco IP Networks (TSHOOT) Foundation Learning Guide

Amir Ranjbar,
CCIE No. 8669

Cisco Press

800 East 96th Street

Indianapolis, IN 46240

Troubleshooting and Maintaining Cisco IP Networks (TSHOOT) Foundation Learning Guide

Amir Ranjbar

Published by:
Cisco Press
800 East 96th Street
Indianapolis, IN 46240 USA

Printed in the United States of America

Second Printing: January 2016

Library of Congress Control Number: 2014955936

ISBN-13: 978-1-58720-455-5

ISBN-10: 1-58720-455-X

Warning and Disclaimer

This book is designed to provide information about the Troubleshooting and Maintaining Cisco IP Networks (TSHOOT) course, which is an element of the CCNP Routing and Switching certification curriculum. Every effort has been made to make this book as complete and as accurate as possible, but no warranty or fitness is implied.

The information is provided on an "as is" basis. The author, Cisco Press, and Cisco Systems, Inc. shall have neither liability nor responsibility to any person or entity with respect to any loss or damages arising from the information contained in this book or from the use of the discs or programs that may accompany it.

The opinions expressed in this book belong to the author and are not necessarily those of Cisco Systems, Inc.

Trademark Acknowledgments

All terms mentioned in this book that are known to be trademarks or service marks have been appropriately capitalized. Cisco Press or Cisco Systems, Inc., cannot attest to the accuracy of this information. Use of a term in this book should not be regarded as affecting the validity of any trademark or service mark.

Special Sales

For information about buying this title in bulk quantities, or for special sales opportunities (which may include electronic versions; custom cover designs; and content particular to your business, training goals, marketing focus, or branding interests), please contact our corporate sales department at corpsales@pearsoned.com or (800) 382-3419.

For government sales inquiries, please contact governmentsales@pearsoned.com.

For questions about sales outside the U.S., please contact international@pearsoned.com.

Feedback Information

At Cisco Press, our goal is to create in-depth technical books of the highest quality and value. Each book is crafted with care and precision, undergoing rigorous development that involves the unique expertise of members from the professional technical community.

Readers' feedback is a natural continuation of this process. If you have any comments regarding how we could improve the quality of this book, or otherwise alter it to better suit your needs, you can contact us through email at feedback@ciscopress.com. Please make sure to include the book title and ISBN in your message.

We greatly appreciate your assistance.

Publisher: Paul Boger	**Associate Publisher:** Dave Dusthimer
Business Operation Manager, Cisco Press: Jan Cornelssen	**Acquisitions Editor:** Mary Beth Ray
Managing Editor: Sandra Schroeder	**Development Editor:** Ellie Bru
Senior Project Editor: Tonya Simpson	**Copy Editor:** Keith Cline
Technical Editor: Ted Kim	**Team Coordinator:** Vanessa Evans
Cover Designer: Mark Shirar	**Composition:** Trina Wurst
Indexer: Lisa Stumpf	**Proofreader:** Debbie Williams

	Americas Headquarters Cisco Systems, Inc. San Jose, CA	**Asia Pacific Headquarters** Cisco Systems (USA) Pte. Ltd. Singapore	**Europe Headquarters** Cisco Systems International BV Amsterdam, The Netherlands

Cisco has more than 200 offices worldwide. Addresses, phone numbers, and fax numbers are listed on the Cisco Website at **www.cisco.com/go/offices.**

CCDE, CCENT, Cisco Eos, Cisco HealthPresence, the Cisco logo, Cisco Lumin, Cisco Nexus, Cisco StadiumVision, Cisco TelePresence, Cisco WebEx, DCE, and Welcome to the Human Network are trademarks; Changing the Way We Work, Live, Play, and Learn and Cisco Store are service marks; and Access Registrar, Aironet, AsyncOS, Bringing the Meeting To You, Catalyst, CCDA, CCDP, CCIE, CCIP, CCNA, CCNP, CCSP, CCVP, Cisco, the Cisco Certified Internetwork Expert logo, Cisco IOS, Cisco Press, Cisco Systems, Cisco Systems Capital, the Cisco Systems logo, Cisco Unity, Collaboration Without Limitation, EtherFast, EtherSwitch, Event Center, Fast Step, Follow Me Browsing, FormShare, GigaDrive, HomeLink, Internet Quotient, IOS, iPhone, iQuick Study, IronPort, the IronPort logo, LightStream, Linksys, MediaTone, MeetingPlace, MeetingPlace Chime Sound, MGX, Networkers, Networking Academy, Network Registrar, PCNow, PIX, PowerPanels, ProConnect, ScriptShare, SenderBase, SMARTnet, Spectrum Expert, StackWise, The Fastest Way to Increase Your Internet Quotient, TransPath, WebEx, and the WebEx logo are registered trademarks of Cisco Systems, Inc. and/or its affiliates in the United States and certain other countries.

All other trademarks mentioned in this document or website are the property of their respective owners. The use of the word partner does not imply a partnership relationship between Cisco and any other company. (0812R)

About the Author

Amir Ranjbar, CCIE No. 8669, is a Certified Cisco Systems Instructor and a senior network consultant. Operating under his own corporation, AMIRACAN Inc., Amir offers his training services to Global Knowledge Network, his consulting expertise to a variety of clients (mainly Internet service providers), and his technical writing skills to Cisco Press (Pearson Education, Inc.). Born in Tehran, Iran, Amir immigrated to Canada in 1983 at the age of 16 and completed his Master's degree in knowledge-based systems (a branch in artificial intelligence [AI]) in 1991. He has been involved in training, consulting, and technical writing for the greater part of his career. Amir Ranjbar can be contacted through his email address aranjbar@amiracan.com.

About the Technical Reviewer

Ted Kim, CCIE No. 22769 (Routing and Switching and Service Provider), has 10 years of experience in the IT industry, with a focus on data center technologies during the past several years. He has experience with designing, implementing, and troubleshooting large enterprise environments. Ted's networking career began at Johns Hopkins as a network engineer, and he has been with Cisco since 2013 as a network consulting engineer.

Dedication

I dedicate this book to my father, Mr. Kavos Ranjbar, whom I lost on January 2, 2013. I wish we could all be so loving, helpful, and generous, yet humble, peaceful, and gentle, just like my dad.

Acknowledgments

This book is the result of work done by many individuals. I would like to offer my sincere gratitude to all of them, whether we worked together directly or otherwise. Mary Beth Ray, Ellie Bru, Tonya Simpson, Keith Cline, Vanessa Evans, Mark Shirar, Trina Wurst, and Lisa Stumpf, please accept my most sincere gratitude for the time and effort you put into this project. I wish I could attend the next Pearson Education social gathering and thank you all in person! Ted Kim, thank you for your technical review and feedback; I hope to meet you someday and thank you in person, too.

Contents at a Glance

Contents

Icons Used in This Book

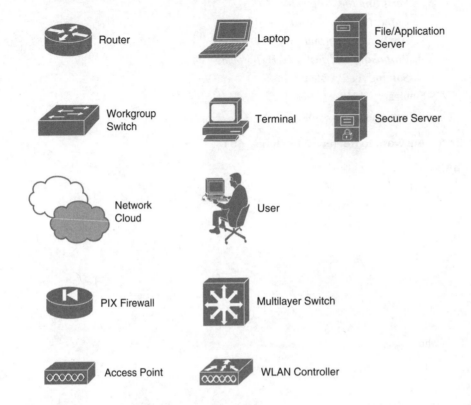

Command Syntax Conventions

The conventions used to present command syntax in this book are the same conventions used in the IOS Command Reference. The Command Reference describes these conventions as follows:

- **Boldface** indicates commands and keywords that are entered literally as shown. In actual configuration examples and output (not general command syntax), boldface indicates commands that are manually input by the user (such as a **show** command).

- *Italic* indicates arguments for which you supply actual values.

- Vertical bars (|) separate alternative, mutually exclusive elements.

- Square brackets ([ ]) indicate an optional element.

- Braces ({ }) indicate a required choice.

- Braces within brackets ([{ }]) indicate a required choice within an optional element.

Introduction

This book is based on the Cisco Systems TSHOOT course, which was recently introduced as part of the CCNP curriculum. It provides troubleshooting and maintenance information and examples that relate to Cisco routing and switching. It is assumed that readers know and understand as much Cisco routing and switching background as covered in the Cisco ROUTE and SWITCH courses. The book is enough to prepare you for the TSHOOT exam, too.

Teaching troubleshooting is not an easy task. This book introduces you to many troubleshooting methodologies and identifies the benefits of different techniques. Technical routing and switching topics are briefly reviewed, but the emphasis is on troubleshooting commands, and most important, this book presents many troubleshooting examples. Chapter review questions will help you evaluate how well you absorbed material within each chapter. The questions are also an excellent supplement for exam preparation.

Who Should Read This Book?

Those individuals who want to learn about modern troubleshooting methodologies and techniques and want to see several relevant examples will find this book very useful. This book is most suitable for those who have some prior routing and switching knowledge but would like to learn more or otherwise enhance their troubleshooting skill set. Readers who want to pass the Cisco TSHOOT exam can find all the content they need to successfully do so in this book. The Cisco Networking Academy CCNP TSHOOT course students will use this book as their official textbook.

Cisco Certifications and Exams

Cisco offers four levels of routing and switching certification, each with an increasing level of proficiency: Entry, Associate, Professional, and Expert. These are commonly known by their acronyms CCENT (Cisco Certified Entry Networking Technician), CCNA (Cisco Certified Network Associate), CCNP (Cisco Certified Network Professional), and CCIE (Cisco Certified Internetworking Expert). There are others, too, but this book focuses on the certifications for enterprise networks.

For the CCNP certification, you must pass exams on a series of CCNP topics, including the SWITCH, ROUTE, and TSHOOT exams. For most exams, Cisco does not publish the scores needed for passing. You need to take the exam to find that out for yourself.

To see the most current requirements for the CCNP certification, go to Cisco.com and click **Training and Events**. There you can find out other exam details such as exam topics and how to register for an exam.

The strategy you use to prepare for the TSHOOT exam might differ slightly from strategies used by other readers, mainly based on the skills, knowledge, and experience you have already obtained. For instance, if you have attended the TSHOOT course, you might take a different approach than someone who learned troubleshooting through on-the-job training. Regardless of the strategy you use or the background you have, this book is designed to help you get to the point where you can pass the exam with the least amount of time required.

How This Book Is Organized

Although this book can be read cover to cover, it is designed to be flexible and allow you to easily move between chapters to cover only the material for which you might need additional remediation. The chapters can be covered in any order, although some chapters are related to and build upon each other. If you do intend to read them all, the order in the book is an excellent sequence to follow.

Each core chapter covers a subset of the topics on the CCNP TSHOOT exam. The chapters cover the following topics:

- Chapter 1 introduces the troubleshooting principles and discusses the most common troubleshooting approaches.

- Chapter 2 defines structured troubleshooting and analyzes all the subprocesses of structured troubleshooting.

- Chapter 3 introduces structured network maintenance and discusses network maintenance processes and procedures. Network maintenance services and tools, along with how you can integrate troubleshooting into the network maintenance process, are also presented in this chapter.

- Chapter 4 reviews the Layer 2 switching and Layer 3 routing processes and shows how to do selective information gathering using the IOS **show** command, **debug** command, ping, and Telnet.

- Chapter 5 discusses troubleshooting tools: traffic-capturing features and tools, information gathering with SNMP, information gathering with NetFlow, and network event notification with EEM.

- Chapters 6 through 10 are all troubleshooting cases. Each chapter is about a different network with many different problems. Each problem is dealt with in the form of a real-life trouble ticket, and it is fixed following the structured troubleshooting methodology using the appropriate approach. All stages of troubleshooting, including fact gathering, are presented with output from Cisco IOS routers and switches. The network diagrams for Chapters 6 through 10 appear at the beginning and end of each chapter. For easier reference, a PDF of these network diagrams is available to download and print out or read on your e-device. Go to ciscopress.com/title/9781587204555 and click on the Downloads tab.

There is also an appendix that has answers to the review questions found at the end of each chapter.

Chapter 1

Troubleshooting Methods

This chapter covers the following topics:

- Troubleshooting principles
- Common troubleshooting approaches
- Troubleshooting example using six different approaches

Most modern enterprises depend heavily on the smooth operation of their network infrastructure. Network downtime usually translates to loss of productivity, revenue, and reputation. Network troubleshooting is therefore one of the essential responsibilities of the network support group. The more efficiently and effectively the network support personnel diagnose and resolve problems, the lower impact and damages will be to business. In complex environments, troubleshooting can be a daunting task, and the recommended way to diagnose and resolve problems quickly and effectively is by following a structured approach. Structured network troubleshooting requires well-defined and documented troubleshooting procedures.

This chapter defines troubleshooting and troubleshooting principles. Next, six different troubleshooting approaches are described. The third section of this chapter presents a troubleshooting example based on each of the six troubleshooting approaches.

Troubleshooting Principles

Troubleshooting is the process that leads to the diagnosis and, if possible, resolution of a problem. Troubleshooting is usually triggered when a person reports a problem. In modern and sophisticated environments that deploy proactive network monitoring tools and techniques, a failure/problem may be discovered and even fixed/resolved before end users notice or business applications get affected by it.

Some people say that a problem does not exist until it is noticed, perceived as a problem, and reported as a problem. This implies that you need to differentiate between a problem, as experienced by the user, and the actual cause of that problem. The time a problem is reported is not necessarily the same time at which the event causing the problem happened. Also, the reporting user generally equates the problem to the symptoms, whereas the troubleshooter often equates the problem to the root cause. For example, if the Internet connection fails on Saturday in a small company, it is usually not a problem, but you can be sure that it will turn into a problem on Monday morning if it is not fixed before then. Although this distinction between symptoms and cause of a problem might seem philosophical, you need to be aware of the potential communication issues that might arise from it.

Generally, reporting of a problem triggers the troubleshooting process. Troubleshooting starts by defining the problem. The second step is diagnosing the problem, during which information is gathered, the problem definition is refined, and possible causes for the problem are proposed. Eventually, this process should lead to a hypothesis for the root cause of the problem. At this time, possible solutions need to be proposed and evaluated. Next, the best solution is selected and implemented. Figure 1-1 illustrates the main elements of a structured troubleshooting approach and the transition possibilities from one step to the next.

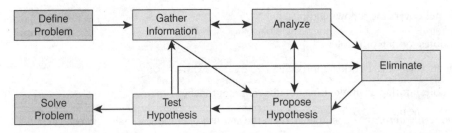

Figure 1-1   *Flow Chart of a Structured Troubleshooting Approach*

Note   It is noteworthy, however, that the solution to a network problem cannot always be readily implemented and an interim workaround might have to be proposed. The difference between a solution and a workaround is that a solution resolves the root cause of the problem, whereas a workaround only alleviates the symptoms of the problem.

Although problem reporting and resolution are definitely essential elements of the troubleshooting process, most of the time is spent in the diagnostic phase. One might even believe that diagnosis is all troubleshooting is about. Nevertheless, within the context of network maintenance, problem reporting and resolution are indeed essential parts of troubleshooting. Diagnosis is the process of identifying the nature and cause of a problem. The main elements of this process are as follows:

- **Gathering information:** Gathering information happens after the problem has been reported by the user (or anyone). This might include interviewing all parties (user) involved, plus any other means to gather relevant information. Usually, the problem report does not contain enough information to formulate a good hypothesis without first gathering more information. Information and symptoms can be gathered directly, by observing processes, or indirectly, by executing tests.

- **Analyzing information:** After the gathered information has been analyzed, the troubleshooter compares the symptoms against his knowledge of the system, processes, and baselines to separate normal behavior from abnormal behavior.

- **Eliminating possible causes:** By comparing the observed behavior against expected behavior, some of the possible problem causes are eliminated.

- **Formulating/proposing a hypothesis:** After gathering and analyzing information and eliminating the possible causes, one or more potential problem causes remain. The probability of each of these causes will have to be assessed and the most likely cause proposed as the hypothetical cause of the problem.

- **Testing the hypothesis:** The hypothesis must be tested to confirm or deny that it is the actual cause of the problem. The simplest way to do this is by proposing a solution based on this hypothesis, implementing that solution, and verifying whether this solved the problem. If this method is impossible or disruptive, the hypothesis can be strengthened or invalidated by gathering and analyzing more information.

All troubleshooting methods include the elements of gathering and analyzing information, eliminating possible causes, and formulating and testing hypotheses. Each of these steps has its merits and requires some time and effort; how and when one moves from one step to the next is a key factor in the success level of a troubleshooting exercise. In a scenario where you are troubleshooting a complex problem, you might go back and forth between different stages of troubleshooting: Gather some information, analyze the information, eliminate some of the possibilities, gather more information, analyze again, formulate a hypothesis, test it, reject it, eliminate some more possibilities, gather more information, and so on.

If you do not take a structured approach to troubleshooting and do troubleshooting in an ad hoc fashion, you might eventually find the solution; however, the process in general will be very inefficient. Another drawback of ad hoc troubleshooting is that handing the job over to someone else is very hard to do; the progress results are mainly lost. This can happen even if the troubleshooter wants to resume his own task after he has stopped for a while, perhaps to take care of another matter. A structured approach to troubleshooting, regardless of the exact method adopted, yields more predictable results in the long run. It also makes it easier to pick up where you left off or hand the job over to someone else without losing any effort or results.

A troubleshooting approach that is commonly deployed both by inexperienced and experienced troubleshooters is called shoot-from-the-hip. After a very short period of gathering information, taking this approach, the troubleshooter quickly makes a change to see if it solves the problem. Even though it may seem like random troubleshooting on the surface, it is not. The reason is that the guiding principle for this method is prior and usually vast knowledge of common symptoms and their corresponding causes, or simply extensive relevant experience in a particular environment or application. This technique might be quite effective for the experienced troubleshooter most times, but it usually does not yield the same results for the inexperienced troubleshooter. Figure 1-2 shows how the "shoot-from-the-hip" approach goes about solving a problem, spending almost no effort in analyzing the gathered information and eliminating possibilities.

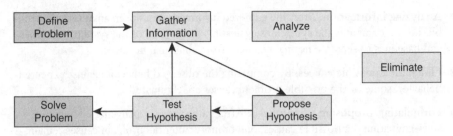

Figure 1-2   *Shoot-from-the-Hip*

Assume that a user reports a LAN performance problem and in 90 percent of the past cases with similar symptoms, the problem has been caused by duplex mismatch between users' workstations (PC or laptop) and the corresponding access switch port. The solution has been to configure the switch port for 100-Mbps full duplex. Therefore, it sounds reasonable to quickly verify the duplex setting of the switch port to which the user connects and change it to 100-Mbps full duplex to see whether that fixes the problem. When it works, this method can be very effective because it takes very little time. Unfortunately, the downside of this method is that if it does not work, you have not come any closer to a possible solution, you have wasted some time (both yours and users'), and you might possibly have caused a bit of frustration. Experienced troubleshooters use this method to great effect. The key factor in using this method effectively is knowing when to stop and switch to a more methodical (structured) approach.

Structured Troubleshooting Approaches

Troubleshooting is not an exact science, and a particular problem can be diagnosed and sometimes even solved in many different ways. However, when you perform structured troubleshooting, you make continuous progress, and usually solve the problem faster than it would take using an ad hoc approach. There are many different structured troubleshooting approaches. For some problems, one method might work better, whereas for others, another method might be more suitable. Therefore, it is beneficial for the troubleshooter to be familiar with a variety of structured approaches and select the best method or combination of methods to solve a particular problem.

A structured troubleshooting method is used as a guideline through a troubleshooting process. The key to all structured troubleshooting methods is systematic elimination of hypothetical causes and narrowing down on the possible causes. By systematically eliminating possible problem causes, you can reduce the scope of the problem until you manage to isolate and solve the problem. If at some point you decide to seek help or hand the task over to someone else, your findings can be of help to that person and your efforts are not wasted. Commonly used troubleshooting approaches include the following:

- **The top-down approach:** Using this approach, you work from the Open Systems Interconnection (OSI) model's application layer down to the physical layer. The OSI seven-layer networking model and TCP/IP four-layer model are shown side by side in Figure 1-3 for your reference.

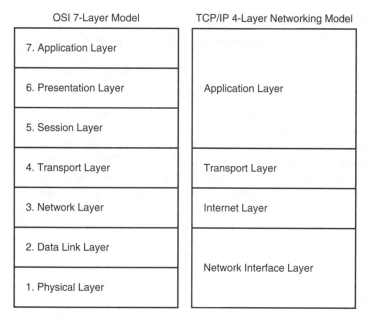

Figure 1-3   *The OSI and TCP/IP Networking Models*

- **The bottom-up approach:** This approach starts from the OSI model's physical layer and moves up toward the application layer.

- **The divide-and-conquer approach:** Using this approach, you start in the middle of the OSI model's stack (usually the network layer), and then, based on your findings, you move up or down the OSI stack.

- **The follow-the-path approach:** This approach is based on the path that packets take through the network from source to destination.

- **The spot-the-differences approach:** As the name implies, this approach compares network devices or processes that are operating correctly to devices or processes that are not operating as expected and gathers clues by spotting significant differences. In case the problem occurred after a change on a single device was implemented, the spot-the differences approach can pinpoint the problem cause by focusing on the difference between the device configurations, before and after the problem was reported.

- **The move-the-problem approach:** The strategy of this troubleshooting approach is to physically move components and observe whether the problem moves with the moved components.

The sections that follow describe each of these methods in more detail.

The Top-Down Troubleshooting Approach

The top-down troubleshooting method uses the OSI model as a guiding principle. One of the most important characteristics of the OSI model is that each layer depends on the underlying layers for its operation. This implies that if you find a layer to be operational, you can safely assume that all underlying layers are fully operational as well.

Let's assume that you are researching a problem of a user that cannot browse a particular website and you find that you can establish a TCP connection on port 80 from this host to the server and get a response from the server (see Figure 1-4). In this situation, it is reasonable to conclude that the transport layer and all layers below must be fully functional between the client and the server and that this is most likely a client or server problem (most likely at application, presentation, or session layer) and not a network problem. Be aware that in this example it is reasonable to conclude that Layers 1 through 4 must be fully operational, but it does not definitively prove this. For instance, nonfragmented packets might be routed correctly, whereas fragmented packets are dropped. The TCP connection to port 80 might not uncover such a problem.

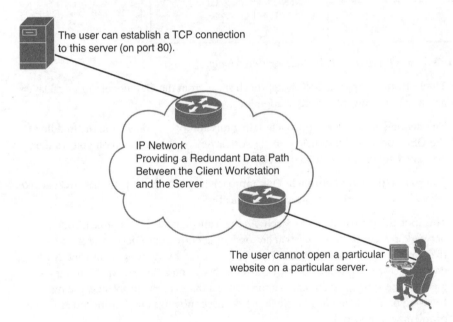

The user can establish a TCP connection
to this server (on port 80).

IP Network
Providing a Redundant Data Path
Between the Client Workstation
and the Server

The user cannot open a particular
website on a particular server.

Figure 1-4 *Application Layer Failure*

Essentially, the goal of the top-down approach is to find the highest OSI layer that is still working. All devices and processes that work on that layer or layers below are then eliminated from the scope of the troubleshooting. It might be clear that this approach is most effective if the problem is on one of the higher OSI layers. It is also one of the most straightforward troubleshooting approaches, because problems reported by users are typically defined as application layer problems, so starting the troubleshooting process at that layer is a natural thing to do. A drawback or impediment to this approach is that you need to have access to the client's application layer software to initiate the troubleshooting process, and if the software is only installed on a small number of machines, your troubleshooting options might be limited.

The Bottom-Up Troubleshooting Approach

The bottom-up troubleshooting approach also uses the OSI model as its guiding principle with the physical layer (bottom layer of the OSI seven-layer network model) as the starting point. In this approach, you work your way layer by layer up toward the application layer and verify that relevant network elements are operating correctly. You try to eliminate more and more potential problem causes so that you can narrow down the scope of the potential problems.

Let's assume that you are researching a problem of a user that cannot browse a particular website and while you are verifying the problem, you find that the user's workstation is not even able to obtain an IP address through the DHCP process (see Figure 1-5). In this situation it is reasonable to suspect lower layers of the OSI model and take a bottom-up troubleshooting approach.

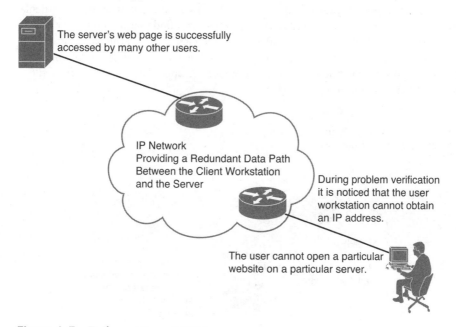

The server's web page is successfully accessed by many other users.

IP Network
Providing a Redundant Data Path
Between the Client Workstation
and the Server

During problem verification it is noticed that the user workstation cannot obtain an IP address.

The user cannot open a particular website on a particular server.

Figure 1-5   *Failure at Lower OSI Layers*

A benefit of the bottom-up approach is that all the initial troubleshooting takes place on the network, so access to clients, servers, or applications is not necessary until a very late stage in the troubleshooting process. In certain environments, especially those where many old and outdated devices and technologies are still in use, many network problems are hardware related. The bottom-up approach is very effective under those circumstances. A disadvantage of this method is that, in large networks, it can be a time-consuming process because a lot of effort will be spent on gathering and analyzing data and you always start from the bottom layer. The best bottom-up approach is to first reduce the scope of the problem using a different strategy and then switch to the bottom-up approach for clearly bounded parts of the network topology.

The Divide-and-Conquer Troubleshooting Approach

The divide-and-conquer troubleshooting approach strikes a balance between the top-down and bottom-up troubleshooting approaches. If it is not clear which of the top-down or bottom-up approaches will be more effective for a particular problem, an alternative is to start in the middle (usually from the network layer) and perform some tests such as ping and trace. Ping is an excellent connectivity testing tool. If the test is successful, you can assume that all lower layers are functional, and so you can start a bottom-up troubleshooting starting from the network layer. However, if the test fails, you can start a top-down troubleshooting starting from the network layer.

Let's assume that you are researching a problem of a user who cannot browse a particular website and that while you are verifying the problem you find that the user's workstation can successfully ping the server's IP address (see Figure 1-6). In this situation, it is reasonable to assume that the physical, data link, and network layers of the OSI model are in good working condition, and so you examine the upper layers, starting from the transport layer in a bottom-up approach.

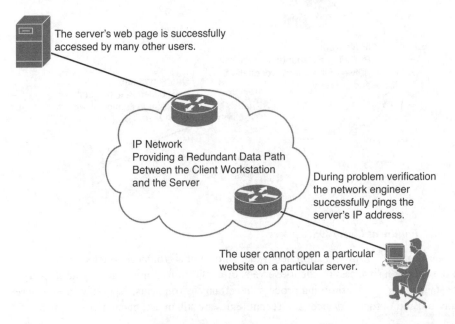

Figure 1-6   *Successful Ping Shifts the Focus to Upper OSI Layers (Divide-and-Conquer Approach)*

Whether the result of the initial test is positive or negative, the divide-and-conquer approach usually results in a faster elimination of potential problems than what you would achieve by implementing a full top-down or bottom-up approach. Therefore, the divide-and-conquer method is considered highly effective and possibly the most popular troubleshooting approach.

The Follow-the-Path Troubleshooting Approach

The follow-the-path approach is one of the most basic troubleshooting techniques, and it usually complements one of the other troubleshooting methods such as the top-down or the bottom-up approach. The follow-the-path approach first discovers the actual traffic path all the way from source to destination. Next, the scope of troubleshooting is reduced to just the links and devices that are actually in the forwarding path. The principle of this approach is to eliminate the links and devices that are irrelevant to the troubleshooting task at hand.

Let's assume that you are researching a problem of a user who cannot browse a particular website and that while you are verifying the problem you find that a trace (tracert) from the user's PC command prompt to the server's IP address succeeds only as far as the first hop, which is the L3 Switch v (Layer 3 or Multilayer Switch v) in Figure 1-7. Based on your understanding of the network link bandwidths and the routing protocol used on this network, you mark the links on the best path between the user workstation and the server on the diagram with numbers 1 through 7, as shown in Figure 1-7.

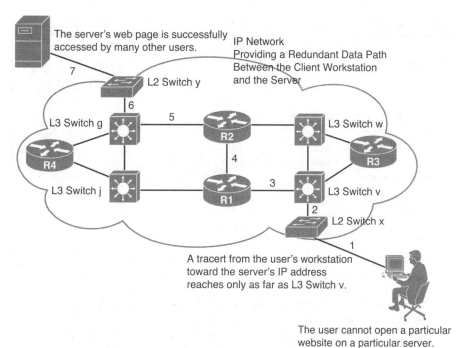

Figure 1-7 *The Follow-the-Path Approach Shifts the Focus to Link 3 and Beyond Toward the Server*

In this situation it is reasonable to shift your troubleshooting approach to the L3 Switch v and the segments beyond, toward the server along the best path. The follow-the-path approach can quickly lead you to the problem area. You can then try and pinpoint the problem to a device, and ultimately to a particular physical or logical component that is either broken, misconfigured, or has a bug.

The Compare-Configurations Troubleshooting Approach

Another common troubleshooting approach is called the compare-configurations approach, also referred to as the spotting-the-differences approach. By comparing configurations, software versions, hardware, or other device properties between working and nonworking situations and spotting significant differences between them, this approach attempts to resolve the problem by changing the nonoperational elements to be consistent with the working ones. The weakness of this method is that it might lead to a working situation, without clearly revealing the root cause of the problem. In some cases, you are not sure whether you have implemented a solution or a workaround.

Example 1-1 shows two routing tables; one belongs to Branch2's edge router, experiencing problems, and the other belongs to Branch1's edge router, with no problems. If you compare the content of these routing tables, as per the compare-configurations (spotting-the-differences) approach, a natural deduction is that the branch with problems is missing a static entry. The static entry can be added to see whether it solves the problem.

Example 1-1 *Spot-the-Differences: One Malfunctioning and One Working Router*

```
------------- Branch1 is in good working order ----------
Branch1# show ip route
<...output omitted...>
10.0.0.0/24 is subnetted, 1 subnets
C   10.132.125.0 is directly connected, FastEthernet4
C   192.168.36.0/24 is directly connected, BVI1
S*  0.0.0.0/0 [254/0] via 10.132.125.1
------------- Branch2 has connectivity problems ----------
Branch2# show ip route
<...output omitted...>
10.0.0.0/24 is subnetted, 1 subnets
C 10.132.126.0 is directly connected, FastEthernet4
C 192.168.37.0/24 is directly connected, BVI1
```

The compare-configurations approach (spotting-the-differences) is not a complete approach; it is, however, a good technique to use undertaking other approaches. One benefit of this approach is that it can easily be used by less-experienced troubleshooting staff to at least shed more light on the case. When you have an up-to-date and accessible set of baseline configurations, diagrams, and so on, spotting the difference between the current configuration and the baseline might help you solve the problem faster than any other approach.

The Swap-Components Troubleshooting Approach

Also called move-the-problem, the swap-components approach is a very elementary troubleshooting technique that you can use for problem isolation: You physically swap components and observe whether the problem stays in place, moves with the component, or disappears entirely. Figure 1-8 shows two PCs and three laptops connected to a LAN switch, among which laptop B has connectivity problems. Assuming that hardware failure is suspected, you must discover whether the problem is on the switch, the cable, or the laptop. One approach is to start gathering data by checking the settings on the laptop with problems, examining the settings on the switch, comparing the settings of all the laptops, and the switch ports, and so on. However, you might not have the required administrative passwords for the PCs, laptops, and the switch. The only data that you can gather is the status of the link LEDs on the switch and the laptops and PCs. What you can do is obviously limited. A common way to at least isolate the problem (if it is not solved outright) is cable or port swapping. Swap the cable between a working device and laptop B (the one that is having problems). Move the laptop from one port to another using a cable that you know for sure is good. Based on these simple moves, you can isolate whether the problem is cable, switch, or laptop related.

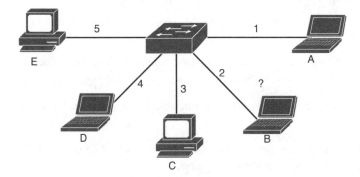

Figure 1-8 *Swap-the-Component: Laptop B Is Having Network Problems*

Just by executing simple tests in a methodical way, the swap-components approach enables you to isolate the problem even if the information that you can gather is minimal. Even if you do not solve the problem, you have scoped it to a single element, and you can now focus further troubleshooting on that element. Note that in the previous example if you determine that the problem is cable related, it is unnecessary to obtain the administrative password for the switch, PCs, and laptops. The drawbacks of this method are that you are isolating the problem to only a limited set of physical elements and not gaining any real insight into what is happening, because you are gathering only very limited indirect information. This method assumes that the problem is with a single component. If the problem lies within multiple devices, you might not be able to isolate the problem correctly.

Troubleshooting Example Using Six Different Approaches

An external financial consultant has come in to help your company's controller with an accounting problem. He needs access to the finance server. An account has been created for him on the server, and the client software has been installed on the consultant's laptop. You happen to walk past the controller's office and are called in and told that the consultant can't connect to the finance server. You are a network support engineer and have access to all network devices, but not to the servers. Think about how you would handle this problem, what your troubleshooting plan would be, and which method or combination of methods you would use.

What possible approaches can you take for this troubleshooting task? This case lends itself to many different approaches, but some specific characteristics can help you decide an appropriate approach:

- You have access to the network devices, but not to the server. This implies that you will likely be able to handle Layer 1–4 problems by yourself; however, for Layer 5–7, you will probably have to escalate to a different person.

- You have access to the client device, so it is possible to start your troubleshooting from it.

- The controller has the same software and access rights on his machine, so it is possible to compare between the two devices.

What are the benefits and drawbacks of each possible troubleshooting approach for this case?

- **Top-down:** You have the opportunity to start testing at the application layer. It is good troubleshooting practice to confirm the reported problem, so starting from the application layer is an obvious choice. The only possible drawback is that you will not discover simple problems, such as the cable being plugged in to a wrong outlet, until later in the process.

- **Bottom-up:** A full bottom-up check of the whole network is not a very useful approach because it will take too much time and at this point, there is no reason to assume that the network beyond the first access switch would be causing the issue. You could consider starting with a bottom-up approach for the first stretch of the network, from the consultant's laptop to the access switch, to uncover potential cabling problems.

- **Divide-and-conquer:** This is a viable approach. You can ping from the consultant's laptop to the finance server. If that succeeds, the problem is most likely at upper layers. For example, a firewall or access control list could be the culprit. If the ping fails, assuming that ping is not blocked in the network, it is safe to assume that the problem is at network or lower layers and you are responsible for fixing it. The advantage of this method is that you can quickly decide on the scope of the problem and whether escalation is necessary.

- **Follow-the-path:** Similar to the bottom-up approach, a full follow-the-path approach is not efficient under the circumstances, but tracing the cabling to the first switch can be a good start if it turns out that the link LED is off on the consultant's PC. This method might come into play after other techniques have been used to narrow the scope of the problem.

- **Compare-configurations:** You have access to both the controller's PC and the consultant's laptop; therefore, compare-configurations is a possible strategy. However, because these machines are not under the control of a single IT department, you might find many differences, and it might therefore be hard to spot the significant and relevant differences. The compare-configurations approach might prove useful later, after it has been determined that the problem is likely to be on the client.

- **Swap-components:** Using this approach alone is not likely to be enough to solve the problem, but if following any of the other methods indicates a potential hardware issue between the consultant's PC and the access switch, this method might come into play. However, merely as a first step, you could consider swapping the cable and the jack connected to the consultant's laptop and the controller's PC, in turn, to see whether the problem is cable, PC, or switch related.

Many combinations of these different methods could be considered here. The most promising methods are top-down or divide-and-conquer. You will possibly switch to follow-the-path or compare-configurations approach after the scope of the problem has been properly reduced. As an initial step in any approach, the swap-components method could be used to quickly separate client-related issues from network-related issues. The bottom-up approach could be used as the first step to verify the first stretch of cabling.

Summary

The fundamental elements of a troubleshooting process are as follows:

- Defining the problem
- Gathering information
- Analyzing information
- Eliminating possible causes
- Formulating a hypothesis
- Testing the hypothesis
- Solving the problem

Some commonly used troubleshooting approaches are as follows:

- Top-down
- Bottom-up

- Divide-and-conquer

- Follow-the-path

- Compare-configurations

- Swap-components

Review Questions

1. Which *three* of the following processes are subprocesses or phases of a trouble-shooting process?

    a. Solve the problem
    b. Eliminate
    c. Compile
    d. Report the problem
    e. Define the problem

2. Which *three* of the following approaches are valid troubleshooting methods?

    a. Swap-components
    b. Ad Hoc
    c. Compare-configurations
    d. Follow-the-path
    e. Hierarchical

3. Which *three* of the following troubleshooting approaches use the OSI reference model as a guiding principle?

    a. Top-down
    b. Bottom-up
    c. Divide-and-conquer
    d. Compare-configurations
    e. Swap-components

4. Which of the following troubleshooting methods would be most effective when the problem is with the Ethernet cable connecting a workstation to the wall RJ-45 jack?

    a. Top-down
    b. Divide-and-conquer
    c. Compare-configurations
    d. Swap-components
    e. Follow-the-path

Chapter 2

Structured Troubleshooting

This chapter covers the following topics:

- Meaning of structured troubleshooting method and procedure

- The subprocesses of structured troubleshooting, the actions taken within each sub-process, and how and when you move from one to another progressively

- Troubleshooting example utilizing the structured troubleshooting method and procedures

Network troubleshooting is not an exact science, and no strict set of procedures, tasks, and steps available guarantees successful diagnosis and resolution of all networking problems in all situations. The troubleshooting process can be guided by structured methods, but it is not static, and its steps are not always the same and might not be executed in the exact same order every time. Each network has its own characteristics; there are an almost unlimited number of possible problems, and the skill set/experience of each troubleshooting engineer is unique. However, to guarantee a certain level of consistency in the way that problems are diagnosed and solved in an organization, it is quite important to identify the main subprocesses of structured troubleshooting and how one should move from one to another as the troubleshooting task progresses.

This chapter defines structured troubleshooting method and procedure, identifies the subprocesses of structured troubleshooting, suggests the order of executing these subprocesses, and specifies what tasks each subprocess consists of. This chapter concludes with an example that demonstrates a successful structured troubleshooting effort using the troubleshooting subprocesses covered, and executing them in the order as suggested in this chapter.

Troubleshooting Method and Procedure

The generic troubleshooting process consists of the following tasks (subprocesses):

1. Defining the problem

2. Gathering information

3. Analyzing the information

4. Eliminating potential causes

5. Proposing a hypothesis (likely cause of the problem)

6. Testing and verifying validity of the proposed hypothesis

7. Solving the problem and documenting the work

A network troubleshooting process can be reduced to a number of elementary subprocesses, as outlined in the preceding list. These subprocesses are not strictly sequential in nature, and many times you will go back and forth through many of these subprocesses repeatedly until you eventually reach the solve the problem stage. Figure 2-1 illustrates the order of deploying the tasks/subprocesses within a structured troubleshooting process using a flowchart. A troubleshooting method provides a guiding principle that helps you move through these processes in a structured way. There is no exact recipe for troubleshooting. Every problem is different, and it is impossible to create a script for all possible problem scenarios.

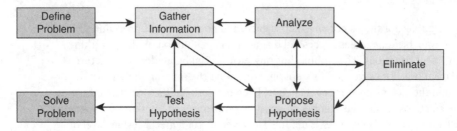

Figure 2-1   *Flow Chart of a Structured Troubleshooting Approach*

Troubleshooting is a skill that requires relevant knowledge and experience. After using different methods several times, you will become more effective at selecting the right method for a particular problem, gathering the most relevant information, and analyzing problems quickly and efficiently. As you gain more experience, you will find that you can skip some steps and adopt more of a shoot-from-the-hip approach, resolving problems more quickly. Regardless, to execute a successful troubleshooting exercise, you must be able to answer the following questions:

- What is the action plan for each of the elementary subprocesses or phases?

- What is it that you actually do during each of those subprocesses?

- What decisions do you need to make?

- What kind of support or resources do you need?

- What kind of communication needs to take place?

- How do you delegate responsibilities properly?

Although the answers to these questions will differ for each individual organization, by planning, documenting, and implementing troubleshooting procedures, the consistency and effectiveness of the troubleshooting processes in your organization will improve.

Defining the Problem

All troubleshooting tasks begin with defining the problem. However, what triggers a troubleshooting exercise is a failure experienced by someone who reports it to the support group. Figure 2-2 illustrates reporting of the problem (done by the user) as the trigger action, followed by verification and defining the problem (done by support group). Unless an organization has a strict policy on how problems are reported, the reported problem can unfortunately be vague or even misleading. Problem reports can look like the following: "When I try to go to this location on the intranet, I get a page that says I don't have permission," "The mail server isn't working," or "I can't file my expense report." As you might have noticed, the second statement is merely a conclusion a user has drawn perhaps merely because he cannot send or receive e-mail. To prevent wasting a lot of time during the troubleshooting process based on false assumptions and claims, the first step of troubleshooting is always verifying and defining the problem. The problem must first be verified, and then defined by you (the support engineer, not the user), and it has to be defined clearly. A good problem definition must also include information about when the problem started, if there have been any recent changes or upgrades, and how widespread the problem is. Knowing that the problem is experienced by a single user only (and not others) or that the problem has affected a group of users is quite valuable; it affects your analysis (eliminating causes and formulating hypotheses about the root cause of the problem) and your choice of the troubleshooting approach.

A good problem description consists of an accurate statement of symptoms and not of interpretations or conclusions. Consequences for the user are, strictly speaking, not part of the problem description itself, but can prove helpful to assess the urgency of the issue. When a problem is reported as "The mail server isn't working," you must contact the user and find out exactly what he has experienced. You will probably define the problem as "When user X starts his e-mail client, he gets an error message saying that the client cannot connect to the server. The user can still access his network drives and browse the Internet."

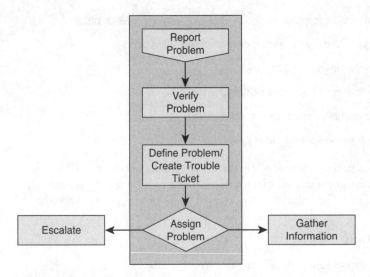

Figure 2-2   *Defining the Problem: The Problem Must First Be Verified and Then Defined by Support Staff*

After you have clearly defined the problem and created the trouble ticket, you have one more step to take before starting the actual troubleshooting process. You must determine whether this problem is your responsibility or if it needs to be escalated to another department or person. For example, assume that the reported problem is this: "When user Y tries to access the corporate directory on the company intranet, she gets a message that says permission is denied. She can access all other intranet pages." You are a network engineer, and you do not have access to the servers. A separate department in your company manages the intranet servers. Therefore, you must know what to do when this type of problem is reported to you as a network problem. You must know whether to start troubleshooting or to escalate it to the server department. It is important that you know which types of problems are your responsibility to act on, what minimal actions you need to take before you escalate a problem, and how you escalate a problem. As Figure 2-2 illustrates, after defining the problem, you assign the problem: The problem is either escalated to another group or department, or it is network support's responsibility to solve it. In the latter case, the next step is gathering information.

Gathering Information

Before gathering information, you should select your initial troubleshooting method and develop an information-gathering plan. As part of this plan, you need to identify what the targets are for the information-gathering process. In other words, you must decide which devices, clients, or servers you want to collect information from or about, and what tools you intend to use to gather that information (assemble a toolkit). Next, you have to acquire access to the identified targets. In many cases, you might have access to these systems as a normal part of your job role; in some cases, however, you might need to get information from systems that you cannot normally access. In this case, you might have to escalate the issue to a different department or person, either to obtain access or to get someone else to gather the information for you. If the escalation process would slow the procedure down and the problem is urgent, you might want to reconsider the troubleshooting method that you selected and first try a method that uses different targets and would not require you to escalate. As you can see in Figure 2-3, whether you can access and examine the devices you identified will either lead to the problem's escalation to another group or department or to the analyzing the information step.

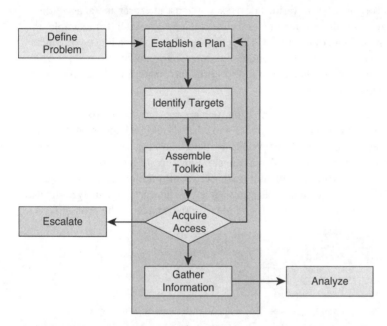

Figure 2-3 *Gathering Information: Lack of Access to Devices Might Lead to Problem Escalation to Another Group.*

The example that follows demonstrates how information gathering can be influenced by factors out of your control, and consequently, it can force you to alter your troubleshooting approach. Imagine that it is 1:00 p.m. now and your company's sales manager has reported that he cannot send or receive e-mail from the branch office where he is working. The matter is quite urgent because he has to send out a response to an important request for proposal (RFP) later this afternoon. Your first reaction might be to start a top-down troubleshooting method by calling him up and running through a series of tests. However, the sales manager is not available because he is in a meeting until 4:30 p.m. One of your colleagues from that same branch office confirms that the sales manager is in a meeting, but left his laptop on his desk. The RFP response needs to be received by the customer before 5:00 p.m. Even though a top-down troubleshooting approach might seem like the best choice, because you will not be able to access the sales manager's laptop, you will have to wait until 4:30 before you can start troubleshooting. Having to perform an entire troubleshooting exercise successfully in about 30 minutes is risky, and it will put you under a lot of pressure. In this case, it is best if you use a combination of the bottom-up and follow-the-path approaches. You can verify whether there are any Layer 1–3 problems between the manager's laptop and the company's mail server. Even if you do not find an issue, you can eliminate many potential problem causes, and when you start a top-down approach at 4:30, you will be able to work more efficiently.

Analyzing the Information

After gathering information from various devices, you must interpret and analyze the information. To interpret the raw information that you have gathered (for example, the output of **show** and **debug** commands, or packet captures and device logs), you might need to research commands, protocols, and technologies. You might also need to consult network documentation to be able to interpret the information in the context of the actual network's implementation.

During the analysis of the gathered information, you are typically trying to determine two things: What is happening on the network and what should be happening. If you discover differences between these two, you can collect clues for what is wrong or at least a direction to take for further information gathering. Figure 2-4 shows that the gathered information, network documentation, baseline information, plus your research results and past experience are all used as input while you interpret and analyze the gathered information to eliminate possibilities and identify the source of the problem.

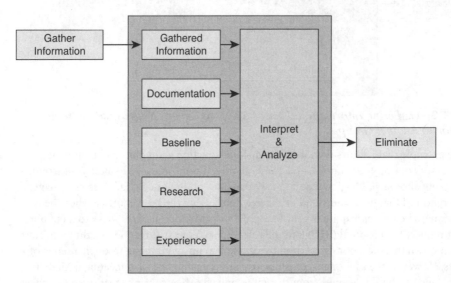

Figure 2-4 *Analyze the Information: Gathered and Existing Information, Knowledge, and Experiences All Considered and Incorporated*

Your perception of what is actually happening is usually formed based on interpretation of the raw data, supported by research and documentation; however, your understanding of the underlying protocols and technologies also plays a role in your success level. If you are troubleshooting protocols and technologies that you are not very familiar with, you will have to invest some time in researching how they operate. Furthermore, a good baseline of the behavior of your network can prove quite useful at the analysis stage. If you know how your network performs and how things work under normal conditions, you can spot anomalies in the behavior of the network and derive clues from those deviations. The benefit of vast relevant past experience cannot be overstated. An experienced network engineer will spend significantly less time (than an inexperienced engineer would) on researching processes, interpreting raw data, and distilling the relevant information from the raw data.

Eliminating Potential Causes

Analyzing the gathered information while considering and incorporating existing information, such as network baseline and documentation, helps you eliminate many potential causes. For example, if a user can successfully ping a certain web server but cannot retrieve its main web page, you will comfortably eliminate many potential problem causes such as physical, data link, and network layer failures or misconfigurations. As Figure 2-5 illustrates, based on the gathered information and any assumptions made, from among all potential causes some are eliminated, leaving other potential causes to be evaluated and proposed in the next step.

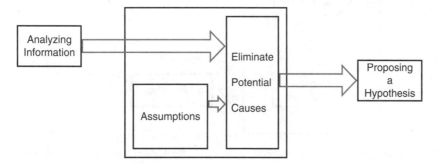

Figure 2-5 *Eliminating Potential Causes: Gathered Information and Assumptions Help You Eliminate Some of the Potential Problem Causes*

You must make note of the important influence that your assumptions have in eliminating the potential causes. Assumptions may or may not be true. If you end up with conflicting conclusions or scenarios that make no sense, you might have to reevaluate your assumptions by gathering more information and analyzing the new information accordingly. For example, if you start troubleshooting a user's inability to access or use a particular service based on the false assumption that he or she could use or access the same service in the past, you might waste a long time in the analysis stage and draw no rational conclusion.

Proposing a Hypothesis (Likely Cause of the Problem)

After eliminating potential problem causes, you are usually left with other potential causes. These potential causes must be ordered based on their likelihood, so that the most likely cause can form the proposed hypothesis. Ordering the remaining potential causes based on their likelihood is once again dependent on your knowledge, past experiences, and assumptions. Figure 2-6 shows that the most likely cause that you propose may or may not lie within your territory or area of responsibility, and it may have to be escalated to another group or department. Figure 2-6 also shows that once the most likely cause has been determined, further fact gathering may be necessary, effectively triggering a new round of analysis, elimination, and proposing a hypothesis.

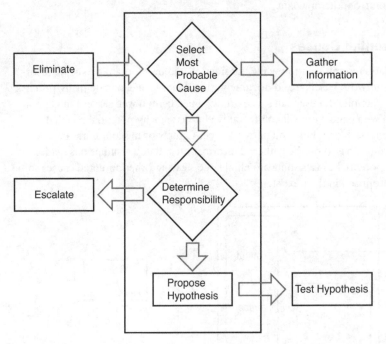

Figure 2-6   *Proposing a Hypothesis: Selecting the Most Probable Cause of the Problem*

The proposed hypothesis leads us to the next stage of the structured troubleshooting process: testing the hypothesis. If at that stage the most probable hypothesis is determined not to be the potential cause, we normally propose the next most likely potential problem and once again go to the test hypothesis stage. This cycle may continue until the problem is solved or we exhaust all possible potential causes without solving the problem. In the latter case, we need to gather more facts and effectively restart the troubleshooting cycle, or we merely have to escalate the problem to more experienced staff or contact external sources such as consulting companies or the Cisco Technical Assistance Center (TAC).

If you decide to escalate the problem, ask yourself whether this ends your involvement in the process. Note that escalating the problem is not the same as solving the problem. You have to think about how long it will take the other party to solve the problem and how urgent the problem is to them. Users affected by the problem might not be able to wait long for the other group to fix the problem. If you cannot solve the problem, but it is too urgent to wait for the problem to be solved through an escalation, you might need to come up with a workaround. A temporary fix alleviates the symptoms experienced by the user, even if it does not address the root cause of the problem.

Testing and Verifying Validity of the Proposed Hypothesis

After a hypothesis is proposed identifying the cause of a problem, the next step is to come up with a possible solution (or workaround) to that problem, and plan an implementation scheme. Usually, implementing a possible solution involves making changes to the network. Therefore, if your organization has defined procedures for regular network maintenance, you must follow your organization's regular change procedures. The next step is to assess the impact of the change on the network and balance that against the urgency of the problem. If the urgency outweighs the impact and you decide to go ahead with the change, it is important to make sure that you have a way to revert to the original situation after you make the change. Even though you have determined that your hypothesis is the most likely cause of the problem and your solution is intended to fix it, you can never be entirely sure that your proposed solution will actually solve the problem. If the problem is not solved, you need to have a way to undo your changes and revert to the original situation. Upon creation of a rollback plan, you can implement your proposed solution according to your organization's change procedures. Verify that the problem is solved and that the change you made did what you expected it to do. In other words, make sure the root cause of the problem and its symptoms are eliminated, and that your solution has not introduced any new problems. If all results are positive and desirable, you move on to the final stage of troubleshooting, which is integrating the solution and documenting your work. Figure 2-7 shows the flow of tasks while you implement and test your proposed hypothesis and either solve the problem or end up rolling back your changes.

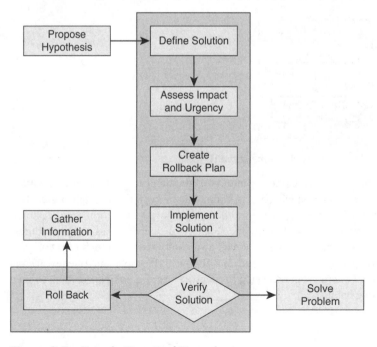

Figure 2-7 *Test the Proposed Hypothesis*

You must have a plan for the situation if it turns out that the problem was not fixed, the symptoms have not disappeared, or new problems have been introduced by the changes that you have made. In this case, you should execute your rollback plan, revert to the original situation, and resume the troubleshooting process. It is important to determine whether the root cause hypothesis was invalid or whether it was simply the proposed solution that did not work.

Solving the Problem and Documenting the Work

After you have confirmed your hypothesis and verified that the symptoms have disappeared, you have essentially solved the problem. All you need to do then is to make sure that the changes you made are integrated into the regular implementation of the network and that any maintenance procedures associated with those changes are executed. You will have to create backups of any changed configurations or upgraded software. You will have to document all changes to make sure that the network documentation still accurately describes the current state of the network. In addition, you must perform any other actions that are prescribed by your organization's change control procedures. Figure 2-8 shows that upon receiving successful results from testing your hypothesis, you incorporate your solution and perform the final tasks such as backup, documentation, and communication, before you report the problem as solved. Note that modern troubleshooting practices require that once the cause of a problem is determined and a solution has been implemented, a recommendation is to be made on how to eliminate or reduce occurrence of similar problems in the future.

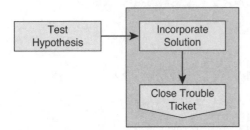

Figure 2-8   *Solve the Problem and Document the Work*

Your troubleshooting job is not complete until you communicate that the problem has been solved. At a minimum, you will have to communicate back to the original user that reported the problem; if you have involved others as part of an escalation process, however, you should communicate with them, too. For any of the processes and procedures described here, each organization must make its own choices in how much of these procedures should be described, formalized, and followed. However, anyone involved in troubleshooting will benefit from reviewing these processes and comparing them to their own troubleshooting habits.

Troubleshooting Example Based on the Structured Method and Procedures

Armando, a member of the network support team at AMIRACAN, Inc., receives a call from Ariana, who works for the accounting department. Ariana complains that the Internet is not accessible from her office workstation; she was trying to access www.cisco.com. At this stage, the problem is reported but the troubleshooting process has not begun yet. Armando followed the structured troubleshooting process, step by step, until he solved the problem and documented his work.

- **Define the problem:** Armando decided to verify the problem by going to Ariana's office. While there, he also found out that Ariana was able to access www.cisco.com yesterday. Armando creates a trouble ticket in the system and defines the problem by accurately stating Ariana's problem along with its date of occurrence, specifying that the problem was verified, and that the problem did not exist 24 hours ago.

- **Gathering information:** Armando decides to access www.cisco.com from his workstation in his office and is successful in doing so. Based on this gathered fact, Armando decides to take a bottom-up approach and start his work from Ariana's office using her workstation. Using Ariana's workstation, Armando notices that the workstation has an IP address, subnet mask, default gateway, and a DNS server address. Armando pings the configured DNS server's address and the ping succeeds 100 percent. However, because no web page can be retrieved from Ariana's workstation, Armando decides to use nslookup to see whether the DNS server returns proper IP addresses for some known URLs. Name resolution fails through the configured DNS address. Armando compares the DNS address configured on Ariana's workstation with the DNS address configured on other workstations in the accounting department, and notices that the DNS address on Ariana's workstation is different from all others.

- **Analyzing the information:** Knowing that Ariana's workstation is the only workstation in the accounting department that cannot access web pages using names, and that her workstation's DNS server address is different from everyone else's, and that the DNS server does not respond to nslookup, Armando associates Ariana's problem with the configured DNS server. Armando refers to the documentation related to user workstations and finds that the DNS server address must be assigned by the DHCP server.

- **Eliminate potential causes:** Armando eliminates physical and data link layer problems.

- **Propose a hypothesis:** Armando suspects that either Ariana's IP information has all been configured manually, or that basic IP information is gathered through Dynamic Host Configuration Protocol (DHCP), but other information, such as DNS server address, has been entered manually (and incorrectly). Armando decides that the invalid DNS address entered manually (and erroneously) is the most likely problem cause.

■ **Test the hypothesis:** Armando modifies Ariana's workstation configuration to obtain its DNS server address through DHCP. Then he checks the result by attempting to access www.cisco.com. He is successful.

■ **Solve the problem and document the work:** Armando enters the solution into the system for this trouble ticket and closes the case. Armando then explains to Ariana that the DNS server IP address must not be entered manually. He explains that using unknown third-party DNS servers can impose serious security threats, too. In the documentation related to the trouble tickets, Armando recommends that users' accounts should not have the privilege to change system settings.

Summary

The generic troubleshooting process consists of the following tasks (subprocesses):

1. Defining the problem

2. Gathering information

3. Analyzing the information

4. Eliminating potential causes

5. Proposing a hypothesis (likely cause of the problem)

6. Testing and verifying validity of the proposed hypothesis

7. Solving the problem and documenting the work

A structured approach to troubleshooting (no matter what the exact method is) will yield more predictable results in the long run and will make it easier to pick up the process where you left off in a later stage or to hand it over to someone else.

The structured troubleshooting begins with problem definition followed by fact gathering. The gathered information, network documentation, baseline information, plus your research results and past experience are all used as input while you interpret and analyze the gathered information to eliminate possibilities and identify the source of the problem. Based on your continuous information analysis and the assumptions you make, you eliminate possible problem causes from the pool of proposed causes until you have a final proposal that takes you to the next step of the troubleshooting process: formulating and proposing a hypothesis. Based on your hypothesis, the problem might or might not fall within your area of responsibility, so proposing a hypothesis is either followed by escalating it to another group or by testing your hypothesis. If your test results are positive, you have to plan and implement a solution. The solution entails changes that must follow the change-control procedures within your organization. The results and all the changes you make must be clearly documented and communicated with all the relevant parties.

Review Questions

1. Which *three* of the following processes are subprocesses of a structured trouble-shooting process?

   a. Eliminate potential causes

   b. Test the hypothesis

   c. Termination

   d. Define the problem

   e. Calculation

   f. Compilation

2. Which *two* of the following resources will help in interpreting and analyzing information gathered during troubleshooting?

   a. Documentation

   b. Network baseline

   c. Packet sniffers

   d. Assumptions

3. Which of the following steps are parts of testing a hypothesis? (Choose four.)

   a. Defining a solution

   b. Creating a rollback plan

   c. Implementing the solution

   d. Defining the problem

   e. Assessing impact and urgency

4. During which *three* of the troubleshooting phases could it be necessary to escalate a problem to a different department?

   a. Defining the problem

   b. Gathering information

   c. Analyzing the facts

   d. Eliminating possible causes

   e. Proposing a hypothesis

   f. Solving the problem

Network Maintenance Tasks and Best Practices

This chapter covers the following topics:

- Structured network maintenance
- Network maintenance processes and procedures
- Network maintenance services and tools
- Integrating troubleshooting into the network maintenance process

Many modern business processes and transactions depend on high availability and reliability of an organization's computer network and computing resources. Downtime can cause significant loss of reputation/revenue. Planning the network maintenance processes and procedures facilitates high availability and cost control. This chapter starts by explaining structured network maintenance and its benefits. Next, common network maintenance tasks are presented, along with how they should be planned and executed. The third section of this chapter introduces critical network maintenance-related services and tools such as network time services, logging services, and how to perform backup and restore. The final section of this chapter describes network maintenance tasks such as documentation, baseline, communication, and change control, which support and integrate with network troubleshooting.

Structured Network Maintenance

Support and maintenance are two of the core tasks that network engineers perform. The objective of network maintenance is to keep the network available with minimum service disruption and at acceptable performance levels. Network maintenance includes regularly scheduled tasks such as making backups and upgrading devices or software. Structured network maintenance provides a guideline that you can follow to maximize network uptime and minimize unplanned outages, but the exact techniques you should use are governed by your company's policies and procedures and your experience and preferences. Network support includes following up on interrupt-driven tasks, such as responding to device and link failures and to users who need help. You must evaluate the commonly practiced models and methodologies used for network maintenance and identify the benefits that these models bring to your organization. You must also select generalized maintenance models and planning tools that fit your organization the best.

A typical network engineer's job description usually includes elements such as installing, implementing, maintaining, and supporting network equipment. The exact set of tasks performed by network engineers might differ between organizations. Depending on the size and type of organization, some or all of the following are likely to be included in that set:

- **Tasks related to device installation and maintenance:** Includes tasks such as installing devices and software, and creating and backing up configurations and software

- **Tasks related to failure response:** Includes tasks such as supporting users that experience network problems, troubleshooting device or link failures, replacing equipment, and restoring backups

- **Tasks related to network performance:** Includes tasks such as capacity planning, performance tuning, and usage monitoring

- **Tasks related to business procedures:** Includes tasks such as documenting, compliance auditing, and service level agreement (SLA) management

- **Tasks related to security:** Includes tasks such as following and implementing security procedures and security auditing

Network engineers must not only understand their own organization's definition of network maintenance and the tasks it includes, but they must also comprehend the policies and procedures that govern how those tasks are performed. In many smaller networks, the process is largely interrupt driven. For example, when users have problems, you start helping them, or when applications experience performance problems, you upgrade links or equipment. Another example is that a company's network engineer reviews and improves the security of the network only when security concerns or incidents are reported. Although this is obviously the most basic method of performing network maintenance, it clearly has some disadvantages, including the following:

- Tasks that are beneficial to the long-term health of the network might be ignored, postponed, or forgotten.

- Tasks might not be executed in order of priority or urgency, but instead in the order they were requested.

- The network might experience more downtime than necessary because problems are not prevented.

You cannot avoid interrupt-driven work entirely because failures will happen and you cannot plan them. However, you can reduce the amount of incident-driven (interrupt-driven) work by proactively monitoring and managing systems.

The alternative to the interrupt-driven model of maintenance is structured network maintenance. Structured network maintenance predefines and plans much of the processes and procedures. This proactive approach not only reduces the frequency and quantity of user, application, and business problems, it also renders the responses to incidents more efficiently. The structured approach to network maintenance has some clear benefits over the interrupt-driven approach, including the following:

- **Reduced network downtime:** By discovering and preventing problems before they happen, you can prevent or at least minimize network downtime. You should strive to maximize mean time between failures (MTBF). Even if you cannot prevent problems, you can reduce the amount of time it takes to fix them by following proper procedures and using adequate tools. You should strive to minimize mean time to repair (MTTR). Maximizing MTBF and minimizing MTTR translates to lower financial damage and higher user satisfaction.

- **More cost-effectiveness:** Performance monitoring and capacity planning allows you to make adequate budgeting decisions for current and future networking needs. Choosing proper equipment and using it to capacity means better price/performance ratio (return on investment, ROI) over the lifetime of your equipment. Lower maintenance costs and network downtime also help to reduce the price/performance ratio.

- **Better alignment with business objectives:** Within the structured network maintenance framework, instead of prioritizing tasks and assigning budgets based on incidents, time and resources are allocated to processes based on their importance to the business. For example, upgrades and major maintenance jobs are not scheduled during critical business hours.

- **Higher network security:** Attention to network security is part of structured network maintenance. If prevention techniques do not stop a breach or attack, detection mechanisms will contain them, and support staff will be notified through logs and alarms. Monitoring allows you to observe network vulnerabilities and needs and to justify plans for strengthening network security.

Network Maintenance Processes and Procedures

Network maintenance involves many tasks. Some of these tasks are nearly universal, whereas others might be deployed by only some organizations or performed in unique ways. Processes such as maintenance planning, change control, documentation, disaster recovery, and network monitoring are common elements of all network maintenance plans. To establish procedures that fit an organization's needs best, network engineers need to do the following:

- Identify essential network maintenance tasks.

- Recognize and describe the advantages of scheduled maintenance.

- Evaluate the key decision factors that affect change control procedures to create procedures that fit the organization's needs.

- Describe the essential elements of network documentation and its function.

- Plan for efficient disaster recovery.

- Describe the importance of network monitoring and performance measurement as an integral element of a proactive network maintenance strategy.

Common Maintenance Tasks

Regardless of the network maintenance model and methodology you choose or the size of your network, certain tasks must be included in your network maintenance plan. The amount of resources, time, and money you spend on these tasks will vary, however, depending on the size and type of your organization. All network maintenance plans need to include procedures to perform the following tasks:

- **Accommodating adds, moves, and changes:** Networks are always undergoing changes. As people move and offices are changed and restructured, network devices such as computers, printers, and servers might need to be moved, and configuration and cabling changes might be necessary. These adds, moves, and changes are a normal part of network maintenance.

- **Installation and configuration of new devices:** This task includes adding ports, link capacity, network devices, and so on. Implementation of new technologies or installation and configuration of new devices is either handled by a different group within your organization, by an external party, or handled by internal staff.

- **Replacement of failed devices:** Whether replacement of failed devices is done through service contracts or done in house by support engineers, it is an important network maintenance task.

- **Backup of device configurations and software:** This task is linked to the task of replacing failed devices. Without good backups of both software and configurations, the time to replace failed equipment or recover from severe device failures will not be trouble-free and might take a long time.

- **Troubleshooting link and device failures:** Failures are inevitable; diagnosing and resolving failures related to network components, links, or service provider connections are essential tasks within a network engineer's job.

- **Software upgrading or patching:** Network maintenance requires that you stay informed of available software upgrades or patches and use them if necessary. Critical performance or security vulnerabilities are often addressed by the software upgrades or patches.

- **Network monitoring:** Monitoring operation of the devices and user activity on the network is also part of a network maintenance plan. Network monitoring can be performed using simple mechanisms such as collection of router and firewall logs or by using sophisticated network monitoring applications.

- **Performance measurement and capacity planning:** Because the demand for bandwidth is continually increasing, another network maintenance task is to perform at least some basic measurements to decide when it is time to upgrade links or equipment and to justify the cost of the corresponding investments. This proactive approach allows one to plan for upgrades (capacity planning) before bottlenecks are formed, congestions are experienced, or failures occur.

- **Writing and updating documentation:** Preparing proper network documentation that describes the current state of the network for reference during implementation, administration, and troubleshooting is a mandatory network maintenance task within most organizations. Network documentation must be kept current.

Network Maintenance Planning

You must build processes and procedures for performing your network maintenance tasks; this is called network maintenance planning. Network maintenance planning includes the following:

- Scheduling maintenance

- Formalizing change-control procedures

- Establishing network documentation procedures

- Establishing effective communication

- Defining templates/procedures/conventions

- Planning for disaster recovery

Scheduling Maintenance

After you have determined the tasks and processes that are part of network maintenance, you can assign priorities to them. You can also determine which of these tasks will be interrupt driven by nature (hardware failures, outages, and so on) and which tasks are parts of a long-term maintenance cycle (software patching, backups, and so on). For the long-term tasks, you will have to work out a schedule that guarantees that these tasks will be done regularly and will not get lost in the busy day-to-day work schedule. For some tasks, such as moves and changes, you can adopt a procedure that is partly interrupt driven (incoming change requests) and partly scheduled: Change requests need not be handled immediately, but during the next scheduled timeframe. This allows you to properly prioritize tasks but still have a predictable lead time that the requesting party knows they can count on for a change to be executed. With scheduled maintenance, tasks that are disruptive to the network are scheduled during off-hours. You can select maintenance windows during evenings or weekends where outages will be acceptable, thereby reducing unnecessary outages during office hours. The uptime of the network will increase as both the number of unplanned outages and their duration will be reduced. To summarize, the benefits of scheduled maintenance include the following:

■ Network downtime is reduced.

■ Long-term maintenance tasks will not be neglected or forgotten.

■ You have predictable lead times for change requests.

■ Disruptive maintenance tasks can be scheduled during assigned maintenance windows, reducing downtime during production hours.

Formalizing Change-Control Procedures

Sometimes it is necessary to make changes to configuration, software, or hardware. Any change that you make has an associated risk due to possible mistakes, conflicts, or bugs. Before making any change, you must first determine the impact of the change on the network and balance this against the urgency of the change. If the anticipated impact is high, you might need to justify the need for the change and obtain authorization to proceed. High-impact changes are usually made during maintenance windows specifically scheduled for this purpose. However, you also need a process for emergency changes. For example, if a broadcast storm occurs in your network and a link needs to be disconnected to break the loop and allow the network to stabilize, you might not be able to wait for authorization and the next maintenance window. In many companies, change control is formalized and answers the following types of questions:

■ Which types of change require authorization and who is responsible for authorizing them?

■ Which changes have to be done during a maintenance window and which changes can be done immediately?

■ What kind of preparation needs to be done before executing a change?

■ What kind of verification needs to be done to confirm that the change was effective?

■ What other actions (such as updating documentation) need to be taken after a successful change?

■ What actions should be taken when a change has unexpected results or causes problems?

■ What conditions allow skipping some of the normal change procedures and which elements of the procedures should still be followed?

Establishing Network Documentation Procedures

An essential part of any network maintenance is building and keeping up-to-date network documentation. Without up-to-date network documentation, it is difficult to correctly plan and implement changes, and troubleshooting is tedious and time-consuming. Usually, documentation is created as part of network design and implementation, but keeping it up-to-date is part of network maintenance. Therefore, any good change-control procedure will include updating the relevant documentation after the change is made. Documentation can be as simple as a few network drawings, equipment and software lists, and the current configurations of all devices. On the other hand, documentation can be extensive, describing all implemented features, design choices that were made, service contract numbers, change procedures, and so on. Typical elements of network documentation include the following:

- **Network drawings:** Diagrams of the physical and logical structure of the network

- **Connection documentation:** Lists of all relevant physical connections, such as patches, connections to service providers, and power circuits

- **Equipment lists:** Lists of all devices, part numbers, serial numbers, installed software versions, software licenses (if applicable), warranty/service information

- **IP address administration:** Lists of the IP subnets scheme and all IP addresses in use

- **Configurations:** A set of all current device configurations or even an archive that contains all previous configurations

- **Design documentation:** A document describing the motivation behind certain implementation choices

Establishing Effective Communication

Network maintenance is usually performed by a team of people and cannot easily be divided into exclusive sets of tasks that do not affect each other. Even if you have specialists who are responsible for particular technologies or set of devices, they will always have to communicate with team members who are responsible for different technologies or other devices. The best means of communication depends on the situation and organization, but a major consideration for choosing a communication method is how easily it is logged and shared with the network maintenance team. Communication is vital both during troubleshooting and technical support and afterward. During troubleshooting, certain questions must be answered, such as the following:

- Who is making changes and when?

- How does the change affect others?

- What are the results of tests that were done, and what conclusions can be drawn?

If actions, test results, and conclusions are not communicated between team members, the process in the hands of one team member can be disruptive to the process handled by another team member. You do not want to create new problems while solving others.

In many cases, diagnosis and resolution must be done by several people or during multiple sessions. In those cases, it is important to have a log of actions, tests, communication, and conclusions. These must be distributed among all those involved. With proper communication, one team member should comfortably take over where another team member has left off. Communication is also required after completion of troubleshooting or making changes.

Defining Templates/Procedures/Conventions (Standardization)

When a team of people execute the same or related tasks, it is important that those tasks be performed consistently. Because people might inherently have different working methods, styles, and backgrounds, standardization makes sure that work performed by different people remains consistent. Even if two different approaches to the same task are both valid, they might yield inconsistent results. One of the ways to streamline processes and make sure that tasks are executed in a consistent manner is to define and document procedures; this is called standardization. Defining and using templates is an effective method of network documentation, and it helps in creating a consistent network maintenance process. The following are some of the types of questions answered by network conventions, templates, and best practices (standardization) documentation:

- Are logging and debug time stamps set to local time or coordinated universal time (UTC)?

- Should access lists end with an explicit "deny any"?

- In an IP subnet, is the first or the last valid IP address allocated to the local gateway?

In many cases, you can configure a device in several different ways to achieve the same results. However, using different methods of achieving the same results in the same network can easily lead to confusion, especially during troubleshooting. Under pressure, valuable time can be wasted in verifying configurations that are assumed incorrect simply because they are configured differently.

Planning for Disaster Recovery

Although the modern MTBF for certain network devices is claimed to be 5, 7, or 10 years or more, you must always consider the possibility of device failure. By having a plan for such occasions and knowing what to do, you can significantly reduce the amount of downtime. One way to reduce the impact of failure is to build redundancy into the network at critical points and eliminate single points of failure. A single point of failure means that a single device or link does not have a backup and its failure can cause major damage to your network operation. However, mainly because of budgetary limitations, it is not always possible to make every single link, component, and device redundant. Disasters, natural and otherwise, must also be taken into account. For example, you could be struck by a disaster such as a flood or fire in the server room. The quicker you can replace failed devices and restore functionality, the quicker your network will be running again. To replace a failed device, you need the following items:

- Replacement hardware

- The current software version for the device

- The current configuration for the device

- The tools to transfer the software and configuration to the device

- Licenses (if applicable)

- Knowledge of the procedures to install software, configurations, and licenses

Missing any of the listed items severely affects the time it takes to replace the device. To make sure that you have these items available when you need them, follow these guidelines:

- **Replacement hardware:** You need to have either spare devices or a service contract with a distributor or vendor that will replace the failed hardware. Typically, this means that you need documentation of the exact hardware part numbers, serial numbers, and service contract numbers for the devices.

- **Current software:** Usually devices are delivered with a particular version of software, which is not necessarily the same as the version that you were running on the device. Therefore, you should have a repository where you store all current software versions in use on your network.

- **Current configuration:** In addition to creating backups of your configurations any time you make a change, you need to have a clear versioning system so that you know which configuration is the most recent.

- **Tools:** You need to have the appropriate tools to transfer software and configurations to the new device, which you should be able to do even if the network is unavailable.

- **Licenses:** If your software requires a license, you need to have that license or know the procedure to obtain a new license.

- **Knowledge:** Because these procedures are used infrequently, you might not have them committed to memory. Having all necessary documentation ready, however, will save time in executing the necessary procedures and will also decrease the risk of making mistakes.

In short, the key factors to a successful disaster recovery are defining and documenting recovery procedures and making sure that you always have the necessary elements available in case a disaster strikes.

Network Maintenance Services and Tools

After you determine and define the network maintenance methods, processes, and procedures to be implemented in your organization, you can choose the tools, applications, and resources for executing your network maintenance tasks in an efficient manner. These tools must be adequate and affordable. Ideally, all the tasks that are part of your maintenance plan should be supported by the products and applications that you choose, with the initial and ongoing costs within your budget. To determine the suitability of a network maintenance toolkit, you must learn to perform the following tasks:

- Identify, evaluate, and implement the elements of a basic network maintenance toolkit.

- Evaluate tools that support the documentation process and select the tools appropriate to your organization.

- Describe how configuration, software, and hardware resource management can improve disaster recovery procedures.

- Describe how network monitoring software benefits the maintenance process.

- Analyze the metrics that could be used to measure network performance and the key elements of the performance measurement process to create a performance measurement plan appropriate to your organization.

You have many tools, applications, and resources from which to choose to support network maintenance processes. These tools and applications vary based on price, complexity, capability, and scalability. Figure 3-1 shows the fundamental tools and applications that belong in network maintenance toolkits.

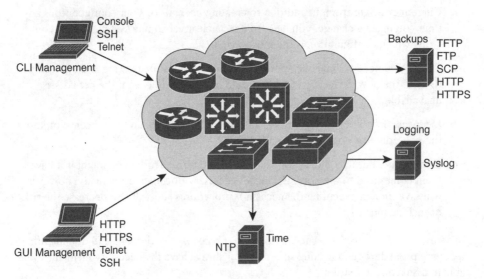

Figure 3-1   *Fundamental Tools and Applications of Network Maintenance Toolkits*

The basic components of a network maintenance toolkit are as follows:

- **Command-line device management:** Cisco IOS Software includes a powerful command-line interface (CLI) that you can use to configure and monitor individual routers and switches. This includes commands such as the **show** commands, the **debug** commands, Embedded Event Manager (EEM) commands, and IP SLA commands. After an initial configuration through the serial console of the device, the CLI is commonly accessed remotely through use of the Telnet or Secure Shell (SSH) protocols. To be able to manage the devices during network outages, an out-of-band management solution can be implemented to allow access to the CLI using the serial console at all times.

- **Graphical user interface (GUI)–based device management:** Cisco provides free GUI-based device management tools for many Cisco routers and switches. Examples of such tools include Cisco Configuration Professional (CCP), Secure Device Manager (SDM), Cisco Configuration Assistant (CCA), and Cisco Network Assistant (CNA).

- **Backup server:** To create backups of the software and configurations of your routers and switches, you need to provide a TFTP, FTP, HTTP, or Secure Copy Protocol (SCP) server. Many operating systems include these services as optional add-ons, and many software packages offer those services, too.

- **Log server:** Basic logging functionality can be provided by sending the router's or switch's log messages to a syslog server using the syslog protocol. Syslog is a standard service on most UNIX-based operating systems or could be provided by installing additional software on the operating system of your choice.

- **Time server:** To synchronize clocks on all your network devices, it is useful to have a Network Time Protocol (NTP) server on your network. You could even synchronize your router and switch clocks to one of the many public time servers available on the Internet.

Network Time Services

To ensure correct time stamps on logging and debug output and to support other time-based features such as the use of certificates or time-based access, it is vital that the clocks of the network devices be properly set and synchronized. You can use the Network Time Protocol to synchronize the clock of a device to the clock of an NTP server, which in turn is synchronized to another server higher up the NTP hierarchy. The position of a device in the NTP hierarchy is determined by its stratum, which serves as an NTP hop count. A stratum 1 server is a server that is directly connected to an authoritative time source such as a radio or atomic clock. A server that synchronizes its clock to a stratum 1 server will become a stratum 2 time source, and so on.

It is common to have a redundant set of servers in the core of the network that are synchronized to an authoritative source or a service provider server, and to configure other devices to synchronize their clocks to these central sources. In large networks, this hierarchy could even consist of multiple levels. You configure time servers using the **ntp server** command. If multiple time servers are configured for redundancy, NTP decides which server is most reliable and synchronizes to that server. Alternatively, a preferred server can be appointed by use of the **prefer** command option on the **ntp server** command. In addition to defining time servers, you can define your local time zone and configure the devices to adapt to daylight savings time. Finally, after you have the time synchronized and the correct time zone has been configured, you configure the router or switch to time stamp its log and debug entries.

Example 3-1 shows the clock of a device that is synchronized to a single time server with IP address 10.1.220.3. The time zone is configured to Pacific standard time (PST), which has a −8 hour offset to UTC. The clock is configured to change to daylight savings time on the second Sunday in March at 2:00 a.m. and back to standard time on the first Sunday in November at 2:00 a.m. The system logging is configured to use the local date and time in the time stamps and to include the time zone in the time stamps. For log entries generated by debugs, the settings are similar, but milliseconds are included in the time stamps for greater accuracy.

Example 3-1 *NTP Example*

```
service timestamps debug datetime msec localtime show-timezone
service timestamps log datetime localtime show-timezone
!
clock timezone PST -8
clock summer-time PDT recurring 2 Sun Mar 2:00 1 Sun Nov 2:00
!
ntp server 10.1.220.3
```

Logging Services

During operation, network devices generate messages called logging messages about events as they happen. There are different types of events, and different events have different levels of significance or severity. Examples of events include interfaces going up and down, configuration changes, and routing protocol adjacencies being established. By default, events are usually logged only to the device's console; however, because the console is usually not easily accessible, let alone monitored, it is worthwhile to collect and store the logs on a server, or at least in a separate piece of memory of the router, to facilitate access to them during troubleshooting procedures. Logging messages can be sent to one or more of the following:

- Console (default)

- Monitor (vty/AUX)

- Buffer (volatile memory)

- Syslog server

- Flash memory (nonvolatile memory)

- Simple Network Management Protocol (SNMP) network management server (as an SNMP trap)

Logging the messages to buffers on the router or switch is a minimal step that guarantees that logs are available on the device, so long as it is not rebooted. On some devices and Cisco IOS Software versions, logging to buffers is turned on by default. To enable buffer logging manually, you can use the logging buffered command to specify that messages should be logged to a buffer in the device's RAM. As an option, you can specify the amount of RAM that should be allocated to this buffer. The buffer is circular, meaning that when the buffer has reached its maximum capacity, the oldest messages will be discarded to allow the logging of new messages. You can display the content of this logging buffer via the **show logging** command. Logging severity levels on Cisco Systems devices are as follows:

(0) Emergency

(1) Alert

(2) Critical

(3) Error

(4) Warning

(5) Notification

(6) Informational

(7) Debugging

When logging is enabled, the severity level can be specified as an option. This causes the device to only log messages with a severity at the configured level or lower numeric value. The default severity level for logging to buffer and console is debugging (7).

You can also adjust the logging severity level of the console. By default, all messages from level 0 to 7 are logged to the console; however, similar to buffer logging, you can configure the severity level as an optional parameter on the **logging console** command.

Logging messages are best to be sent to a syslog server. Doing so allows you to store the logs of all your network devices centrally. When logging messages are sent to a syslog server, logs are no longer lost when the networking device crashes or reboots. You can configure one or more syslog servers by entering the **logging** *host* command. By default, only messages of severity level 6 or lower are logged to the syslog server. This can be changed, similar to buffer or console logging, but unlike these other commands, the severity is configured by entering the **logging trap** *level* command. This command applies to all configured syslog hosts. Figure 3-2 shows three logging commands configured on a device and an explanation for each command.

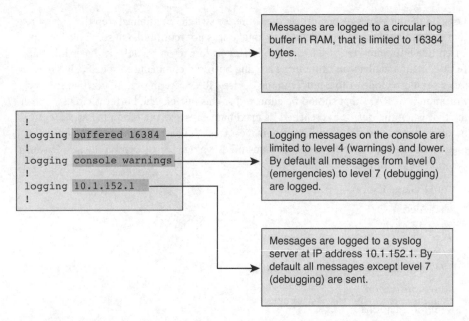

Figure 3-2   *A Logging Command Example with Explanation*

Performing Backup and Restore

An essential element of any network maintenance toolkit is a backup server to/from which device configurations and Cisco IOS Software can be copied and restored. The simplest and most commonly implemented service is TFTP, which does not require any configuration on the network devices. The server is set up to serve and receive files without any need for authentication or identification, other than specifying the name of the configuration or software file itself. The fact that the protocol does not require any authentication and that all content is sent across the network in clear text makes it a nonsecure mechanism. More secure protocols such as FTP, SCP, and HTTP or HTTPS can also be used as a means of transferring configurations and software (backup and restore). To use any of these more-secure protocols, you must specify the username and password that are used to authenticate to the server. For all of these protocols, the credentials can be specified as part of the Uniform Resource Locator (URL) that is used with the **copy** command. The username and password are specified by placing the username and password as *user-name:password@* before the server name or IP address in the URL. Example 3-2 shows how to copy the startup configuration using FTP to a server with the IP address 10.1.152.1 and a file named RO1-test.cfg using the user name Germany and password Brazil.

Example 3-2 *Performing Backup Using FTP with Username and Password*

```
RO1# copy startup-config ftp://Germany:Brazil@10.1.152.1/RO1-test.cfg
Address or name of remote host [10.1.152.1]?
Destination filename [RO1-test.cfg]?
Writing RO1-test.cfg !
2323 bytes copied in 0.268 secs (8668 bytes/sec)
```

For SCP, HTTP, and HTTPS you use a similar syntax, replacing the URL prefix ftp://
with scp://, http://, or https://, respectively. Specifying the username and password on
the command line is somewhat cumbersome and suffers from the fact that the password
is displayed in clear text on the screen, which is less desirable from a security stand-
point. To circumvent this issue, the username and password can be specified in the configuration, instead of on the command line, for the FTP, HTTP, and HTTPS protocols.
Example 3-3 shows how to store FTP and HTTP usernames and passwords in the configuration and perform an FTP backup without having to type the username and password.

Example 3-3 *Storing FTP, HTTP Usernames and Passwords in Configuration*

```
RO1(config)# ip ftp username Germany
RO1(config)# ip ftp password Brazil
RO1(config)# ip http client username Holland
RO1(config)# ip http client password 0 Argentina
RO1(config)# exit
RO1# copy startup-config ftp://10.1.152.1/RO1-test.cfg
Address or name of remote host [10.1.152.1]?
Destination filename [RO1-test.cfg]?
Writing RO1-test.cfg ! 2323 bytes copied in 0.304 secs (7641 bytes/sec)
```

The same configuration commands are used for both HTTP and HTTPS. The only difference is the protocol identifier in the URL. It is important to know that even though FTP
and HTTP require authentication, these protocols send credentials in clear text. HTTPS
and SCP use encryption to ensure confidentiality of both the transmitted credentials and
the content of the transferred file. When possible, use secure protocols such as HTTPS
and SCP. When using SCP, you can use the local user database instead of writing the
username and the password in the command line. For SCP to work, SSH must first be
configured properly. After completing the SSH configuration, you can use an SCP client
to securely copy files to and from the IOS file system. Example 3-4 shows a local username and password (cisco and cisco123, respectively) configured on router R1, 768-bit
RSA keys generated, and SSH timeout and authentication retries are configured. After
configuring SSH, a file (test-scp.txt) is copied from flash memory to an SCP server at
address 10.10.10.3 using the local username cisco.

Example 3-4 *Configuring SSH and Copying a File from Local Flash Memory to an SCP Server*

```
R1(config)# username cisco privilege 15 password 0 cisco123
R1(config)# ! SSH must be configured and functioning
R1(config)# crypto key generate rsa
The name for the keys will be: R1.lab.local
Choose the size of the key modulus in the range of 360 to 2048 for your General
Purpose Keys. Choosing a key modulus greater than 512 may take a few minutes.

How many bits in the modulus [512]: 768
% Generating 768 bit RSA keys, keys will be non-exportable...[OK]

R1(config)# ip ssh time-out 120
R1(config)# ip ssh authentication-retries 5
R1(config)# ip scp server enable
R1(config)# exit
R1# copy flash: scp:
Source filename []? test-scp.txt
Address or name of remote host []? 10.10.10.3
Destination username [Router]? Cisco
Destination filename [test-scp.txt]?
Writing test-scp.txt
Password:
!
30 bytes copied in 13.404 secs (2 bytes/sec)
```

Creating backups of configurations should be an integral part of your network maintenance routines. After any change, you should create backups, copying the configuration
file to nonvolatile RAM (NVRAM) on the device and to a network server. If you have
sufficient flash storage space on the device, you might find it useful to not only build a
configuration archive on the server, but in the flash memory of the device, too. A feature that can be helpful in the creation of configuration archives, either locally on the
device or remotely on a server, is the configuration archiving feature that is part of the
Configuration Replace and Configuration Rollback feature that was introduced in Cisco
IOS Software Release 12.3(7)T. Example 3-5 shows how to set up the configuration
archive. The configuration archive is set up by entering the **archive** command in global
configuration mode, which gets you into the config-archive configuration mode. In this
configuration submode, you can specify the parameters for the archive. The only mandatory parameter is the base file path. This path will be used as the base filename and is
appended with a number for each subsequent archived configuration. The path is specified in URL notation and can either be a local or a networked path supported by the
Cisco IOS file system. Not all types of local flash storage are supported, so check your
device's flash type for support of this feature if you want to store your configuration
archive locally instead of on a server. The configuration **path** command can include the
variables **$h** for the device's host name and **$t** to include a time and date stamp in the

filename. If you do not make use of the **$t** variable, a numeric version number is automatically appended to the filename.

Example 3-5 *Setting Up the Configuration Archive*

```
Router(config)# archive
Router(config-archive)# path flash:/config-archive/$h-config
Router(config-archive)# write-memory
Router(config-archive)# time-period 10080
```

After you specify the location of the archive, it is ready to be used, and archive copies of the configuration can be created manually by issuing the **archive config** command. However, the biggest advantage of this feature is the way you can use it to create and update a configuration archive automatically. By adding the **write-memory** option to the archive configuration section, you can trigger an archive copy of the running configuration to be created any time the running configuration is copied to NVRAM. It is also possible to generate archive copies of the configuration periodically by specifying the **time-period** option followed by a time period, specified in minutes. Each time the configured time period elapses, a copy of the running configuration will be archived (see Example 3-4).

You can verify the presence of the archived configuration files by using the **show archive** command. In addition to the files themselves, this command displays the most recent archived file and the filename for the next archive to be created, as demonstrated in Example 3-6.

Example 3-6 show archive *Command's Output*

```
RO1# show archive
There are currently 5 archive configurations saved.
The next archive file will be named flash:/config-archive/RO1-config-6
Archive # Name
0
1 flash:/config-archive/RO1-config-1
2 flash:/config-archive/RO1-config-2
3 flash:/config-archive/RO1-config-3
4 flash:/config-archive/RO1-config-4
5 flash:/config-archive/RO1-config-5 <- Most Recent
```

By creating backups, either by manually copying the files or through use of configuration archiving, you have something to fall back to when disaster strikes. If the configuration of a device is lost through human error, hardware failure, or when a device needs to be replaced, you can copy the last archived configuration to the NVRAM of the device and boot it to restore it to the exact same configuration that you had stored in your archive. Another common event when you might want to restore the device to its last archived configuration is when you have made a change or a series of changes and they did not work out as expected. If these changes were made during a regularly scheduled maintenance window, you can often perform the same procedure as if you have lost a configuration entirely. You copy the last archived known-good configuration to the NVRAM of the device and reload it. However, if you made these changes during normal network operation (for example, while troubleshooting a problem), reloading the device could be a disruptive operation and not acceptable unless you have no other option.

This situation is what the configuration replace feature was designed to deal with. The **configure replace** command enables you to replace the currently running configuration on the router with a saved configuration. It does so by comparing the running configuration with the configuration file appointed by the **configure replace** command and then creates a list of differences between the files. Based on the discovered differences, various Cisco IOS configuration commands are generated that will change the existing running configuration to the replacement configuration. Example 3-7 makes a simple demonstration of this command. The advantages of this method are as follows: Only parts of the configuration that differ will be changed, the device does not need to be reloaded (most important advantage), and existing commands are not reapplied. This manner of rolling back to an existing archived configuration is the least-disruptive method you can use. Within the documentation at Cisco.com, the **configure replace** command is sometimes referred to as configuration rollback, although the command itself does not include rollback as a keyword. It is noteworthy that the **show archive config differences** command can be used to display the differences between the running configuration and the archive.

Example 3-7   *A Simple Demonstration of the* **configure replace** *Command*

```
RO1# configure terminal
Enter configuration commands, one per line. End with CNTL/Z.
RO1(config)# hostname TEST
TEST(config)# ^Z
TEST# configure replace flash:config-archive/RO1-config-5 list
This will apply all necessary additions and deletions
to replace the current running configuration with the
contents of the specified configuration file, which is
assumed to be a complete configuration, not a partial
configuration. Enter Y if you are sure you want to proceed. ? [no]: yes
!Pass 1

!List of Commands:
no hostname TEST
hostname RO1
end




Total number of passes: 1
Rollback Done

RO1#
```

Example 3-7 shows that the hostname of a device is changed and then the configuration is rolled back to the most current archived configuration. The command option **list** is added to the configure replace command to show the configuration commands that are being applied by the configuration replacement. As you can see from the example, the change that was made is undone, without affecting any other parts of the configuration. Although this command was designed to complement the configuration archiving feature, you can use the **configure replace** command with any complete Cisco IOS configuration file.

Integrating Troubleshooting into the Network Maintenance Process

Troubleshooting is a process that takes place as part of many different network maintenance tasks. For example, it might be necessary to troubleshoot issues that arise after implementation of new devices. Similarly, it could be necessary to troubleshoot after a network maintenance task such as a software upgrade. Consequently, troubleshooting processes should be integrated into network maintenance procedures and vice versa. When troubleshooting procedures and maintenance procedures are properly aligned, the overall network maintenance process will be more effective.

Network maintenance involves many different tasks, some of which are listed within Figure 3-3. For some of these tasks, such as supporting users, responding to network failures, or disaster recovery, troubleshooting is a major component of the tasks. Tasks that do not revolve around fault management, such as adding or replacing equipment, moving servers and users, and performing software upgrades, will regularly include troubleshooting processes, too. Hence, troubleshooting should not be seen as a standalone process, but as an essential skill that plays an important role in many different types of network maintenance tasks.

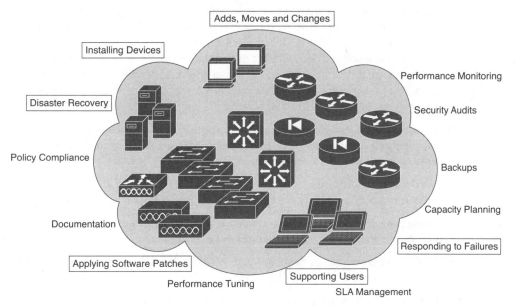

Figure 3-3 *Troubleshooting Plays an Important Role in Many Network Maintenance Tasks*

To troubleshoot effectively, you must rely on many processes and resources that are part of the network maintenance process. You need to have access to up-to-date and accurate documentation. You rely on good backup and restore procedures to be able to roll back changes if they do not resolve the problem that you are troubleshooting. You need to have a good baseline of the network so that you know which conditions are supposed to be normal on your network and what kind of behavior is considered abnormal. Also, you need to have access to logs that are properly time stamped to find out when particular events have happened. So in many ways, the quality of your troubleshooting processes depends significantly on the quality of your network maintenance processes. Therefore, it makes sense to plan and implement troubleshooting activities as part of the overall network maintenance process and to make sure that troubleshooting processes and maintenance processes are aligned and support each other, making both processes more effective.

Network Documentation and Baseline

Having accurate and current network documentation can tremendously increase the speed and effectiveness of troubleshooting processes. Having good network diagrams can especially help in quickly isolating problems to a particular part of the network, tracing the flow of traffic, and verifying connections between devices. Having a good IP address schematic and patching administration is invaluable, too, and can save a lot of time while trying to locate devices and IP addresses. Network documentation is expected to include the following items:

- **Network diagrams:** Accurate physical and logical diagrams are both required and extremely helpful.

- **Labeling interfaces and cables:** Clearly label all cables and configure a description for all interfaces. Unlabeled or mislabeled cable can seriously impede your troubleshooting efforts. When labeling cables, obey your organization's labeling scheme. The labeling scheme must be documented and made available near the wire cabinet, so troubleshooting staff can access it during the maintenance or troubleshooting tasks. When configuring a description for an interface, describe where it is connected and add other useful information such as remote interface, IP address, or even a tech support phone number to be called if the interface goes down.

- **Device interconnections specifications:** A spreadsheet or database listing and explaining all connections between internal devices, connections to external entities such as service providers, and all power circuits.

- **Hardware and software inventory:** A spreadsheet or database of all devices (including part numbers and serial numbers), spare parts, and software versions and licenses.

- **Addressing scheme:** A document that specifies all IP addresses of all devices, including physical, logical, and management interfaces.

- **Device configurations:** A hard copy and soft copy of all device configurations and possibly an archive with multiple versions.

- **Design documentation:** A document that explains all design choices made and their interdependencies and assumptions.

However, documentation that is wrong or outdated is often worse than having no documentation at all. If the documentation that you have is inaccurate or out-of-date, you might start working with information that is wrong and you might end up drawing the wrong conclusions and potentially lose a lot of time before you discover that the documentation is incorrect and cannot be relied upon.

Although everyone who is involved in network maintenance will agree that updating documentation is an essential part of network maintenance tasks, they will all recognize that in the heat of the moment, when you are troubleshooting a problem that is affecting network connectivity for many users, documenting the process and any changes that you are making is one of the last things on your mind. There are several ways to alleviate this problem. First, make sure that any changes you make during troubleshooting are handled in accordance with normal change procedures (if not during the troubleshooting process itself, then at least after the fact). You might loosen the requirements concerning authorization and scheduling of changes during major failures, but you have to make sure that after the problem has been solved or a workaround has been implemented to restore connectivity, you always go through any of the standard administrative processes like updating the documentation. Because you know that you will have to update the documentation afterward, there is an incentive to keep at least a minimal log of the changes that you make while troubleshooting.

One good policy to keep your documentation accurate, assuming that people will forget to update the documentation, is to schedule regular checks of the documentation. However, verifying documentation manually is tedious work, so you will probably prefer to implement an automated system for that. For configuration changes, you could implement a system that downloads all device configurations on a regular basis and compares the configuration to the last version to spot any differences. There are also various IOS features such as the Configuration Archive, Rollback feature, and the Embedded Event Manager that can be leveraged to create automatic configuration backups, to log configuration commands to a syslog server, or to even send out configuration differences via e-mail.

An essential troubleshooting technique is to compare what is happening on the network to what is expected or to what is normal on the network. Whenever you spot abnormal behavior in an area of the network that is experiencing problems, there is a good chance that it is related to the problems. It could be the cause of the problem, or it could be another symptom that might help point toward the underlying root cause. Either way, it is always worth investigating abnormal behavior to find out whether it is related to the problem. For example, suppose you are troubleshooting an application problem, and while you are following the path between the client and the server, you notice that one of the routers is also a bit slow in its responses to your commands. You execute the **show processes cpu** command and notice that the average CPU load over the past 5 seconds was 97 percent and over the last 1 minute was around 39 percent. You might wonder if this router's high CPU utilization might be the cause of the problem you are troubleshooting. On one hand, this could be an important clue that is worth investigating, but on the other hand, it could be that your router regularly runs at 40 percent to 50 percent CPU and it is not related to this problem at all. In this case, you could potentially waste a lot of time trying to find the cause for the high CPU load, while it is entirely unrelated to the problem at hand.

The only way to know what is normal for your network is to measure the network's behavior continuously. Knowing what to measure is different for each network. In general, the more you know, the better it is, but obviously this has to be balanced against the effort and cost involved in implementing and maintaining a performance management system. The following list describes some useful data to gather and create a baseline:

- **Basic performance statistics:** Interface load for critical network links, CPU load, and memory usage of routers and switches are essential statistics to gather. These values can be polled and collected on a regular basis using SNMP and graphed for visual inspection.

- **Accounting of network traffic:** Remote Monitoring (RMON), Network Based Application Recognition (NBAR), or NetFlow statistics can be used to profile different types of traffic on the network.

- **Measurements of network performance characteristics:** The IP SLA feature in Cisco IOS can be used to measure critical performance indicators such as delay and jitter across the network infrastructure.

These baseline measurements are useful for troubleshooting, but they are also useful inputs for capacity planning, network usage accounting, and SLA monitoring. Clearly, a synergy exists between gathering traffic and performance statistics as part of regular network maintenance and using those statistics as a baseline during troubleshooting. Moreover, after you have the infrastructure in place to collect, analyze, and graph network statistics, you can also leverage this infrastructure to troubleshoot specific performance problems. For example, if you notice that a router crashes once a week and you suspect a memory leak as the cause of this issue, you could decide to graph the router's memory usage for a certain period of time to see whether you can find a correlation between the crashes and the memory usage. Some of the protocols that can help you gather information and statistics on your network and build a credible baseline are SNMP, RMON, NetFlow, and Cisco IP SLA.

Communication

Communication is an essential part of the troubleshooting process. To review, the main phases of structured troubleshooting are as follows:

- Define the problem

- Gather information

- Analyze the information

- Eliminate what cannot be the problem cause

- Formulate a hypothesis about the likely cause of the problem

- Test your hypothesis

- Solve the problem

Figure 3-4 shows several spots where, while performing structured troubleshooting, communication is necessary if not inevitable.

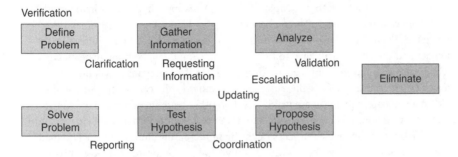

Figure 3-4   *Communication Is Needed In All Phases of the Structured Troubleshooting Process*

Within each phase of the troubleshooting process, communication plays a role:

- **Define the problem:** Even though this is the first step of the structured troubleshooting, it is triggered by the user reporting the problem. Reporting the problem and defining the problem are not the same. When someone reports a problem, it is often too vague to act on it immediately. You have to verify the problem and gather as much information as you can about the symptoms from the person who reported the problem. Asking good questions and carefully listening to the answers is essential in this phase. You might ask questions such as these: "What do you mean exactly when you say that something is failing? Did you make any changes before the problem started? Did you notice anything special before this problem started? When did it last work? Has it ever worked?" After you communicate with the users and perhaps see the problems for yourself, you make a precise and clear problem definition. Clearly, this step is all about communication.

- **Gather information:** During this phase of the process, you will often depend on other engineers or users to gather information for you. You might need to obtain information contained in server or application logs, configurations of devices that you do not manage, information about outages from a service provider, or information from users in different locations, to compare against the location that is experiencing the problem. Clearly, communicating what information you need and how that information can be obtained determines how successfully you can acquire the information you really need.

- **Analyze information and eliminate possibilities:** In itself, interpretation and analysis is mostly a solitary process, but there are still some communication aspects to this phase. First of all, you cannot be experienced in every aspect of networking. So, if you find that you are having trouble interpreting certain results or if you lack knowledge about certain processes, you can ask specialists on your team to help you out. Also, there is always a chance that you are misinterpreting results, misreading information, making wrong assumptions, or are having other flaws in your interpretation and analysis. A different viewpoint can often help in these situations, so discussing your reasoning and results with teammates to validate your assumptions and conclusions can be very helpful, especially when you are stuck.

- **Propose and test a hypothesis:** Most of the time, testing a hypothesis involves making changes to the network. These changes may be disruptive, and users may be impacted. Even if you have decided that the urgency of the problem outweighs the impact and the change will have to be made, you should still communicate clearly what you are doing and why you are doing it. Even if your changes will not have a major impact on the users or the business, you should still coordinate and communicate any changes that you are making. When other team members are working on the same problem, you have to make sure that you are not both making changes. Any results from the elimination process might be rendered invalid if a change was made during the information-gathering phase and you were not aware of it. Also, if two changes are made in quick succession and it turns out that the problem was resolved, you will not know which of the two changes actually fixed it. This does not mean that you cannot be working on the same problem as a team, but you have to adhere to certain rules. Having multiple people working on different parts of the network, gathering information in parallel or pursuing different strategies, can help in finding the cause faster. During a major disaster, when every minute counts, the extra speed that you can gain by working in parallel may prove valuable. However, any changes or other disruptive actions should be carefully coordinated and communicated.

- **Solve the problem:** Clearly, this phase also involves some communication. You must report back to the person who originally reported the problem that the problem has been solved. Also, you must communicate this to any other people who were involved during the process. Finally, you will have to go through any communication that is involved in the normal change processes, to make sure that the changes that you made are properly integrated in the standard network maintenance processes.

Sometimes it is necessary to escalate the problem to another person or another group. Common reasons for this could be that you do not have sufficient knowledge and skills and you want to escalate the problem to a specialist or to a more senior engineer, or that you are working in shifts and you need to hand over the problem as your shift ends. Handing the troubleshooting task over to someone else does not only require clear communication of the results of your process, such as gathered information and conclusions that you have drawn, but it also includes any communication that has been going on up to this point. This is where an issue-tracking or trouble ticketing system can be of tremendous value, especially if it integrates well with other means of communication such as e-mail.

Finally, another communication process that requires some attention is how to communicate the progress of your troubleshooting process to the business (management or otherwise). When you are experiencing a major outage, there will usually be a barrage of questions from business managers and users: What are you doing to repair this issue? How long will it take before it is solved? Can you implement any workarounds? What do you need to fix this? Although these are all reasonable questions, the truth is that many of these questions cannot be answered until the cause of the problem is found. At the same time, all the time spent communicating about the process is taken away from the actual troubleshooting effort itself. Therefore, it is worthwhile to streamline this process (for instance, by having one of the senior team members act as a conduit for all communication). All questions are routed to this person, and any updates and changes are communicated to him; this person will then update the key stakeholders. This way, the engineers who are actually working on the problem can work with a minimal amount of distraction.

Change Control

Change control is one of the most fundamental processes in network maintenance. By strictly controlling when changes are made, defining what type of authorization is required and what actions need to be taken as part of that process, you can reduce the frequency and duration of unplanned outages and thereby increase the overall uptime of your network. You must therefore understand how the changes made as part of trouble-shooting fit into the overall change processes. Essentially, there is not anything different between making a change as part of the maintenance process or as part of troubleshoot-ing. Most of the actions that you take are the same. You implement the change, verify that it achieved the desired results, roll back if it did not achieve the desired results, back up the changed configurations or software, and document/communicate your changes. The biggest difference between regular changes and emergency changes is the authoriza-tion required to make a change and the scheduling of the change. Within change-control procedures, there is always an aspect of balancing urgency, necessity, impact, and risk. The outcome of this assessment will determine whether a change can be executed imme-diately or if it will have to be scheduled at a later time.

The troubleshooting process can benefit tremendously from having well-defined and well-documented change processes. It is uncommon for devices or links just to fail from one moment to the next. In many cases, problems are triggered or caused by some sort of change. This can be a simple change, such as changing a cable or reconfiguring a set-ting, but it may also be more subtle, like a change in traffic patterns due to the outbreak of a new worm or virus. A problem can also be caused by a combination of changes, where the first change is the root cause of the problem, but the problem is not triggered until you make another change. For example, imagine a situation where somebody acci-dentally erases the router software from its flash. This will not cause the router to fail immediately, because it is running IOS from its RAM. However, if that router reboots because of a short power failure a month later, it will not boot, because it is missing the IOS in its flash memory. In this example, the root cause of the failure is the erased soft-ware, but the trigger is the power failure. This type of problem is harder to catch, and only in tightly controlled environments will you be able to find the root cause or prevent this type of problem. In the previous example, a log of all privileged EXEC commands executed on this router can reveal that the software had been erased at a previous date. You can conclude that one of the useful questions you can ask during fact gathering is "Has anything been changed?" The answer to this question can very likely be found in the network documentation or change logs if network policies enforce rigid documenta-tion and change-control procedures.

Summary

Tasks performed by network engineers can be classified into the following general categories:

- Tasks related to device installation and maintenance
- Tasks related to failure response
- Tasks related to network performance
- Tasks related to business procedures
- Tasks related to security

There are two network maintenance models: interrupt driven and structured. The structured network maintenance model has the following advantages over its interrupt-driven counterpart:

- Reduced network downtime
- More cost-effectiveness
- Better alignment with business objectives
- Higher network security

All network maintenance plans need to include procedures to perform the following tasks:

- Accommodating adds, moves, and changes
- Installing and configuring new devices
- Replacing failed devices
- Backing up device configurations and software
- Troubleshooting link and device failures
- Upgrading or patching software
- Monitoring the network
- Performance measurement and capacity planning
- Writing and updating documentation

Network maintenance planning includes the following:

- Scheduling maintenance
- Change-control procedures
- Network documentation
- Effective communication

- Defining templates/procedures/conventions
- Disaster recovery

Benefits of scheduled maintenance include the following:

- You reduce network downtime.
- Long-term maintenance tasks will not be neglected or forgotten.
- You have predictable lead times for change requests.
- Disruptive maintenance tasks can be scheduled during assigned maintenance windows, reducing downtime during production hours.

Typical elements of network documentation include the following:

- Network drawings
- Connection documentation
- Equipment lists
- IP address administration
- Configurations
- Design documentation

To perform successful disaster recovery when a device fails, you need to have the following saved and available:

- Replacement hardware
- The current software version for the device
- The current configuration for the device
- The tools to transfer the software and configuration to the device
- Licenses (if applicable)
- Knowledge of the procedures to install software, configurations, and licenses

The basic components of a network maintenance toolkit are as follows:

- CLI-based device management
- GUI-based device management
- Backup server
- Log server
- Time server

Logging messages can be sent to one or more of the following destinations:

- Console (default)

- Monitor (vty/AUX)

- Buffer (volatile memory)

- Syslog server

- Flash memory (nonvolatile memory)

- SNMP network management server (as an SNMP trap)

Logging severity levels on Cisco Systems devices are as follows:

    (0) Emergency

    (1) Alert

    (2) Critical

    (3) Error

    (4) Warning

    (5) Notification

    (6) Informational

    (7) Debugging

The three main motivations for measuring network performance are as follows:

- Capacity planning

- Diagnosing performance problems

- SLA compliance

TFTP, FTP, SCP, HTTP, and HTTPS can all be used to transfer files between your network and backup devices. FTP, SCP, HTTP, and HTTPS are more secure than TFTP because they require authentication. SCP and HTTPS are most secure because they also incorporate encryption.

A feature that can prove helpful in the creation of configuration archives, either locally on the device or remotely on a server, is the configuration archiving feature that is part of the Configuration Replace and Configuration Rollback feature that was introduced in Cisco IOS Software Release 12.3(7)T.

To successfully recover from a disaster, you need the following:

- Up-to-date configuration backups

- Up-to-date software backups

- Up-to-date hardware inventories

- Configuration and software provisioning tools

Network documentation is expected to include the following items:

- Network diagrams
- Labeling interfaces and cables
- Device interconnections specifications
- Hardware and software inventory
- Addressing scheme
- Device configurations
- Design documentation

The data that you need to gather and include in your network baseline document must include the following:

- Basic performance statistics
- Accounting of network traffic
- Measurements of network performance characteristics

Review Questions

1. Which *three* of the following are benefits of a structured approach to network maintenance?

   a. Maintenance processes are better aligned to business needs.
   b. Hardware discounts can be negotiated with the reseller.
   c. The overall security of the network will be higher.
   d. The total unplanned network downtime will be lower.
   e. Users will never have to wait to get support.
   f. Network maintenance can be outsourced to lower the cost.

2. Network maintenance planning includes all except which of the following?

   a. Scheduling maintenance
   b. Change-control procedures
   c. Network documentation
   d. Effective communication
   e. Defining templates/procedures/conventions
   f. Network security design

3. Which *two* of the following are benefits of scheduled maintenance?

   a. Network engineers will not have to work outside regular work hours.
   b. Lead times for change requests will be more predictable.
   c. Disruptive maintenance tasks can be scheduled during assigned maintenance windows.
   d. No change will be necessary or allowed during regular business hours.

4. Which factors should be considered during the implementation of change procedures?

5. Which *three* of the following items do you need to have to replace a failed device?

   a. Replacement hardware for the failed device

   b. Proof of purchase of the failed device

   c. TAC support for the failed device

   d. The current configuration of the failed device

   e. The current software version of the failed device

   f. The original box that the failed device was shipped in

6. Network monitoring is a fundamental aspect of a proactive network management strategy. True or False?

   a. True

   b. False

7. Which *five* of the following protocols can be used to transfer a configuration file from a router to a server to create a configuration backup?

   a. HTTPS

   b. HTTP

   c. FTP

   d. SNMP

   e. TFTP

   f. SCP

8. Which of the following commands is the correct command to copy the running configuration of a router to a file named test.cfg residing on an FTP server with IP address 10.1.1.1, using the username admin and password cisco?

   a. copy running-config ftp://10.1.1.1/test.cfg user admin password cisco

   b. copy running-config ftp://10.1.1.1/test.cfg/user:admin /password:cisco

   c. copy running-config ftp://admin:cisco@10.1.1.1/test.cfg

   d. archive running-config ftp://10.1.1.1/test.cfg user admin password cisco

   e. None of these are correct; FTP does not require authentication.

9. What command enables you to manually create an archive copy of the running configuration?

10. Which of the following commands is the correct command to restore the current configuration to the archived configuration file RO1-archive-config-5 residing in flash?

   a. archive rollback flash:/RO1-archive-config-5

   b. configure replace flash:/RO1-archive-config-5

   c. copy flash:/RO1-archive-config-5 running-config

   d. archive restore flash:/RO1-archive-config-5

11. What command enables you to configure a switch to log system messages to a syslog server at IP address 10.1.1.1?

12. Which *two* of the following are processes that benefit from the implementation of a network performance measurement system?

   a. Disaster recovery
   b. Change management
   c. Capacity planning
   d. SLA compliance

13. Which of the following phases of the structured troubleshooting process does not have communication as a major component?

   a. Defining the problem
   b. Solving the problem
   c. Eliminating causes
   d. Gathering information

Chapter 4

Basic Switching and Routing Process and Effective IOS Troubleshooting Commands

This chapter covers the following topics:

- Basic Layer 2 switching process

- Basic Layer 3 routing process

- Selective information gathering using IOS **show** commands, **debug** commands, ping, and Telnet

Ethernet LAN switching is a commonly used technology in current enterprise networks. Layer 2 and Layer 3 switching are a major part of campus networks, and they can also be found in data centers and some WAN solutions. It is therefore essential to have a good understanding of campus routing and switching technologies. It is also important for a network engineer to be able to diagnose and resolve problems associated with these technologies.

This chapter covers the basic Layer 2 switching and basic Layer 3 routing by presenting and analyzing an example for each process. The third section of this chapter provides some useful filtering and redirecting techniques to be used while using the **show** command. Furthermore, some basic hardware (CPU, memory, interface) diagnostic commands, **ping** and **telnet**, and effective use of the **debug** command, are presented and explained.

Basic Layer 2 Switching Process

A good understanding of the processes involved in Layer 2 switching is essential to any engineer who is involved in network troubleshooting. VLAN-based switched infrastructures are at the core of every campus network and being able to diagnose and resolve Layer 2 switching problems in these environments is a fundamental skill that any network engineer should have. This section first reviews the Layer 2 switching process and the associated switch data structures. Next, you will learn how to gather information from these data structures using Cisco IOS Software commands. Finally, you will learn how to interpret and analyze the gathered information in order to verify the proper operation of the Layer 2 switching process or to pinpoint and resolve problems.

Ethernet Frame Forwarding (Layer 2 Data Plane)

As a network engineer, you must have an in-depth knowledge of the core processes performed by hosts and network devices. When things break down and devices do not function as they should, a good understanding of processes helps you determine where exactly a process breaks down. In addition, you will be able to determine which parts of the network are functioning correctly and which parts are not functioning correctly. This section examines the processes that take place when two IP hosts communicate over a switched LAN. The focus here is at the IP and lower layers; this means that the host application is in working condition and matters such as name to IP address resolution are functional. To limit the scope of the discussion to the processes involved in Layer 2 switching, assume that the two hosts reside on a common subnet (VLAN). Because the actual application being used is irrelevant to this discussion, imagine that the user of Host A would like to test connectivity to Host B using ping as per the network shown in Figure 4-1.

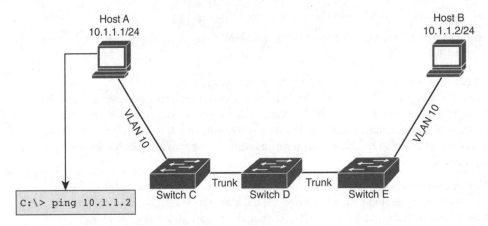

Figure 4-1   *Host A Tests Connectivity to Host B on the Same VLAN (Subnet)*

This process can be broken down into the following steps:

Step 1.   Host A will look up the destination (Host B) IP address in its routing table and determine that it is on a directly connected network.

Step 2.   Because Host B is directly reachable, Host A will consult its Address Resolution Protocol (ARP) cache to find the MAC address of Host B.

Step 3.   If the ARP cache on Host A does not contain an entry for the IP address of Host B, it will send out an ARP request as a broadcast to obtain the MAC address of Host B (see Figure 4-2).

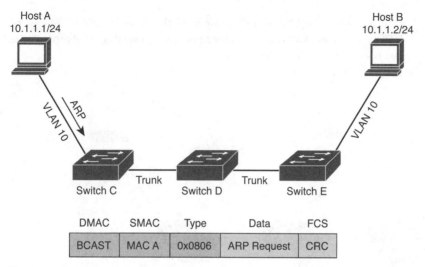

Figure 4-2 *Host A Sends a Broadcast ARP Request to Obtain Host B's MAC Address*

Step 4.   Switch C checks the VLAN of the port upon which it receives the frame, records the source MAC address in its MAC address table, and associates it to that port and VLAN. Switch C will perform a lookup in its MAC address table to try to find the port that is associated to the broadcast MAC address.

The MAC address table never contains an entry for the broadcast MAC address (FFFF:FFFF:FFFF). Therefore, Switch C will flood the frame on all ports in that VLAN, including all trunks that this VLAN is allowed, that are active, and that are not pruned on (except the port it came in from). Switches D and E repeat this process as they receive the frame (see Figure 4-3).

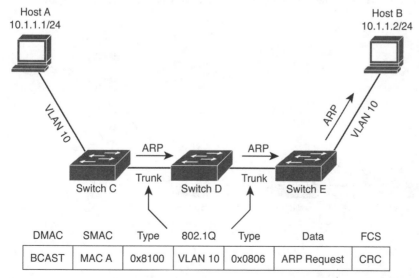

Figure 4-3 *Switch Floods Broadcast Frame to All but the Sending Interface (Within the Same VLAN)*

Step 5. Host B receives the ARP request, records the IP address and MAC address of Host A in its own ARP cache, and then proceeds to send an ARP reply as a unicast back to Host A (see Figure 4-4).

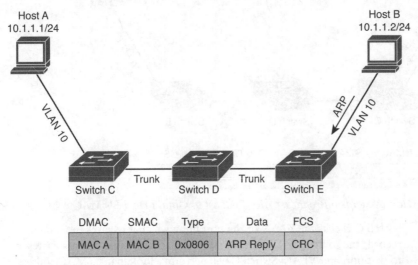

Figure 4-4 *Host B Sends a Unicast ARP Reply Back to Host A*

Step 6. The switches will check the VLAN of the port they received the frame on, and because all switches now have an entry in their MAC address table for the MAC address of Host A, they will forward the frame containing the ARP reply on the path to Host A only, not flooding it out on any other port. At the same time, they will record Host B's MAC address and corresponding interface and VLAN in their MAC address table if they did not already have that entry (see Figure 4-5).

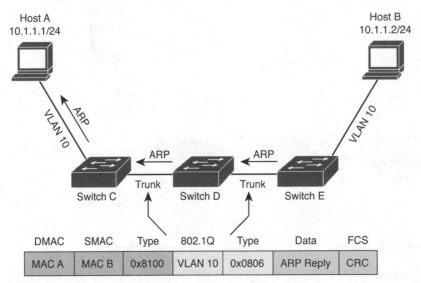

Figure 4-5 *Switches Forward the ARP Reply (Unicast) Frame Toward Host A*

Step 7. Host A receives the ARP reply and records the IP and MAC address of Host B in its ARP cache. Now it is ready to send the original IP packet.

Step 8. Host A encapsulates the IP packet (which encapsulates an ICMP echo request) in a unicast frame destined for Host B and sends it out. Note that the Ethernet type field of 0x0800 indicates that the frame is encapsulating an IP packet.

Step 9. The switches again consult their MAC address tables, find an entry for Host B's MAC address, and forward it on the path toward Host B (see Figure 4-6).

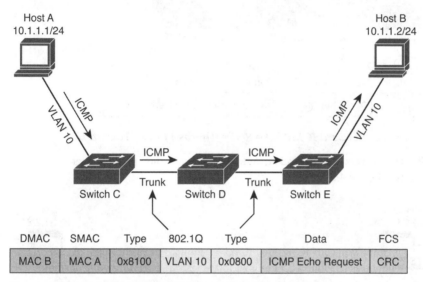

Figure 4-6 *Switches Forward ICMP Echo Request (Unicast) Frame Toward Host B*

Step 10. Host B receives the packet and responds to Host A (by sending an ICMP echo-reply packet).

Step 11. The switches again consult their MAC address tables and forward the frame straight to Host A, without any flooding (see Figure 4-7).

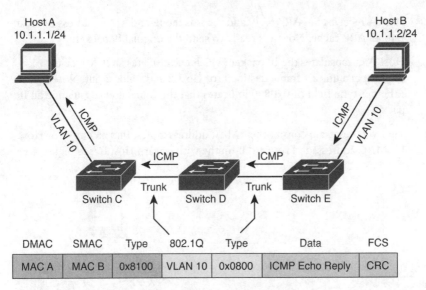

Figure 4-7   *Switches Forward ICMP Echo Reply (Unicast) Frame Toward Host A*

> **Step 12.**   Host A receives the packet, and this concludes this simple packet exchange
> (see Figure 4-8).

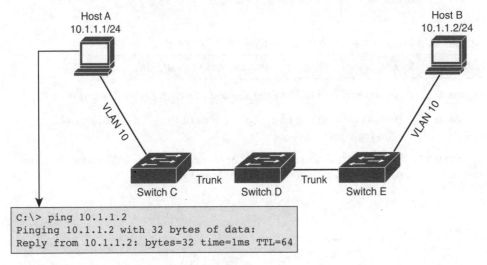

Figure 4-8   *Host A Receives ICMP Echo Reply Back from Host B*

Although this process might seem trivial, listing the steps clearly shows that even for
the simplest communication, an elaborate chain of events takes place. If at any point
this chain is broken due to faulty cabling, failing devices, or misconfiguration, the communication will fail. Therefore, you must leverage your knowledge of these processes to
diagnose and solve problems in a switched environment. Possible issues that could cause
the communication to fail include the following:

- Physical problems

- Bad, missing, or miswired cables

- Bad ports

- Power failure

- Device problems

- Software bugs

- Performance problems

- Misconfiguration

- Missing or wrong VLANs

- Misconfigured VLAN Trunking Protocol (VTP) settings

- Wrong VLAN setting on access ports

- Missing or misconfigured trunks

- Native VLAN mismatch

- VLANs not allowed on trunk

Note   Please note that this list is not complete, and is focused on Layer 1 and Layer 2 issues. For example, a firewall may stop the Internet Control Message Protocol (ICMP) packets. Sometimes the very first ICMP echo request times out because of the requirement for an ARP request, which is not necessary on the following ICMP echo requests.

To keep the focus specifically on LAN switching, this chapter does not discuss any generic physical problems. However, you will learn how specific commands available on the Cisco Catalyst LAN switches could supplement your troubleshooting toolkit to help troubleshoot data link and physical layer problems.

Layer 2 Switching Verification

A common method to troubleshoot Layer 2 switching problems is to follow the path of the frames through the switches. Following the actual frames themselves in real time takes a lot of time and effort because it requires packet captures at various points in the network; that is neither practical nor feasible. Instead of trying to follow the frame in real time, you must follow the trail of the frame. The objective is to confirm that frames have passed through the switches and to verify how each switch made its forwarding decisions. If you find a point where the trail suddenly stops or if you find that the information that the switch uses to forward frames does not match your expectations, you will gain important clues. These clues will help in reducing the scope of the possible problem areas, and it helps in formulating a hypothesis on the cause of the problem; it may even outright point at the cause of the problem. Consequently, a troubleshooter needs to learn how to follow the trail of the frame, and know which data structure proves whether frames have passed through the switch.

One key data structure that you can consult is the switch's MAC address table. In this table, the switch registers the source MAC address of each frame that it receives, and records the port and VLAN on which the frame was received. When you see an entry for a particular MAC address in this table, it proves that at some point, usually up to 5 minutes ago, this switch received frames from that source. This does not necessarily tell you anything about a particular frame or how long ago the last frame was received. Therefore, it might be a good practice to clear the MAC entry from the table by using the **clear mac-address-table dynamic** command and verify that the MAC address is learned again when you reinitiate the connection. Second, the MAC address table enables you to verify that frames are received on the port and VLAN where they are expected. If the output does not match your expectations and assumptions, use it as a clue in forming a hypothesis about the cause of the problem. Because there are many possible findings and conclusions that you might draw from, the following is a short list of some common findings and plausible conclusions:

- **Frames are not received on the correct VLAN:** This could point to VLAN or trunk misconfiguration as the cause of the problem.

- **Frames are received on a different port than you expected:** This could point to a physical problem, spanning-tree issues, or duplicate MAC addresses.

- **The MAC address is not registered in the MAC address table:** This tells you that the problem is most likely upstream from this switch. You should retrace your steps and investigate between the last point where you know that frames were received and this switch.

The next step is to use your knowledge of the forwarding process combined with the information you can gather using the switch's diagnostic commands output to determine what the next step in the process must be. Again, you should validate the facts that you gather about the switch's forwarding behavior against your expectations and assumptions. After you have confirmed that the behavior of the switch matches your expectations, you have successfully reduced the possible scope of the problem: You have confirmed that everything works as expected up to this point.

You must definitely have a good grasp of the switch diagnostic commands and use them effectively. You will use these commands to gather the information from the switch that is needed to validate your assumptions. Some commonly used diagnostic commands that help you obtain information about the Layer 2 switching process, VLANs, and trunks are as follows:

- **show mac-address-table:** This is the main command to verify Layer 2 forwarding. It shows you the MAC addresses learned by the switch and their corresponding port and VLAN associations. This command gives you an indication if frames sourced by a particular host have succeeded in reaching this switch. It will also help you verify whether these frames were received on the correct inbound interface. Note that if the MAC address table becomes full, no more learning can happen. During trouble-shooting, always check to see whether the table is full.

- **show vlan:** This command enables you to verify VLAN existence and port-to-VLAN associations. This command lists all VLANS that were created on the switch (either manually or through VTP). It will also list the ports that are associated to each of the VLANs. Note that trunks are not listed because they do not belong to any particular VLAN.

- **show interfaces trunk:** This command displays all interfaces that are configured as trunks. It will also display on each trunk which VLANs are allowed and what the native VLAN is.

- **show interfaces switchport:** This command combines some of the information found in **show vlan** and **show interfaces trunk** commands. It is most useful if you are not looking for a switch-wide overview of trunk or VLAN related information, but if you would rather have a quick summary of all VLAN-related information for a single interface.

- **show platform forward** *interface-id*: You can use many parameters with this command and find out how the hardware would forward a frame that matches the specified parameters, on the specified interface.

- **traceroute mac:** You specify a source and destination MAC address with this command to see the list of switch hops that a frame from that source MAC address to that destination MAC address passes through. Use this command to discover the Layer 2 path frames take from the specified source MAC address to the specified destination MAC address. This command requires that Cisco Discovery Protocol (CDP) be enabled on all the switches in the network (or at least within the path).

Based on the information they provide, the commands listed can be categorized. To display the MAC address table, use the **show mac-address-table** command. To display VLAN database and port-to-VLAN mapping, use the **show vlan** command. To see the trunk port settings and port-to-VLAN associations, use the **show interfaces switchport** and **show interfaces trunk** commands. To directly verify frame forwarding, use the **show platform forward** and the **traceroute mac** commands.

Basic Layer 3 Routing Process

TCP/IP is the dominant networking protocol suite within modern networks. Internet Protocol (IP) routing takes place in almost all parts of an enterprise network, and it facilitates communication within a campus network, between branch and headquarter offices, to and from the Internet, and among virtual private network (VPN) sites. Border Gateway Protocol (BGP) is the only routing protocol capable of inter-autonomous system or interdomain routing. Enhanced Interior Gateway Routing Protocol (EIGRP) and Open Shortest Path First (OSPF) Protocol are the most preferred intra autonomous system or interior routing protocols within nontransit enterprise networks. A good understanding of EIGRP, OSPF, BGP, route redistribution mechanisms, network layer connectivity in general, and the ability to diagnose and resolve problems associated with these technologies is therefore essential to any network engineer.

For most connectivity problems in IP networks, the network layer is the point where troubleshooting efforts start. Examining network layer connectivity between two hosts helps determine whether the problem cause is at the same, lower, or higher layer than the network layer of the Open Systems Interconnection (OSI) model. If network layer connectivity between two hosts is functional, the problem is more likely to be caused by application issues or it may be due to security-related settings or problems. However, lack of network layer connectivity indicates that the problem is at or below the network layer. A network engineer should have the skills and knowledge to diagnose and resolve these problems in an efficient manner. This can be accomplished by comprehending the processes and data structures used by routers to forward IP packets and the Cisco IOS tools that can be used to diagnose those types of problems.

IP Packet Forwarding (Layer 3 Data Plane)

To troubleshoot Layer 3 connectivity, you need to have a good understanding of the processes involved in routing a packet from a host through multiple routers to the final destination. Figure 4-9 shows an IP network with IP Hosts A and B on the opposite ends of the network, interconnected by two networks and Routers C, D, and E.

Figure 4-9   *Identify the Processes and Data Structures Involved in Sending Packets from Host A to Host B and Back*

As a network support and troubleshooting professional, you need to be able to answer the following questions about the data structures used and the processes involved in the packet exchange process between Hosts A and B, on all the devices:

1. Which decisions does Host A make, what information does it need, and which actions does it perform to successfully send a packet destined for Host B to the first hop Router C?

2. Which decisions does Router C make, what information does it need, and which actions does it perform to successfully send the packet from Host A destined for Host B to the next hop, Router D?

3. Which decisions does Router D make, what information does it need, and which actions does it perform to successfully send the packet from Host A destined for Host B to the next hop, Router E? Is the answer to this question the same as the answer to the previous question or are there any differences?

4. Which decisions does Router E make, what information does it need, and which actions does it perform to successfully send the packet from Host A destined for Host B to its final destination, Host B?

5. Are there any differences in the processes and information required to successfully transmit return packets from Host B back to Host A?

If the source host or any of the routers in the path are not capable of forwarding packets, because of the lack of proper configuration or the required forwarding information, the packets are dropped, and Layer 3 connectivity is lost.

The sequence of the major processes, decisions, and actions that take place on the end devices and the intermediate devices (routers) is as follows:

1. When Host A starts the process to send a packet to Host B, it first determines whether the destination network is the same or different from its own local subnet. This is done by comparing the destination IP address (10.1.4.2) to its own IP address and subnet mask (10.1.1.1/24). Host A concludes that the destination is not local, and therefore it attempts to forward the packet to its default gateway, which is known through manual configuration or learned through Dynamic Host Configuration Protocol (DHCP). To encapsulate the packet in an Ethernet frame, Host A needs the MAC address of the default gateway. This can be resolved using the Address Resolution Protocol (ARP). Host A will either already have an entry in its ARP cache for the default gateway IP address or, alternatively, it will send out an ARP request to obtain the information and populate the cache.

2. Router C de-encapsulates the IP packet from the received Ethernet frame and examines the destination IP address of the IP packet. Router C decrements the Time To Live (TTL) field in the IP header of the packet by one. If this causes the TTL field to be set to zero, Router C will discard the packet and send an Internet Control Message Protocol (ICMP) "time exceeded" message back to the source, Host A. If the TTL of the packet is not reduced to zero, the router performs a forwarding table lookup to find the longest prefix that matches the destination IP address of the packet being processed. In this example, Router C finds the entry 10.1.4.0/24 as the best match for the destination address of the packet (10.1.4.2). Two important parameters are associated with this entry: the next-hop IP address 10.1.2.2 and the egress interface Serial 0. This serial interface uses the High-Level Data Link Control (HDLC) protocol on Layer 2. Because this protocol does not require a MAC address or other form of Layer 2 address for the next-hop IP address, no further lookups are necessary. Router C encapsulates the packet (datagram) in an HDLC frame and transmits it out of interface Serial 0.

3. Router D goes through the same general process as Router C. It also finds an entry for prefix 10.1.4.0/24 in its forwarding table. In this case, the next hop is 10.1.3.2, and the egress interface is FastEthernet 0. The biggest difference with the previous step is the Layer 2 protocol of the egress interface. Because this is a Fast Ethernet interface, the router might have to make use of ARP to resolve the next-hop IP address 10.1.3.2 to a MAC address. Normally, Router D has this address recorded in its Cisco Express Forwarding (CEF) adjacency table and need not use ARP. Router D encapsulates the packet in an Ethernet frame and forwards it to the next hop, Router E.

4. The process on Router E is similar to the process on Router C and Router D. The most important difference is that the entry for prefix 10.1.4.0/24 that Router E finds in the routing table is listed as being directly connected to interface FastEthernet 1. Therefore, instead of forwarding the packet to a next-hop router, Router E forwards the packet directly to the destination Host B on the connected network. Because the Layer 2 protocol in this example is again Ethernet, Router E consults its ARP cache to find the MAC address for Host B (10.1.4.2). Host B's MAC address might or might not be present in Router E's ARP cache. Therefore, Router E might have to send an ARP request out and obtain Host B's MAC address. Router E encapsulates the packet in an Ethernet frame destined for Host B and transmits the frame out of its FastEthernet 1 interface. When Host B receives the packet, this concludes the transmission of a packet from Host A to Host B.

5. The process in sending return packets from Host B to Host A is similar. However, the information used in the lookups in the routing table and Layer 3 to Layer 2 mapping tables, such as the ARP cache, is different. For the return packets, the destination IP address is 10.1.1.1; so instead of entries for subnet 10.1.4.0/24, entries for subnet 10.1.1.0/24 will have to be present in all router forwarding tables. These entries will have different associated egress interfaces and next-hop IP addresses. As a result, the corresponding ARP cache entries for those next hops need to be present, and these differ from the entries that were used on the path from Host A to Host B. Consequently, you cannot conclude that if packets are successfully forwarded from Host A to Host B, return packets from Host B to Host A will automatically be successful, too. This is a wrong assumption made by many people.

When you find that there is no network layer connectivity between two hosts, a good method to troubleshoot the problem is to track the path of the packet from router to router, similar to the method of tracking the path of a frame from switch to switch to diagnose Layer 2 problems. Along the way, you have to verify the availability of a matching route in the forwarding table for the destination of the packet and, subsequently, the availability of a Layer 3 to Layer 2 address mapping for the next hop for those technologies that require a Layer 2 address, such as Ethernet. For any type of application that requires two-way communication, you have to track the packets in both directions. Availability of the correct routing information and Layer 3 to Layer 2 mappings for packets traveling in one direction does not imply that the correct information is available for packets traveling in the opposite direction, too.

Based on the processes that take place in the example presented in Figure 4-9, as packets from Host A are forwarded across multiple router hops (Routers C, D, and E) to Host B, the correct values for the packet and frame header address fields are shown in Table 4-1.

Table 4-1 *Frame and Packet Header Address Fields in Transit*

Packet Position	Source IP Address	Destination IP Address	Source MAC Address	Destination MAC Address
From Host A to Router C	10.1.1.1	10.1.4.2	Host A's MAC address	MAC address of interface Fa0 on router C
From Host A to Router C	10.1.1.1	10.1.4.2	Not applicable	Not applicable
From Router D to Router E	10.1.1.1	10.1.4.2	MAC address of Router D's Fa0 interface	MAC address of router E's Fa0 interface
From Router E to Host B	10.1.1.1	10.1.4.2	MAC address of router E's Fa1 interface	Host B's MAC address

To forward packets, a router combines information from various control plane data structures. The most important of these data structures is the routing table. Unlike switches, which flood a frame to all ports if its destination MAC address is not known by the MAC address table, routers drop any packet for which they cannot find a matching entry in the routing table. When a packet has to be forwarded, the routing table is searched for the longest possible prefix that matches the destination IP address of the packet. Associated with this entry is an egress interface and, in most cases, a next-hop IP address.

Executing different table lookups and combining the information to construct a frame every time a packet needs to be routed is an inefficient approach to forwarding IP packets. To improve this process and increase the performance of IP packet-switching operations on routers, Cisco has developed Cisco Express Forwarding (CEF). This advanced Layer 3 IP switching mechanism can be used on all routers, and is at the core of the Layer 3 switching technology used in Cisco Catalyst multilayer switches. On most platforms, the CEF switching method is enabled by default.

CEF combines the information from the routing table and other data structures, such as Layer 3 to Layer 2 mapping tables, into two new data structures: the Forwarding Information Base (FIB) and the CEF adjacency table. The FIB mostly reflects the routing table with all the recursive lookups resolved. A lookup in the FIB results in a pointer to an adjacency entry in the CEF adjacency table. Similar to an entry from the routing table, an adjacency table entry can consist of an egress interface only for a point-to-point interface or an egress interface and next-hop IP address for a multipoint interface.

Using IOS Commands to Verify IP Packet Forwarding

To determine the information that is used to forward packets, you can verify the availability of a specific routing entry (prefix) in the routing table or the CEF FIB table.

Note   Since the release of RFC 3222 in 2001, the routing table is also called Routing Information Base (RIB) by many. Note that during discussions about protocols such as BGP and OSPF, the collection of the best paths to different destinations are referred to as BGP RIB or OSPF RIB, too. However, you must remember that BGP, OSPF, or any protocol's best path to any destination might or might not be installed in the IP routing table (or the generic IP RIB). The reason is that when there are multiple alternatives, the IP process installs paths with the smallest administrative distance in the IP routing table (or the generic IP RIB).

The choice of whether to check the IP routing table or the FIB depends on exactly what you are trying to diagnose. To diagnose control plane problems, such as the exchange of routing information by routing protocols, the **show ip route** command is a clear choice because it contains all the control plane details for a route, such as the advertising routing protocol, routing source, administrative distance, and routing protocol metrics. To diagnose problems more closely related to the data plane (for example, by tracking the exact traffic flow between two hosts through the network), the FIB is often the best choice because it contains all the details that are necessary to make packet-switching decisions.

To display the content of the IP routing table, you can use the following commands:

- **show ip route** *ip-address*: Supplying the destination IP address as an option to the **show ip route** command causes the router to perform a routing table lookup for that IP address and display the best route that matches the address and all associated control plane details. (Note that the default route will never be displayed as a match for an IP address.)

- **show ip route** *network mask*: The provided network and mask as options to this command request the routing table to be searched for an exact match (for that network and mask). If an exact match is found, this entry is displayed with all of its associated control plane details.

- **show ip route** *network mask* **longer-prefixes**: The longer-prefixes option causes the router to display all prefixes in the routing table that fall within the prefix specified by the network and mask parameters. This command can prove useful to diagnose problems related to route summarization.

To display the content of the CEF FIB table, you can use the following commands:

- **show ip cef** *ip-address*: This command is similar to the **show ip route** *ip-address* command, but it searches the FIB rather than the routing table. Therefore, the displayed results do not include any routing protocol-related information, but only the information necessary to forward packets. (Note that this command will display the default route if it is the best match for a particular IP address.)

- **show ip cef** *network mask*: This is similar to the **show ip route** *network mask* command, but it displays information from the FIB rather than the routing table (RIB).

- **show ip cef exact-route** *source destination*: This command displays the exact adjacency that will be used to forward a packet with source and destination IP addresses, as specified by the source and destination parameters. The main reason to use this command is in a situation when you are tracking a packet flow across the routed network but the routing table and FIB contain two or more equal routes for a particular prefix. In this case, the CEF mechanisms will balance the traffic load across the multiple adjacencies associated with that prefix. By use of this command, you can determine which of the possible adjacencies is used to forward packets for a specific source and destination IP address pair.

After the egress interface and, in case of multipoint interfaces, a next-hop IP address for the destination of a packet has been determined by the routing table or FIB, the router needs to construct a frame for the data link layer protocol associated with the egress interface. Depending on the data link layer used on the egress interface, the header of this frame will require some connection specific parameters, such as source and destination MAC addresses for Ethernet, DLCI for Frame Relay, or virtual path/channel identifier (VPI/VCI) for ATM. These data link layer parameters are stored in various different data structures. For point-to-point (sub)interfaces, the relation between the interface and data link identifier or address is usually statically configured. For multipoint (sub) interfaces, the relation between the next-hop IP address and the data link identifier and address can be manually configured or dynamically resolved through some form of an address resolution protocol. The commands to display the statically configured or dynamically obtained mappings are unique for each data link layer technology. Research the command references for the data link layer protocol that you are troubleshooting to find the appropriate commands. Use the **show ip arp** command to verify the dynamic IP address to Ethernet MAC address mappings that were resolved and stored by ARP in the ARP table. Routers cache this information for 4 hours by default. If you need to refresh the content of the ARP cache, you can enter the **clear ip arp** command to clear all or a particular entry from the ARP cache.

When CEF is used as the switching method, the information from the various Layer 2 data structures is used to construct a frame header for each adjacency that is listed in the adjacency table. You can display the full frame header that will be used to encapsulate the packet via the **show adjacency detail** command. In addition, this command displays packet and byte counters for all traffic that was forwarded using this particular adjacency entry. Certain troubleshooting cases require verifying the Layer 3 to Layer 2 mappings. If the routing table or the FIB lists the correct next-hop IP address and egress interface for a particular destination, but packets do not arrive at that next hop, you should verify the Layer 3 to Layer 2 mappings for the data link protocol that is used on the egress interface. Specifically, verify that a correct frame header is constructed to encapsulate the packets and forward them to the next hop.

Selective Information Gathering Using IOS show Commands, debug Commands, Ping, and Telnet

Much of the total time spent on troubleshooting processes is usually spent on the information-gathering stage. One of the challenges during this process is how to gather only the relevant information. Collecting and processing a lot of irrelevant information is distracting and a waste of time. Learning how to efficiently and effectively apply the basic tools that support the elementary diagnostic processes that you repeatedly exercise is worthwhile. Learning the Cisco IOS **show** commands used for collecting and filtering information and the commands used to test connectivity problems is vital to the support staff's troubleshooting strength. Other relevant and beneficial skills are collecting real-time information using Cisco IOS **debug** commands and diagnosing basic hardware-related problems.

Filtering and Redirecting show Command's Output

You must learn how to apply filtering to Cisco IOS **show** commands to optimize your information gathering. During troubleshooting, you are often looking for specific information. For example, you might be looking for a particular prefix in the routing table, or you might want to verify whether a specific MAC address has been learned on an interface. Sometimes you need to find out the percentage of CPU time that is being used by a process such as the IP Input process. Using the **show ip route** command and the **show mac-address-table** command, you can display the IP routing table and the MAC address table, and using the **show processes cpu** command, you can check the CPU utilization for all processes on a Cisco router or switch. However, because the routing table and MAC address table can contain thousands to tens of thousands of entries, scanning through these tables to find a particular entry is neither viable nor realistic. Also, if you cannot find the entry that you are searching for, does it really mean that it is not in the table or that you simply did not spot it? Repeating the command and not seeing what you are looking for again still does not guarantee that you did not simply miss it. The list of processes on a router or switch is not hundreds or thousands of entries long; you could indeed just look through the full list and find a single process such as the IP Input process. But if you want to repeat the command every minute to see how the CPU usage for the IP Input process changes over time, displaying the whole table might not be desirable. In all these cases, you are interested in only a small subset of the information that the commands can provide. Cisco IOS Software provides options to limit or filter the output that it displays.

To limit the output of the **show ip route** command, you can optionally enter a specific IP address on the command line. Doing so causes the router to execute a routing table lookup for that specific IP address. If the router finds a match in the routing table, it displays the corresponding entry with all its details. If the router does not find a match in the routing table, it displays the "% Subnet not in table" message (see Example 4-1). Keep in mind that if the gateway of last resort (default route) is present in the IP routing table, but no entry matches the IP address you entered, the router again responds with the "% Subnet not in table" message even though packets for that destination are forwarded using the gateway of last resort.

Example 4-1 *Filtering Output of the* **show ip route** *Command*

```
RO1# show ip route 10.1.193.3
Routing entry for 10.1.193.0/30
  Known via "connected", distance 0, metric 0 (connected, via interface)
  Redistributing via eigrp 1
  Routing Descriptor Blocks:
  * directly connected, via Serial0/0/1
      Route metric is 0, traffic share count is 1


RO1# show ip route 10.1.193.10
% Subnet not in table
```

Another option to limit the output of the **show ip route** command to a particular sub-set of routing information that you are interested in is typing a prefix followed by the optional **longer-prefixes** keyword, as demonstrated in Example 4-2. The router will then list all subnets that fall within the prefix that you have specified (including that prefix itself, if it is present in the routing table). If the network that you are troubleshooting has a good hierarchical IP numbering plan, the **longer-prefixes** command option can prove useful for displaying addresses from a particular part of the network. You can display all subnets of a particular branch office or data center, for example, using the summary address for these blocks and the **longer-prefixes** keyword.

Example 4-2 *Using the* **longer-prefixes** *Keyword with the* **show ip route** *Command*

```
CRO1# show ip route 10.1.193.0 255.255.255.0 longer-prefixes
Codes: C - connected, S - static, R - RIP, M - mobile, B - BGP
       D - EIGRP, EX - EIGRP external, O - OSPF, IA - OSPF inter area
       N1 - OSPF NSSA external type 1, N2 - OSPF NSSA external type 2
       E1 - OSPF external type 1, E2 - OSPF external type 2
       i - IS-IS, su - IS-IS summary, L1 - IS-IS level-1, L2 - IS-IS level-2
       ia - IS-IS inter area, * - candidate default, U - per-user static route
       o - ODR, P - periodic downloaded static route
Gateway of last resort is not set
     10.0.0.0/8 is variably subnetted, 46 subnets, 6 masks
C       10.1.193.2/32 is directly connected, Serial0/0/1
C       10.1.193.0/30 is directly connected, Serial0/0/1
D       10.1.193.6/32 [90/20517120] via 10.1.192.9, 2d01h, FastEthernet0/1
                      [90/20517120] via 10.1.192.1, 2d01h, FastEthernet0/0
D       10.1.193.4/30 [90/20517120] via 10.1.192.9, 2d01h, FastEthernet0/1
                      [90/20517120] via 10.1.192.1, 2d01h, FastEthernet0/0
D       10.1.193.5/32 [90/41024000] via 10.1.194.6, 2d01h, Serial0/0/0.122
```

Unfortunately, **show** commands do not always have the option that allows you to filter the output down to exactly what you need. You can still perform a more generic way of filtering. The output of Cisco IOS **show** commands can be filtered by appending a pipe character (|) to the **show** command followed by one of the keywords **include**, **exclude**, or **begin**, and then a *regular expression*. Regular expressions are patterns that can be used to match strings in a piece of text. In its simplest form, you can use it to match words or text fragments in a line of text, but full use of the regular expression syntax allows you to build complex expressions that match specific text patterns. Example 4-3 shows usage of the **include**, **exclude**, and **begin** keywords with the **show processes cpu**, **show ip interface brief**, and the **show running-config** commands.

Example 4-3 *Using* **include**, **exclude**, *and* **begin** *Keywords with* **show** *Commands*

```
RO1# show processes cpu | include IP Input
  71    3149172   7922812      397  0.24%  0.15%  0.05%   0 IP Input

SW1# show ip interface brief | exclude unassigned
Interface            IP-Address      OK? Method Status            Protocol
Vlan128              10.1.156.1      YES NVRAM  up                up

SW1# show running-config | begin line vty
line vty 0 4
 transport input telnet ssh
line vty 5 15
 transport input telnet ssh
!
end
```

In Example 4-3, you are only interested in the IP Input process in the output of the **show processes cpu** command, so you select only the lines that contain the string "IP Input" by using the command **show processes cpu | include IP Input**.

You can exclude lines from the output through use of the **| exclude** option, which, for example, can be useful on a switch where you are trying to obtain all of the IP addresses on the interfaces with the **show ip interface brief** command. On a switch that has many interfaces (ports), the output of this command will also list all the interfaces that have no IP address assigned. If you are looking for the interfaces that have an IP address only, these lines obscure the output. If you know that all interfaces without an IP address have the string "unassigned" in place of the IP address, as you can see in Example 4-3, you can exclude those lines from the output by issuing the command **show ip interface brief | exclude unassigned**. Finally, using **| begin** enables you to skip all command output up to the first occurrence of the regular expression pattern. In Example 4-3, you are only interested in checking the configuration for the vty lines, and you know that the vty configuration commands are at the bottom of the router's running configuration file. So, you jump straight to the vty configuration point by issuing the command **show running-config | begin line vty**.

Cisco IOS Software Release 12.3(2)T introduced the **section** option, which enables you to select and display a specific section or lines from the configuration that match a particular regular expression and any following associated lines. For example, Example 4-4 demonstrates using the command **show running-config | section router eigrp** to display the EIGRP configuration section only.

Example 4-4   *Using the* **|** section *and the* **^** *Options to Filter the Output of the* **show** *Commands*

```
RO1# show running-config | section router eigrp
router eigrp 1
 network 10.1.192.2 0.0.0.0
 network 10.1.192.10 0.0.0.0
 network 10.1.193.1 0.0.0.0
 no auto-summary

RO1# show processes cpu | include ^CPU|IP Input
CPU utilization for five seconds: 1%/0%; one minute: 1%; five minutes: 1%
  71    3149424   7923898        397 0.24%  0.04%  0.00%   0 IP Input
```

If you used **show running-config | section router**, however, all lines that include the expression router and the configuration section that follows that line would be displayed. In other words, all routing protocol configuration sections would be displayed and the rest of the configuration wouldn't. This makes **| section** more restrictive than the **| begin** option, but more useful than the **| include** option when you want to select sections instead of only lines that contain a specific expression. Although the **show running-config** command is the most obvious candidate for the use of the **| section** option, this option can also be applied to any **show** command that separates its output in sections. For example, if you want to display only the standard access lists in the output of the **show access-lists** command, you could achieve that by issuing the command **show access-lists | section standard**.

The **include, exclude, begin,** and **section** options are usually followed by just a word or text fragment, but it is possible to use regular expressions for more granular filtering. For example, the second command used in Example 4-4 uses the caret (^) character, which is used to denote that a particular string will be matched only if it occurs at the beginning of a line. The expression **^CPU** will therefore only match lines that *start* with the characters "CPU" and not any line that contains the string "CPU". The same line uses the pipe character (|) (without a preceding and following space) as part of a regular expression to signify a logical OR. As a result, the **show processes cpu | include ^CPU|IP Input** command displays only the lines that start with the string "CPU" or contain the string "IP Input".

Other useful options that can be used with the pipe character after the **show** command are **redirect, tee,** and **append.** The output of a **show** command can be redirected, copied or appended to a file by using the pipe character, followed by the options **redirect, tee,** or **append** and a URL that denotes the file. Example 4-5 depicts a sample usage of these options with the **show tech-support, show ip interface brief,** and **show version** commands.

Example 4-5   *Using the* redirect, append, *and* tee *Options with the IOS* show *Commands*

```
RO1# show tech-support | redirect tftp://192.168.37.2/show-tech.txt
! The redirect option does not display the output on the console
RO1# show ip interface brief | tee flash:show-int-brief.txt
! The tee option displays the output on the console and sends it to the file
Interface                IP-Address        OK? Method Status          Protocol
FastEthernet0/0          10.1.192.2        YES manual up              up
FastEthernet0/1          10.1.192.10       YES manual up              up
Loopback0                10.1.220.1        YES manual up              up


RO1# dir flash:
Directory of flash:/

   1  -rw-    23361156    Mar 2 2009 16:25:54 -08:00  c1841-advipservicesk9mz.1243.bin
   2  -rw-          680    Mar 7 2009 02:16:56 -08:00  show-int-brief.txt


RO1# show version | append flash:show-commands.txt
RO1# show ip interface brief | append flash:show-commands.txt
! The append option allows you to add the command output to an existing file
RO1# more flash:show-commands.txt
Cisco IOS Software, 1841 Software (C1841-ADVIPSERVICESK9-M), Version 12.4(23),
RELEASE SOFTWARE (fc1)
Technical Support: http://www.cisco.com/techsupport
Copyright (c) 1986-2008 by Cisco Systems, Inc.
Compiled Sat 08-Nov-08 20:07 by prod_rel_team
ROM: System Bootstrap, Version 12.3(8r)T9, RELEASE SOFTWARE (fc1)
RO1 uptime is 3 days, 1 hour, 22 minutes
<...output omitted...>
Interface                IP-Address        OK? Method Status          Protocol
FastEthernet0/0          10.1.192.2        YES manual up              up
FastEthernet0/1          10.1.192.10       YES manual up              up
Loopback0                10.1.220.1        YES manual up              up
```

When you use the | **redirect** option on a **show** command, the output will not display on the screen, but will be redirected to a text file instead. This file can be stored locally on the device's flash memory or it can be stored on a network server such as a TFTP or FTP server. The | **tee** option is similar to the | **redirect** option, but this command both displays the output on your screen and copies it to a text file. Finally, the | **append** option is analogous to the | **redirect** option, but it allows you to append the output to a file instead of replacing that file. The use of this command option makes it easy to collect the output of several **show** commands in a text file one after the other. A prerequisite for this option is that the file system that you are writing to must support "append" operations; so, for instance, a TFTP server cannot be used in this case.

Testing Network Connectivity Using Ping and Telnet

The ping utility is a popular network connectivity testing tool that has been part of Cisco IOS Software since the first version of IOS. The ping utility has some extended options that are useful for testing specific conditions, including the following:

- **repeat** *repeat-count*: By default, the Cisco IOS **ping** command sends out five ICMP echo-request packets. The **repeat** option enables you to specify how many echo-request packets are sent. This proves particularly useful when you are troubleshooting a packet-loss situation. The repeat option enables you to send out hundreds to thousands of packets to help pinpoint a pattern in the occurrence of the packet loss. For example, if you see a pattern where every other packet is lost, resulting in exactly 50 percent packet loss, you might have a load-balancing situation with packet loss on one path.

- **size** *datagram-size*: This option enables you to specify the total size of the ping packet (including headers) in bytes that will be sent. In combination with the **repeat** option, you can send a steady stream of large packets and generate some load. The quickest way to generate a heavy load using the **ping** command is to combine a very large repeat number, a size set to 1500 bytes, and the **timeout** option set to 0 seconds. When used with the Don't Fragment (df-bit) option (discussed after Example 4-6), the size option allows you to determine the maximum transmission unit (MTU) along the path to a particular destination IP address.

- **source** [*address* | *interface*]: This option enables you to set the source IP address or interface of the ping packet. The IP address has to be one of the local device's own IP addresses. If this option is not used, the router will select the IP address of the egress interface as the source of the ping packets. Example 4-6 shows a case where a simple ping succeeds, but the ping with the source IP address set to the IP address of the FastEthernet 0/0 interface fails. You can conclude from the successful initial ping that the local router has a working path to the destination IP address 10.1.156.1. For the second ping, because a different source address is used, the return packets will have a different destination IP address. The most likely explanation for the failure of the second ping is that at least one of the routers on the return path does not have a route to the address/subnet of the FastEthernet 0/0 interface (used as source in the second ping). There might be several other reasons for this, too. For example, an access list on one of the transit routers might be blocking the IP address of the Fa0/0 interface. Specifying the source IP address or interface proves useful when you want to check two-way reachability to/from a network/address other than the router's egress interface's IP address/network.

Example 4-6 *Ping Extended Option: Source*

```
RO1# ping 10.1.156.1
Type escape sequence to abort.
Sending 5, 100-byte ICMP Echos to 10.1.156.1, timeout is 2 seconds:
!!!!!
Success rate is 100 percent (5/5), round-trip min/avg/max = 1/2/4 ms
```

```
RO1# ping 10.1.156.1 source FastEthernet 0/0
Type escape sequence to abort.
Sending 5, 100-byte ICMP Echos to 10.1.156.1, timeout is 2 seconds:
Packet sent with a source address of 10.1.192.2
.....
Success rate is 0 percent (0/5)
```

- **df-bit:** This option sets the Don't Fragment bit in the IP header to indicate that routers should not fragment this packet. If it is larger than the MTU of the outbound interface, the router should drop the packet and send an ICMP "Fragmentation needed and DF bit set" message back to the source. This option can prove very useful when you are troubleshooting MTU-related problems. By setting the **df-bit** option and combining it with the size option, you can force routers along the path to drop the packets if they would have to fragment them. By varying the size and looking at which point the packets start being dropped, you can determine the MTU. Example 4-7 shows successful ping results when packet size of 1476 bytes is used; however, ping packets with a size of 1477 bytes are not successful. The M in the output of the **ping** command signifies that an ICMP "Fragmentation needed and DF bit set message" was received. From this, you can conclude that somewhere along the path to the destination there must be a host that has an MTU of 1476 bytes. A possible explanation for this could be usage of a generic routing encapsulation (GRE) tunnel, which typically has an MTU of 1476 bytes (1500 bytes default MTU minus 24 bytes for the GRE and IP headers).

Example 4-7   *Ping Extended Option:* **df-bit**

```
RO1# ping 10.1.221.1 size 1476 df-bit
Type escape sequence to abort.
Sending 5, 1476-byte ICMP Echos to 10.1.221.1, timeout is 2 seconds:
Packet sent with the DF bit set
!!!!!
Success rate is 100 percent (5/5), round-trip min/avg/max = 184/189/193 ms

RO1# ping 10.1.221.1 size 1477 df-bit
Type escape sequence to abort.
Sending 5, 1477-byte ICMP Echos to 10.1.221.1, timeout is 2 seconds:
Packet sent with the DF bit set
M.M.M
Success rate is 0 percent (0/5)
```

There are more extended options available for ping through the interactive dialog. If you type **ping** without any additional options and press Enter, you are prompted with a series of questions about the source and destination and all the ping options. In Example 4-8, the sweep range of sizes option is highlighted. This option allows you to send a series of packets that increase in size and can be useful to determine the smallest MTU along a path, similar to the previous example.

Example 4-8 ping *Extended Option: Sweep Range of Sizes*

```
RO1# ping
Protocol [ip]:
Target IP address: 10.1.221.1
Repeat count [5]: 1
Datagram size [100]:
Timeout in seconds [2]:
Extended commands [n]: y
Source address or interface:
Type of service [0]:
Set DF bit in IP header? [no]: yes
Validate reply data? [no]:
Data pattern [0xABCD]:
Loose, Strict, Record, Time stamp, Verbose[none]:
Sweep range of sizes [n]: y
Sweep min size [36]: 1400
Sweep max size [18024]: 1500
Sweep interval [1]:
Type escape sequence to abort.
Sending 101, [1400..1500]-byte ICMP Echos to 10.1.221.1, timeout is 2 seconds:
Packet sent with the DF bit set
!!!!!!!!!!!!!!!!!!!!!!!!!!!!!!!!!!!!!!!!!!!!!!!!!!!!!!!!!!!!!!!!!!!!!!!!!
!!!!!!!M.M.M.M.M.M.M.M.M.M.M.M.
Success rate is 76 percent (77/101), round-trip min/avg/max = 176/184/193 ms
```

When you want to determine the MTU of a particular path, a lot of times you do not really have a good initial guess, and it might take you many tries to find the exact MTU. In Example 4-8, the router is instructed to send packets starting at a size of 1400 bytes, sending a single packet per size and increasing the size 1 byte at a time until a size of 1500 bytes is reached. Again, the DF bit is set on the packets. The result is that the router sent out 101 consecutive packets, the first one was 1400 bytes, the last one was 1500 bytes, 77 of the pings were successful, and 24 failed. Again, this means that there must be a link along the path that has an MTU of 1476 bytes. It is important to note that because some applications cannot reassemble fragmented packets, if the network fragments that application's packet, the application will fail. Sometimes by discovering the MTU of a path, the application can be configured to not send packets larger than the MTU so that fragmentation does not happen. That is why it is sometimes necessary to find out the MTU of a path.

Note   The various symbols generated in ping output are described as follows:

!: Each exclamation point indicates receipt of a reply.

.: Each period indicates the network server timed out while waiting for a reply.

U: A destination unreachable error protocol data unit (PDU) was received.

Q: Source quench (destination too busy).

M: Could not fragment.

?: Unknown packet type.

&: Packet lifetime exceeded.

Telnet is an excellent companion to ping for testing transport layer connections from the command line. Assume that you are troubleshooting a problem where someone has trouble sending e-mail through a particular Simple Mail Transfer Protocol (SMTP) server. Taking a divide-and-conquer approach, you ping the server, and it is successful. This means that the network layer between your device and the server is operational. Now you have to investigate the transport layer. You could configure a client and start a top-down troubleshooting procedure, but it is more convenient if you first establish whether Layer 4 is operational. The Telnet protocol can prove useful in this situation. If you want to determine whether a particular TCP-based application is active on a server, you can attempt a Telnet connection to the TCP port of that application. In Example 4-9, a Telnet connection to port 80 (HTTP) on a server shows success, and a Telnet connection to port 25 (SMTP) is unsuccessful.

Example 4-9   *Using Telnet to Test the Transport Layer*

```
RO1# telnet 192.168.37.2 80
Trying 192.168.37.2, 80 ... Open
GET
<html><body><h1>It works!</h1></body></html>
[Connection to 192.168.37.2 closed by foreign host]



RO1# telnet 192.168.37.2 25
Trying 192.168.37.2, 25 ...
% Connection refused by remote host
```

Even though the Telnet server application uses the TCP well-known port number 23 and Telnet clients connect to that port by default, you can specify a specific port number on the client and connect to any TCP port that you want to test. The connection is either accepted (as indicated by the word Open in Example 4-9), or it is refused, or times out. The **Open** response indicates that the port (application) you attempted is active, and the other results require further investigation. For applications that use an ASCII-based session protocol, you might even see an application banner or you might be able to trigger some responses from the server by typing in some keywords (as in Example 4-9). Good examples of these types of protocols are SMTP, FTP, and HTTP.

Collecting Real-Time Information Using Cisco IOS debug Commands

First, it is important to caution readers that because debugging output is assigned high priority in the CPU process, it can render the system unusable. For this reason, use **debug** commands only to troubleshoot specific problems or during troubleshooting sessions with Cisco technical support staff. Moreover, it is best to use **debug** commands during periods of lower network traffic and fewer users.

All **debug** commands are entered in privileged EXEC mode, and most **debug** commands take no arguments. All **debug** commands can be turned off by retyping the command and preceding it with a **no.** To display the state of each debugging option, enter the **show debugging** command in the Cisco IOS privileged EXEC mode. The **no debug all** command turns off all diagnostic output. Using the **no debug all** command is a convenient way to ensure that you have not accidentally left any **debug** commands turned on. To list and see a brief description of all the **debug** command options, enter the **debug ?** command. The following is a short list of useful debug options:

- **debug interface** *interface-slot/number*: Provides debug messages for specific physical ports on the device.

- **debug ip icmp:** Used to troubleshoot connectivity issues, from the output you can see whether the device is sending or receiving ICMP messages.

- **debug ip packet:** Used to troubleshoot end-to-end communication. It should always be used with an access control list (ACL).

- **debug eigrp packets hello:** Used to troubleshoot neighbor establishment. It shows the frequency of the sent and the received hello packets.

- **debug ip ospf adjacency:** Provides information about events concerning adjacency relationships with other OSPF routers.

- **debug ip ospf events:** Provides information about all OSPF events.

- **debug ip bgp updates:** Provides information about routes you have advertised/ received from your BGP peer.

- **debug ip bgp events:** Provides information about any BGP event, such as neighbor state changes.

- **debug spanning-tree bpdu receive:** Used to confirm the bridge protocol data unit (BPDU) flow on switches.

For the sake of brevity, the **debug ip packet** command is the only one that is discussed further. This command can be used along with an access list and the optional keyword detail: **debug ip packet** [*access list-number*][**detail**].

This command displays general IP debugging information and IP security option (IPSO) security transactions. The option to use an access list with the **debug ip packet** command enables you to limit the scope of it to those packets that match the access list. The **detail** option of this debug displays detailed IP packet-debugging information. This information includes the packet types and codes and source and destination port numbers.

If a communication session is closing when it should not be, an end-to-end connection problem may be the cause. The **debug ip packet** command is useful for analyzing the messages traveling between the local and remote hosts. IP packet debugging captures the packets that are process switched including received, generated, and forwarded packets. Example 4-10 shows sample output from the **debug ip packet** command.

Example 4-10   debug ip packet *Sample Output*

```
IP: s=172.69.13.44 (Fddi0), d=10.125.254.1 (Serial2), g=172.69.16.2, forward
IP: s=172.69.1.57 (Ethernet4), d=10.36.125.2 (Serial2), g=172.69.16.2, forward
IP: s=172.69.1.6 (Ethernet4), d=255.255.255.255, rcvd 2
IP: s=172.69.1.55 (Ethernet4), d=172.69.2.42 (Fddi0), g=172.69.13.6, forward
IP: s=172.69.89.33 (Ethernet2), d=10.130.2.156 (Serial2), g=172.69.16.2, forward
IP: s=172.69.1.27 (Ethernet4), d=172.69.43.126 (Fddi1), g=172.69.23.5, forward
IP: s=172.69.1.27 (Ethernet4), d=172.69.43.126 (Fddi0), g=172.69.13.6, forward
IP: s=172.69.20.32 (Ethernet2), d=255.255.255.255, rcvd 2
IP: s=172.69.1.57 (Ethernet4), d=10.36.125.2 (Serial2), g=172.69.16.2, access denied
```

Diagnosing Hardware Issues Using Cisco IOS Commands

The three main categories of failure causes in a network are as follows: hardware failures, software failures (bugs), and configuration errors. One could argue that performance problems form a fourth category, but performance problems are symptoms rather than failure causes. Having a performance problem means that there is a difference between the expected behavior and the observed behavior of a system. Sometimes the system is functioning as it should, but the results are not what were expected or promised. In this case, the problem is not technical, but organizational, in nature and cannot be resolved through technical means. However, there are situations where the system is not functioning as it should. In this case, the system behaves differently than expected, but the underlying cause is a hardware failure, a software failure, or a configuration error. The focus here is on diagnosing and resolving configuration errors. There are a number of reasons for this focus. Hardware and software can really be swapped out only if they are suspected to be the cause of the problem, so the actions that can be taken to resolve the problem are limited.

The detailed information necessary to pinpoint a specific hardware or software problem is often not publicly available, and therefore hardware and software troubleshooting are processes that are generally executed as a joint effort with a vendor (or a reseller or partner for that vendor). Documentation of the configuration and operation of software features is generally publicly available, and therefore configuration problems can often be diagnosed without the need for direct assistance from the vendor or reseller. However, even if you decide to focus your troubleshooting effort on configuration errors initially, as your work progresses and you eliminate common configuration problems from the equation, you might pick up clues that hardware components are the root cause of the problem. You will then need to do an initial analysis and diagnosis of the problem, before it is escalated to the vendor. The move-the-problem method is an obvious candidate to approach suspected hardware problems, but this method works well only if the problem is strictly due to a broken piece of hardware. Performance problems that might be caused by hardware failures generally require a more subtle approach and require more detailed information gathering. When hardware problems are intermittent, they are harder to diagnose and isolate.

Due to its nature, diagnosing hardware problems is highly product and platform dependent. However, you can use a number of generic commands to diagnose performance-related hardware issues on all Cisco IOS platforms. Essentially, a network device is a specialized computer, with a CPU, RAM, and storage, to say the least. This allows the network devise to boot and run the operating system. Next, interfaces are initialized and started, which allows for reception and transmission of network traffic. Therefore, when you decide that a problem you are observing on a given device may be hardware related, it is important that you verify the operation of these generic components. The most commonly used Cisco IOS commands used for this purpose are the **show processes cpu**, **show memory**, and **show interface** commands, as covered in the sections that follow.

Checking CPU Utilization

Both routers and switches have a main CPU that executes the processes that constitute Cisco IOS Software. Processes are scheduled to share the available CPU cycles and take turns executing their code. The **show processes cpu** command provides you with an overview of all processes currently running on the router, including a display of the total CPU time that the processes have consumed over their lifetime; plus their CPU usage over the last 5 seconds, 1 minute, and 5 minutes. The first line of output from the **show processes cpu** command displays the percentages of the CPU cycles. From this information, you can see whether the total CPU usage is high or low and which processes might be causing the CPU load. By default, the processes are sorted by process ID, but they can be sorted based on the 5-second, 1-minute, and 5-minute averages. Figure 4-10 shows a sample output of the **show processes cpu** command entered with the 1-minute **sort** option.

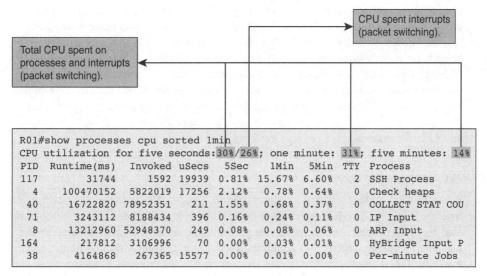

Figure 4-10   *The* **show processes** cpu *Command Output Example*

The example depicted in Figure 4-10 shows that over the past minute 31 percent of the available CPU has been used and the "SSH Process" was responsible for roughly half of these CPU cycles (15.67 percent) over that period. However, the next process in this sorted list is the "Check heaps" process, which has consumed only 0.78 percent of the total available CPU time over the last minute and the list quickly drops off after that. You might wonder what the remaining 15 percent CPU cycles recorded over the last minute were spent on. On the router used to generate the output depicted in Figure 4-10, the same CPU that is used to run the operating system processes is also responsible for packet switching. The CPU is interrupted to suspend the current process that it is executing, switch one or more packets, and resume the execution of scheduled processes. The CPU time spent on interrupt-driven tasks can be calculated by adding the CPU percentages for all processes and then subtracting that total from the total CPU percentage listed at the top. For the 5-second CPU usage, this figure is actually even listed separately behind the slash. This means that in the example shown in Figure 4-10, 30 percent of the total available CPU cycles over the past 5 seconds were used, out of which 26 percent were spent in interrupt mode and 4 percent for the execution of scheduled processes.

Because of this, it is quite normal for routers to be running at high CPU loads during peaks in network traffic. In those cases, most of the CPU cycles will be consumed in interrupt mode. If particular processes consistently use large chunks of the available CPU time, however, this could be a clue that a problem exists associated with that particular process. However, to be able to draw any definitive conclusions, you need to have a baseline of the CPU usage over time. Keep in mind that the better caching mechanisms reduce the number of CPU interrupts and, consequently, the CPU utilization attributable to interrupts. For example, Cisco Express Forwarding (CEF) in distributed mode allows most packet switching to happen on the line card without causing any CPU interrupts.

On LAN switches, the essential elements of the **show processes cpu** command output are the same as routers, but the interpretation of the numbers tends to be a bit different. Switches have specialized hardware that handle the switching task, so the main CPU should in general not be involved in this. When you see a high percentage of the CPU time being spent in interrupt mode, this usually indicates that the forwarded traffic is being forwarded in software instead of by the ternary content-addressable memory (TCAM). Punted traffic is the traffic that is processed and forwarded through less-efficient means for a reason, such as tunneling or encryption. After you have determined that the CPU load is abnormally high and you decide to investigate further, you generally have to resort to platform-specific troubleshooting commands to gain more insight into what is happening.

Checking Memory Utilization

Similar to CPU cycles, memory is a finite resource shared by the various processes that together form the Cisco IOS operating system. Memory is divided into different pools and used for different purposes: the processor pool contains memory that can be used by the scheduled processes, and the I/O pool is used to temporarily buffer packets during packet switching. Processes allocate and release memory, as needed, from the processor pool, and generally there is more than enough free memory for all the processes to share. Example

4-11 shows sample output from the **show memory** command. In this example, the processor memory is shown on the first line, and the I/O memory is shown on the second line. Each row shows the total memory available, used memory, and free memory. The least amount of free memory and the most amount of free memory over the measurement interval (device dependent, but usually 5 minutes) are also displayed at each row.

Example 4-11   show memory *Command Output*

```
RO1# show memory
              Head      Total(b)     Used(b)      Free(b)     Lowest(b)    Largest(b)
Processor   820B1DB4    26534476     19686964     6847512     6288260      6712884
      I/O    3A00000     6291456      3702900     2588556     2511168      2577468
```

Typically, the memory on routers and switches is more than enough to do what they were designed for. However, in particular deployment scenarios, for example if you decide to run Border Gateway Protocol (BGP) on your router and carry the full Internet routing table, you might need more memory than the typical amount recommended for the router. Also, whenever you decide to upgrade Cisco IOS Software on your router, you should verify the recommended amount of memory for the new software version.

As with CPU usage, it is useful to create a baseline of the memory usage on your routers and switches and graph the utilization over time. You should monitor memory utilization over time and be able to anticipate when your devices need memory upgrade or a complete system upgrade. If a router or switch does not have enough free memory to satisfy the request of a process, it will log a memory allocation failure, signified by a "%SYS-2MALLOCFAIL" message. The result of this is that the process cannot get the memory that it requires, and this might result in unpredictable disruptions or failures. Apart from the processes using up the memory through normal use, there is a possibility for memory leak. Caused by a software defect, a process that does not properly release memory (causing memory to "leak" away) eventually leads to memory exhaustion and memory-allocation failures. Creating a baseline and graphing memory usage over time allows us to monitor for these types of failures, too.

Checking Interfaces

Checking the performance of the device interfaces while troubleshooting, especially while hardware faults are suspected, is as important as checking your device's CPU and memory utilization. The **show interfaces** command is a valuable Cisco IOS troubleshooting command. Example 4-12 shows sample output of this command for a FastEthernet interface.

Example 4-12   show interfaces *Command Output*

```
RO1# show interfaces FastEthernet 0/0
FastEthernet0/0 is up, line protocol is up
<...output omitted...>
  Last input 00:00:00, output 00:00:01, output hang never
```

```
Last clearing of "show interface" counters never
Input queue: 0/75/1120/0 (size/max/drops/flushes); Total output drops: 0
Queueing strategy: fifo
Output queue: 0/40 (size/max)
5 minute input rate 2000 bits/sec, 3 packets/sec
5 minute output rate 0 bits/sec, 1 packets/sec
   110834589 packets input, 1698341767 bytes
   Received 61734527 broadcasts, 0 runts, 0 giants, 565 throttles
   30 input errors, 5 CRC, 1 frame, 0 overrun, 25 ignored
   0 watchdog
   0 input packets with dribble condition detected
   35616938 packets output, 526385834 bytes, 0 underruns
   0 output errors, 0 collisions, 1 interface resets
   0 babbles, 0 late collision, 0 deferred
   0 lost carrier, 0 no carrier
   0 output buffer failures, 0 output buffers swapped out
```

The output of the **show interfaces** command lists a number of key statistics, which are briefly described as follows:

- **Input queue drops:** Input queue drops (and the related ignored and throttle counters) signify that at some point more traffic was delivered to the router than it could process. This does not necessarily indicate a problem, because it could be normal during traffic peaks. However, it might indicate that the CPU cannot process packets in time. If this number is consistently high and the dropped packets are causing application failures, the reasons must be detected and resolved.

- **Output queue drops:** Input packet drops indicate congestion on the interface. Seeing output drops is normal when the aggregate input traffic rate is higher than the output traffic rate on an interface. However, even if this is considered normal behavior, it leads to packet drops and queuing delays. Applications that are sensitive to delay and packet loss, such as Voice over IP, will have serious quality issues in those situations. This counter is a good indicator that you need to implement a congestion management mechanism to provide good quality of service (QoS) to your applications.

- **Input errors:** This counter indicates the number of errors such as cyclic redundancy check (CRC) errors, experienced during reception of frames. High numbers of CRC errors could indicate cabling problems, interface hardware problems, or in an Ethernet-based network, duplex mismatches.

- **Output errors:** This counter indicates the number of errors, such as collisions, during the transmission of frames. In most Ethernet-based networks today, full-duplex transmission is the norm, and half-duplex is the exception. In full-duplex operation, collisions cannot occur, and therefore collisions, and especially late collisions, often indicate duplex mismatches.

The absolute number of drops or errors in the output of the **show interfaces** command
is not very significant. The error counters should be evaluated against the total number
of input and output packets. For example, a total of 25 CRC errors in relation to 123
input packets is reason for concern, whereas 25 CRC errors for 1,458,349 packets is
not a problem at all. Furthermore, note that these counters accumulate from the time
the router boots, so the numbers displayed on the output might be accumulated over
months. Therefore, it is difficult to diagnose a problem that has been happening over 2
days based on these statistics. After you have decided that you need to investigate the
interface counters in more detail, it is good practice to reset the interface counters by
using the **clear counters** command, let it accumulate statistics for a specific period, and
then re-evaluate the outcome. If you repeatedly want to display selected statistics to see
how the counters are increasing, it is useful to filter the output. Using a regular expression to include only the lines in which you are interested can prove quite useful in this
case. In Example 4-13, the output is limited to the lines that start with the word Fast,
include the word errors, or include the word packets.

Example 4-13   *Filtering Output of the* show interfaces *Command*

```
RO1# show interfaces FastEthernet 0/0 | include ^Fast|errors|packets
FastEthernet0/0 is up, line protocol is up
  5 minute input rate 3000 bits/sec, 5 packets/sec
  5 minute output rate 2000 bits/sec, 1 packets/sec
     2548 packets input, 257209 bytes
     0 input errors, 0 CRC, 0 frame, 0 overrun, 0 ignored
     0 input packets with dribble condition detected
     610 packets output, 73509 bytes, 0 underruns
     0 output errors, 0 collisions, 0 interface resets
```

The **show processes cpu, show memory**, and **show interfaces** commands form a limited
toolkit of hardware troubleshooting commands, but they are a good starting point to
collect some initial clues to either confirm that the problem may be hardware related
or to eliminate hardware problems from the list of potential problem causes. After you
have decided that the cause of the problem might be hardware related, research the
more specific hardware troubleshooting tools that are available for the platform that you
are working with. Many additional hardware troubleshooting features and commands are
supported in the Cisco IOS Software, including the following:

- **show controllers:** The output of this command varies based on interface hardware
  type. In general, this command provides more detailed packet and error statistics for
  each type of hardware and interface.

- **show platform:** The output of this command can be helpful to troubleshoot a
  router crash. In case you have to open a Cisco TAC Service Request to troubleshoot
  a device's crash, be sure to collect and include this information prior to opening
  the case. On many Cisco LAN switches, this command can be used to examine the
  TCAM and other specialized switch hardware components.

- **show inventory:** This command lists the hardware components of a router or switch. The output includes the product code and serial number for each component. This is very useful for documenting your device and for ordering replacement or spare parts.

- **show diag:** On routers, you can use this command to gather even more detailed information about the hardware than the output provided by the **show inventory** command. For example, the output of this command includes the hardware revision of the individual components. In case of known hardware issues, this command can be used to determine whether the component is susceptible to a particular hardware fault.

- **Generic Online Diagnostics (GOLD):** GOLD is a platform-independent framework for runtime diagnostics. It includes command-line interface (CLI)-based access to boot and health monitoring, plus on-demand and scheduled diagnostics. GOLD is available on many of the mid-range and high-end Catalyst LAN switches and high-end routers such as the 7600 series and CRS-1 routers.

- **Time Domain Reflectometer (TDR):** Some of the Catalyst LAN switches support the TDR feature. This feature enables you to detect cabling problems such as open or shorted unshielded twisted-pair (UTP) wire pairs.

Summary

To display the MAC address table, use the **show mac-address-table** command. Use the **clear mac-address-table dynamic** command to clear the dynamically learned entries of the MAC address table. To display VLAN database and port-to-VLAN mapping, use the **show vlan** command. To see the trunk port settings and port-to-VLAN associations, use the **show interfaces switchport** and **show interfaces trunk** commands. To directly verify frame forwarding, use the **show platform forward** and the **traceroute mac** commands.

To display the content of the IP routing table, you can use the **show ip route** command. To display the content of the CEF FIB table, you can use the **show ip cef** command. The **show adjacency detail** command displays the CEF adjacency table. The **show ip arp** command displays the contents of the IP ARP cache table, and the **clear ip arp** command clears its contents.

The output of Cisco IOS **show** commands can be filtered by appending a pipe character (|) to the **show** command followed by one of the keywords **include, exclude,** or **begin,** and then a *regular expression.*

Other useful options that can be used with the pipe character after the **show** command are **redirect, tee,** and **append.** The output of a **show** command can be redirected, copied, or appended to a file by using the pipe character, followed by the options **redirect, tee,** or **append** and a URL that denotes the file.

The ping utility has some useful extended options such as **repeat** *repeat-count,* **size** *datagram-size,* **source** [*address* | *interface*], and **df-bit.**

If you want to determine whether a particular TCP-based application is active on a server, you can attempt a Telnet connection to the TCP port of that application. The connection is either accepted (indicated by the word *Open*), or it is refused, or times out. The Open response indicates that the port (application) you attempted is active, and the other results require further investigation.

Use the **debug** command (with caution) along with a variety of its options to get real-time information about the active processes and traffic handled by your network device. It is best if **debug** is focused (by using specific parameters) or is used with access lists, both for trouble-shooting effectiveness and for device CPU utilization sake.

Cisco IOS Software includes many commands to diagnose hardware operation. Due to their nature, many of those commands and features are product and platform specific. Essential commands common to both routers and switches include the following:

- **show processes cpu**
- **show memory**
- **show interfaces**

The **show processes cpu** command gives you an overview of all processes currently running on the router, the total amount of CPU time that they have consumed over their lifetime, and their CPU usage over the past 5 seconds. This command also displays a 1-minute and a 5-minute weighted average of CPU utilization for all processes.

Both routers and switches have an amount of generic RAM, used by processes and for temporary packet buffering. Not having sufficient free memory can cause memory-allocation problems. Establishing a baseline can help discover these issues before they cause disruption.

The output of the **show interfaces** command includes statistics such as input and output errors, CRC errors, collisions, and queue drops. Error statistics should be related to total packet statistics. Use the **clear counters** command to reset the interface counters and ensure that you are observing recent data. Use output filtering to limit the output to the fields that you are interested in viewing.

Other commands that can be useful in troubleshooting hardware related problems include the following:

- **show controllers**
- **show platform**
- **show inventory**
- **show diag**

Review Questions

1. Figure 4-11 shows a frame containing an ARP reply from Host B in response to a request from Host A as it traverses the 802.1Q trunk between the switches. What is the destination MAC address for that frame?

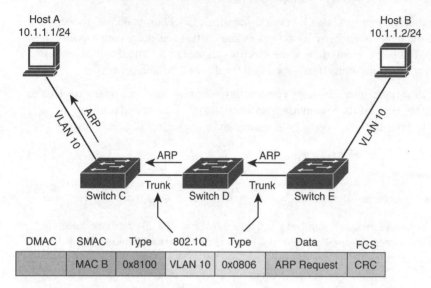

Figure 4-11 *What Is the Destination MAC Address for the Frame?*

    a. The MAC address of Host A

    b. The MAC address of Host B

    c. The broadcast MAC address ffff.ffff.ffff

    d. The 801.1Q multicast MAC address 0180.C200.0000

2. Figure 4-12 shows a frame encapsulating an ARP reply from Host B in response to a request from Host A as it traverses the 802.1Q trunk between the switches. Which *two* items do the values 0x0806 and 0x8100 in the type fields represent?

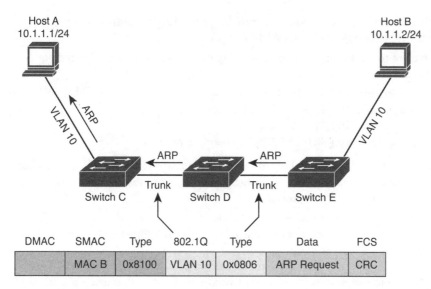

Figure 4-12 *What Do 0x0806 and 0x0800 Represent?*

    a. The value 0x0806 indicates that this frame is an 802.1Q frame.

    b. The value 0x8100 indicates that this frame is an 802.1Q frame.

    c. The value 0x0806 indicates that the data inside this frame belongs to the ARP protocol.

    d. The value 0x8100 indicates that the data inside this frame belongs to the ARP protocol.

3. Which *three* of the following items are recorded in the MAC address table of a switch?

    a. MAC address

    b. Switch port

    c. IP address

    d. VLAN

    e. Trunk or access port status

    f. Type

4. What command combines information from the **show vlan** and **show interfaces trunk** commands, in addition to other VLAN-related information, such as the voice VLAN of an interface?

5. What data structure of a switch can provide proof that frames from a particular host have passed through the switch?

6. Which of the following commands will display all subnets contained in the prefix 10.1.32.0/19?

   a. show ip route 10.1.32.0 /19 longer-prefixes

   b. show ip route 10.1.32.0 255.255.224.0 subnets

   c. show ip route 10.1.32.0 /19 subnets

   d. show ip route 10.1.32.0 255.255.224.0 longer-prefixes

7. You execute the command **show ip route 10.1.1.1**, and the response of the router is "% Subnet not in table." Which of the following is the most accurate conclusion you can draw from this response?

   a. The host entry 10.1.1.1/32 is not in the routing table.

   b. There is no route in the routing table that matches IP address 10.1.1.1. All packets to that destination will be dropped.

   c. There is no specific route in the routing table that matches IP address 10.1.1.1. Packets to that destination may be forwarded by the default route, if it is present.

   d. The classful network 10.0.0.0 is not present in the routing table.

8. Which of the following commands displays the part of the running configuration that contains all statements for the EIGRP routing protocol?

   a. show running-config | section router eigrp

   b. show running-config | include router eigrp

   c. show running-config | exclude router eigrp

   d. show running-config | start router eigrp

   e. None of these options are correct; this requires using a regular expression.

9. Which of the following commands displays the output of the command **show ip interface brief** on screen and copies the output of the command to the file show-output.txt on TFTP server 10.1.1.1?

   a. show ip interface brief | tee tftp://10.1.1.1/show-output.txt

   b. show ip interface brief | append tftp://10.1.1.1/show-output.txt

   c. show ip interface brief | redirect tftp://10.1.1.1/show-output.txt

   d. show ip interface brief | copy tftp://10.1.1.1/show-output.txt

   e. None of these options are correct; **show** command output can be copied only to a file in the flash memory of the device.

10. Which of the following Cisco IOS commands will send 154 ICMP request packets of 1400 bytes each with the Don't Fragment bit set to IP address 10.1.1.1?

   a. ping 10.1.1.1 -l 1400 -r 154 -f

   b. ping 10.1.1.1 size 1400 repeat 154 df-bit

   c. ping 10.1.1.1 repeat 154 size 1400 df 1

   d. None of these options are correct; this can be accomplished only by use of the extended ping interactive dialog.

11. You execute the command **telnet 192.168.37.2 80**, and the response of the router is "Trying 192.168.37.2, 80 ... Open." Which conclusion can you draw from this response?

   a. The web server on host 192.168.37.2 is running and serving files.
   b. There is a service running on TCP port 80 on host 192.168.37.2, and it accepts connections.
   c. The server on 192.168.37.2 is accepting Telnet connections.
   d. No conclusions can be drawn about the server. The word *Open* just means that the IP address could be found in the routing table.

12. You execute the command **show processes cpu**, and the output includes CPU utilization for 5 seconds: 30%/26%. Which *two* of the following statements are correct?

   a. The total CPU load over the past 5 seconds was 56 percent.
   b. The total CPU load over the past 5 seconds was 30 percent.
   c. The percentage of CPU time spent on scheduled processes was 26 percent.
   d. The percentage of CPU time spent on scheduled processes was 4 percent.

Chapter 5

Using Specialized Maintenance and Troubleshooting Tools

This chapter covers the following topics:

- Categories of troubleshooting tools

- Traffic-capturing features and tools

- Information gathering with SNMP

- Information gathering with NetFlow

- Network event notification with EEM

Information gathering is essential to both troubleshooting and maintenance. Information is either gathered on a need basis, such as during a troubleshooting effort, or continuously as part of baseline creation. Sometimes network events trigger information gathering. In addition to the **debug** and **show** commands available in the Cisco IOS command-line interface (CLI), there are many specialized network maintenance and troubleshooting tools. You can use these tools for information gathering, fault detection, creating baseline, and even capacity planning and proactive network management. These tools and applications typically require communication with the network devices, and several different underlying technologies can govern this communication. Network support professionals must familiarize themselves with the commonly used network management platforms and troubleshooting tools and learn to perform the following tasks:

- Identify the tools and their underlying technologies to support the troubleshooting process.

- Enable Switched Port Analyzer (SPAN) and Remote SPAN (RSPAN) to facilitate the use of packet sniffers.

- Configure routers and switches for communication with Simple Network Management Protocol (SNMP) or NetFlow-based network management systems to facilitate the collection of device and traffic statistics that are part of a network baseline.

- Configure routers and switches to send SNMP traps to provide fault notification to SNMP-based network management systems.

- Write simple Embedded Event Manager (EEM) applets to take actions when particular events take place.

Categories of Troubleshooting Tools

A generic troubleshooting process consists of several phases or subprocesses. Some of these are primarily mental; an example is the elimination process. Some of these processes are administrative in nature, such as documenting and reporting the changes and solutions. Finally, some of these are more technical in nature, such as the gathering and analysis of information. The processes that benefit the most from the deployment of network maintenance and troubleshooting tools are the processes that are technical in nature:

- **Defining the problem:** One of the main objectives of deploying a proactive network management strategy is to learn about potential problems before users report that they are experiencing outages or performance degradation. Network monitoring and event reporting systems can notify the network support team of events as they happen, giving them lead time to battle the problem before the users notice and report them.

- **Gathering information:** This is one of the most essential steps in the troubleshooting process, and it is incident driven and targeted. It is beneficial to be able to leverage any tool to obtain detailed information about events in an effective way.

- **Analyzing:** A major aspect of interpreting and analyzing the gathered information is comparing it against the network baseline. The ability to differentiate between normal and abnormal behavior can yield important clues about the potential problem cause. Collecting statistics about network behavior and network traffic is therefore a key process to support troubleshooting data analysis.

- **Testing the hypothesis:** Testing a hypothesis commonly involves making changes to the network. This might entail the need to roll back these changes if they do not resolve the problem or cause new ones. Tools that enable easy rollback of changes are therefore important to an efficient troubleshooting process.

With the exception of configuration rollback, which is more a generic change management tool than a specific troubleshooting tool, the mechanisms mentioned fall into one of the following three categories:

- **Collection of information:** This is the typical information gathering that you do during the troubleshooting process itself. This can also be done during a special project about analyzing and improving network performance or security. After the information is gathered, it is interpreted and analyzed. The outcome of this process during a troubleshooting task is eliminating unlikely root causes of problems and forming hypotheses about possible causes of problems. In scenarios not related to troubleshooting, the information gathered is used to make proposals for improvements. Examples for this type of information gathering are capturing of network traffic using tools such as sniffers, or debugging output of device processes.

- **Continuous collection of information to establish a baseline:** This operation entails establishing a set of key network performance indicators. Based on these indicators, statistics about the network behavior over a long period of time are collected. These statistics form a baseline that you can use to judge whether the network behavior that you observe is normal. This process also provides historical data that you can correlate to events. Examples of this are collection of statistics through use of the SNMP and traffic accounting by use of NetFlow technology.

- **Notification of network events:** This method, instead of continuously collecting information, is based on events triggering devices to report specific information. Examples of this are the reporting of events through syslog messages or SNMP traps and the definition and the reporting of specific events through the use of the EEM that is part of Cisco IOS Software.

What these categories all have in common is that their functionality depends on interaction between a tool or an application running on a host and the network devices. In the first two categories, the information is pulled from the network elements to the application or tool, whereas in the last category the information is pushed to the application or tool by the network devices. A broad spectrum of tools and applications can perform the processes mentioned, but it is unfeasible to mention them all, let alone compare and contrast them. However, many of these tools depend on the same underlying technologies and protocols for the communication between the application and the network devices. Examples of such technologies and protocols are syslog, SNMP, and NetFlow, plus network event notification technologies. Apart from understanding the main benefits that a particular tool or application brings to the network troubleshooting process, it is therefore also important for an engineer to know how to enable the necessary communication between the network devices and the tools and applications.

Traffic-Capturing Features and Tools

Packet sniffers, also called network or protocol analyzers, are important and useful tools for network engineers. Using these tools, you can look for and observe protocol errors like retransmissions or session resets. Captured traffic can also be helpful when diagnosing communication problems between two hosts. If you can spot where packets start to go missing, for example, this will help in pinpointing the problem. Packet sniffers are powerful tools because they capture large amounts of very detailed data, but that can also be a drawback. Unless you know exactly what you are looking for and you know how to set up a filter so that only the traffic you are interested in is displayed, it can be very hard to analyze packet captures. Figure 5-1 displays a sample screen from a protocol analyzer. The first four packets shown on the screen are the four-way Dynamic Host Control Protocol (DHCP) exchange resulting in an IP address lease from a DHCP server to a DHCP client. The next three packets are gratuitous Address Resolution Protocol (ARP) from an IP device.

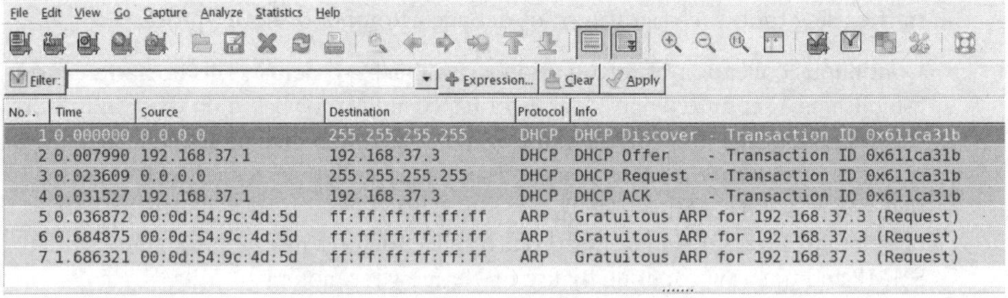
File Edit View Go Capture Analyze Statistics Help
Filter:
Expression... Clear Apply
No. Time Source Destination Protocol Info
1 0.000000 0.0.0.0 255.255.255.255 DHCP DHCP Discover - Transaction ID 0x611ca31b
2 0.007990 192.168.37.1 192.168.37.3 DHCP DHCP Offer - Transaction ID 0x611ca31b
3 0.023609 0.0.0.0 255.255.255.255 DHCP DHCP Request - Transaction ID 0x611ca31b
4 0.031527 192.168.37.1 192.168.37.3 DHCP DHCP ACK - Transaction ID 0x611ca31b
5 0.036872 00:0d:54:9c:4d:5d ff:ff:ff:ff:ff:ff ARP Gratuitous ARP for 192.168.37.3 (Request)
6 0.684875 00:0d:54:9c:4d:5d ff:ff:ff:ff:ff:ff ARP Gratuitous ARP for 192.168.37.3 (Request)
7 1.686321 00:0d:54:9c:4d:5d ff:ff:ff:ff:ff:ff ARP Gratuitous ARP for 192.168.37.3 (Request)

Figure 5-1 *Sample Screenshot from a Protocol Analyzer*

Various tools on the market (some free and some for a fee) are available for packet capturing and packet analysis. These tools can be either software based and installed on a regular computer or they can be appliance-style devices (with specialized hardware) that can capture vast amounts of data in real time. Whichever tool you select, it is always important to learn the filtering capabilities of the product so that you can select just the information that you are interested in. Furthermore, one of the issues that you generally run into is that it is not always practical or even possible to install the software on the device that is the subject of your troubleshooting. On servers, and even on certain clients, the installation of software is often tightly controlled (and in many cases, prohibited). Sometimes it is the capturing of a large amount of data that is not possible or allowed on the server or client. Fortunately, a solution to this problem exists. If you cannot perform packet capturing on a particular device itself, then from the switch that the device is connected to, you can transport the traffic that you want to capture to another device that has the software installed.

SPAN

The Switched Port Analyzer (SPAN) feature of Cisco Catalyst switches allows copying the traffic from one or more switch interfaces or VLANs to another interface on the same switch. You connect the system with the protocol analyzer capability to an interface on the switch; this will be the destination interface of SPAN. Next, you configure the switch to send a copy of the traffic from one or more interfaces or VLANs to the SPAN destination interface, where the protocol analyzer can capture and analyze the traffic. The traffic that is copied and sent to the SPAN destination interface can be the incoming traffic, outgoing traffic, or both, from the source interfaces. The source and destination interfaces (or VLANs) all reside on the same switch.

Figure 5-2 shows a switch that is configured to send traffic from the source interface Fa0/7 to the destination interface Fa0/8 using the SPAN feature. The objective is to capture all the traffic sent or received by the server connected to interface Fa0/7, in order to help troubleshooting a problem related to that server. A packet sniffer is connected to interface Fa0/8. The switch is instructed to copy all the traffic that it sends and receives on interface

Fa0/7 to interface Fa0/8. This is done using the **monitor session** *session_number* command shown on the top of Figure 5-2. Each SPAN session has a unique session identifier; in this particular case, the configured SPAN session number is 1. The source ports or VLANs are identified by use of the **monitor session** *session_number* **source** *interface* command, and the destination port is identified by use of the **monitor session** *session_number* **destination** *interface* command. The session number is what binds the commands together to form a single session. On the bottom of Figure 5-2, the configuration of the SPAN session is verified using the **show monitor session** *session-number* command. The output of this command shows that both incoming and outgoing traffic are sent from Fa0/7 to Fa0/8. Also, the frame type of native indicates Ethernet frames rather than 802.1Q frames. The last line indicating ingress as disabled means that on the destination interface Fa0/8 (where the sniffer is connected), ingress traffic is not accepted as per the current configuration.

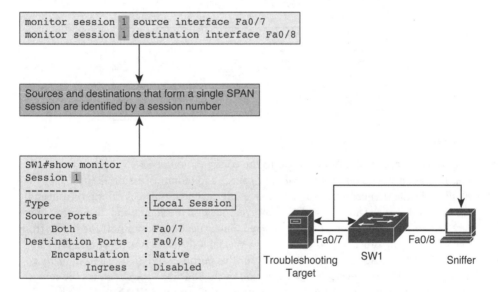

Figure 5-2 *SPAN Configuration Example*

RSPAN

Using the Remote Switched Port Analyzer (RSPAN) feature, however, you can copy traffic from ports or VLANs on one switch (let's call it the source switch) to a port on a different switch (destination switch). A VLAN must be designated as the RSPAN VLAN and not be used for any other purposes. The RSPAN VLAN receives traffic from the ports or VLANs on the source switch. The RSPAN VLAN then transports the traffic through one or more switches all the way to the destination switch. On the destination switch, the traffic is then copied from the RSPAN VLAN to the destination port. Be aware that each switching platform has certain capabilities and imposes certain restrictions on the usage of RSPAN/SPAN. You can discover these limitations and capabilities of such in the corresponding device documentation. Figure 5-3 shows an example of RSPAN configuration on two LAN switches connected by an 802.1Q trunk.

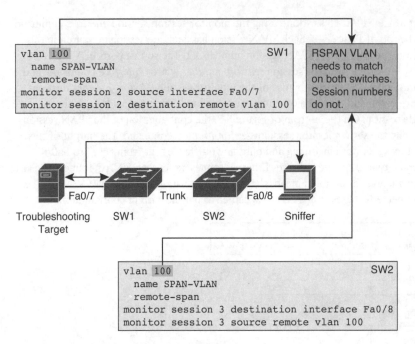

Figure 5-3   *RSPAN Configuration Example*

The configuration of RSPAN is similar to the configuration of SPAN in the sense that it uses the **monitor session** *session_number* **source** and **monitor session** *session_ number* **destination** commands to define the interface that traffic is captured from and the interface that traffic is copied to. However, because the source and destination interface are now on two different switches, a medium is needed to transport the traffic from one switch to the other. This is done using a special RSPAN VLAN. As you can see in Figure 5-3, the VLAN number 100 is used for this purpose, and it is created similarly to any other VLAN. However, the configuration of the RSPAN VLAN requires the **remote-span** command within the VLAN configuration mode, and this VLAN needs to be defined on all switches and allowed on all the trunks within the path between the source and destination switches. On the source switch, the RSPAN VLAN is configured as the destination for the SPAN session through use of the **monitor session** *session_number* **destination remote vlan** *vlan_number* command, and in a similar way the destination switch is configured to use the RSPAN VLAN as the source of the SPAN session through use of the **monitor session** *session_number* **source remote vlan** *vlan_number* command. The RSPAN VLAN needs to match on the source and destination switches, but the session numbers do not need to match. The session numbers are local identifiers that define the relationship between sources and destinations for a session on a single switch. The session numbers are not communicated between switches. In Figure 5-4, the **show monitor** command is used to verify the configuration of RSPAN on the source and destination switches.

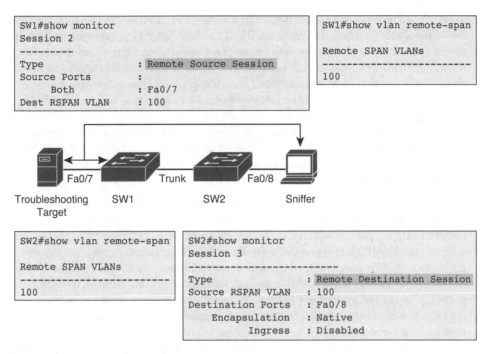

Figure 5-4 *Verifying RSPAN Configuration*

From the output of the **show monitor** command in Figure 5-4, notice that on the source switch (SW1), the session is identified as a Remote Source Session, whereas on the destination switch (SW2), it is marked as a Remote Destination Session. In addition to verifying the correct configuration of the RSPAN session, it is important that you verify the fact that the VLAN is configured correctly as an RSPAN VLAN on both switches. The **show vlan remote-span** command enables you to verify this. Finally, if pruning is enabled on the trunks within the path between source and destination switches, you should verify that the RSPAN VLAN is allowed on those trunks.

Information Gathering with SNMP

Simple Network Management Protocol (SNMP) and NetFlow are two main technologies that are used to gather statistics from Cisco switches and routers. Although there is a certain amount of overlap between the types of data they can collect, SNMP and NetFlow each have a different focus. SNMP's focus is primarily on the collection of various statistics from network devices. Routers and switches (and other network devices) keep statistics about the operation of their processes and interfaces locally. These statistics can be viewed through the CLI or graphical user interface (GUI), which is enough if all you need is a snapshot view of particular statistics or parameters at a single moment of time. However, if you want to collect and analyze these statistics over time, you can take advantage of SNMP. SNMP makes use of an SNMP network management station (NMS) and one or more SNMP agents. Agents are special processes running on the devices we would like to monitor and collect information about. You can query the SNMP agent by use of the SNMP protocol (for example, SNMP Get and Get-Next) and obtain the values for the parameters or counters of interest. By periodically querying (polling) the SNMP agent, the SNMP NMS can collect valuable ongoing information and statistics and store them. This data can then be processed and analyzed in various ways. Averages, minimums, maximums, and so on can be calculated, the data can be graphed, and thresholds can be set to trigger a notification process when they are exceeded. Statistics gathering with SNMP is considered a pull-based system because the NMS polls devices periodically to obtain the values of the objects that it is set up to collect. An NMS can query about numerous objects. These objects are organized and identified in a hierarchical model called a Management Information Base (MIB).

To configure a router for SNMP-based access is fairly simple. Although SNMP Version 3 is the official current standard, Version 2c is still the most widely used version. SNMPv3 offers enhanced security, through authentication and encryption. In SNMPv2c, access to the SNMP agent is granted based on an SNMP community string. An SNMP community string is comparable to a shared password; it must match between the NMS and the agent. Two different SNMP community strings are usually defined, one for read-only access and another one for read-write access. For statistics gathering, only read access is required, and therefore a read-write community is optional and does not need to be defined. Although it is not strictly necessary, it is also beneficial to define the SNMP contact and location. Because these parameters can be collected using SNMP, the support contact and physical location of a device can be retrieved. Another useful configuration, especially when creating a baseline or graphing interface-related variables, is the **snmp-server ifindex persist** command. This command guarantees that the SNMP interface index for each interface will stay the same, even if the device is rebooted. Without this command, you could run into a situation where the interface's ifindex changes after a reboot and counters for that interface are no longer correctly graphed. Figure 5-5 displays a simple set of SNMP configuration commands on a router.

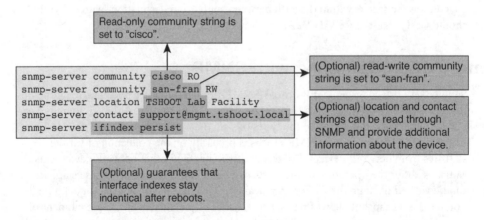

Figure 5-5 *A Simple SNMP Configuration Example*

In the example shown in Figure 5-5, the read-only community string is set to cisco, and the read-write community is set to san-fran. Furthermore, the location is set to TSHOOT Lab Facility, the contact is set to support@mgmt.tshoot.local, and ifindex is set to persistent. For increased security, you can define access lists to allow only SNMP access from certain subnets. Finally, in scenarios where access needs to be granted for only a small collection of MIB objects, an SNMP view can be defined together with a specific community string. Then, access to those MIBs will be granted only if the requestor has a matching community.

Information Gathering with NetFlow

NetFlow has a different focus and uses different underlying mechanisms. A NetFlow-enabled device, such as a router or Layer 3 switch, will collect information about the IP traffic that is flowing through (transit through) the device. The NetFlow feature classifies traffic by flow. A flow is identified as a collection of packets that have the same essential header fields, such as source IP address, destination IP address, protocol number, type of service (TOS) field, port number (if applicable), plus the ingress interface. For each individual flow, the number of packets and bytes is tracked and accounted. This information is kept in a flow cache. Flows are expired from the cache when the flows are terminated or time out.

NetFlow is currently supported on most router platforms. Among Cisco LAN switches, the 4500 and 6500 series Catalyst switches support NetFlow as well. You can enable this feature as a standalone feature on a router (interfaces) and examine the NetFlow cache using the proper CLI commands. This can be a useful tool during troubleshooting, because it enables you to see the flow entries being created as packets enter the router. In that sense, you could utilize NetFlow as a diagnostic tool. However, the biggest strength of the NetFlow technology is that in addition to keeping a local cache and temporary accounting of the flows on the device itself, the flow information can be exported to a NetFlow collector. Before entries are expired from the cache, the flow information, consisting of the key packet headers and additional information such as packet counts, byte counts, egress interface, flow start, and flow duration, is sent to the flow collector. The collector receives the flow information and records it in a database. Although the content of the packet payloads is not recorded, the flow information transferred to the collector by the router essentially contains a full view of all the traffic that has transited through the router. Enabling NetFlow and exporting the flows from a number of key routers, referred to as NetFlow Data Export (NDE), can yield a fairly complete view of all the traffic on the network. After collection, the NetFlow data can be processed and graphed.

To export NetFlow information to a collector, you must first enable NetFlow accounting (collection) on the desired router interfaces. This is done using the **ip flow ingress** interface configuration mode IOS command. You also need to configure three more items:

1. **Configure the version of the NetFlow protocol:** The most commonly used and supported version is NetFlow Version 5. The most current and flexible version is NetFlow Version 9, which is the recommended version only if your collector supports it. Consult the documentation of your collector to find out which versions of NetFlow are supported.

2. **Configure the IP address and UDP port number of the collector:** There is no default port number for NetFlow, so check the documentation of your collector to make sure that the port number on your collector and the exporting router match.

3. **Specify the source interface:** Because the collector is configured with and verifies the source IP address of the incoming packets, it is important that the NetFlow packets are always sourced from the same router interface. Using a loopback interface as the source interface for NetFlow ensures that the packets will always be sourced from the same address, regardless of the interface used to transmit the NetFlow packets.

Figure 5-6 shows a router with its Fa0/0 and Fa0/1 interfaces enabled to collect NetFlow information for ingress traffic. The definition of a flow is unidirectional, so if you want to account for both inbound and outbound traffic, the feature needs to be turned on for both interfaces. The Cisco IOS router command **ip flow ingress** replaces the old **ip route-cache flow** command. The NetFlow information is exported to a collector with the IP address 10.1.152.1 (at UDP port 9996), the packet format version is 5, and interface loopback 0's IP address is used as the source of the outgoing IP packet.

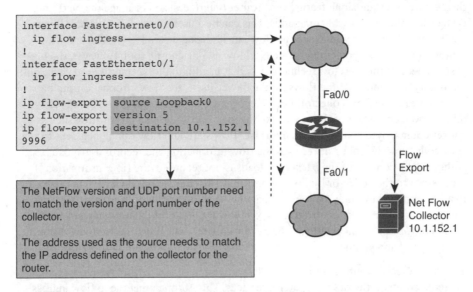

Figure 5-6 *A Simple NetFlow Configuration Example*

After the router starts caching and accounting flow information locally in its memory, you can display the NetFlow cache content by issuing the **show ip cache flow** command. This command can prove very useful when troubleshooting connection problems

because it shows the active flows that are sending packets through the router.
Example 5-1 shows partial output of the **show ip cache flow** command on a router.

Example 5-1   show ip cache flow *Command Output*

```
RO1# show ip cache flow
<...output omitted>
SrcIf         SrcIPaddress    DstIF    DstIPaddress     Pr   SrcP  DstP  Pkts
Se0/0/0.121   10.1.194.10     Null     224.0.0.10       58   0000  0000  27
Se0/0/0.121   10.1.194.14     Null     224.0.0.10       58   0000  0000  28
Fa0/0         10.1.192.5      Null     224.0.0.10       58   0000  0000  28
Fa0/1         10.1.192.13     Null     224.0.0.10       58   0000  0000  27
Fa0/1         10.1.152.1      Local    10.1.220.2       01   0000  0303  1
Se0/0/1       10.1.193.6      Null     224.0.0.10       58   0000  0000  28
Fa0/1         10.1.152.1      Se0/0/1  10.1.163.193     11   0666  E75E  1906
Se0/0/1       10.1.163.193    Fa0/0    10.1.152.1       11   E75E  0666  1905
```

The output filtering options for **show** commands can be used to select only those IP
addresses that you are interested in. For example, for the sample output in Example 5-1,
the command **show ip cache flow | include 10.1.163.193** could have been used to limit
the output to only those flows that have 10.1.163.193 as the source or destination IP
address.

In contrast to SNMP, NetFlow uses a "push"-based model. The collector will simply
be listening to NetFlow traffic, and the routers will be in charge of sending NetFlow
data to the collector, based on changes in their flow cache. Another difference between
NetFlow and SNMP is that NetFlow only gathers traffic statistics, whereas SNMP can
also collect many other performance indicators, such as interface errors, CPU usage, and
memory usage. However, the traffic statistics collected using NetFlow have a lot more
granularity than the traffic statistics that can be collected using SNMP.

Network Event Notification

A key element of a proactive network management strategy is fault notification. When a
significant event such as a failure or intrusion happens on a network, the support group
should not be notified of it through user reports or complaints. It is best if network
devices report that event to a central system and the support group becomes aware of
the issue before problems associated with the event are noticed and reported by users.
In addition to learning about the event earlier, the support group will also have the
advantage of getting a report of the underlying event rather than a mere description of
symptoms. Two popular protocols that are used for this purpose are syslog and SNMP.
In addition, the EEM feature in Cisco IOS provides an advanced method to create custom events and define actions to be taken in response to those events.

Syslog is a simple protocol used by an IP device (syslog client) to send text-based log
messages to another IP device (syslog server). These messages are the same messages that
are displayed on the console of Cisco routers and switches. The syslog protocol allows

these messages to be forwarded across the network to a central log server that collects and stores the messages from all the devices. By itself, this constitutes only a very basic form of event notification and collection: The network device notifies the log server, and the log message is stored. However, the network support team must be notified of significant events. Fortunately, syslog capabilities are included as a component of many network management systems, and these systems often include advanced mechanisms to notify network support engineers of significant events.

SNMP allows an agent running on a network device to be queried by an SNMP manager for various matters, including configuration settings, counters, and statistics. In addition to responding to polling, the agent can be configured to send messages to the SNMP manager based on the occurrence of events, such as an interface going down or device configuration change. These messages are called traps and do not contain user-readable text; instead, they include SNMP MIB objects and the associated variables. Consequently, traps must always be processed by an SNMP-based network management system that can interpret and process the MIB object information contained in the trap.

Both syslog messages and SNMP traps use predefined messages that are embedded in Cisco IOS Software. These messages can be triggered on predefined conditions, and the content of each message is fixed. The number and variety of defined syslog messages and SNMP traps is extensive, and as a result, they will fulfill the fault-notification needs of most organizations. However, special cases arise at times when you would like to be notified of a particular condition or event that is not part of the standard set of log messages and events included in Cisco IOS. For these special cases, Cisco IOS Software has a feature called Embedded Event Manager (EEM), which enables you to define custom events and corresponding actions.

Figure 5-7 shows a router configured with the commands that enable SNMP trap notification. This task is performed in two steps. In the first step, one or more trap receivers are defined, and in the second step, sending traps is enabled.

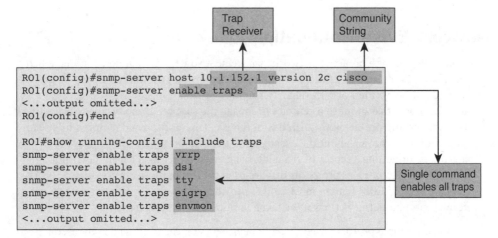

Figure 5-7 *A Sample Configuration for Enabling SNMP Traps*

Trap receivers are configured using the **snmp-server host** *host* **traps [version {1 | 2c | 3}] community-string** command. By default, Cisco routers send SNMP Version 1 traps, but higher versions can be configured explicitly. If you want a router to send specific traps, each desired trap must be encoded with the **snmp-server enable traps** *notification-type* command. However, to enable all trap types with a single command, you must use the **snmp-server enable traps** command. This command will not appear in the configuration as a command because it executes a macro that enables all available categories of traps. This effect is visible in the output of the **show running-config | include traps** command in Figure 5-7. SNMP and syslog both act on predefined triggers and send predefined messages. Both protocols allow for a limited amount of filtering, but it is not possible to define entirely new event triggers or messages.

The EEM framework enables the creation of custom policies that trigger actions based on events. Events can be triggered based on various Cisco IOS subsystems such as syslog messages, Cisco IOS counter changes, SNMP MIB object changes, SNMP traps, CLI command execution, timers, and many other options. Actions can consist of sending SNMP traps or syslog messages, executing CLI commands, sending e-mail, or even running tool command language (TCL) scripts. Thus, EEM enables you to create very powerful and complex policies.

Example 5-2 shows how to implement a policy using the Cisco IOS EEM feature. Assume that all network engineers within an organization are granted privileged access to the routers and switches and can make changes if necessary. The rule is that only Level 3 support engineers are allowed to make emergency changes if required, but Level 1 and 2 engineers always need to obtain authorization before making any change to the system. Whenever an engineer configures a router or switch, a %SYS-5-CONFIG_I message is logged to the syslog server. However, this message is logged as a syslog level five "notification" message and does not show up in the logs as a high-priority item. There is a requirement that a message must be logged as soon as anybody enters configuration mode; that is in addition to the %SYS-5-CONFIG_I message that is logged after configuration mode is exited. This message should be logged as a critical message and an informational message should be logged reminding the engineer of the existing change-control policies.

Example 5-2 *An EEM Configuration Example*

```
Router(config)# event manager applet CONFIG-STARTED
Router(config-applet)# event cli pattern "configure terminal" sync no skip no
  occurs 1
Router(config-applet)# action 1.0 syslog priority critical msg "Configuration mode
  was entered"
Router(config-applet)# action 2.0 syslog priority informational msg "Change control
  policies apply. Authorized access only."
```

The simple EEM applet shown in Example 5-2 accomplishes the policy requirements using the following four command lines:

1. The **event manager applet CONFIG-STARTED** command creates an applet called CONFIG-STARTED.

2. The event that should trigger this applet is defined on the second line using the command **event cli pattern "configure terminal" sync no skip no occurs 1**. This line effectively says that the policy should be triggered if a command that includes **"configure terminal"** is entered. The occurs 1 option forces the event to be triggered on a single occurrence of the CLI pattern.

3. The **action 1.0 syslog priority critical msg "Configuration mode was entered"** command defines an action named 1.0 (actions are sorted in alphabetical order) and instructs the router to log a critical message containing the text "Configuration mode was entered."

4. The **action 2.0 syslog priority informational msg "Change control policies apply. Authorized access only."** command defines an action named 2.0 and instructs the router to log an informational message containing the text "Change control policies apply. Authorized access only."

Example 5-3 shows the effect and result of the EEM policy discussed in Example 5-2. As soon as a user enters the IOS global configuration mode, two messages appear. The first message is a critical message (syslog level 2) stating "%HA_EM-2-LOG: CONFIG-STARTED: Configuration mode was entered," and the second message is an informational message (syslog level 6) stating %HA_EM-6-LOG: CONFIG-STARTED: "Change control policies apply. Authorized access only."

Example 5-3   *A Sample EEM Policy Result*

```
RO1# conf t
Enter configuration commands, one per line.  End with CNTL/Z.
RO1(config)#
Mar 13 03:24:41.473 PDT: %HA_EM-2-LOG: CONFIG-STARTED: Configuration mode was entered
Mar 13 03:24:41.473 PDT: %HA_EM-6-LOG: CONFIG-STARTED: Change control policies
  apply. Authorized access only.
```

Examples 5-2 and 5-3 demonstrated a simple implementation of EEM and its policy results. Bear in mind, however, that the EEM is a very powerful tool, and by incorporating the use of the TCL scripting language tool, you can implement a complete distributed notification system. Please note that complete coverage of EEM is beyond the scope of this chapter. However, you can find more information about the latest version and features of EEM at Cisco.com.

Summary

Different phases of the troubleshooting process can benefit from specific types of troubleshooting tools:

- **Defining the problem:** Network monitoring and event reporting tools

- **Gathering information:** Incident driven, targeted information-gathering tools

- **Analyzing:** Baseline-creation and traffic-accounting tools

- **Testing the hypothesis:** Configuration rollback tools

Examples of network monitoring and event reporting tools include the following:

- Logging system messages to syslog

- Event notification using SNMP

- Event notification using the EEM

Examples of incident-related information gathering are SPAN and RSPAN (used for traffic capturing).

The following are examples of baseline-creation and traffic-accounting tools:

- Statistics gathering using SNMP

- Traffic accounting using NetFlow

Packet sniffers can be used to capture packets to allow detailed analysis of packet flows. Taking packet captures at various points in the network allows you to spot potential differences.

The SPAN feature allows traffic to be copied from one or more source ports or source VLANs to a port on the same switch for capture and analysis. The RSPAN feature allows traffic to be copied from one or more source ports or source VLANs on one switch to a port on another switch by use of a special RSPAN VLAN. The RSPAN VLAN needs to be carried between the source and destination switches by use of trunks. RSPAN cannot cross Layer 3 boundaries.

Two main technologies that can be used to create a baseline of network usage and performance are SNMP and NetFlow.

SNMP is a standard protocol and is a pull model where the NMS polls devices for specific information. Cisco IOS NetFlow is based on the collection of detailed traffic profiles, and it is considered a push model. The NetFlow-enabled device pushes flow information to a collector, as traffic flows through the device. NetFlow is a Cisco router-specific feature.

Routers and switches can notify network management stations of significant events using two common methods: syslog and SNMP. In addition, you can use the EEM feature in Cisco IOS to create custom events and define actions to be taken in response to the event.

Review Questions

1. Which of the following phases or subprocesses of structured troubleshooting normally is least likely to make use of specialized troubleshooting protocols, tools, and utilities?

   a. Defining the problem

   b. Gathering information

   c. Analyzing information

   d. Eliminating impossible or unlikely causes

   e. Testing the hypothesis

2. Which of the following items are most useful for collecting information to establish a baseline? (Choose two.)

   a. SNMP

   b. NetFlow

   c. EEM

   d. Ping

3. Which of the following items is not generally used for the purpose of automatic notification of network events?

   a. Syslog

   b. Protocol analyzer/packet sniffer

   c. SNMP traps

   d. EEM

4. Which of the following Catalyst switch features allows traffic from particular interfaces or VLANs to be duplicated and sent to another interface?

   a. Syslog

   b. EEM

   c. SPAN

   d. NetFlow

5. Which of the following commands enables you to verify configuration of a SPAN session?

   a. monitor session

   b. session monitor

   c. show monitor session *session number*

   d. show session

6. As of which version of SNMP has enhanced security through authentication and encryption been offered?

   a. Version 1

   b. Version 2

   c. Version 2c

   d. Version 3

   e. Version 4

7. Which command enables you to display a router's NetFlow cache content?

   a. show ip cache flow

   b. show netflow cache

   c. show nde flow cache

   d. show ip cache

8. Which of the following Cisco IOS features enables you to create custom events and define actions to be taken in response to those events?

   a. SPAN/RSPAN

   b. Syslog

   c. NetFlow

   d. EEM

9. Which of the following network management actions is considered a pull operation?

   a. SNMP Get

   b. SNMP trap

   c. Syslog

   d. NetFlow data export

   e. EEM action

10. Which *two* of the following commands are necessary to configure a switch to copy all traffic from interface Fa0/1 to a packet sniffer on interface Fa0/5?

   a. monitor session 1 source interface Fa0/1

   b. span session 1 destination interface Fa0/5

   c. span session 1 destination remote interface Fa0/5

   d. monitor session 1 destination interface Fa0/5

   e. span session 1 source interface Fa0/1

   f. span session 1 destination remote interface Fa0/5

11. Which of the following best describes EEM?

   a. It is a framework that allows for the creation of custom events and corresponding actions.

   b. It is a technology that allows traffic to be copied from one switch port to another to allow it to be captured.

   c. It is a protocol that allows statistics to be gathered from a device and notifications to be sent by that same device.

   d. It is a technology that enables the collection of detailed traffic profiles.

12. Which of the following best describes SNMP?

   a. It is a framework that allows for the creation of custom events and corresponding actions.

   b. It is a technology that allows traffic to be copied from one switch port to another to allow it to be captured.

   c. It is a protocol that allows particular information (defined as MIBs) on an IP device to be set and/or gathered by a network management service.

   d. It is a technology that enables the collection of detailed traffic profiles.

13. Which of the following best describes NetFlow?

   a. It is a framework that allows for the creation of custom events and corresponding actions.

   b. It is a technology that allows traffic to be copied from one switch port to another to allow it to be captured.

   c. It is a protocol that allows statistics to be gathered from a device and notifications to be sent by that same device.

   d. It is a technology that enables the collection of detailed traffic profiles.

14. Which of the following best describes SPAN?

   a. It is a framework that allows for the creation of custom events and corresponding actions.

   b. It is a technology that allows traffic to be copied from one switch port to another so that the traffic can be captured.

   c. It is a protocol that allows statistics to be gathered from a device and notifications to be sent by that same device.

   d. It is a technology that enables the collection of detailed traffic profiles.

Chapter 6

Troubleshooting Case Study: SECHNIK Networking

This chapter presents three troubleshooting cases at SECHNIK Networking, a fictitious company, based on the topology shown in Figure 6-1. Each troubleshooting case includes a few configuration errors. Configuration errors will be dealt with as real-world troubleshooting scenarios. Certain technologies are explained briefly to refresh your memory.

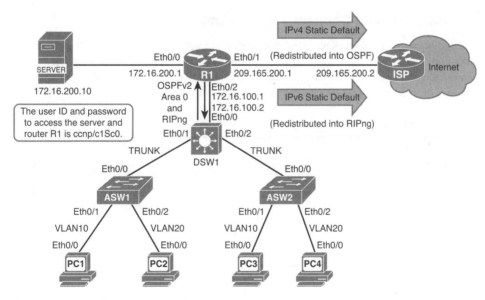

Figure 6-1 *SECHNIK Networking Network Diagram*

> **Note**   The networks presented in this and the following chapters use Cisco routers to simulate the servers and personal computers (PCs); keep that in mind as you observe the output shown in the examples presented.

SECHNIK Networking Trouble Ticket 1

On Monday morning, four employees have reported network connectivity problems. They all claim that the issues did not exist on Friday before they left work. The following is the list of their complaints:

- Kimberly, the user on PC1, cannot access data on the server at 172.16.200.10.

- Andrew, the user on PC2, cannot access the Internet. He is trying to access a server at 209.165.200.2.

- Carol, the user on PC3, cannot use Secure Shell (SSH) to connect to the server at 172.16.200.10.

- Mithun, the user on PC4, said that he would like to access the Internet through IPv6. He added that because this worked for Andrew, it should also work for him. He requested to use IPv6 address 2001:DB8:D1:A5:C8::2 for a connectivity test.

Troubleshooting PC1's Connectivity Problem

Kimberly, the user of PC1, has reported that she cannot access the server with IP address 172.16.200.10. The first thing we need to do is verify the problem and make a troubleshooting plan. Example 6-1 shows a ping to the server at 172.16.200.10 failed. We also know that PC1 could communicate with this server 1 business day ago.

Example 6-1   *Verify PC1's Connectivity Problem*

```
PC1# ping 172.16.200.10
% Unrecognized host or address, or protocol not running.
PC1#


PC3# show ip int brief
Interface            IP-Address      OK? Method Status              Protocol
Ethernet0/0          192.168.10.2    YES DHCP   up                  up


PC3# ping 172.16.200.10
Type escape sequence to abort.
Sending 5, 100-byte ICMP Echos to 172.16.200.10, timeout is 2 seconds:
!!!!!
Success rate is 100 percent (5/5), round-trip min/avg/max = 3/205/1003 ms
```

We can take the bottom-up troubleshooting approach and start at the physical and data link layer and move our way up.

Gathering Information

Having decided to take the bottom-up approach, we examine the Ethernet interface on PC1. As the output of Example 6-2 shows, PC1's interface is up, but it has no IP address. Example 6-2 also shows that ASW1's Ethernet 0/1 connecting to PC1 is configured correctly. The problem does not seem to be at the physical or data link layers. PC1 is supposed to obtain its address through Dynamic Host Configuration Protocol (DHCP), but that has obviously failed for some reason.

Example 6-2 *Checking the Ethernet Interface of PC1*

```
PC1# show ip interface brief
Interface            IP-Address      OK? Method Status         Protocol
Ethernet0/0          unassigned      YES DHCP   up             up
PC1#


ASW1# show running-config interface ethernet 0/1
Building configuration...

Current configuration : 134 bytes
!
interface Ethernet0/1
 description PC1
 switchport access vlan 10
 switchport mode access
 duplex auto
 spanning-tree portfast
end
ASW1#
```

Analyzing Information, Eliminating Causes, and Gathering Further Information

PC3 is in the same VLAN as PC1 (VLAN 10) and it has successfully obtained its address through DHCP, but it is connected to ASW2 (see Example 6-1). We can conclude that the DHCP server is up and reachable from VLAN 10; in other words, we eliminate DHCP server as cause. It is therefore logical to examine ASW1's uplink to DSW1 next. Example 6-3 shows the result of checking the configuration of the trunk link from both ends, from ASW1 and from DSW1.

Example 6-3 *Checking the Configuration of a Trunk Link from Both Ends*

```
ASW1# show interfaces description
Interface                 Status          Protocol Description
Et0/0                     up              up       link to DSW1
Et0/1                     up              up       PC1
Et0/2                     up              up       PC2
< output omitted >
ASW1#


ASW1# show interfaces trunk
Port        Mode            Encapsulation Status          Native vlan
Et0/0       on              802.1q        trunking        1


Port        Vlans allowed on trunk
Et0/0       1,20


Port        Vlans allowed and active in management domain
Et0/0       1,20


Port        Vlans in spanning tree forwarding state and not pruned
Et0/0       1,20
ASW1#


DSW1# show interfaces trunk
Port        Mode            Encapsulation Status          Native vlan
Et0/1       on              802.1q        trunking        1
Et0/2       on              802.1q        trunking        1


Port        Vlans allowed on trunk
Et0/1       1,10,20
Et0/2       1,10,20


Port        Vlans allowed and active in management domain
Et0/1       1,10,20
Et0/2       1,10,20


Port        Vlans in spanning tree forwarding state and not pruned
Et0/1       1,10,20
Et0/2       1,10,20
DSW1#
```

Proposing Hypotheses

The output of Example 6-3 shows us that DSW1 allows VLANs 1, 10, 20 in the trunk (Ethernet 0/1) connected to ASW1. However, ASW1 only allows VLANs 1 and 20 in the trunk (Ethernet 0/0) connected to DSW1. We can propose that a contributing cause for PC1's problem is that VLAN 10 is not allowed on the trunk (Ethernet 0/0) configuration on ASW1.

Testing the Hypotheses and Solving the Problem

Example 6-4 shows us changing the configuration on ASW1 to allow VLAN 10 on the trunk (Ethernet 0/0) connection to DSW1. Example 6-4 also shows that subsequent to the change, we try to ping the server (172.16.200.10) from PC1 and it succeeds.

Example 6-4   *Correcting Trunk Allowed VLAN Configuration*

```
ASW1# configure terminal
Enter configuration commands, one per line.  End with CNTL/Z.
ASW1(config)# interface eth 0/0
ASW1(config-if)# switchport trunk allowed vlan add 10
ASW1(config-if)# end
*Aug  4 23:38:29.314: %SYS-5-CONFIG_I: Configured from console by console
ASW1# show interfaces trunk

Port          Mode              Encapsulation  Status         Native vlan
Et0/0         on                802.1q         trunking       1

Port          Vlans allowed on trunk
Et0/0         1,10,20

Port          Vlans allowed and active in management domain
Et0/0         1,10,20

Port          Vlans in spanning tree forwarding state and not pruned
Et0/0         1,20
ASW1#


PC1# ping 172.16.200.10
Type escape sequence to abort.
Sending 5, 100-byte ICMP Echos to 172.16.200.10, timeout is 2 seconds:
!!!!!
Success rate is 100 percent (5/5), round-trip min/avg/max = 2/4/8 ms
PC1#
```

We must document our work and notify the user and any other party involved that the problem is solved.

Troubleshooting Ethernet Trunks

Common trunk configuration errors include the following:

■ Trunk type (ISL versus 802.1Q) mismatch

■ Switchport mode mismatch

■ Native VLAN mismatch (applicable to 802.1Q)

■ Allowed VLANs mismatch or error

When you configure the switchport mode in interface configuration mode, you have the following choices:

■ **Dynamic auto:** The Ethernet interface starts in access mode, but it will switch to trunk mode if the adjacent neighbor suggests it using the Dynamic Trunking Protocol (DTP).

■ **Dynamic desirable:** The Ethernet interface starts in access mode, but it will suggest to the adjacent neighbor to switch to trunk mode (using DTP). The interface will go into trunk mode only if the adjacent neighbor agrees.

■ **Trunk:** The Ethernet interface starts in trunk mode. It does not generate DTP messages, but it will respond positively to adjacent neighbor's suggestion to switch to trunk mode.

■ **Access:** The Ethernet interface starts in access mode. It does not generate DTP messages, and it will not agree to adjacent neighbor's suggestion to switch to trunk mode.

■ **Nonegotiate:** The Ethernet interface starts in trunk mode with DTP completely disabled. It does not generate DTP messages, and it will not respond to adjacent neighbor's suggestion to switch to trunk mode. This option should only be used if both sides of the link are configured identically with it.

The output of the **show interfaces trunk** and the **show interface** *Ethernet x/y* **switchport** commands helps you determine the current configuration of Ethernet interfaces (see Example 6-5). Those outputs are also useful to compare the settings of the two ends of an interswitch link.

Example 6-5 *Helpful Trunk Troubleshooting Commands*

```
DSW1# show interfaces trunk

Port        Mode          Encapsulation  Status    Native vlan
Et0/1       on            802.1q         trunking  1
Et0/2       on            802.1q         trunking  1


Port        Vlans allowed on trunk
Et0/1       1,10,20
```

```
Et0/2        1,10,20


Port         Vlans allowed and active in management domain
Et0/1        1,10,20
Et0/2        1,10,20


Port         Vlans in spanning tree forwarding state and not pruned
Et0/1        none
Et0/2        none
DSW1#
DSW1# show interface ethernet0/1 switchport
Name: Et0/1
Switchport: Enabled
Administrative Mode: trunk
Operational Mode: trunk
Administrative Trunking Encapsulation: dot1q
Operational Trunking Encapsulation: dot1q
Negotiation of Trunking: On
Access Mode VLAN: 1 (default)
Trunking Native Mode VLAN: 1 (default)
Administrative Native VLAN tagging: enabled
Voice VLAN: none
Administrative private-vlan host-association: none
Administrative private-vlan mapping: none
Administrative private-vlan trunk native VLAN: none
Administrative private-vlan trunk Native VLAN tagging: enabled
Administrative private-vlan trunk encapsulation: dot1q
Administrative private-vlan trunk normal VLANs: none
Administrative private-vlan trunk associations: none
Administrative private-vlan trunk mappings: none
Operational private-vlan: none          .
Trunking VLANs Enabled: 1,10,20
Pruning VLANs Enabled: 2-1001
Capture Mode Disabled
Capture VLANs Allowed: ALL


Appliance trust: none
DSW1#
```

Troubleshooting PC2's Connectivity Problem

Andrew, the user of PC2, has reported that he cannot access the Internet. Specifically, the address of the server he is trying to reach is 209.165.200.2. The first thing we need to do is verify the problem and make a troubleshooting plan. Example 6-6 shows a ping to the server at 209.165.200.2 from PC2 failing. We know that PC2 could communicate with this server last week.

Example 6-6   *Verifying the Internet Connectivity Problem at PC2*

```
PC2# ping 209.165.200.2
Type escape sequence to abort.
Sending 5, 100-byte ICMP Echos to 209.165.200.2, timeout is 2 seconds:
.....
Success rate is 0 percent (0/5)
PC2#
PC2# show ip interface brief
Interface            IP-Address      OK? Method Status              Protocol
Ethernet0/0          192.168.20.2    YES DHCP   up                  up
PC2#
```

Gathering Information

It is a good idea to check and see whether other users and PCs have Internet connectivity problems similar to PC2. We test Internet connectivity from other PCs, and they all have identical problems as PC2. This is a simple swap-the-component troubleshooting approach that allows us to decide whether the problem originates in PC2 itself or if the problem originates elsewhere (thus affecting many other devices).

Next, we check whether R1 has connectivity to the Internet as well as connectivity to the PCs inside the network. Example 6-7 shows that R1 can successfully ping 209.165.200.2 (Internet), and it can also ping 192.168.20.2 (PC2).

Example 6-7   *Information Gathering: Check R1's Inside and Outside Connectivity*

```
R1# ping 209.165.200.2
Type escape sequence to abort.
Sending 5, 100-byte ICMP Echos to 209.165.200.2, timeout is 2 seconds:
!!!!!
Success rate is 100 percent (5/5), round-trip min/avg/max = 1/5/10 ms
R1#
R1# ping 192.168.20.2
Type escape sequence to abort.
Sending 5, 100-byte ICMP Echos to 192.168.20.2, timeout is 2 seconds:
!!!!!
Success rate is 100 percent (5/5), round-trip min/avg/max = 4/7/11 ms
R1#
```

Based on the ping results at R1, we can conclude that our connection to the Internet service provider (ISP) is good and that no connectivity problems exist between the PCs and the edge router (R1). The configuration problems that could affect Internet connectivity include Network Address Translation (NAT), access control lists (ACLs), and routing. We know that the PCs inside are using private IP addresses, so checking the NAT configuration on R1 seems like a logical next step. Example 6-8 shows the output of **show ip nat** statistics and **show interfaces description** commands on R1. Based on the output, NAT is not working (Total active translations: 0), outside interface is configured as Ethernet 0/1, and inside interface is configured as Ethernet 0/2. The output of **show interfaces description** verifies that these interfaces are configured as planned. The output of **show ip nat statistics** also shows us that access list 1 is used to match the source address of the packets coming in through inside interface.

Example 6-8   *Information Gathering: NAT Configuration on R1*

```
R1# show ip nat statistics
Total active translations: 0 (0 static, 0 dynamic; 0 extended)
Outside interfaces:
  Ethernet0/1
Inside interfaces:
  Ethernet0/2
Hits: 0  Misses: 0
CEF Translated packets: 0, CEF Punted packets: 17
Expired translations: 0
Dynamic mappings:
-- Inside Source
[Id: 1] access-list 1 interface Ethernet0/1 refcount 0
nat-limit statistics:
 max entry: max allowed 0, used 0, missed 0
R1#
R1# show interface description
Interface                 Status         Protocol Description
Et0/0                     up             up       link to SERVER
Et0/1                     up             up       link to INTERNET
Et0/2                     up             up       link to DSW1
R1#
R1# show access-list 1
R1#
R1# show access-list
Standard IP access list 21
    10 permit 192.168.0.0, wildcard bits 0.0.255.255
    20 permit 172.16.0.0, wildcard bits 0.0.255.255
R1#
R1# show ip interface | include Outgoing|Inbound
  Outgoing access list is not set
  Inbound  access list is not set
  Outgoing access list is not set
  Inbound  access list is not set
  Outgoing access list is not set
  Inbound  access list is not set
  Outgoing access list is not set
```

```
  Inbound  access list is not set
  Outgoing access list is not set
  Inbound  access list is not set
R1#
```

The logical next step is to check validity of access list 1. We used the **show access-list 1** command (see Example 6-8) and found that this access list does not exist. However, the output of the **show access-list** command that we tried immediately after tells us that there is an access list 21 with a configuration suitable for our NAT needs. However, before we use access list 21 for NAT purposes, to be safe, we check to determine whether an access list is applied to any interface on R1. The last section in Example 6-8, where we typed the command **show ip interface | include Outgoing|Inbound**, shows that no ip access list is applied to any of the R1 interfaces.

Proposing a Hypothesis, Testing the Hypothesis, and Solving the Problem

We have discovered that the access list used for NAT is mistakenly typed as access list 1 instead of access list 21. We remove the old command referring to access list 1, and we configure a new NAT command referencing access list 21 instead. As you can see in Example 6-9, after the correction was made on R1, we can successfully reach/ping the 206.165.200.2 device on the Internet from PC2.

Example 6-9 *Information Gathering: NAT Configuration on R1*

```
R1# show run | include ip nat inside source
ip nat inside source list 1 interface Ethernet0/1 overload
R1#
R1# conf t
Enter configuration commands, one per line.  End with CNTL/Z.
R1(config)# no ip nat inside source list 1 interface Ethernet0/1 overload
R1(config)# ip nat inside source list 21 interface Ethernet0/1 overload
R1(config)#end
*Aug  5 15:21:22.814: %SYS-5-CONFIG_I: Configured from console by console
R1# copy run start
Destination filename [startup-config]?
Building configuration...
Compressed configuration from 2094 bytes to 1245 bytes[OK]
R1#


PC2# ping 209.165.200.2
Type escape sequence to abort.
Sending 5, 100-byte ICMP Echos to 209.165.200.2, timeout is 2 seconds:
!!!!!
Success rate is 100 percent (5/5), round-trip min/avg/max = 2/7/11 ms
PC2#
```

We must document our work and notify the user and any other party involved that the problem is solved.

Troubleshooting NAT

Common NAT misconfigurations include the following:

- Inside and outside interfaces are not configured properly.

- The ACL used for NAT is not correctly configured.

- The NAT IP address pool is not correctly configured.

- The inside global address is not advertised, causing routing and reachability problems from outside.

Aside from NAT configuration errors, you need to familiarize yourself with some NAT-related caveats:

- **Some applications are not NAT friendly:** Certain applications such as IP telephony call-setup protocols make a reference to the host IP address (before translation). This will cause the Voice over IP (VoIP) traffic (the actual call) to be dropped, because the IP packet destination addresses are private addresses and unreachable. Usage of these applications with NAT requires special configurations and workarounds.

- **NAT contributes to the total end-to-end delay:** Packets subject to NAT experience more delay than they would without NAT. If you experience significant delays due to translations, it is possible that the NAT device is doing excessive NAT translations.

- **Using NAT over a VPN:** IP address translation performed by NAT modifies the IP header checksum as well. If the IP header checksum is used in the integrity check performed by a security protocol, the IP packet will be rejected. There are workarounds for these cases.

- **NAT will hide the IP address information:** End-to-end troubleshooting can be challenging with NAT. A good understanding of the NAT process is crucial before starting the troubleshooting process.

It is important for you to be aware that there is a new NAT configuration method using the NAT Virtual Interface (NVI) feature. The configuration syntax for NAT and NVI differ slightly. With NAT NVI, you do not need to define NAT inside and NAT outside interfaces; you only need to enable interfaces for NAT. Furthermore, the command that translates the addresses does not include the keyword **inside**. Example 6-10 shows a legacy NAT configuration followed by an NVI configuration.

Example 6-10   *Example of Legacy NAT Versus NVI*

```
R1(config)# interface fastethernet 0/0
R1(config-if)# ip nat inside
R1(config-if)# interface fastethernet 0/1
R1(config-if)# ip nat outside
R1(config-if)# exit
R1(config)# ip nat inside source static 192.168.0.1 209.165.200.2


R1(config)# interface fastethernet 0/0
R1(config-if)# ip nat enable
R1(config-if)# interface fastethernet 0/1
R1(config-if)# ip nat enable
R1(config-if)# exit
R1(config)# ip nat source static 192.168.0.1 209.165.200.2
```

The NVI feature enables NAT traffic flows on the virtual interface, eliminating the need to specify inside and outside domains. When a domain is specified, translation rules are applied either before or after route decisions are applied, depending on the traffic flow from inside to outside or outside to inside. Translation rules are applied to a domain only after the route decision for an NVI is applied.

The **show ip nat translations** command shows which interfaces are acting as the inside and outside interfaces and the current number of static and dynamic translations. When troubleshooting NAT, **clear ip nat translation *** is a useful command. It removes all active dynamic translations from the NAT table. *Inside global* address is an IP address of an internal device as it appears to the external network. *Inside local* address is an IP address assigned to a device on the internal network. *Outside local* address is an IP address of an external device as it appears to the internal network. *Outside global* address is an IP address assigned to an external device. The **debug ip nat** command shows translations as they occur. The IP identification number can be used to match the packets in the output with the packets captured with a protocol analyzer.

Troubleshooting PC3's Connectivity Problem

Carol, the user of PC3, has reported that she cannot use SSH (Secure Shell) to access the server at 172.16.200.10. Carol was able to access this server from her PC before. The first thing we need to do is verify the problem and make a troubleshooting plan. Example 6-11 shows our SSH attempt (using the user account ccnp) to server at 172.16.200.10 from PC3 failing.

Example 6-11   *Verifying SSH Connection Problem from PC3*

```
PC3>ssh -l ccnp 172.16.200.10
% Destination unreachable; gateway or host down

PC3>
```

To solve this problem, we can take a top-down approach. Because the SSH application is not working, we can attempt a basic connectivity test to the server at 172.16.200.10 using ping next.

Gathering Information

Example 6-12 shows that ping from PC3 to server 172.16.200.10 has failed, too. Taking a top-down approach, we must check the data link layer next.

Example 6-12 *Performing a Basic Connectivity Test from PC3 to the SSH Server*

```
PC3>ping 172.16.200.10
% Unrecognized host or address, or protocol not running.
PC3>



ASW2# show interfaces description
Interface                 Status           Protocol  Description
Et0/0                     up                   up           link to DSW1
Et0/1                     admin down down      PC3
Et0/2                     up                   up           PC4
< output omitted >
ASW2#
```

A next simple fact-gathering step is to check the status of the Ethernet interfaces on ASW2. As you can see in Example 6-12, the output of the **show interfaces description** command shows interface Ethernet 0/1 (where PC3 connects) as admin down.

Eliminating Possibilities, Proposing a Hypothesis, and Testing the Hypothesis

The Ethernet 0/1 interface on ASW2 being shut down explains why PC3 is experiencing connectivity problems. With this fact gathered, other network configuration problems are possible but less likely. We must bring this interface up to determine whether that is the only problem affecting PC3's connectivity, or whether we need to do more fact gathering. As you can see in Example 6-13, after bringing the interface Ethernet 0/1 up on ASW2, PC3 can successfully make an SSH connection to the server at 172.16.200.10 (using user ID ccnp).

Example 6-13 *Testing the Hypothesis: Bring Up Interface Ethernet 0/1 on ASW2*

```
ASW2# configure terminal
Enter configuration commands, one per line.  End with CNTL/Z.
ASW2(config)# interface ethernet 0/1
ASW2(config-if)# no shut
ASW2(config-if)#
*Aug  5 18:17:41.402: %LINK-3-UPDOWN: Interface Ethernet0/1, changed state to up
```

```
*Aug  5 18:17:42.407: %LINEPROTO-5-UPDOWN: Line protocol on Interface Ethernet0/1,
  changed state to up
ASW2(config-if)# end
ASW2#
*Aug  5 18:17:44.457: %SYS-5-CONFIG_I: Configured from console by console
ASW2# copy run start
Destination filename [startup-config]?
Building configuration...
Compressed configuration from 1849 bytes to 934 bytes[OK]
ASW2#


PC3>
*Aug  5 18:18:23.373: %DHCP-6-ADDRESS_ASSIGN: Interface Ethernet0/0 assigned DHCP
  address 192.168.10.2, mask 255.255.255.0, hostname PC3

PC3>ssh -l ccnp 172.16.200.10
Password:

SERVER>exit

[Connection to 172.16.200.10 closed by foreign host]
PC3>
```

It seems that there was a single problem preventing PC3 from connecting to the network and making an SSH session to the desired server. We must now complete all documentation and notify the user and any other party involved that the problem is solved.

Troubleshooting Network Device Interfaces

To verify a network device interface status, you can use the **show ip interface** *interface slot/number* and **show ip interface brief** commands. The status refers to the hardware layer and reflects whether the interface is receiving the detected signal from the other end. The line protocol refers to the data link layer and reflects whether the data link layer protocol keepalives are being received. Possible problems for an interface not being operational:

- **Interface is up and the line protocol is down:** Some possible causes are no keep-alives, mismatch in encapsulation type, and a clock-rate issue.

- **Line protocol and the interface are both down:** A cable might not be attached to a switch, or the other end of the connection may be administratively down.

- **Interface Status shows as admin down:** The interface has been shut down administratively and must be configured with the **no shutdown** command.

Troubleshooting PC4's IPv6 Connectivity Problem

Mithun, the user of PC4, has reported that he cannot access the device with the IPv6 address 2001:DB8:D1:A5:C8::2 on the Internet. He has informed us, however, that he was able to access this server from his PC last week, and that PC2 can access this server with no problems at this moment.

The first thing we need to do is verify the problem and make a troubleshooting plan. Example 6-14 shows our ping attempt from PC4 failing, but ping to the same server from PC2 succeeds.

Example 6-14 *Verifying IPv6 Connectivity Problem from PC4*

```
PC4# ping 2001:db8:d1:a5:c8::2
Type escape sequence to abort.
Sending 5, 100-byte ICMP Echos to 2001:DB8:D1:A5:C8::2, timeout is 2 seconds:
NNNNN
Success rate is 0 percent (0/5)
PC4#


PC2#
PC2# ping 2001:db8:d1:a5:c8::2
Type escape sequence to abort.
Sending 5, 100-byte ICMP Echos to 2001:DB8:D1:A5:C8::2, timeout is 2 seconds:
.!!!!
Success rate is 80 percent (4/5), round-trip min/avg/max = 2/3/6 ms
PC2#
```

Based on this initial information, using the compare-configurations approach makes the best sense. It is reasonable to assume that the IPv6 connectivity to the Internet using our ISP is operational.

Gathering Information

Comparing the configuration of PC4 and PC2, as you can see in Example 6-15, it is noticeable that PC2 is configured with the **ipv6 address autoconfig** command on its Ethernet 0/0 interface, but PC4 is missing that command on its Ethernet 0/0 interface.

Example 6-15 *Comparing Configurations: Spotting PC4 and PC2 IPv6 Differences*

```
PC4# show ipv6 interface brief
Ethernet0/0            [up/up]
   FE80::A8BB:CCFF:FE00:A000
< output omitted >
PC4#
PC4# show running-config interface ethernet 0/0
```

```
Building configuration...

Current configuration : 78 bytes
!
interface Ethernet0/0
 ip address dhcp
 no ip route-cache
 ipv6 enable
end
PC4#


PC2#
PC2# show running-config interface ethernet 0/0
Building configuration...

Current configuration : 90 bytes
!
interface Ethernet0/0
 ip address dhcp
 no ip route-cache
 ipv6 address autoconfig
end
PC2#
```

To verify the IPv6 address of PC4 on its Ethernet 0/0, on top of Example 6-15 you can see that we use the **show ipv6 interface brief** command. The output shows that PC4 has a link-local address (FE80::A8BB:CCFF:FE00:A000) on this interface, but not a routable IPv6 address.

Eliminating Possibilities, Proposing a Hypothesis, and Testing the Hypothesis

Without a routable IP address, PC4 cannot communicate with devices outside its local link. Lack of a routable IPv6 address is definitely our hypothesis. If configuring PC4's Ethernet 0/0 interface with the **IPv6 address autoconfig** command is in accordance to our network documentation and policies, we will make the change and test our hypothesis. If the PC4 connectivity problems are solved, we can close this case. Example 6-16 shows our work with regard to fixing the configuration of PC4.

Example 6-16   *Testing The Hypothesis: Fixing PC4's IPv6 Address Configuration*

```
PC4# config terminal
Enter configuration commands, one per line.  End with CNTL/Z.
PC4(config)# interface ethernet 0/0
PC4(config-if)# ipv6 address autoconfig
PC4(config-if)# end
```

```
PC4#
*Aug  5 20:22:14.185: %SYS-5-CONFIG_I: Configured from console by console

PC4# ping 2001:db8:d1:a5:c8::2
Type escape sequence to abort.
Sending 5, 100-byte ICMP Echos to 2001:DB8:D1:A5:C8::2, timeout is 2 seconds:

*Aug  5 20:22:18.564: %DHCP-6-ADDRESS_ASSIGN: Interface Ethernet0/0 assigned DHCP
  address 192.168.20.4, mask 255.255.255.0, hostname PC4
.!!!!
Success rate is 80 percent (4/5), round-trip min/avg/max = 4/6/10 ms
PC4#

PC4# copy running-config startup-config
Destination filename [startup-config]?
Building configuration...
Compressed configuration from 900 bytes to 584 bytes[OK]
PC4#
```

It seems that there was a single problem preventing PC4's IPv6 connectivity. We must now complete all documentation and notify the user and any other party involved that the problem is solved.

Troubleshooting IPv6 Address Assignment on Clients

You can configure IPv6 hosts with an IPv6 address or obtain an IPv6 address in several different ways:

- Manual configuration with the host portion configured

- Manual configuration with the host portion autogenerated

    - The host portion of IPv6 address can be autogenerated using EUI-64.

    - The host portion of IPv6 address can be autogenerated randomly (and optionally securely).

- Stateless address autoconfiguration (SLAAC) based on local IPv6 router's router advertisements (RA)

- Stateful autoconfiguration using DHCPv6

- SLAAC can be complemented with DHCPv6 for other information, such as DNS address and domain name; this is referred to as the DHCPv6 Lite method.

SLAAC enables a host to generate its own address based on the local IPv6 router's RA announcing the local network's address and subnet mask. The IPv6 host creates a global unicast address by combining its interface's EUI-64 address or a randomly generated address with the link prefix learned from the RA. DHCPv6 is available for IPv6. The

DHCPv6 client can obtain configuration parameters from a server either through a rapid two-message exchange (SOLICIT, REPLY) or through a normal four-message exchange (SOLICIT, ADVERTISE, REQUEST, REPLY). DHCPv6 can also be used to complement SLAAC. Relying on SLAAC only, hosts lack information such as DNS address, domain name, and so forth. This method is known as DHCPv6 Lite; DHCPv6 does not assign addresses to clients and it only provides configuration information other than IPv6 address, prefix length (subnet mask), and gateway address. Clients must obtain routable IPv6 addresses through some other means (for example, using SLAAC).

Using the **show ipv6 interface** command, you can verify that the IPv6 address is configured on the device. You can also determine whether it was configured with stateless autoconfiguration. The other way to check whether the client has obtained the IPv6 address is to use the **show ipv6 interface brief** command. If you have a client configured to obtain IPv6 address using DHCPv6, you can verify that the client received the IPv6 address by using the **show ipv6 dhcp** interface command. If you are using DHCPv6 Lite, the output differs slightly. There is only the domain name and the DNS server information, but no IPv6 address.

SECHNIK Networking Trouble Ticket 2

After completion of some upgrades performed by the network engineer called Peter, certain users have reported connectivity problems from their workstations. The following is the list of what has been reported:

- Kimberly, the user of PC1, has reported that she cannot access the Internet any more.

- Peter explained to you that he tried to configure a security feature where users could only establish an SSH session to the server (172.16.200.10), but nobody would be able to establish a session from the server. However, things are not working as planned. Andrew, the user on PC2, now cannot use SSH to connect to the server.

- Peter also performed port security configuration on access layer switches. However, Mithun, the user of PC4, has reported that his PC cannot obtain an IP address from the DHCP server any more.

Our challenge is to make the implemented security features work, while we fix the connectivity issues reported by the users.

Troubleshooting PC1's Internet Connectivity Problem

Kimberly, the user of PC1, has reported that she cannot access the Internet; specifically, she cannot access the server with IP address 209.165.201.225. Kimberly said that other users cannot access this server either and that she could access this server before Peter (network engineer) made the recent changes.

The first thing we need to do is verify the problem and make a troubleshooting plan. Example 6-17 shows our ping attempt from PC1 to the server at 209.165.201.225 failing.

Example 6-17 *Verifying PC1's Connectivity Problem to the Internet*

```
PC1# ping 209.165.201.225
Type escape sequence to abort.
Sending 5, 100-byte ICMP Echos to 209.165.201.225, timeout is 2 seconds:
.....
Success rate is 0 percent (0/5)
PC1#
```

Because other users cannot access this server on the Internet, it is reasonable to assume there is a network problem rather than a specific PC problem. Kimberly does not have other problems, so it is not feasible to use the bottom-up approach; divide-and-conquer starting at the network layer suits this problem best. We can use the follow-the-path technique to discover the problem area.

Gathering Information

Deploying the follow-the-path technique, doing an IP trace from PC1 to the destination 209.165.201.225, makes sense. Doing so reveals (see Example 6-18) that there seems to be a routing loop, as the packet bounces back and forth between 172.16.100.1 (R1) and 172.16.100.2 (DSW1).

Example 6-18 *Information Gathering Using IP Traceroute at PC1*

```
PC1# traceroute 209.165.201.225
Type escape sequence to abort.
Tracing the route to 209.165.201.225
VRF info: (vrf in name/id, vrf out name/id)
  1 192.168.10.1 1 msec 4 msec 3 msec
  2 172.16.100.1 5 msec 2 msec 6 msec
  3 172.16.100.2 2 msec 1 msec 1 msec
  4 172.16.100.1 5 msec 8 msec 2 msec
  5 172.16.100.2 5 msec 1 msec 8 msec
  6 172.16.100.1 8 msec 4 msec 12 msec
...
PC1#
```

Continuing with our information gathering, it is best to examine the routing table for DWS1 and R1. Example 6-19 displays the result. As you can see, DSW1 has received default information through Open Shortest Path First (OSPF) Protocol from R1. Therefore, DSW1 uses R1 (172.16.100.1) as its gateway of last resort. This seems reasonable. However, R1's routing table shows a static default (0.0.0.0/0) with the ISP's address (209.165.200.2) as the next hop, which is reasonable. However, R1's routing table has yet another static route to 209.165.201.0/24, which uses 172.16.100.2 (R1's Ethernet 0/0) as its next hop. This static route matches the network at which the server that Kimberly (using PC1) is trying to reach resides. This network is out at the Internet; therefore, this static route is invalid and should be removed.

Example 6-19   *Information Gathering: Examining DSW1 and R1's Routing Tables*

```
DSW1# show ip route
Codes: L - local, C - connected, S - static, R - RIP, M - mobile, B - BGP
< output omitted >


Gateway of last resort is 172.16.100.1 to network 0.0.0.0

O*E2  0.0.0.0/0 [110/1] via 172.16.100.1, 00:10:25, Ethernet0/0
      2.0.0.0/32 is subnetted, 1 subnets
C        2.2.2.2 is directly connected, Loopback0
      172.16.0.0/16 is variably subnetted, 2 subnets, 2 masks
C        172.16.100.0/24 is directly connected, Ethernet0/0
L        172.16.100.2/32 is directly connected, Ethernet0/0
      192.168.10.0/24 is variably subnetted, 2 subnets, 2 masks
C        192.168.10.0/24 is directly connected, Vlan10
L        192.168.10.1/32 is directly connected, Vlan10
      192.168.20.0/24 is variably subnetted, 2 subnets, 2 masks
C        192.168.20.0/24 is directly connected, Vlan20
L        192.168.20.1/32 is directly connected, Vlan20
O E2  192.168.22.0/24 [110/20] via 172.16.100.1, 00:10:25, Ethernet0/0
DSW1#


R1#show ip route
Codes: L - local, C - connected, S - static, R - RIP, M - mobile, B - BGP
< output omitted >


Gateway of last resort is 209.165.200.2 to network 0.0.0.0

S*    0.0.0.0/0 [1/0] via 209.165.200.2
      1.0.0.0/32 is subnetted, 1 subnets
C        1.1.1.1 is directly connected, Loopback0
      172.16.0.0/16 is variably subnetted, 4 subnets, 3 masks
C        172.16.100.0/24 is directly connected, Ethernet0/2
L        172.16.100.1/32 is directly connected, Ethernet0/2
C        172.16.200.0/28 is directly connected, Ethernet0/0
L        172.16.200.1/32 is directly connected, Ethernet0/0
O     192.168.10.0/24 [110/11] via 172.16.100.2, 00:09:48, Ethernet0/2
O     192.168.20.0/24 [110/11] via 172.16.100.2, 00:09:48, Ethernet0/2
      192.168.22.0/24 is variably subnetted, 2 subnets, 2 masks
```

```
C        192.168.22.0/24 is directly connected, Loopback22
L        192.168.22.1/32 is directly connected, Loopback22
      209.165.200.0/24 is variably subnetted, 2 subnets, 2 masks
C        209.165.200.0/30 is directly connected, Ethernet0/1
L        209.165.200.1/32 is directly connected, Ethernet0/1
S     209.165.201.0/24 [1/0] via 172.16.100.2
R1#
```

Proposing a Hypothesis, Testing the Hypothesis, and Solving the Problem

Having a hypothesis that it is the invalid static route on R1 causing a routing loop and preventing PC1 to reach the server 206.165.201.255 at the Internet, we remove the static route from R1 (see Example 6-20).

Example 6-20   *Testing the Hypothesis: Remove Invalid Static Route and Observe the Result*

```
R1# show running-config | include route
 default-router 192.168.10.1
 default-router 192.168.20.1
router ospf 1
ip route 0.0.0.0 0.0.0.0 209.165.200.2
ip route 209.165.201.0 255.255.255.0 172.16.100.2
ipv6 route ::/0 2001:DB8:D1:A5:C8::2
ipv6 router rip RIPNG
R1#


R1# configure terminal
Enter configuration commands, one per line.  End with CNTL/Z.
R1(config)# no ip route 209.165.201.0 255.255.255.0 172.16.100.2
R1(config)# end
*Aug  6 17:35:41.550: %SYS-5-CONFIG_I: Configured from console by console
R1# copy run start
Destination filename [startup-config]?
Building configuration...
Compressed configuration from 2203 bytes to 1305 bytes[OK]
R1#


PC1# ping 209.165.201.225
Type escape sequence to abort.
Sending 5, 100-byte ICMP Echos to 209.165.201.225, timeout is 2 seconds:
!!!!!
Success rate is 100 percent (5/5), round-trip min/avg/max = 4/7/10 ms
PC1#
```

As you can see in Example 6-20, after removing the invalid static route from R1, PC1 can ping the server at 209.165.201.225. We must now complete all documentation and notify the user and any other party involved that the problem is solved.

Troubleshooting Network Layer Connectivity

When you find that there is no network layer connectivity between two hosts, a good method to troubleshoot the problem is to track the path of the packet from router to router, similar to the method of tracking the path of a frame from switch to switch to diagnose Layer 2 problems. Along the way, you have to verify the availability of a matching route in the forwarding table for the destination of the packet and, subsequently, the availability of a Layer 3 to Layer 2 address mapping for the next hop for those technologies that require a Layer 2 address, such as Ethernet. For any type of application that requires two-way communication, you have to track the packets in both directions. Availability of the correct routing information and Layer 3 to Layer 2 mappings for packets traveling in one direction does not imply that the correct information is available for packets traveling in the opposite direction, too.

To forward packets, a router combines information from various control plane data structures. The most important of these data structures is the routing table. Unlike switches, which flood a frame to all ports if its destination MAC address is not known by the MAC address table, routers drop any packet for which they cannot find a matching entry in the routing table. When a packet has to be forwarded, the routing table is searched for the longest possible prefix that matches the destination IP address of the packet. Associated with this entry is an egress interface and, in most cases, a next-hop IP address.

For point-to-point egress interfaces, such as a serial interface running Point-to-Point Protocol (PPP) or High-Level Data Link Control (HDLC), a point-to-point Frame Relay, or point-to-point Asynchronous Transfer Mode (ATM) subinterface, a next-hop IP address is not mandatory, because all the information that is necessary to construct the frame and encapsulate the packet can be derived from the egress interface itself. For example, in the case of Frame Relay, a point-to-point subinterface has a single associated data-link connection identifier (DLCI), so there is no need to map the next-hop IP address to a DLCI to be able to construct the Frame Relay frame header and encapsulate the packet. For multipoint egress interfaces, such as Ethernet interfaces or multipoint Frame Relay or ATM subinterfaces, the next-hop IP address is a mandatory element because it is used to find the correct Layer 2 destination address or other Layer 2 identifier to construct the frame and encapsulate the packet. The mapping between the next-hop IP address and the Layer 2 address or identifier is stored in a data structure specific for that Layer 2 protocol. For example, in the case of Ethernet, this information is stored in the Address Resolution Protocol (ARP) cache, and in the case of Frame Relay, the information is stored in the Frame Relay map table. Consequently, a routing table lookup may need to be followed up by a lookup in a Layer 3 to Layer 2 mapping table to gather all the necessary information required to construct a frame, encapsulate the packet, and transmit it.

Executing different table lookups and combining the information to construct a frame every time a packet needs to be routed is an inefficient approach to forwarding IP packets. To improve this process and increase the performance of IP packet-switching operations on routers, Cisco has developed Cisco Express Forwarding (CEF). This advanced Layer 3 IP switching mechanism can be used on all routers, and is at the core of the Layer 3 switching technology used in Cisco Catalyst multilayer switches. On most platforms, the CEF switching method is enabled by default.

CEF combines the information from the routing table and other data structures, such as Layer 3 to Layer 2 mapping tables, into two new data structures: the Forwarding Information Base (FIB) and the CEF adjacency table. The FIB mostly reflects the routing table with all the recursive lookups resolved. A lookup in the FIB results in a pointer to an adjacency entry in the CEF adjacency table. Similar to an entry from the routing table, an adjacency table entry can consist of an egress interface only for a point-to-point interface or an egress interface and next-hop IP address for a multipoint interface.

To determine the information that is used to forward packets, you can verify the availability of specific routing entry (prefix) in the routing table or the CEF FIB table. Note that during discussions about protocols such as Border Gateway Protocol (BGP) and Open Shortest Path First (OSPF) Protocol, the collection of the best paths to different destinations are often referred to as BGP Routing Information Base (RIB) or OSPF RIB. However, you must remember that BGP, OSPF, or any protocol's best path to any destination might or might not be installed in the IP routing table (or the generic IP RIB). The reason is that when there are multiple alternatives, the IP process installs paths with the smallest administrative distance (AD) in the IP routing table (or the generic IP RIB).

The choice of whether to check the IP routing table or the FIB depends on exactly what you are trying to diagnose. To diagnose control plane problems, such as the exchange of routing information by routing protocols, the **show ip route** command is a clear choice because it contains all the control plane details for a route, such as the advertising routing protocol, routing source, AD, and routing protocol metrics. To diagnose problems more closely related to the data plane (for example, by tracking the exact traffic flow between two hosts through the network), the FIB is often the best choice because it contains all the details that are necessary to make packet-switching decisions.

To display the content of the IP routing table, you can use the following commands:

- **show ip route** *ip-address*: Supplying the destination IP address as an option to the **show ip route** command causes the router to perform a routing table lookup for that IP address and display the best route that matches the address and all associated control plane details. (Note that the default route will never be displayed as a match for an IP address.)

- **show ip route** *network mask*: The provided *network* and *mask* as options to this command request the routing table to be searched for an exact match (for that network and mask). If an exact match is found, this entry is displayed with all of its associated control plane details.

- **show ip route** *network mask* **longer-prefixes:** The **longer-prefixes** option causes the router to display all prefixes in the routing table that fall within the prefix specified by the *network* and *mask* parameters. This command can prove useful to diagnose problems related to route summarization.

To display the content of the CEF FIB table, you can use the following commands:

- **show ip cef** *ip-address*: This command is similar to the **show ip route** *ip-address* command, but it searches the FIB rather than the routing table. Therefore, the displayed results do not include any routing protocol-related information, but only the information necessary to forward packets. (Note that this command will display the default route if it is the best match for a particular IP address.)

- **show ip cef** *network mask*: This is similar to the **show ip route** *network mask* command, but it displays information from the FIB rather than the routing table (RIB).

- **show ip cef exact-route** *source destination*: This command displays the exact adjacency that will be used to forward a packet with source and destination IP addresses, as specified by the source and destination parameters. The main reason to use this command is in a situation when you are tracking a packet flow across the routed network but the routing table and FIB contain two or more equal routes for a particular prefix. In this case, the CEF mechanisms will balance the traffic load across the multiple adjacencies associated with that prefix. By use of this command, you can determine which of the possible adjacencies is used to forward packets for a specific source and destination IP address pair.

After the egress interface and, in case of multipoint interfaces, a next-hop IP address for the destination of a packet has been determined by the routing table or FIB, the router needs to construct a frame for the data link layer protocol associated with the egress interface. Depending on the data link layer used on the egress interface, the header of this frame will require some connection specific parameters, such as source and destination MAC addresses for Ethernet, DLCI for Frame Relay, or virtual path/channel identifier (VPI/VCI) for ATM. These data link-layer parameters are stored in various different data structures. For point-to-point (sub)interfaces, the relation between the interface and data link identifier or address is usually statically configured. For multipoint (sub) interfaces, the relation between the next-hop IP address and the data-link identifier and address can be manually configured or dynamically resolved through some form of an address resolution protocol. The commands to display the statically configured or dynamically obtained mappings are unique for each data link layer technology. Research the command references for the data link layer protocol that you are troubleshooting to find the appropriate commands. Commands that enable you to verify the Layer 3 to Layer 2 mappings include the following:

- **show ip arp:** You can use this command to verify the dynamic IP address to Ethernet MAC address mappings that were resolved by ARP. Routers cache this information for four hours by default. If you need to refresh the content of the ARP cache, you can enter the **clear ip arp** command to clear all or a particular entry from the ARP cache.

■ **show frame-relay map:** This command lists all the mappings of next-hop IP addresses on multipoint (sub)interfaces to the DLCI of the corresponding permanent virtual circuit (PVC). These mappings may have been manually configured or dynamically resolved using Frame Relay Inverse ARP. In addition, this command lists any DLCIs that were manually associated to specific point-to-point subinterfaces.

When CEF is used as the switching method, the information from the various Layer 2 data structures is used to construct a frame header for each adjacency that is listed in the adjacency table. You can display the full frame header that will be used to encapsulate the packet via the **show adjacency detail** command. In addition, this command displays packet and byte counters for all traffic that was forwarded using this particular adjacency entry. Certain troubleshooting cases require verifying the Layer 3 to Layer 2 mappings. If the routing table or the FIB lists the correct next-hop IP address and egress interface for a particular destination, but packets do not arrive at that next hop, you should verify the Layer 3 to Layer 2 mappings for the data link protocol that is used on the egress interface. Specifically, verify that a correct frame header is constructed to encapsulate the packets and forward them to the next hop.

Troubleshooting PC2's SSH Connectivity Problem

Peter, the network engineer, has reported that he tried to implement a security policy so that users can only establish SSH sessions to server 172.16.200.10. Also, the policy does not allow any sessions initiated at the server. Unfortunately his attempt in implementing this policy has failed. Andrew, the user at PC2, cannot establish an SSH session to the server.

Verifying and Defining the Problem

We must first verify that PC2 indeed cannot establish an SSH session to server 172.16.200.10. Example 6-21 shows that the attempt to make an SSH session to the server from PC2 fails. However, using Telnet from the server to port 22 (SSH) with destination 1.1.1.1 is successful.

The problem is defined as follows:

Authorized users cannot establish an SSH session to server 172.16.200.10 after security feature implementation. We must implement the security feature properly; yet, authorized users must be able to establish an SSH session to this server. Sessions initiated from the server must not be allowed.

Example 6-21   *Verifying the Problem: PC2 Cannot SSH to Server 172.16.200.10*

```
PC2# ssh -l ccnp 172.16.200.10
% Destination unreachable; gateway or host down

PC2#
```

```
SERVER# telnet 1.1.1.1 22
Trying 1.1.1.1, 22 ... Open
SSH-1.99-Cisco-1.25
```

We can take the follow-the-path approach and find out whether SSH to the server is possible from any device along the path between PC2 and the server. Most importantly, we need to find out what security feature Peter has implemented and correct it.

Gathering Information

Using Telnet to a port other than port 23 is a troubleshooting technique that enables us, without a username, to find out whether a service is active on a device. A Telnet to port 22 (SSH) also enables us to find out which version of SSH is honored on the server. Example 6-22 shows that from R1 we are able to connect to the server at port 22. The server response after the open message indicates SSH Version 1. However, our same attempt from DSW1 failed. Using the IOS **debug ip icmp** command and the same attempt from PC2, however, we receive the message "ICMP: dst (192.168.20.2) administratively prohibited unreachable rcv from 172.16.100.1." Because 172.16.100.1 is one of R1's IP addresses, it is natural to inspect R1 for a possible access list misconfiguration. Note that if PC2 received a TCP RST (reset) message, you would see a "%Connection refused by remote host" message instead. In that case, we would not suspect an access list issue and would suspect that the SSH application is not running on the server.

Note   Another useful technique to investigate problems related to TCP-based application sessions (for example, SSH using port 22) is using the **debug ip tcp packet in port 22** command. This enables you to see all incoming TCP packets with a source or destination port number 22.

You must, however, be cautious with the **debug** command on production devices because it can produce a lot of output and use up your device's CPU cycles.

Example 6-22   *Information Gathering Using* telnet *and* debug *Commands*

```
R1# telnet 172.16.200.10 22
Trying 172.16.200.10, 22 ... Open
SSH-1.99-Cisco-1.25


DSW1# telnet 172.16.200.10 22
Trying 172.16.200.10, 22 ...
% Destination unreachable; gateway or host down
DSW1#


PC2# debug ip icmp
```

```
ICMP packet debugging is on
PC2# telnet 172.16.200.10 22
Trying 172.16.200.10, 22 ...
% Destination unreachable; gateway or host down
PC2#
*Aug  7 15:12:30.857: ICMP: dst (192.168.20.2) administratively prohibited
  unreachable rcv from 172.16.100.1
PC2#
```

As shown in Example 6-23, using the **show running-config** and the appropriate filters, we find out quickly that there is an access list 111 applied in the *outbound* direction to the Ethernet 0/0 of router R1. According to our diagram and the output of the **show interface description** command, interface Ethernet 0/0 connects to the server. You can see the content of access list 111 by using the **show access-list 111** command.

Example 6-23   *Information Gathering Using* show *Commands*

```
R1# show running-config | include ^interface|access-group
interface Loopback0
interface Loopback22
interface Ethernet0/0
 ip access-group 111 out
< output omitted >
R1#
R1# show interface description
Interface               Status          Protocol Description
Et0/0                       up              up       link to SERVER
Et0/1                       up              up       link to INTERNET
Et0/2                       up              up      link to DSW1
< output omitted >
R1#
R1# show access-list 111
Extended IP access list 111
    10 permit tcp 192.168.0.0 0.0.255.255 host 172.16.200.10 established
R1#
```

Proposing a Hypothesis and Testing the Hypothesis

Considering the content of access list 111 and the fact that it is applied to R1's Ethernet 0/0 interface in the outbound direction, no device (other than R1 itself) would be able to initiate a session with the server 172.16.200.10. The reason is that the initiating TCP packet (first of the three legs of the TCP handshake) is missing the ACK flag and the access list with the **established** keyword only permits (lets out) packets that have the ACK flag set. If you wonder how (why) we could establish a session from R1 itself to the server, the reason is that outbound access lists applied to router interfaces do not apply to the traffic generated by the router itself.

Correcting the access list would require an access list applied in the inbound direction of R1's Ethernet 0/0 interface that would allow TCP traffic from the server only if it has an ACK flag (established). This way, server-initiated sessions will not be allowed in by the Ethernet 0/0 interface, but server response (second leg of TCP handshake) will be allowed in because it has the ACK flag (established).

As you can see in Example 6-24, to test our hypothesis, after creating the new access list 112 we applied it to the Ethernet 0/0 interface in the inbound direction and removed the access list 111 that was applied in the outbound direction. Example 6-24 also shows that after the change was made to R1, PC2 is able to SSH to the server. Also, a Telnet session initiated from the server is refused.

Example 6-24   *Testing the Hypothesis and Solving the ACL Problem on R1*

```
R1# config term
Enter configuration commands, one per line.  End with CNTL/Z.
R1(config)# access-list 112 permit tcp host 172.16.200.10 192.168.0.0 0.0.255.255
  established
R1(config)# interface ethernet 0/0
R1(config-if)# ip access-group 112 in
R1(config-if)# no ip access-group 111 out
R1(config-if)# end
*Aug  7 15:18:42.672: %SYS-5-CONFIG_I: Configured from console by console
R1# copy run start
Destination filename [startup-config]?
Building configuration...
Compressed configuration from 2284 bytes to 1333 bytes[OK]
R1#


PC2#
PC2# ssh -l ccnp 172.16.200.10
Password:
SERVER>exit

[Connection to 172.16.200.10 closed by foreign host]
PC2#


SERVER#
SERVER# telnet 1.1.1.1 22
Trying 1.1.1.1, 22 ...

% Destination unreachable; gateway or host down
SERVER#
```

Our mission is accomplished: The SSH session from PC2 is now working, but sessions initiated at the server itself are blocked by R1. We must now complete all documentation and notify the user and any other party involved that the problem is solved.

TCP Three-Way Handshake

The TCP is one of the core protocols of the TCP/IP suite. TCP provides a reliable means of data transport. TCP establishes the connection by using a process that is called the three-way handshake. Control bits in the TCP header indicate the progress and status of the connection. The three-way handshake processing is as follows:

- Establishes that the destination device is present on the network

- Verifies that the destination device has an active service and is accepting requests on the destination port number that the initiating client intends to use for the session

- Informs the destination device that the source client intends to establish a communication session on that port number

This process involves setting the SYN bit and ACK bit in the segment header between the two devices. Another important function that is performed during connection establishment is that the first device informs the second device of the ISN, which is used to track data bytes on this connection. FTP, HTTP, HTTPS, SMTP, IMAP, POP3, Telnet, SSH, or any other protocol that uses TCP for transport, has three-way handshake performed as connection is opened. Figure 6-2 demonstrates a TCP three-way handshake.

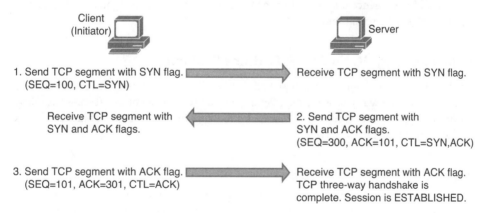

Figure 6-2 *TCP Three-Way Handshake*

The TCP connection setup procedure is as follows:

1. The connection requestor (client) sends a synchronization segment to the receiving (server) device (with SYN bit set); this starts the handshake process. The synchronization segment specifies the number of the port to which the sender wants to connect. The synchronization segment also contains the initial sequence number (ISN) value to be used by the acknowledgment process.

2. The receiving device (server) responds with a segment that has the SYN bits and ACK bits set to negotiate the connection and acknowledge receipt of the synchronization segment from the sender (client). The receiving device's (server) response includes the sequence number of the next byte of data that is expected from the sender (client). The next sequence number is the current ISN of the sender (client), incremented by one.

3. The initiating device (client) acknowledges the synchronization segment of the receiver (server). The SYN bit is unset in the TCP header, which confirms that the three-way handshake is completed.

TCP performs sequencing of segments with a forward reference acknowledgment. The forward reference acknowledgment comes from the receiving device (server) and tells the sending device (client) which segment it is expecting to receive next. One of the functions of TCP is to make sure that each segment reaches its destination. The TCP services on the destination host acknowledge the data that it has received from the source application. The complex operation of TCP is simplified here in a number of ways. Simple incremental numbers are used as the sequence numbers and acknowledgments, although in reality the sequence numbers track the number of bytes that are received. In a TCP simple acknowledgment, the sending computer transmits a segment, starts a timer, and waits for acknowledgment before transmitting the next segment. If the timer expires before receipt of the segment is acknowledged, the sending computer retransmits the segment and starts the timer again. Imagine that each segment is numbered before transmission. At the receiving station, TCP reassembles the segments into a complete message. If a sequence number is missing in the series, that segment and all subsequent segments may be retransmitted.

Troubleshooting PC4's DHCP Address Problem

Peter, the network engineer, has reported that he tried to implement port security on access switch ASW2. Unfortunately, Peter's attempt to implement this feature has failed. Mithun says that ever since Peter's changes, his computer (PC4) cannot obtain an IP address from the DHCP server.

Verifying and Defining the Problem

We must first verify that PC4 indeed cannot obtain an IP address through DHCP. Example 6-25 shows that PC4's Ethernet 0/0 has no IP address and that restarting the interface to initiate a DHCP process and obtain an IP address does not help.

The problem is defined as follows:

PC4 is configured as a DHCP client, but it cannot obtain an IP address from the DHCP server. This symptom was first noticed after implementation of port security on access switch ASW2.

Example 6-25 *Verifying the Problem: DHCP on PC4 Fails to Obtain IP Address*

```
PC4# show ip interface brief
Interface              IP-Address      OK? Method Status              Protocol
Ethernet0/0            unassigned      YES DHCP   up                  up
< output omitted >


PC4# conf term
Enter configuration commands, one per line.  End with CNTL/Z.
PC4(config)# interface ethernet 0/0
PC4(config-if)# shut
*Aug  7 19:20:36.912: %LINK-5-CHANGED: Interface Ethernet0/0, changed state to
  administratively down
*Aug  7 19:20:37.913: %LINEPROTO-5-UPDOWN: Line protocol on Interface Ethernet0/0,
  changed state to down
PC4(config-if)# no shut
PC4(config-if)# end
PC4#
*Aug  7 19:20:41.660: %LINK-3-UPDOWN: Interface Ethernet0/0, changed state to up
*Aug  7 19:20:42.661: %LINEPROTO-5-UPDOWN: Line protocol on Interface Ethernet0/0,
  changed state to up
PC4#
*Aug  7 19:20:42.719: %SYS-5-CONFIG_I: Configured from console by console
PC4# show ip interface brief
Interface              IP-Address      OK? Method Status              Protocol
Ethernet0/0            unassigned      YES DHCP   up                  up
< output omitted >


PC4#
```

Gathering Information

Based on the information we have, it is only natural to target ASW2 right away and check its port security configuration. Based on the information we have, this is the most natural approach, and in troubleshooting terms we call it the shooting-from-the-hip approach. Example 6-26 shows the output of the **show port-security** command on ASW2. You can see that port security has been applied to ASW2's interface Ethernet 0/0, there has been a security violation, and the violation action is shutdown. Checking the status of ASW2's Ethernet 0/0, in Example 6-26, confirms that this interface is down (err-disabled).

Example 6-26 *Information Gathering: Checking Port Security Status on ASW2*

```
ASW2# show port-security
Secure Port   MaxSecureAddr  CurrentAddr  SecurityViolation  Security Action
                  (Count)        (Count)        (Count)
---------------------------------------------------------------------------
```

```
      Et0/0              1                  1                1 Shutdown
-----------------------------------------------------------------------------
Total Addresses in System (excluding one mac per port)    : 0
Max Addresses limit in System (excluding one mac per port) : 4096
ASW2#

ASW2# show interface ethernet 0/0
Ethernet0/0 is down, line protocol is down (err-disabled)
  Hardware is AmdP2, address is aabb.cc00.a500 (bia aabb.cc00.a500)
  Description: link to DSW1
< output omitted>


ASW2#
ASW2# show interface description
Interface                Status        Protocol Description
Et0/0                    down          down     link to DSW1
Et0/1                    up            up       PC3
Et0/2                    up            up       PC4
< output omitted >
```

Based on our network diagram and the output of the **show interface description** command (shown at the bottom of Example 6-26), interface Ethernet 0/0, where port security has been implemented, is the interface that connects to DSW1.

Proposing a Hypothesis, Testing a Hypothesis, and Solving the Problem

It seems that port security has been implemented on Ethernet 0/0 interface of ASW2 erroneously. Based on this hypothesis, we need to perform the following tasks to test the hypothesis and solve the problem:

1. Remove port security commands applied to ASW2's Ethernet 0/0 interface.

2. Apply port security to Ethernet 0/1 (connecting to PC3) with PC3's MAC address, and apply port security to Ethernet 0/2 (connecting to PC4) with PC4's MAC address.

3. Verify port security configuration on ASW2.

4. Test that PC4 can obtain an IP address using DHCP.

As Example 6-27 shows, we check the current commands applied to ASW2 interface Ethernet 0/0 and remove the erroneous port security commands. We also restart (**shutdown** followed by **no shutdown**) interface Ethernet 0/0 to make it operational again.

Example 6-27 *Removing the Erroneous Port Security Configuration on ASW2*

```
ASW2# show running-config interface ethernet 0/0
Building configuration...

Current configuration : 247 bytes
!
interface Ethernet0/0
 description link to DSW1
 switchport trunk encapsulation dot1q
 switchport trunk allowed vlan 1,10,20
 switchport mode trunk
 switchport port-security
 switchport port-security mac-address 0000.0000.1111
 duplex auto
end
ASW2#



ASW2# conf term
Enter configuration commands, one per line.  End with CNTL/Z.
ASW2(config)# interface ethernet 0/0
ASW2(config-if)# no switchport port-security
ASW2(config-if)# no switchport port-security mac-address 0000.0000.1111
ASW2(config-if)# shutdown
ASW2(config-if)# no shutdown
ASW2(config-if)#
*Aug  7 19:25:11.733: %LINK-5-CHANGED: Interface Ethernet0/0, changed state to
  administratively down
ASW2(config-if)#
*Aug  7 19:25:13.933: %LINK-3-UPDOWN: Interface Ethernet0/0, changed state to up
ASW2(config-if)#
*Aug  7 19:25:14.937: %LINEPROTO-5-UPDOWN: Line protocol on Interface Ethernet0/0,
  changed state to up
ASW2(config-if)# end
ASW2#
*Aug  7 19:25:18.816: %SYS-5-CONFIG_I: Configured from console by console
ASW2#
```

Next, as you can see in Example 6-28, we display the content of ASW2's MAC address table and record PC3 and PC4's MAC addresses learned through Ethernet 0/1 (VLAN 10) and Ethernet 0/2 (VLAN 20), respectively. Next, we add correct **port-security** commands to those interfaces with the recorded MAC addresses, and then save the configuration.

Example 6-28   *Reconfiguring Port Security on ASW2*

```
ASW2# show mac address-table
          Mac Address Table
-------------------------------------------

Vlan    Mac Address       Type        Ports
----    -----------       -------     -----
   1    aabb.cc00.a400    DYNAMIC     Et0/0
   1    aabb.cc00.a720    DYNAMIC     Et0/0
  10    aabb.cc00.a200    DYNAMIC     Et0/1
  10    aabb.cc80.a700    DYNAMIC     Et0/0
  20    aabb.cc00.a300    DYNAMIC     Et0/2
  20    aabb.cc80.a700    DYNAMIC     Et0/0
Total Mac Addresses for this criterion: 6
ASW2#
ASW2# config term
Enter configuration commands, one per line.  End with CNTL/Z.
ASW2(config)# interface ethernet 0/1
ASW2(config-if)# switchport port-security mac-address  aabb.cc00.a200
ASW2(config-if)# switchport port-security
ASW2(config-if)# exit
ASW2(config)# interface ethernet 0/2
ASW2(config-if)# switchport port-security mac-address  aabb.cc00.a300
ASW2(config-if)# switchport port-security
ASW2(config-if)# end
ASW2#copy
*Aug  7 19:30:29.143: %SYS-5-CONFIG_I: Configured from console by console
ASW2# copy run start
Destination filename [startup-config]?
Building configuration...
Compressed configuration from 2007 bytes to 1022 bytes[OK]
ASW2#
```

As you can see in Example 6-29, we check the status of port security on ASW2 and notice that it is applied correctly to interfaces Ethernet 0/1 and Ethernet 0/2 with no violations recorded. Finally, we make sure that PC4 can now obtain its IP address through DHCP by restarting its Ethernet interface; this is shown at the bottom of Example 6-29.

Example 6-29   *Verifying Port Security on ASW2 and Proper Operation of PC4*

```
ASW2# show port-security
Secure Port  MaxSecureAddr  CurrentAddr  SecurityViolation  Security Action
                (Count)                    (Count)            (Count)
--------------------------------------------------------------------------------
```

```
      Et0/1               1                     1                 0    Shutdown
      Et0/2               1                     1                 0    Shutdown
------------------------------------------------------------------------------
Total Addresses in System (excluding one mac per port)    : 0
Max Addresses limit in System (excluding one mac per port) : 4096
ASW2#


PC4# conf term
Enter configuration commands, one per line.  End with CNTL/Z.
PC4(config)# int ethernet 0/0
PC4(config-if)# shut
PC4(config-if)# no shut
PC4(config-if)# end
*Aug  7 19:32:30.143: %LINK-5-CHANGED: Interface Ethernet0/0, changed state to
  administratively down
*Aug  7 19:32:31.144: %LINEPROTO-5-UPDOWN: Line protocol on Interface Ethernet0/0,
  changed state to down
PC4#
*Aug  7 19:32:33.610: %SYS-5-CONFIG_I: Configured from console by console
PC4#
*Aug  7 19:32:33.610: %LINK-3-UPDOWN: Interface Ethernet0/0, changed state to up
*Aug  7 19:32:34.610: %LINEPROTO-5-UPDOWN: Line protocol on Interface Ethernet0/0,
  changed state to up

PC4#
PC4# show ip int brief
Interface             IP-Address       OK? Method Status              Protocol
Ethernet0/0           192.168.20.4     YES DHCP   up                  up
< output omitted >

PC4#
*Aug  7 19:32:37.755: %DHCP-6-ADDRESS_ASSIGN: Interface Ethernet0/0 assigned DHCP
  address 192.168.20.4, mask 255.255.255.0, hostname PC4
PC4#
```

We have fixed the port security configuration on ASW2, and PC4 can now obtain its IP address through DHCP. We must now complete all documentation and notify the user and any other party involved that the problem is solved.

Troubleshooting Error-Disabled Ports

Common reasons for an interface falling into error-disabled state include the following:

■ **Port security:** Using port security administrator can specify which hosts can connect to a specific interface or how many MAC addresses can be learned on a single interface. If a frame is received with an unauthorized source MAC address or if too many MAC addresses are learned, the interface is in violation. The interface goes into error-disabled state only if violation action is set to shutdown. Violation actions restrict and protect will not force the interface into error-disabled state.

- **Spanning-tree BPDU Guard:** BPDU Guard is used to protect access ports, where LAN switches are not supposed to connect. Interfaces where the PortFast feature is enabled are great candidates for the BPDU Guard feature. PortFast puts the interface into forwarding state shortly (2 to 3 seconds) after it is enabled by the administrator. If a BPDU is received on an interface with BPDU Guard enabled, the interface will shut down to prevent a Layer 2 loop.

- **Unidirectional Link Detection:** UDLD is commonly used on fiber-optic connections where physically separated fiber strands are used for transmitting and receiving data; UDLD is also useful in full-duplex copper connections. Failure of either transmitting or sending circuit can result in a Layer 2 loop. UDLD mechanism will prevent a Layer 2 loop by shutting down unidirectional interfaces.

- **EtherChannel misconfiguration:** When you are configuring EtherChannel, it is important that all parameters are identical between interfaces that are bundled. Misconfigured EtherChannel can cause interfaces to be put into error-disabled state. A common misconfiguration problem is speed and duplex mismatch.

- **Other reasons:** DHCP snooping rate-limiting, non-Cisco gigabit interface converter (GBIC) inserted, excessive collisions (broadcast storms), duplex mismatch, flapping link, and Port Aggregation Protocol (PAgP) flapping can also cause an interface to go into err-disabled state.

You can use the **show errdisable detect** command to discover all the possible reasons why a port can become error-disabled. An error-disabled interface can be detected in many ways. On an error-disabled interface, the green LED changes to orange. Syslog generates a log when an interface goes into error-disabled state. You can also set up a Simple Network Management Protocol (SNMP) trap for this purpose. To check interface status, use the **show interfaces interface** *slot/number* command. The output of **show interfaces status err-disabled** command shows the reason for each interface that has gone into error-disabled state. Finally, after fixing the error that cause the interface to go into error-disabled state, do not forget to restart the interface using the interface configuration mode **shutdown** and **no shutdown** commands in sequence. Some switches allow you to configure a time after which the switch will automatically attempt to bring up an interface that has gone into error-disabled state.

SECHNIK Networking Trouble Ticket 3

Users at SECHNIK Networking have filed new problems with regard to their workstation connectivity. Users of PC1 and PC2 lack connectivity altogether, but the user of PC3 has reported on IPv6 connectivity problem to the Internet. Peter, the network engineer, has reported that due to maintenance work being done in the server, he wants router R1's interface connecting to this server to remain shut down.

Troubleshooting PC1 and PC2's Internet Connectivity Issues

Users of PC1 and PC2 have reported that their workstations are not operational this morning. They noticed that as they attempted to access the Internet.

Verifying and Defining the Problem

To verify the problem, we access PC1 and PC2, and as you can see in Example 6-30, pinging the Internet server 209.165.201.225, which we know is up and reachable, failed on both PCs. The problem definition is simple: PC1 and PC2 have IPv4 network connectivity problems and cannot access the Internet. We can take the bottom-up approach, keeping in mind that it is possible that the same problem is affecting both PCs.

Example 6-30 *Verifying PC1 and PC2's Reported Internet Connectivity Problems*

```
PC1# ping 209.165.201.225
% Unrecognized host or address, or protocol not running.


PC2# ping 209.165.201.225
% Unrecognized host or address, or protocol not running.
```

Gathering Information

The first step in our information-gathering process is to check the Ethernet interface status on PC1 and PC2. As you can see in Example 6-31, the Ethernet interface on both PCs is up but lacks an IP address. Knowing that the PCs are DHCP clients, we restart the interfaces to force the DHCP process, but DHCP fails and no IP address is obtained.

Example 6-31 *Information Gathering: PC1's and PC2's Ethernet Interface Status*

```
PC1#
PC1# show ip interface brief
Interface              IP-Address      OK? Method    Status            Protocol
Ethernet0/0            unassigned      YES DHCP      up                up
Ethernet0/1            unassigned      YES NVRAM     administratively down down
Ethernet0/2            unassigned      YES NVRAM     administratively down down
Ethernet0/3            unassigned      YES NVRAM     administratively down down
PC1#


PC2#
PC2# conf term
Enter configuration commands, one per line.  End with CNTL/Z.
PC2(config)# interface ethernet 0/0
PC2(config-if)# shut
```

```
PC2(config-if)# no shut
PC2(config-if)# end
PC2#
*Aug  8 17:29:19.895: %SYS-5-CONFIG_I: Configured from console by console
PC2# show ip interface brief
Interface             IP-Address      OK? Method  Status                 Protocol
Ethernet0/0           unassigned      YES DHCP    up                     up
Ethernet0/1           unassigned      YES NVRAM   administratively down down
Ethernet0/2           unassigned      YES NVRAM   administratively down down
Ethernet0/3           unassigned      YES NVRAM   administratively down down
PC2#
```

Because router R1 is the DHCP server for both VLAN 10 and 20 (where PC1 and PC2 reside), we check its configuration (see Example 6-32) and find no abnormality there. However, because DSW1, which is a multilayer switch, is on the path between these PCs and router R1, we must make sure the DHCP relay is properly configured on DSW1. As you can see in Example 6-32, on VLAN 10 interface, DSW1 is pointing to 172.16.100.1, which is the IP address of interface Ethernet 0/2 of R1. However, on VLAN 20 interface, DSW1 is pointing to 172.16.200.1, which is the IP address of interface Ethernet 0/0 of R1.

Example 6-32   *Information Gathering: DHCP Configuration on R1 and DSW1*

```
R1# show running-config | section dhcp
ip dhcp excluded-address 192.168.10.1
ip dhcp excluded-address 192.168.20.1
ip dhcp pool POOL-VLAN10
 network 192.168.10.0 255.255.255.0
 domain-name tshoot.com
 default-router 192.168.10.1
 dns-server 172.16.250.10
 lease 7
ip dhcp pool POOL-VLAN20
 network 192.168.20.0 255.255.255.0
 domain-name tshoot.com
 default-router 192.168.20.1
 dns-server 172.16.250.10
 lease 7
R1#


DSW1# show running-config | begin interface Vlan10
interface Vlan10
 ip address 192.168.10.1 255.255.255.0
 ip helper-address 172.16.100.1
 ip ospf 1 area 0
 ipv6 address 2001:DB8:A::1/64
```

```
 ipv6 enable
 ipv6 rip RIPNG enable
!
interface Vlan20
 ip address 192.168.20.1 255.255.255.0
 ip helper-address 172.16.200.1
 ip ospf 1 area 0
 ipv6 address 2001:DB8:14::1/64
 ipv6 enable
 ipv6 rip RIPNG enable
!
< output omitted >
!
DSW1#
```

It is best to test reachability of both addresses from DSW1. We must test reachability of 172.16.100.1 using interface VLAN 10 as the source, and we must test reachability of 172.16.200.1 using interface VLAN 20 as the source. We must also make a note to investigate why a single address of R1, preferably from a loopback interface, is not used instead. As you can see in Example 6-33, neither ping worked, and that prompted us to check DSW1's routing table. DSW1 is directly connected to 172.16.100.0 through interface Ethernet 0/0, but DSW1 has no route to 172.16.200.1.

Example 6-33 *Information Gathering: Source-Specific Ping from DSW1*

```
DSW1# ping 172.16.100.1 source vlan10
Type escape sequence to abort.
Sending 5, 100-byte ICMP Echos to 172.16.100.1, timeout is 2 seconds:
Packet sent with a source address of 192.168.10.1
.....
Success rate is 0 percent (0/5)
DSW1#
DSW1# ping 172.16.200.1 source vlan20
Type escape sequence to abort.
Sending 5, 100-byte ICMP Echos to 172.16.200.1, timeout is 2 seconds:
Packet sent with a source address of 192.168.20.1
.....
Success rate is 0 percent (0/5)
DSW1#
DSW1# show ip route
Codes: L - local, C - connected, S - static, R - RIP, M - mobile, B - BGP
< output omitted >
Gateway of last resort is not set

      2.0.0.0/32 is subnetted, 1 subnets
C        2.2.2.2 is directly connected, Loopback0
```

```
        172.16.0.0/16 is variably subnetted, 2 subnets, 2 masks
C          172.16.100.0/24 is directly connected, Ethernet0/0
L          172.16.100.2/32 is directly connected, Ethernet0/0
        192.168.10.0/24 is variably subnetted, 2 subnets, 2 masks
C          192.168.10.0/24 is directly connected, Vlan10
L          192.168.10.1/32 is directly connected, Vlan10
        192.168.20.0/24 is variably subnetted, 2 subnets, 2 masks
C          192.168.20.0/24 is directly connected, Vlan20
L          192.168.20.1/32 is directly connected, Vlan20
DSW1#
```

We must check router R1's routing configuration and find out why it is not advertising network 172.16.200.0 and why it does not respond to the pings we initiated from DSW1 using interface VLAN 10 (172.16.10.1) and interface VLAN 20 (172.16.20.1). As you can see in Example 6-34, the network 172.16.200.0 does not show up in R1's routing table. Also, the output of **show ip protocols** command reveals that OSPF is configured as passive on all interfaces, including Ethernet 0/2, which is facing DSW1. The output of **show running-config** confirms that OSPF has the passive-interface default configuration. Finally, output of **show ip interface brief** reveals interface Ethernet 0/0 as administratively shut down. This explains why network 172.16.200.0 does not show up in R1 and DSW1's routing table. However, this fact is in accordance to Peter's report about the work he is doing on the server, and he wants R1's Ethernet 0/0 to remain shut down at this time.

Example 6-34 *Information Gathering: Investigating Routing Configuration on R1*

```
R1# show ip route
Codes: L - local, C - connected, S - static, R - RIP, M - mobile, B - BGP
< output omitted >

Gateway of last resort is 209.165.200.2 to network 0.0.0.0

S*     0.0.0.0/0 [1/0] via 209.165.200.2
       1.0.0.0/32 is subnetted, 1 subnets
C         1.1.1.1 is directly connected, Loopback0
       172.16.0.0/16 is variably subnetted, 2 subnets, 2 masks
C         172.16.100.0/24 is directly connected, Ethernet0/2
L         172.16.100.1/32 is directly connected, Ethernet0/2
       192.168.22.0/24 is variably subnetted, 2 subnets, 2 masks
C         192.168.22.0/24 is directly connected, Loopback22
L         192.168.22.1/32 is directly connected, Loopback22
       209.165.200.0/24 is variably subnetted, 2 subnets, 2 masks
C         209.165.200.0/30 is directly connected, Ethernet0/1
L         209.165.200.1/32 is directly connected, Ethernet0/1
R1#
R1# show ip protocols
*** IP Routing is NSF aware ***
```

```
Routing Protocol is "ospf 1"
  Outgoing update filter list for all interfaces is not set
  Incoming update filter list for all interfaces is not set
  Router ID 192.168.22.1
  It is an autonomous system boundary router
 Redistributing External Routes from,
    connected
  Number of areas in this router is 1. 1 normal 0 stub 0 nssa
  Maximum path: 4
  Routing for Networks:
  Routing on Interfaces Configured Explicitly (Area 0):
    Ethernet0/2
  Passive Interface(s):
    Ethernet0/0
    Ethernet0/1
    Ethernet0/2
    Ethernet0/3
    Loopback0
    Loopback22
  Routing Information Sources:
    Gateway         Distance      Last Update
  Distance: (default is 110)


R1# show running-config | section ospf
router ospf 1
 redistribute connected
 passive-interface default
 default-information originate
R1#
R1# show ip interface brief
Interface          IP-Address      OK? Method    Status                Protocol
Ethernet0/0        172.16.200.1    YES NVRAM  administratively down down
Ethernet0/1        209.165.200.1 YES NVRAM  up                          up
Ethernet0/2        172.16.100.1    YES NVRAM  up                              up
Ethernet0/3        unassigned      YES NVRAM  up                              up
Loopback0          1.1.1.1         YES NVRAM  up                              up
Loopback22         192.168.22.1  YES NVRAM  up                          up
R1#
```

Proposing a Hypothesis and Testing the Hypothesis

Based on the information gathered, our hypothesis is that R1 should not have OSPF configured as passive on interface Ethernet 0/2 (because it prevents R1 from sending OSPF Hello messages on this interface and prevents the formation of a neighbor relationship with DSW1). Example 6-35 shows that once this change is made on R1, it forms

a neighbor relation with DSW1, and upon routing information exchange, networks
172.16.10.0/24 and 172.16.20.0/24 show up as OSPF entries in R1's IP routing table.

Example 6-35 *Proposing and Testing a Hypothesis: R1 Routing Changes Needed*

```
R1# config term
Enter configuration commands, one per line.  End with CNTL/Z.
R1(config)# router ospf 1
R1(config-router)# no passive-interface ethernet 0/2
R1(config-router)#
*Aug  8 17:41:06.093: %OSPF-5-ADJCHG: Process 1, Nbr 2.2.2.2 on Ethernet0/2 from
  LOADING to FULL, Loading Done
R1(config-router)# end
R1#
*Aug  8 17:41:08.861: %SYS-5-CONFIG_I: Configured from console by console
R1# show ip ospf neighbor

Neighbor ID     Pri   State         Dead Time   Address         Interface
2.2.2.2           1   FULL/DR       00:00:32    172.16.100.2    Ethernet0/2
R1# show ip route
Codes: L - local, C - connected, S - static, R - RIP, M - mobile, B - BGP
       D - EIGRP, EX - EIGRP external, O - OSPF, IA - OSPF inter area
       N1 - OSPF NSSA external type 1, N2 - OSPF NSSA external type 2
       E1 - OSPF external type 1, E2 - OSPF external type 2
       i - IS-IS, su - IS-IS summary, L1 - IS-IS level-1, L2 - IS-IS level-2
       ia - IS-IS inter area, * - candidate default, U - per-user static route
       o - ODR, P - periodic downloaded static route, H - NHRP, l - LISP
       + - replicated route, % - next hop override


Gateway of last resort is 209.165.200.2 to network 0.0.0.0

S*     0.0.0.0/0 [1/0] via 209.165.200.2
       1.0.0.0/32 is subnetted, 1 subnets
C         1.1.1.1 is directly connected, Loopback0
       172.16.0.0/16 is variably subnetted, 2 subnets, 2 masks
C         172.16.100.0/24 is directly connected, Ethernet0/2
L         172.16.100.1/32 is directly connected, Ethernet0/2
O      192.168.10.0/24 [110/11] via 172.16.100.2, 00:00:09, Ethernet0/2
O      192.168.20.0/24 [110/11] via 172.16.100.2, 00:00:09, Ethernet0/2
       192.168.22.0/24 is variably subnetted, 2 subnets, 2 masks
C         192.168.22.0/24 is directly connected, Loopback22
L         192.168.22.1/32 is directly connected, Loopback22
       209.165.200.0/24 is variably subnetted, 2 subnets, 2 masks
C         209.165.200.0/30 is directly connected, Ethernet0/1
L         209.165.200.1/32 is directly connected, Ethernet0/1
R1#
```

Furthermore, because R1's interface Ethernet 0/0 (with IP address 172.16.200.1) is shut down at this time, the DHCP relay configuration on DSW1's interface VLAN 20 should not use 172.16.200.1 for **ip helper-address**. In Example 6-36, we change the **ip helper-address** configuration on DSW's interface VLAN 20 to point to 172.16.100.1. This address belongs to R1's Ethernet 0/2 interface facing DSW1. This configuration will now be consistent with DSW1's interface VLAN 10's **ip helper-address** configuration.

Example 6-36   *Proposing and Testing a Hypothesis: Modifying* ip helper-address

```
DSW1# conf t
Enter configuration commands, one per line.  End with CNTL/Z.
DSW1(config)# interface vlan 20
DSW1(config-if)# no ip helper-address 172.16.200.1
DSW1(config-if)# ip helper-address 172.16.100.1
DSW1(config-if)# end
DSW1#
*Aug  8 17:47:15.453: %SYS-5-CONFIG_I: Configured from console by console
DSW1# copy run start
Destination filename [startup-config]?
Building configuration...
Compressed configuration from 2532 bytes to 1301 bytes[OK]
DSW1#
```

Solving the Problem

After making the changes to R1 and DSW1, we must confirm that PC1 and PC2 problems are now solved. Example 6-37 shows that PC1 and PC2 have both obtained IP addresses through DHCP and that they can both ping the Internet server 209.165.201.225 successfully.

Example 6-37   *Solving the Problem: Testing Connectivity from PC1 and PC2*

```
PC1# show ip interface brief
Interface            IP-Address      OK? Method Status                Protocol
Ethernet0/0          192.168.10.3    YES DHCP   up                    up
Ethernet0/1          unassigned      YES NVRAM  administratively down down
Ethernet0/2          unassigned      YES NVRAM  administratively down down
Ethernet0/3          unassigned      YES NVRAM  administratively down down
PC1# ping 209.165.201.225
Type escape sequence to abort.
Sending 5, 100-byte ICMP Echos to 209.165.201.225, timeout is 2 seconds:
!!!!!
Success rate is 100 percent (5/5), round-trip min/avg/max = 3/205/1004 ms
PC1#
```

```
PC2# show ip interface brief
Interface              IP-Address      OK? Method Status                Protocol
Ethernet0/0            192.168.20.2    YES DHCP   up                    up
Ethernet0/1            unassigned      YES NVRAM  administratively down down
Ethernet0/2            unassigned      YES NVRAM  administratively down down
Ethernet0/3            unassigned      YES NVRAM  administratively down down
PC2# ping 209.165.201.225
Type escape sequence to abort.
Sending 5, 100-byte ICMP Echos to 209.165.201.225, timeout is 2 seconds:
!!!!!
Success rate is 100 percent (5/5), round-trip min/avg/max = 6/207/1007 ms
PC2#
```

We must now complete all documentation and notify the user and any other party involved that the problems are solved.

Troubleshooting DHCP

During troubleshooting cases involving DHCP, consider the following potential issues:

- **Server misconfiguration:** Confirm that DHCP pools, default gateways, DNS server addresses, and excluded IP addresses are correctly configured on the DHCP server.

- **Duplicate IP addresses:** There might be a host in the network whose IP address is statically configured. If the DHCP server hands out that same IP address to a client, the two IP hosts will have duplicate IP addresses and will have IP connectivity issues.

- **Redundant services not working:** You can set up redundant DHCP servers. The redundant servers must be able to communicate and coordinate IP address assignments. If interserver communication fails, servers may end up serving duplicate IP addresses. In many cases, redundant DHCP servers have mutually exclusive address pools and they do not need to communicate and coordinate address assignment.

- **DHCP pool runs out of addresses:** A DHCP pool has a finite number of IP addresses. If this pool gets depleted, requests for new IP addresses will be rejected.

- **A router not forwarding addresses:** If your DHCP server is not in the same subnet as the DHCP clients, the intermediary Layer 3 devices need to be configured as relay agents with the **ip helper-address** command. A router does not by default forward broadcast messages; that includes the DHCPDISCOVER broadcast message.

- **Client is not requesting an IP address:** Client must be configured to acquire an IP address through DHCP.

The passive-interface Command

Interior routing protocols (IGP) have traditionally been activated on Cisco router interfaces using the **network** statement within the routing protocol configuration mode. When routing protocols were classless, no wildcard masks were used along with the **network** statement. However, when we started implementing classless networks, Cisco router IOS allowed us enter a wildcard mask along with the **network** statement. The wildcard mask specifies how many bits of the **network** statement must match an interface IP address, so that the routing protocol gets activated on that interface. Currently, the modern method of activating a routing protocol on a Cisco router interface is by entering a command within the interface configuration mode; this command specifies a protocol along with its process ID or tag (if applicable). This new method does not require usage of wildcard masks and is well received and appreciated by network engineers. Activating a routing protocol on an interface implies two actions:

1. The network address associated to the interface over which the IGP is activated will be advertised by the routing protocol.

2. The IGP will send control packets such as hello (if applicable), and routing updates, out of that interface.

The **passive-interface** *interface* command directs the routing protocol not to send control packets out of an interface. If the protocol is activated on an interface but that interface is configured as passive, the network connected through that interface will be advertised (through other interfaces), but the routing protocol will not send control packets such as "hello" and "routing updates" out of that interface. Hence no neighbor relations will be established over that interface.

Note RIPv2 does *not* build a neighbor adjacency/relationship. The **passive-interface** *interface* command directs RIPv2 not to send updates out of an interface. This command does *not* stop RIPv2 from accepting updates coming in from that interface.

The **passive-interface default** command directs the routing protocol to mark all interfaces as passive. This is a modern and conservative approach to router configuration. If you mark all interfaces as passive, you must then mark specific interfaces with the **no passive-interface** *interface* command to allow the routing protocol to send control packets out of that interface and (if applicable) build neighbor relations through that interface.

Note that the **passive-interface** *interface* command only stops the routing protocol from sending control packets such as "hello" and "routing update" out of that interface. This command does not affect whether a network is advertised or not. The following list specifies how this command influences the behavior of particular routing protocols:

- The **passive-interface** *interface* command will direct Open Shortest Path First (OSPF) Protocol and Enhanced Interior Gateway Routing Protocol (EIGRP) not send hello packets out of the specified interface. As a result, no neighbor relation will be build out of that interface and no routing updates will be sent or received.

■ The **passive-interface** *interface* command will direct RIPv2 not to send updates out of the specified interface, but the protocol *will* accept incoming updates from that interface. Denying update coming from that interface can be accomplished with the **distribute-list** command (in the inbound direction).

■ The **passive-interface** *interface* command is not applicable to the Border Gateway Protocol (BGP).

Troubleshooting PC3's Internet Connectivity Issues

SECHNIK Networking has been informed by their current ISP that they are changing their router's interface IPv6 address from 2001:DB8:D1:A5:C8::2 to 2001:DB8:D1:A5:C8::33. Peter, the network engineer, has made the changes necessary on router R1 (SECHNIK's edge router) and informed the ISP that the work has been completed. However, Carol, the user of PC3, has immediately reported that she can no longer access the IPv6 server with the address 2001:DB8:AA::B.

Verifying and Defining the Problem

To verify the problem, we make a visit to Carol's office and using PC3, we try to ping the IPv6 server 2001:DB8:AA::B. As you can see in Example 6-38, the ping did indeed fail. We can define the problem as PC3 has an IPv6 Internet connectivity problem. Specifically, PC3 can no longer access the server with IPv6 address 2001:DB8:AA::B. This problem only started after the ISP changed their router's IPv6 address and Peter made changes to router R1's configuration accordingly.

Example 6-38   *Verifying PC3's IPv6 Internet Connectivity Problem*

```
PC3# ping 2001:DB8:AA::B
Type escape sequence to abort.
Sending 5, 100-byte ICMP Echos to 2001:DB8:AA::B, timeout is 2 seconds:

% No valid route for destination
Success rate is 0 percent (0/1)
PC3#
```

Gathering Information

As the first step in the information gathering, it is best to try a trace from PC3 to the desired server (at 2001:DB8:AA::B). The result of the trace shown in Example 6-39 tells us that the trace packet makes it through two hops, which happen to be the multilayer switch DSW1 and router R1, before it fails.

Example 6-39 *Gathering Information: IPv6 Trace from PC3 to 2001:DB8:AA::B*

```
PC3# trace 2001:db8:AA::B
Type escape sequence to abort.
Tracing the route to 2001:DB8:AA::B

  1 2001:DB8:A::1 25 msec 1 msec 9 msec
  2 2001:DB8:11::1 4 msec 10 msec 1 msec
  3  *  *  *
  4  *  *  *
  5  *  *  *
  6  *  *  *
  7  *
PC3#
```

We can conclude that the IPv6 configuration on PC3 and the IPv6 configuration on the network are both good, because the trace packet makes it all the way to the edge router R1 before failing. Naturally, the suspect would be R1's configuration after the ISP changes were made. Performing the IPv6 trace from PC3 is a divide-and-conquer method, and the result of the trace leads us to a follow-the-path approach. We can now focus our information gathering on R1. As you can see in Example 6-40, the output of **show ipv6 interface brief** on R1 displays interface Ethernet 0/1 (facing the service provider) as up with the correct IPv6 address 2001:DB8:D1:A5:C8::1. After a ping to IPv6 address 2001:DB8:AA::B from R1 fails, we use the **show ipv6 route** command to see R1's IPv6 routing table. In Example 6-40, R1's routing table shows a static default route pointing to 2001:DB8:D1:A5:C8::2, ISP's old IPv6 address.

Example 6-40 *Gathering Information: Examining Router R1's IPv6 Configuration*

```
R1# show ipv6 interface brief
Ethernet0/0            [administratively down/down]
    FE80::A8BB:CCFF:FE00:9200
    2001:DB8:AC:10:C8::1
Ethernet0/1            [up/up]
    FE80::A8BB:CCFF:FE00:9210
    2001:DB8:D1:A5:C8::1
Ethernet0/2            [up/up]
    FE80::A8BB:CCFF:FE00:9220
    2001:DB8:11::1
< output omitted >
R1#
R1# ping 2001:DB8:AA::B
Type escape sequence to abort.
Sending 5, 100-byte ICMP Echos to 2001:DB8:AA::B, timeout is 2 seconds:
.....
Success rate is 0 percent (0/5)
```

```
R1#
R1# show ipv6 route
IPv6 Routing Table - default - 8 entries
Codes: C - Connected, L - Local, S - Static, U - Per-user Static route
       B - BGP, R - RIP, H - NHRP, I1 - ISIS L1
       I2 - ISIS L2, IA - ISIS interarea, IS - ISIS summary, D - EIGRP
       EX - EIGRP external, ND - ND Default, NDp - ND Prefix, DCE - Destination
       NDr - Redirect, O - OSPF Intra, OI - OSPF Inter, OE1 - OSPF ext 1
       OE2 - OSPF ext 2, ON1 - OSPF NSSA ext 1, ON2 - OSPF NSSA ext 2, l - LISP
S    ::/0 [1/0]
       via 2001:DB8:D1:A5:C8::2
R    2001:DB8:A::/64 [120/2]
      via FE80::A8BB:CCFF:FE00:A800, Ethernet0/2
C    2001:DB8:11::/64 [0/0]
      via Ethernet0/2, directly connected
L    2001:DB8:11::1/128 [0/0]
      via Ethernet0/2, receive
R    2001:DB8:14::/64 [120/2]
      via FE80::A8BB:CCFF:FE00:A800, Ethernet0/2
C    2001:DB8:D1:A5::/64 [0/0]
      via Ethernet0/1, directly connected
L    2001:DB8:D1:A5:C8::1/128 [0/0]
      via Ethernet0/1, receive
L    FF00::/8 [0/0]
      via Null0, receive
R1#
R1# show running-config | include ipv6 route
ipv6 route ::/0 2001:DB8:D1:A5:C8::2
ipv6 route ::/0 2001:DB8:D1:A5:C8::33 2
ipv6 router rip RIPNG
R1#
```

The final step in information gathering at router R1 is displaying the static IPv6 route configurations within the running configuration. As you can see in Example 6-40, there are two static routes in R1's running configuration. The first one pointing to ISP's old IPv6 address has a default AD of 1, and the second one pointing to ISP's new IPv6 address was configured by Peter with an AD of 2 (for some unknown reason). The item with the lower AD is installed in R1's IPv6 routing table.

Proposing a Hypothesis and Testing the Hypothesis

Based on the information gathered so far, the old static default IPv6 route pointing to ISP's old IPv6 has not been removed. We have no reason to keep the AD of the new static default IPv6 route pointing to ISP's new IPv6 address at 2. We can modify this static default IPv6 route to have the default AD of 1. Example 6-41 shows our work related to these modifications.

Example 6-41 *Testing the Hypothesis: Modifying the Static IPv6 Routes in R1*

```
R1# config term
Enter configuration commands, one per line.  End with CNTL/Z.
R1(config)# no ipv6 route ::/0 2001:DB8:D1:A5:C8::2
R1(config)# no ipv6 route ::/0 2001:DB8:D1:A5:C8::33 2
R1(config)#
R1(config)# ipv6 route ::/0 2001:DB8:D1:A5:C8::33
R1(config)# end
R1#copy
*Aug  9 21:48:49.009: %SYS-5-CONFIG_I: Configured from console by console
R1# copy running-config startup-config
Destination filename [startup-config]?
Building configuration...
Compressed configuration from 2179 bytes to 1300 bytes[OK]
R1#
R1# ping 2001:db8:AA::B
Type escape sequence to abort.
Sending 5, 100-byte ICMP Echos to 2001:DB8:AA::B, timeout is 2 seconds:
!!!!!
Success rate is 100 percent (5/5), round-trip min/avg/max = 2/3/6 ms
R1#
```

Following the proposed changes to the edge router R1, ping to the IPv6 server with the IPv6 address 2001:db8:AA::B succeeds.

Solving the Problem

We must ascertain that PC3 can now ping the IPv6 server with the IPv6 address 2001:db8:AA::B. Example 6-42 shows that we can now successfully ping the IPv6 server 2001:db8:AA::B.

Example 6-42 *Solving the Problem: PC3 Can Now Ping the IPv6 Server*

```
PC3# ping 2001:DB8:AA::B
Type escape sequence to abort.
Sending 5, 100-byte ICMP Echos to 2001:DB8:AA::B, timeout is 2 seconds:
!!!!!
Success rate is 100 percent (5/5), round-trip min/avg/max = 2/6/13 ms
PC3#
```

We must now complete all documentation and notify the user and any other party involved that the problems are solved.

IPv6 Review

IPv6 offers several benefits:

- It offers a vast address space.

- It is extensible due to the IPv6 extension header.

- It has built-in support for security and mobility.

- The IPv6 header is simplified.

- IPv6 routers do not fragment IPv6 packets. They merely send an ICMPv6 "packet too big" message to the source of the packet and specify next segment's MTU (maximum transmission unit).

- IPv6 can coexist with IPv4, and it maintains a separate routing table from IPv4.

With no broadcast in IPv6, there are three types of addresses only:

- **Unicast:** For one-to-one communication

- **Multicast:** For one-to-many communication.

- **Anycast:** The same IPv6 address assigned to multiple servers allows clients to reach the nearest server offering the required service or content.

IPv6 address has 128 bits. Each 4 bits is represented using a hexadecimal digit. An IPv6 address has eight sections, with four hexadecimal digits in each. IPv6 addresses can be abbreviated by eliminating leading 0s and by representing contiguous fields containing all 0s with a double colon. You can only do this once in an IPv6 address. Current routing options for IPv6 in Cisco routers include the following:

- Static routes

- OSPFv3

- EIGRP for IPv6

- RIP next generation (RIPng)

- Intermediate System-to-Intermediate System (IS-IS) Protocol for IPv6

- Multiprotocol BGP (mBGP)

Summary

This chapter presented three troubleshooting tickets at SECHNIK Networking, a fictitious company, based on the topology shown in Figure 6-3.

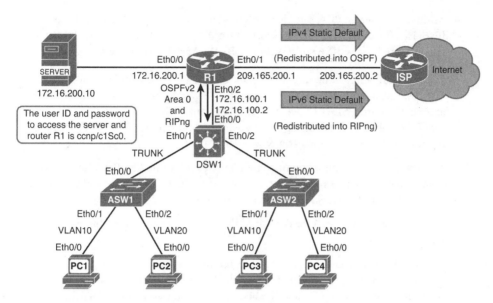

Figure 6-3 *SECHNIK Networking Network Diagram*

Trouble ticket 1: On Monday morning four employees have reported network connectivity problems. They all claimed that the issues did not exist on Friday before they left work. The following is the list of their complaints and the solutions we offered:

1. Kimberly, the user on PC1, cannot access data on the server at 172.16.200.10.

This problem was caused by the trunk configuration error on ASW1's interface Ethernet 0/0. The trunk between DSW1's interface Ethernet 0/1 and ASW1's interface Ethernet 0/0 must allow VLANs 10 and 20. However, during information gathering using the **show interfaces trunk** command, we discovered that ASW1's Ethernet 0/0 configuration only allows VLANs 1 and 20.

2. Andrew, the user on PC2, cannot access the Internet. He is trying to access a server at 209.165.200.2.

This problem was caused by a NAT configuration error on the edge router R1. During information gathering, we discovered that the **ip nat** statement refers to an incorrect/missing access list.

3. Carol, the user on PC3, cannot use SSH to connect to the server at 172.16.200.10.

Even though this problem was reported as PC3 having trouble building an SSH session to server 172.16.200.10, during information gathering we first discovered that PC3 cannot even ping this server. Then we noticed that PC3's interface does not even have an IP address and it is down. This led us to investigate the status of the Ethernet 0/1 interface on ASW2 (connecting to PC3). This interface we discovered in administratively down state, and that happened to be the cause/root of PC3's problems.

4. Mithun, the user on PC4, said that he would like to access the Internet through IPv6. He added that because this worked for Andrew, it should also work for him. He requested to use IPv6 address 2001:DB8:D1:A5:C8::2 for a connectivity test.

During information gathering, we discovered that PC4 does not have an IPv6 address. Knowing that PCs must acquire their IPv6 address through stateless address autoconfiguration (SLAAC), we compared PC3 and PC4's configuration and noticed that PC4, unlike PC3, is missing the **ipv6 address autoconfig** command. This was the root of PC3's IPv6 connectivity problems.

Trouble ticket 2: After completion of some upgrades performed by Peter, the network engineer, certain users have reported connectivity problems from their workstations. The following is the list of what was reported and the solutions we offered:

1. Kimberly, the user of PC1, has reported that she cannot access the Internet any more.

During information gathering, we discovered that packets from PCs going toward devices in network 209.165.201.0/24 on the Internet bounce back and forth between the edge router R1 and the multilayer distribution switch DSW1. This is a typical symptom of routing loops. While examining R1's routing table, we noticed that an erroneous static route on R1 causes packets matching 209.165.201.0/24 to be sent to DSW1's Ethernet 0/0 IP address (172.16.100.2). DSW1, using its default route, then sent those packets back to router R1. After removing the erroneous static route from R1's configuration, packets followed their natural path, using R1's default route toward the ISP, and the problem was solved.

2. Peter explained to you that he tried to configure a security feature where users could only establish an SSH session to the server (172.16.200.10), but nobody would be able to establish a session from the server. However, things are not working as planned. Andrew, the user on PC2, cannot use SSH to connect to the server.

During information gathering, we narrowed this problem down to an erroneous ACL configuration applied to interface Ethernet 0/0 of router R1 in the outbound direction. We configured a new ACL and applied it to R1's interface Ethernet 0/0 in the inbound direction. We also removed the old erroneous ACL that was applied to this interface in the outbound direction. This solved the SSH server security problems.

3. Peter also performed port security configuration on access layer switches. However, Mithun, the user of PC4, has reported that his PC cannot obtain an IP address from the DHCP server any more.

During information gathering, we discovered that the port security feature that Peter had in mind was erroneously applied to ASW2's uplink interface Ethernet 0/0 toward DSW1. This feature must be applied to access interfaces toward PCs, with the MAC address of each PC correctly configured on the corresponding access interface. After applying these changes, all PCs' operation resumed while we implemented the port-security feature as desired.

Trouble ticket 3: The following is the list of the problems users at SECHNIK Networking have filed and the corresponding solutions we offered:

1. Users of PC1 and PC2 lack connectivity altogether.

During information gathering, we discovered two problems. First, the **passive-interface default** command on R1's OSPF configuration was stopping OSPF Hellos from building an OSPF neighbor adjacency between R1 and DSW1. As a result, R1 had no route back to the networks where the DHCP clients reside. The second problem we discovered was a DHCP relay agent configuration error on DSW1. The **ip helper-address** on DSW1's interface VLAN 20 pointed to the IP address 172.16.200.1. This address belongs to R1's Ethernet 0/0 interface, which Peter had shut down for administrative reasons. The **no passive-interface Ethernet 0/2** command on R1's OSPF configuration and correcting the **ip helper-address** command on DSW1's VLAN 20 interface solved all the DHCP client's problems.

2. User of PC3 has reported an IPv6 connectivity problem to the Internet.

During information gathering, we discovered that after the ISP modified their router's IPv6 address, even though Peter entered a new IPv6 static default command on the edge router R1, IPv6 Internet connectivity was broken. While examining R1's IPv6 routing table, we discovered that Peter has not removed the old static route; yet, the new static route he configured had an AD of 2. The higher AD of the new and valid static default route rendered it useless in the presence of the old (and incorrect) static default with the default AD of 1. Removing the old static default route and modifying the new static default route configured with the default AD of 1 fixed all the IPv6 connectivity problems.

Review Questions

1. There is no connectivity between devices in your network. You suspect that the issue is trunk link configuration between switches. What commands could you use to verify the configuration of the trunk ports/interfaces? (Choose two.)

   a. show interfaces trunk
   b. show running-config
   c. show trunking
   d. show vlan trunk

2. Is the following a NAT NVI configuration?

```
ip nat source static 10.0.0.1 209.165.200.211
```

   a. Yes.
   b. No. This is a legacy NAT configuration.
   c. There is not enough information to deduce the answer.
   d. Both. NAT NVI and regular NAT configuration would both work with this statement.

3. How did Router1 acquire an IPv6 address on Ethernet 0/0?

```
Router1# show ipv6 interface
Ethernet0/0 is up, line protocol is up
  IPv6 is enabled, link-local address is FE80::A8BB:CCFF:FE00:500
  No Virtual link-local address(es):
  Stateless address autoconfig enabled
  Global unicast address(es):
  2001:DB8:A:0:A8BB:CCFF:FE00:500, subnet is 2001:DB8:A::/64 [EUI/CAL/PRE]
  valid lifetime 2591961 preferred lifetime 604761
< output omitted >
```

    a. Using DHCPv6.

    b. Using DHCPv6 Lite.

    c. Using stateless autoconfiguration.

    d. It was manually configured.

4. Which of the following static routes will send only traffic destined for the 172.16.14.0/24 network to the next-hop IP address of 192.168.5.5?

    a. ip route 172.16.14.0 255.0.0.0 192.168.5.5

    b. ip route 172.16.14.0 255.255.255.0 192.168.5.5

    c. ip route 192.168.5.5 172.16.14.0 0.0.0.255

    d. ip route 192.168.5.5 172.16.14.0

5. Which command sequence will allow only traffic from the 172.16.16.0/24 network to enter the Ethernet 0/0 interface?

    a.
```
access-list 25 permit 172.16.16.0 0.0.255.255
!
interface ethernet 0/0
 ip access-list 25 out
```

    b.
```
access-list 25 permit 172.16.16.0 0.0.0.255
!
interface ethernet 0/0
 ip access-list 25 in
```

    c.
```
access-list 25 permit 172.16.16.0 0.0.0.255
!
interface ethernet 0/0
 ip access-group 25 in
```

    d.
```
access-list 25 permit 172.16.16.0 0.0.0.255
!
interface ethernet 0/0
 ip access-group 25 out
```

6. Which of the following port security violation modes will disable the port if a violation occurs?

   a. Restrict
   b. Protect
   c. Shutdown
   d. All of these

7. Which of the following statements correctly describes OSPF passive interface?

   a. Passive interfaces do not send Hello messages.
   b. Passive interfaces accept routing updates.
   c. Passive interfaces send routing updates.
   d. When you configure OSPF, every interface is passive by default.

8. Which command can you use to enable IPv6 routing on a router?

   a. ipv6 unicast-routing
   b. ipv6 routing
   c. ip routing ipv6
   d. ip routing unicast-ipv6

Chapter 7

Troubleshooting Case Study: TINC Garbage Disposal

This chapter presents four troubleshooting cases (tickets) at TINC Garbage Disposal, a fictitious company, based on the topology shown in Figure 7-1. TINC has hired SECHNIK Networking for technical support. As employees of SECHNIK, we need to solve all problems reported by the customer (TINC Garbage Disposal) and document them. Each troubleshooting case includes a few configuration errors. Configuration errors will be dealt with as real-world troubleshooting scenarios. Certain technologies are explained briefly to refresh your memory.

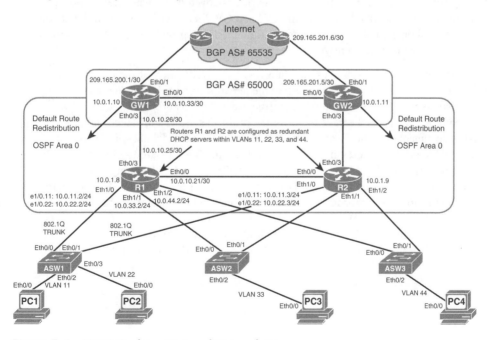

Figure 7-1 *TINC Garbage Disposal Network Diagram*

> **Note**   The networks presented in this and the following chapters use Cisco routers to simulate the servers and personal computers (PCs); keep that in mind as you observe the output shown in the examples presented.

TINC Garbage Disposal Trouble Ticket 1

Donovan works as an IT and network support employee for TINC Garbage Disposal. We (at SECHNIK Networking) have been contacted by Donovan. Donovan has reported the following network problems and needs help with them:

- During the maintenance of GW1, we realized that GW2 does not serve as the backup gateway to the Internet. At this moment GW1 is operating, and there is Internet connectivity through it. However, I have a strong suspicion that if GW1 fails, our network will lose Internet connectivity.

- Users of PC1 and PC2 have reported that they cannot access the Internet. I cannot figure out what is causing this problem.

Troubleshooting Lack of Backup Internet Connectivity Through GW2

Based on what Donovan (the IT and network support engineer at TINC Garbage Disposal) has reported, the edge gateway (router) GW2 does not act as an alternative or backup for Internet connectivity if GW1 fails. He discovered that while he was doing some maintenance work on GW1. Both GW1 and GW2 must have working Internet connectivity at all times, and if one goes down, the other must provide Internet connectivity to TINC's network transparently.

The first step in troubleshooting should always be the verification of the reported problem. We cannot fail GW1 and see whether the network sustains Internet connectivity. The reason is that if the problem is in fact true, we will be disturbing active business flows and processes. So, we need to verify the problem another way. According to TINC's documentation, both routers R1 and R2 must have the default route in their routing tables; default routes are redistributed from the Border Gateway Protocol (BGP) routing process into the Open Shortest Path First (OSPF) Protocol routing process at the gateway routers GW1 and GW2. As shown in Example 7-1, we used the **show ip route** and the **show ip ospf database** commands on R1 and find out that the default route is only learned from GW1. As you can verify using Figure 7-1, the IP route 0.0.0.0 points to 10.0.10.26, which is GW1's interface Eth0/3 IP address, and the OSPF link ID 0.0.0.0 is advertised by the router ID 209.165.200.1, which is GW1's interface E0/1's IP address.

Example 7-1 *Verifying the Problem from Router R1, Nondisruptively*

```
R1# show ip route
Codes: L - local, C - connected, S - static, R - RIP, M - mobile, B - BGP
       D - EIGRP, EX - EIGRP external, O - OSPF, IA - OSPF inter area
       N1 - OSPF NSSA external type 1, N2 - OSPF NSSA external type 2
       E1 - OSPF external type 1, E2 - OSPF external type 2
       i - IS-IS, su - IS-IS summary, L1 - IS-IS level-1, L2 - IS-IS level-2
       ia - IS-IS inter area, * - candidate default, U - per-user static route
       o - ODR, P - periodic downloaded static route, H - NHRP, l - LISP
       + - replicated route, % - next hop override

Gateway of last resort is 10.0.10.26 to network 0.0.0.0

O*E2  0.0.0.0/0 [110/1] via 10.0.10.26, 00:01:26, Ethernet0/3
      10.0.0.0/8 is variably subnetted, 14 subnets, 3 masks
C        10.0.10.20/30 is directly connected, Ethernet0/0
L        10.0.10.21/32 is directly connected, Ethernet0/0
C        10.0.10.24/30 is directly connected, Ethernet0/3
L        10.0.10.25/32 is directly connected, Ethernet0/3
O        10.0.10.28/30 [110/20] via 10.0.44.3, 00:04:38, Ethernet1/2
                       [110/20] via 10.0.33.3, 00:04:38, Ethernet1/1
                       [110/20] via 10.0.11.3, 00:04:38, Ethernet1/0.11
                       [110/20] via 10.0.10.22, 00:04:38, Ethernet0/0
O        10.0.10.32/30 [110/20] via 10.0.10.26, 00:02:27, Ethernet0/3
C        10.0.11.0/24 is directly connected, Ethernet1/0.11
L        10.0.11.2/32 is directly connected, Ethernet1/0.11
C        10.0.22.0/24 is directly connected, Ethernet1/0.22
L        10.0.22.2/32 is directly connected, Ethernet1/0.22
C        10.0.33.0/24 is directly connected, Ethernet1/1
L        10.0.33.2/32 is directly connected, Ethernet1/1
C        10.0.44.0/24 is directly connected, Ethernet1/2
L        10.0.44.2/32 is directly connected, Ethernet1/2
R1#
R1# show ip ospf database

            OSPF Router with ID (10.0.44.2) (Process ID 1)

                Router Link States (Area 0)

Link ID        ADV Router        Age       Seq#        Checksum Link count
10.0.44.2      10.0.44.2         211       0x80000005 0x001C51 6
10.0.44.3      10.0.44.3         316       0x80000003 0x0096CA 6
209.165.200.1  209.165.200.1     212       0x80000003 0x00A41F 2
209.165.201.5  209.165.201.5     218       0x80000002 0x00CEE2 2
```

```
            Net Link States (Area 0)


Link ID         ADV Router      Age        Seq#        Checksum
10.0.10.22      10.0.44.3       342        0x80000001  0x00D88F
10.0.10.25      10.0.44.2       211        0x80000001  0x00F568
10.0.10.29      10.0.44.3       316        0x80000001  0x00173C
10.0.10.34      209.165.201.5   218        0x80000001  0x0053E5
10.0.11.3       10.0.44.3       342        0x80000001  0x009ED8
10.0.33.3       10.0.44.3       342        0x80000001  0x00ABB5
10.0.44.3       10.0.44.3       342        0x80000001  0x003224


            Type-5 AS External Link States


Link ID         ADV Router      Age        Seq#        Checksum Tag
0.0.0.0         209.165.200.1   146        0x80000001  0x002A47 1
R1#
```

This verifies Donovan's suspicion that redundant Internet connectivity through GW2 is not present, and if GW1 fails, Internet connectivity at TINC will be lost. Now that we have verified the problem, we need a plan. We know from TINC's documentation (see notes on Figure 7-1) that GW1 and GW2 are supposed to redistribute the default route from BGP into OSPF and advertise it to R1 and R2. We can take a divide-and-conquer approach and start information gathering from the network layer, focused on routing protocols.

Information Gathering

We start information gathering at R2 using the **show ip ospf neighbor** command. R2 has several interfaces, but we expect it to have discovered and built neighbor relations with both R1 and GW2. Example 7-2 shows that R2 has indeed discovered R1 (with router ID 10.0.44.2) through five interfaces (and subinterfaces), and it has discovered GW2 (with router ID 209.165.201.5) once through interface Eth0/3.

Example 7-2 *Information Gathering: R2 Has OSPF Neighbor Relationship with Both R1 and GW2*

```
R2# show ip ospf neighbor

Neighbor ID      Pri  State          Dead Time   Address        Interface
10.0.44.2         1   FULL/BDR       00:00:39    10.0.44.2      Ethernet1/2
10.0.44.2         1   FULL/BDR       00:00:39    10.0.33.2      Ethernet1/1
10.0.44.2         1   FULL/BDR       00:00:39    10.0.11.2      Ethernet1/0.11
209.165.201.5     1   FULL/BDR       00:00:39    10.0.10.30     Ethernet0/3
10.0.44.2         1   FULL/BDR       00:00:39    10.0.10.21     Ethernet0/0
R2#
```

We now have evidence that OSPF is running on GW2 and it has built a neighbor relationship at least with R2. We must find out why GW2 is not advertising a default router to its neighbors. As stated earlier, based on TINC's documentation, the OSPF default must be redistributed from BGP (originated from BGP). Turning our information gathering focus to GW2, we decide to access GW2. On GW2 the first thing that gets our attention is the log messages indicating BGP neighbor 209.165.201.6 has been removed from the session and that notification has been sent to this neighbor who is in the wrong autonomous system. Example 7-3 shows these log messages.

Example 7-3 *Information Gathering: Logging Messages Indicate BGP Configuration Problem with Respect to Neighbor's ASN*

```
GW2#
*Aug 19 00:56:23.460: %BGP-3-NOTIFICATION: sent to neighbor 209.165.201.6 passive
  2/2 (peer in wrong AS) 2 bytes FFFF
*Aug 19 00:56:23.460: %BGP-4-MSGDUMP: unsupported or mal-formatted message received
  from 209.165.201.6:
FFFF FFFF FFFF FFFF FFFF FFFF FFFF FFFF 0039 0104 FFFF 00B4 D1A5 C9E1 1C02 0601
0400 0100 0102 0280 0002 0202 0002 0246 0002 0641 0400 00FF FF
*Aug 19 00:56:31.676: %BGP-3-NOTIFICATION: sent to neighbor 209.165.201.6 passive
  2/2 (peer in wrong AS) 2 bytes FFFF
*Aug 19 00:56:31.676: %BGP-4-MSGDUMP: unsupported or mal-formatted message received
  from 209.165.201.6:
FFFF FFFF FFFF FFFF FFFF FFFF FFFF FFFF 0039 0104 FFFF 00B4 D1A5 C9E1 1C02 0601
0400 0100 0102 0280 0002 0202 0002 0246 0002 0641 0400 00FF FF
*Aug 19 00:56:32.470: %BGP-3-NOTIFICATION: sent to neighbor 209.165.201.6 active
  2/2 (peer in wrong AS) 2 bytes FFFF
*Aug 19 00:56:32.470: %BGP-4-MSGDUMP: unsupported or mal-formatted message received
  from 209.165.201.6:
FFFF FFFF FFFF FFFF FFFF FFFF FFFF FFFF 0039 0104 FFFF 00B4 D1A5 C9E1 1C02 0601
0400 0100 0102 0280 0002 0202 0002 0246 0002 0641 0400 00FF FF
*Aug 19 00:56:37.590: %BGP_SESSION-5-ADJCHANGE: neighbor 209.165.201.6 IPv4 Unicast
  topology base removed from session BGP notification sent
GW2# show ip bgp summary
BGP router identifier 209.165.201.5, local AS number 65000
BGP table version is 2, main routing table version 2
1 network entries using 148 bytes of memory
1 path entries using 64 bytes of memory
1/1 BGP path/bestpath attribute entries using 136 bytes of memory
1 BGP AS-PATH entries using 24 bytes of memory
0 BGP route-map cache entries using 0 bytes of memory
0 BGP filter-list cache entries using 0 bytes of memory
BGP using 372 total bytes of memory
BGP activity 1/0 prefixes, 1/0 paths, scan interval 60 secs


Neighbor        V    AS MsgRcvd MsgSent  TblVer  InQ OutQ Up/Down  State/PfxRcd
10.0.10.33      4 65000       7       6       2    0    0 00:03:22            1
209.165.201.6   4 65335       2       2       1    0    0 00:00:00  Closing
GW2#
```

While at GW2, we try the **show ip bgp summary** command (see Example 7-3 again). This command's output shows that GW2 has an established BGP session with GW1 (10.0.10.33) within ASN 65000. The output also shows a nonoperational neighbor relationship with 209.165.201.6 within ASN 65335.

Analyzing Information, Eliminating Possibilities, and Proposing a Hypothesis

GW2 is supposed to have an established external BGP (eBGP) session with the Internet service provider (ISP) at 209.165.201.6 (see Figure 7-1), but the service provider's ASN is actually 65535, not 65335. This explains the log messages we saw on GW2 indicating a wrong ASN for the neighbor. We can eliminate possible OSPF or redistribution errors (for now) and propose that the problem is due to an error in BGP **neighbor** statement specifying a wrong ASN for the neighbor. Clearly if the BGP session with the ISP router is down, we cannot be receiving a default route from it, and no default route exists so that it can be redistributed into OSPF.

Proposing a Hypothesis, Testing the Hypothesis, and Solving the Problem

As shown in the output of Example 7-4, to test our hypothesis, we display the BGP section of the running-config first. Next, we remove the **neighbor** statement with the wrong ASN and add the new **neighbor** statement with the correct (65535) ASN.

Example 7-4   *Testing the Hypothesis: Fixing BGP Neighbor's ASN*

```
GW2# show running-config | section bgp
router bgp 65000
 bgp log-neighbor-changes
 neighbor 10.0.10.33 remote-as 65000
 neighbor 10.0.10.33 next-hop-self
 neighbor 209.165.201.6 remote-as 65335
GW2#
GW2# config term
Enter configuration commands, one per line.  End with CNTL/Z.
GW2(config)# router bgp 65000
GW2(config-router)# no neighbor 209.165.201.6 remote-as 65335
GW2(config-router)# neighbor 209.165.201.6 remote-as 65535
GW2(config-router)# end
GW2# wr
Building configuration...
[OK]
GW2#
GW2# show ip bgp summary
BGP router identifier 209.165.201.5, local AS number 65000
BGP table version is 3, main routing table version 3
1 network entries using 148 bytes of memory
2 path entries using 128 bytes of memory
```

```
2/1 BGP path/bestpath attribute entries using 272 bytes of memory
1 BGP AS-PATH entries using 24 bytes of memory
0 BGP route-map cache entries using 0 bytes of memory
0 BGP filter-list cache entries using 0 bytes of memory
BGP using 572 total bytes of memory
BGP activity 1/0 prefixes, 2/0 paths, scan interval 60 secs


Neighbor          V    AS     MsgRcvd  MsgSent  TblVer  InQ OutQ   Up/Down   State/PfxRcd
10.0.10.33        4    65000     10       10       3      0   0    00:06:09             1
209.165.201.6     4    65535      6        5       2      0   0    00:00:15             1
GW2#
```

After fixing the incorrect ASN that was configured for our ISP (eBGP) neighbor, we check the status of the neighbor relationship using the **show ip bgp summary** command again. Within a few seconds, the relationship is established. The output of this command is also shown in Example 7-4. Note that when the BGP relation/session is established, the output of the **show ip bgp summary** command, under the Up/Down column, shows the number of prefixes received from the neighbor instead of the word *established*.

We must now return to R1 and R2 and make sure that they both have two default routes in their OSPF databases, one from GW1 (209.165.200.1) and another from GW2 (209.165.201.5). Example 7-5 shows the output of **show ip ospf database** on both R1 and R2.

Example 7-5   *Solving the Problem: Checking Redundant Default Routes*

```
R1# show ip ospf database

            OSPF Router with ID (10.0.44.2) (Process ID 1)

                Router Link States (Area 0)

Link ID          ADV Router       Age        Seq#        Checksum Link count
10.0.44.2        10.0.44.2        470        0x80000003 0x00204F 6
10.0.44.3        10.0.44.3        472        0x80000003 0x0096CA 6
209.165.200.1    209.165.200.1    434        0x80000003 0x00A41F 2
209.165.201.5    209.165.201.5    435        0x80000003 0x00CCE3 2


                Net Link States (Area 0)

Link ID          ADV Router       Age        Seq#        Checksum
10.0.10.22       10.0.44.3        499        0x80000001 0x00D88F
10.0.10.25       10.0.44.2        470        0x80000001 0x00F568
10.0.10.29       10.0.44.3        472        0x80000001 0x00173C
10.0.10.34       209.165.201.5    435        0x80000001 0x0053E5
10.0.11.3        10.0.44.3        499        0x80000001 0x009ED8
```

```
10.0.33.3        10.0.44.3        499        0x80000001 0x00ABB5
10.0.44.3        10.0.44.3        499        0x80000001 0x003224


                Type-5 AS External Link States


Link ID          ADV Router       Age        Seq#       Checksum Tag
0.0.0.0          209.165.200.1    394        0x80000001 0x002A47 1
0.0.0.0          209.165.201.5    111        0x80000001 0x000B61 1
R1#



R2# show ip ospf database

          OSPF Router with ID (10.0.44.3) (Process ID 1)

              Router Link States (Area 0)

Link ID          ADV Router       Age        Seq#       Checksum Link count
10.0.44.2        10.0.44.2        499        0x80000003 0x00204F 6
10.0.44.3        10.0.44.3        499        0x80000003 0x0096CA 6
209.165.200.1    209.165.200.1    464        0x80000003 0x00A41F 2
209.165.201.5    209.165.201.5    463        0x80000003 0x00CCE3 2

                Net Link States (Area 0)


Link ID          ADV Router       Age        Seq#       Checksum
10.0.10.22       10.0.44.3        526        0x80000001 0x00D88F
10.0.10.25       10.0.44.2        499        0x80000001 0x00F568
10.0.10.29       10.0.44.3        499        0x80000001 0x00173C
10.0.10.34       209.165.201.5    463        0x80000001 0x0053E5
10.0.11.3        10.0.44.3        526        0x80000001 0x009ED8
10.0.33.3        10.0.44.3        526        0x80000001 0x00ABB5
10.0.44.3        10.0.44.3        526        0x80000001 0x003224


                Type-5 AS External Link States


Link ID          ADV Router       Age        Seq#       Checksum Tag
0.0.0.0          209.165.200.1    423        0x80000001 0x002A47 1
0.0.0.0          209.165.201.5    138        0x80000001 0x000B61 1
R2#
```

We must now complete the documentation and inform Donovan at TINC Garbage Disposal and any other party involved that the problem is solved.

Troubleshooting BGP Neighbor Relationships

BGP is a TCP-based application. Therefore, before neighbors send the BGP OPEN message, which initiates the process for establishing a BGP neighbor relationship, they must complete a TCP three-way handshake. Once the TCP three-way handshake is successfully completed, the BGP open message, which includes the sender's router ID, ASN, hold time, and BGP version, is sent from one neighbor to the other. If there are no configuration conflicts with the aforementioned parameters that are sent from one neighbor to the other, the neighbor relationship is established. Next, the neighbors do full exchange of best paths to all known and permitted prefixes. (Filters may prevent a router to send all known prefixes to certain neighbors.) After that, BGP neighbors only exchange hello messages unless there is a change; in that case, they send update (reachable and unreachable) messages to each other. In case of any type of error, BGP neighbors send notification messages to each other, specifying the cause of the conflict.

If for any reason the TCP three-way handshake cannot complete, the BGP open message is not sent, and the relationship will not get established. That happens if no IP connectivity exists between peers or if TCP port 179 (BGP well-known port number) is blocked by an access control list (ACL) or firewall. Also, If the BGP **neighbor** statement specifies a particular address of a neighbor (such as its loopback 0 interface address), and that address is unreachable, the TCP three-way handshake will never succeed. Neighbor relationships can fail to establish if there are BGP configuration errors such as specifying the wrong ASN for a neighbor. Moreover, when a message arrives from the neighbor, the source address of the packet must match the address configured for that neighbor. For internal BGP (iBGP) neighbors, if you use the neighbor's Loopback 0 interface, for example, the neighbor must have the **update-source loopback0** command option. Another possible cause for failure of BGP neighbor relationship can be authentication error. Finally, for eBGP neighbors, if an IP address is specified that is not directly connected, the **ebgp-multihop** command must be used to specify how many hops it takes to reach the neighbor's IP address. The default IP packet Time To Live (TTL) for iBGP messages is 255 and for eBGP messages is 1.

The neighbor relationship between two BGP routers (speakers) can be in one of the following states:

- **Idle:** The router is searching the IP routing table to find a path to reach the neighbor.

- **Active:** The router is still trying (up to 16 retries) to complete a TCP three-way handshake.

- **Connect:** The router found a route to the neighbor and has completed the TCP three-way handshake.

- **Open Sent:** After completion of the TCP three-way handshake, the BGP open was message sent to the neighbor.

- **Open Confirm:** The router received an open message from the neighbor who has agreed to the parameters for establishing a BGP session.

- **Established:** Peering is established; update and hello messages will follow.

To troubleshoot a case where a BGP neighbor will not get established, use the following commands and techniques:

- Use the **show ip bgp summary** command to display the state of all BGP peers.

- Verify IP connectivity to the neighbor's address using extended ping and traceroute.

- Verify the existence of the IP route to the neighbor's address with the **show ip route** command.

- Discover additional information with the **show ip bgp neighbor** command.

- Use the **debug ip bgp** command options to obtain more information and clues about the problem. For example, **debug ip bgp events** displays the state transitions for peers.

Troubleshooting PC1's Connectivity Problem

Other than the fact that PC1 has no Internet connectivity, we do not have much information about this case to begin with. It is better to capture and discover more information while the problem is being reported. Information such as when the problem started, who else is having or not having the same problem, what and when any changes have taken place, and so on, could help us in our approach and focus.

As usual, the first thing we need to do is to verify that PC1 is indeed having Internet connectivity problems. Example 7-6 shows the attempt to ping the Internet server with IP address 209.165.201.225 failing.

Example 7-6 *Verifying the Problem: PC1 Does Not Have Internet Connectivity*

```
PC1# ping 209.165.201.225
% Unrecognized host or address, or protocol not running.

PC1#
```

Gathering Information

Based on the little information we have, we can take the follow-the-path approach and simply start by checking the status of PC1's Ethernet interface. Example 7-7 shows the output of **show ip interface brief** and **show interfaces Ethernet 0/0** commands we tried on PC1. Based on the first command's output, PC1's Ethernet 0/0 is up, but it failed to receive an IP address through Dynamic Host Configuration Protocol (DHCP). The second command's output also shows interface Ethernet 0/0 as up; it also reveals the interface MAC address as aabb.cc00.9300.

Example 7-7 *Information Gathering: Checking PC1's Ethernet Interface Status*

```
PC1# show ip interface brief
Interface              IP-Address     OK? Method Status        Protocol
Ethernet0/0            unassigned     YES DHCP   up            up
< ...output omitted ...>
PC1#
PC1# show interface ethernet 0/0
Ethernet0/0 is up, line protocol is up
  Hardware is AmdP2, address is aabb.cc00.a000 (bia aabb.cc00.a000)
< ...output omitted ...>
PC1#
```

As the next step in the follow-the-path approach, we must examine switch SW1. We
must check and make sure that PC1's MAC address is learned through SW1's interface
Eth0/2. As shown in Example 7-8, we tried the **show mac address-table aabb.cc00.
a000**, but the output is a blank table. PC1's MAC address has not been learned by SW1
through interface Eth0/2 or any other interface. This definitely explains why PC1 has
connectivity problems and cannot obtain an IP address through DHCP.

Example 7-8 *Information Gathering: Examining SW1's MAC Address Table*

```
SW1# show mac address-table address aabb.cc00.a000
          Mac Address Table
-------------------------------------------

Vlan    Mac Address     Type      Ports
----    -----------     --------  -----
SW1#
```

Analyzing Information and Gathering Further Information

Analyzing the fact that the PC1 interface Ethernet 0/0 is up, yet its MAC address has not
been learned by SW1 through interface Ethernet 0/2, leads us to suspect that a special
configuration on SW1 Ethernet 0/2 is stopping SW1 from learning PC1's MAC address.

We must do further information gathering to confirm or reject our suspicion. Example
7-9 shows the output of the **show running-config interface Ethernet 0/2** command on
SW1. As you can see, SW1 has the **switchport port-security mac-address** command
with the MAC address 123f.123f.123f. This is not PC1's MAC address. Furthermore,
SW1's Ethernet 0/2 interface also has the **switchport port-security violation protect** command configured. This command essentially ignores frames with other MAC
addresses and refuses to learn them.

Example 7-9 also shows the output of the **show port-security interface Ethernet 0/2**
command we tried next, on switch SW1. As you can see, this command's output shows

the last source address as aabb.cc00.a000, which is PC1's MAC address. The security violation count is 0, because with a violation action of protect, this counter does not increment; if the violation action were restrict, this counter would increment.

Example 7-9   *Information Gathering: Examining SW1's Eth0/2 Configuration*

```
SW1# show running-config interface ethernet 0/2
Building configuration...


Current configuration : 216 bytes
!
interface Ethernet0/2
 switchport access vlan 11
 switchport mode access
 switchport port-security
 switchport port-security violation protect
 switchport port-security mac-address 123f.123f.123f
 duplex auto
end


SW1#
SW1# show port-security interface ethernet 0/2
Port Security                       : Enabled
Port Status                         : Secure-up
Violation Mode                  : Protect
Aging Time                      : 0 mins
Aging Type                      : Absolute
SecureStatic Address Aging : Disabled
Maximum MAC Addresses   : 1
Total MAC Addresses         : 1
Configured MAC Addresses : 1
Sticky MAC Addresses        : 0
Last Source Address             : aabb.cc00.a000
Last Source Address VlanId : 11
Security Violation Count       : 0

SW1#
```

Proposing a Hypothesis, Testing the Hypothesis, and Solving the Problem

Based on the gathered information, we conclude that while the port security was configured on SW1 interface Ethernet 0/2, the wrong MAC address, not belonging to PC1, was entered. Our proposed hypothesis is to remove the offending MAC address and replace it with PC1's true MAC address table. We should also propose changing the port security's violation action to restrict instead of protect with restrict violation count increments, which would make troubleshooting a lot easier.

Example 7-10 shows us disabling port security, removing the wrong MAC address, adding PC1's MAC address, and enabling port security on SW1's Ethernet 0/2 interface. Following those commands, we issue the **show mac-address interface Ethernet 0/2** command, which now shows that PC1's MAC address is learned by the SW1 switch through interface Ethernet 0/2.

Example 7-10 *Testing a Hypothesis: Correcting Port Security on Switch SW1*

```
SW1# config term
Enter configuration commands, one per line.  End with CNTL/Z.
SW1(config)# interface ethernet 0/2
SW1(config-if)# no switchport port-security
SW1(config-if)# switchport port-security violation restrict
SW1(config-if)# no switchport port-security mac-address 123f.123f.123f
SW1(config-if)# switchport port-security mac-address aabb.cc00.a000
SW1(config-if)# switchport port-security
SW1(config-if)# end
SW1#w
*Aug 20 02:09:44.239: %SYS-5-CONFIG_I: Configured from console by console
SW1# wr
Building configuration...
[OK]
SW1#
SW1# show mac address-table interface ethernet 0/2
          Mac Address Table
-------------------------------------------

Vlan    Mac Address       Type        Ports
----    -----------       --------    -----
 11     aabb.cc00.a000    STATIC      Et0/2
Total Mac Addresses for this criterion: 1
SW1#
```

Finally, we must verify that PC1's Internet connectivity problem is now solved. Example 7-11 shows that PC1 can now ping the server with IP address 209.165.201.225 and that the problem is solved.

Example 7-11 *Solving the Problem: PC1 Can Now Ping the Internet Server*

```
PC1# ping 209.165.201.225
Type escape sequence to abort.
Sending 5, 100-byte ICMP Echos to 209.165.201.225, timeout is 2 seconds:
!!!!!
Success rate is 100 percent (5/5), round-trip min/avg/max = 1/202/1003 ms
PC1#
```

We must document our work and notify the user and any other party involved that the problem is solved.

Troubleshooting Port Security

You can implement port security on an interface with statically configured MAC addresses or by dynamically learned MAC addresses. When you statically configure the MAC address, you mean to restrict usage of that switch interface to that particular MAC address. Otherwise, when you do not statically configure the MAC address and merely specify how many (maximum) MAC addresses can be learned on that interface, you mean to restrict usage of that particular interface to a specific number of (one or two, for example) MAC addresses. When you assign secure MAC addresses to a secure port, the port does not forward ingress traffic that has source addresses outside the group of defined addresses. If you limit the number of secure MAC addresses to one, and assign a single secure MAC address, the device attached to that port has the full bandwidth of the port. When the maximum number of secure MAC addresses is reached on a secure port and the source MAC address of the ingress traffic differs from any of the identified secure MAC addresses, port security applies the configured violation action.

After you have set the maximum number of secure MAC addresses on a port, secure addresses can be inserted in the address table in one of the following ways:

- You can statically configure all secure MAC addresses by using the **switchport port-security mac-address** *mac_address* interface configuration command.

- You can allow the port to dynamically configure secure MAC addresses with the MAC addresses of connected devices (also called sticky learning).

- You can statically configure a number of addresses and allow the rest to be dynamically configured.

Following boot, a reload, or a link-down condition, port security does not populate the address table with dynamically learned MAC addresses until the port receives ingress traffic. A security violation occurs if the maximum number of secure MAC addresses has been added to the address table and the port receives traffic from a MAC address that is not in the address table. You can configure the port for one of three violation modes: protect, restrict, or shutdown. Port security with sticky MAC addresses provides many of the same benefits as port security with static MAC addresses, but sticky MAC addresses can be learned dynamically. Port security with sticky MAC addresses retains dynamically learned MAC addresses during a link-down condition. If you enter a **write memory** or **copy running-config startup-config** command, port security with sticky MAC addresses saves dynamically learned MAC addresses in the startup-config file, and the port does not have to learn addresses from ingress traffic after boot or a restart.

When configuring port security violation modes, note the following information:

- **protect:** Drops packets with unknown source addresses until you remove a sufficient number of secure MAC addresses to drop below the maximum value

- **restrict:** Drops packets with unknown source addresses until you remove a sufficient number of secure MAC addresses to drop below the maximum value and causes the security violation counter to increment

- **shutdown:** Puts the interface into the error-disabled state immediately and sends an SNMP trap notification

If the **show mac address-table** command does not reveal a specific MAC address (that you expect) in the MAC address table, most likely the switch is blocking all the frames from that source. To troubleshoot this type of situation, use the following guidelines:

- Verify the interface status with the **show interface** command. The access interface connecting the host to the network must be in up/up state.

- Check the MAC table for dynamic and static entries with the **show mac address-table** command. You can distinguish entries according to the interface, VLAN, and type.

- Check the port security overall status with the **show port-security** command. You can see on which interfaces port security is actually applied, what kind of violation mode is set for each interface, and check all the relevant counters.

- Check the port security status on the interface with the **show port-security interface ethernet** *x/y* command. The command reveals some additional information about the port security status of the specific interface.

- Check the port security configuration with the **show running-config** and **show startup-config** commands.

Troubleshooting PC2's Connectivity Problem

After fixing PC1's Internet connectivity, we learn that all other PCs except PC2 (which is in VLAN 22) can access the Internet. Based on the recent experience we just had with the port security configuration error on SW1, we asked Donovan to check SW1's interface Eth0/3 configuration. According to TINC's network diagram (Figure 7-1), PC2 is connected to SW1's interface Eth0/3. Donovan reported back that the port security configuration on SW1's interface Eth0/3 is fine and that it has PC2's MAC address configured correctly. To give us assurance, he copied and sent us the interface configuration.

We have no choice but to first verify the problem; then we need to choose an approach and start information gathering. As shown in Example 7-12, the attempt to ping the Internet server with IP address 209.165.201.225 from PC2 fails, and we receive the "% Unrecognized host or address, or protocol not running" message. This message made us curious to check the interface status of PC2; we find out that PC2's interface is up, but has no IP address, which is supposed to be gained through DHCP (see Example 7-12).

Example 7-12   *Verifying the Problem: PC2 Does Not Have Internet Connectivity*

```
PC2# ping 209.165.201.225
% Unrecognized host or address, or protocol not running.

PC2#
PC2# show ip interface brief
Interface                IP-Address        OK? Method Status            Protocol
Ethernet0/0              unassigned        YES DHCP   up                 up
< ...output omitted ...>
```

First of all, it is clear that without an IP address, PC2 will not be able to access the
Internet server (209.165.201.225). Therefore, our first goal must be to fix that issue.
If we find and fix the problem so that PC2 obtains an IP address, we will check to see
whether it can access the Internet. If PC2 still fails to access the Internet, we must continue our troubleshooting; otherwise, the problem is solved and we can close it.

Knowing that PC1, which is also connected to SW1, has obtained an IP address through
DHCP and communicates with Internet servers, it is not likely that the network as a
whole has Internet connectivity problems. However, because PC1 and PC2 belong to
different VLANs and IP subnets, we can take the follow-the-path approach and make
use of the spot-the-difference technique along the path to find the culprit that stops
PC2 from obtaining an IP address through DHCP.

Gathering Information

Based on TINC's network documentation and diagram (Figure 7-1), R1 and R2 are configured to act as redundant DHCP servers for VLANs 11, 22, 33, and 44. Therefore, we inspect
the DHCP configuration on R1 and R2 and notice that their configurations for all VLANs
are identical and seem correct. Example 7-13 shows R1's DHCP-related configuration.

Example 7-13   *DHCP Configuration on Router R1 for VLANs 11 and 12*

```
R1# show running-config
< ...output omitted... >
!
ip dhcp excluded-address 10.0.11.1 10.0.11.10
ip dhcp excluded-address 10.0.22.1 10.0.22.10
ip dhcp excluded-address 10.0.11.128 10.0.11.255
ip dhcp excluded-address 10.0.22.128 10.0.22.255
ip dhcp excluded-address 10.0.33.1 10.0.33.10
ip dhcp excluded-address 10.0.44.1 10.0.44.10
ip dhcp excluded-address 10.0.33.128 10.0.33.255
ip dhcp excluded-address 10.0.44.128 10.0.44.255
!
ip dhcp pool VLAN11_CLIENTS
 network 10.0.11.0 255.255.255.0
```

```
 default-router 10.0.11.1
!
ip dhcp pool VLAN22_CLIENTS
 network 10.0.22.0 255.255.255.0
 default-router 10.0.22.1
!
ip dhcp pool VLAN33_CLIENTS
 network 10.0.33.0 255.255.255.0
 default-router 10.0.33.1
!
ip dhcp pool VLAN44_CLIENTS
 network 10.0.44.0 255.255.255.0
 default-router 10.0.44.1
!
< ...output omitted... >
R1#
```

The next logical step in information gathering would be to inspect the trunk configuration between R1 (interface Eth1/0) and SW1 (interface Eth0/0) and spot and differences with respect to VLANs 11 and 12. Example 7-14 displays the configuration of interface Eth1/0 on R1 with respect to VLANs 11 and 12, which looks correct.

Example 7-14 *Trunk Configuration on R1 Interface Eth1/0 for VLANs 11 and 12*

```
R1# show running-config
< ...output omitted... >
!
interface Ethernet1/0
 no ip address
!
interface Ethernet1/0.11
 encapsulation dot1Q 11
 ip address 10.0.11.2 255.255.255.0
 standby 1 ip 10.0.11.1
 standby 1 priority 110
 standby 1 preempt
!
interface Ethernet1/0.22
 encapsulation dot1Q 22
 ip address 10.0.22.2 255.255.255.0
 standby 2 ip 10.0.22.1
 standby 2 priority 110
 standby 2 preempt
!
< ...output omitted... >
R1#
```

Next, we inspect the trunk interfaces (Eth0/0 and Eth0/1) on switch SW1 using the **show interfaces trunk** command. As shown in Example 7-15, both trunk interfaces are configured for trunking with native VLAN 1 and they both allow all VLANs (1–4094). However, the allowed and active VLANs in those trunks are only VLANs 1 and 11.

Example 7-15   *Checking the Trunk Interfaces on Switch SW1*

```
SW1# show interfaces trunk


Port                 Mode          Encapsulation  Status         Native vlan
Et0/0                on                 802.1q     trunking       1
Et0/1                on                 802.1q     trunking       1


Port                 Vlans allowed on trunk
Et0/0                1-4094
Et0/1                1-4094


Port                 Vlans allowed and active in management domain
Et0/0                1,11
Et0/1                1,11


Port                 Vlans in spanning tree forwarding state and not pruned
Et0/0                1,11
Et0/1                1,11
SW1#
SW1#
```

Eliminating Possibilities, Proposing a Hypothesis, and Testing the Hypothesis

With the latest information we have gathered about switch SW1's uplink trunk interfaces toward R1 and R2, the possibility of VLAN 22 not being allowed in those trunks is eliminated. The remaining hypothesis is that either VLAN 22 does not exist in switch SW1 or that it is down or shut down. To test our hypothesis, we use both **show vlan id 22** and **show vlan** commands on switch SW1. The results shown in Example 7-16 confirm that VLAN 22 does not exist in SW1.

Example 7-16   *Testing the Hypothesis: Check to See Whether VLAN 22 Exists on SW1*

```
SW1# show vlan id 22
VLAN id 22 not found in current VLAN database
SW1#
SW1# show vlan
```

```
VLAN Name                             Status    Ports
---- -------------------------------- --------- ------------------------------
1    default                          active    Et1/0, Et1/1, Et1/2, Et1/3
                                                Et2/0, Et2/1, Et2/2, Et2/3
                                                Et3/0, Et3/1, Et3/2, Et3/3
                                                Et4/0, Et4/1, Et4/2, Et4/3
                                                Et5/0, Et5/1, Et5/2, Et5/3
11   VLAN0011                         active    Et0/2
1002 fddi-default                     act/unsup
1003 token-ring-default               act/unsup
1004 fddinet-default                  act/unsup
1005 trnet-default                    act/unsup


VLAN    Type  SAID       MTU   Parent RingNo BridgeNo Stp  BrdgMode Trans1 Trans2
----    ----- ---------- ----- ------ ------ -------- ---- -------- ------ -----
1       enet  100001     1500  -      -      -        -    -        0      0
11      enet  100011     1500  -      -      -        -    -        0      0
1002    fddi  101002     1500  -      -      -        -    -        0      0
1003    tr    101003     1500  -      -      -        -    -        0      0
1004    fdnet 101004     1500  -      -      -        ieee -        0      0
1005    trnet 101005     1500  -      -      -        ibm  -        0      0


Primary Secondary Type              Ports
------- --------- ----------------- -------------------------------------------

SW1#
```

Solving the Problem

We need to create VLAN 22 on switch SW1. As shown in Example 7-17, after creating VLAN 22, we used the **show vlan id 22** command to ensure that VLAN 22 exists and is active on SW1.

Example 7-17   *Solve the Problem: Create VLAN 22 on Switch SW1*

```
SW1#
SW1# conf term
Enter configuration commands, one per line.  End with CNTL/Z.
SW1(config)# vlan 22
SW1(config-vlan)# end
% Applying VLAN changes may take few minutes.  Please wait...

SW1#
*Aug 21 04:18:55.527: %SYS-5-CONFIG_I: Configured from console by console
SW1# show vlan id 22
```

```
VLAN Name                             Status    Ports
---- -------------------------------- --------- ------------------------------
22   VLAN0022                         active    Et0/0, Et0/1, Et0/3


VLAN Type  SAID       MTU   Parent RingNo BridgeNo Stp  BrdgMode Trans1 Trans2
---- ----- ---------- ----- ------ ------ -------- ---- -------- ------ ------
22   enet  100022     1500  -      -      -        -    -        0      0


Primary Secondary Type              Ports
------- --------- ----------------- ------------------------------------------


SW1#



PC2#
PC2# Ping 209.165.201.225
Type escape sequence to abort.
Sending 5, 100-byte ICMP Echos to 209.165.201.225, timeout is 2 seconds:
!!!!!
Success rate is 100 percent (5/5), round-trip min/avg/max = 1/202/1008 ms
PC2#
```

Finally, as shown in example 7-17, we return to PC2 to see whether it can now access the Internet server. Ping 209.165.201.225 succeeds, and the problem is solved. We must document our work and notify the user and any other party involved.

Troubleshooting VLANs

Use the following checklist during VLAN troubleshooting:

- Verify the status of all the relevant interfaces with the **show interface** command. The interface must be in the up/up state.

- Check the VLAN database with the **show vlan** command. This command enables you to verify which VLANs exist and to view port-to-VLAN mapping. Trunks are not listed because they do not belong to any particular VLAN.

- Check trunk interfaces with the **show interfaces trunk** command and the **show interfaces switchport** command. Using these commands, you can discover all interfaces that are configured as trunks and find out per trunk information about the configured trunk mode, encapsulation type, native VLAN, and allowed VLANs.

- Check the MAC table for dynamic and static entries in a particular VLAN with the **show mac-address-table** command. This is the main command to verify Layer 2 forwarding. It shows you the MAC addresses that are learned by the switch and their corresponding port and VLAN associations.

The native VLAN is used to carry untagged traffic across an 802.1Q trunk. The default native VLAN is set to VLAN 1, but can be changed on each trunk interface. The native VLAN must be the same on both sides of a trunk interface. Native VLAN mismatch between the two ends of a trunk is a common mistake. Native VLAN misconfiguration generates traffic leak between two VLANs, which results in strange forwarding behavior and possible fatal errors in protocols such as Spanning Tree Protocol (STP).

Cisco Discovery Protocol (CDP) monitors the native VLANs and displays a notification if a mismatch is detected. Mismatch messages are displayed every minute and they look like the following:

%CDP-4-NATIVE_VLAN_MISMATCH: Native VLAN mismatch discovered on GigabitEthernet1/0/25 (100), with sw1 GigabitEthernet1/0/25 (300).

STP is also able to detect native VLAN mismatches and can block the affected VLAN on the interface. This will result in notifications such as:

- **%SPANTREE-2-RECV_PVID_ERR:** Received BPDU with inconsistent peer vlan id 300 on GigabitEthernet1/0/25 VLAN100.

- **%SPANTREE-2-BLOCK_PVID_PEER:** Blocking GigabitEthernet1/0/25 on VLAN0300. Inconsistent peer vlan.

- **%SPANTREE-2-BLOCK_PVID_LOCAL:** Blocking GigabitEthernet1/0/25 on VLAN0100. Inconsistent local vlan.

The native VLAN is typically untagged on 802.1Q trunks. This can lead to a security vulnerability because it is possible to create frames that are encapsulated with two 802.1Q tags. If the attacker uses native VLAN for the outer tag and the victim's VLAN for the inner tag, the switch strips the outer tag and forwards the remaining single-tagged frame toward the destination VLAN across a trunk port. This is called a VLAN hopping attack and can be prevented with the **vlan dot1q tag native** command, which explicitly tags the native VLAN as well. For older switches, which do not support this feature, you can remove the native VLAN from the allowed VLAN on that trunk.

You can use the **show interfaces trunk** and the **show interfaces interface** *slot/number* **switchport** commands to verify the configured native VLAN and other trunk parameters.

TINC Garbage Disposal Trouble Ticket 2

Donovan, who works as an IT and network support engineer at TINC Garbage Disposal, has sent us (at SECHNIK Networking) an e-mail asking for help with the following items:

- The router GW1 has router GW2 as the only OSPF neighbor. We need to find out why GW1 does not have an adjacency with router R1. We need to make all the necessary changes so that G1 forms an OSPF neighbor relation with R1.

- All the routers in the network are configured for remote access via Secure Shell (SSH) Version 2. However, for an unknown reason, PC4 cannot access R2, even though it can access GW1, GW2, and R1. This problem needs to be solved.

■ Routers R1 and R2 keep generating log messages indicating a duplicate IP address. This problem needs attention right away because some suspect an IOS bug is causing it.

Troubleshooting GW1's OSPF Neighbor Relation Problem with Router R1

We have been informed that router GW1 must have an OSPF neighbor relationship with routers GW2 and R1. However, there is no OSPF neighbor relationship currently between router's GW1 and R1. Our troubleshooting task is to fix this, but we must first verify the problem.

Verifying the Problem

Example 7-18 shows that we tried the **show ip ospf neighbor** command on router GW1, and the output displays merely one neighbor with the router ID 10.0.1.11. We then try the **show ip ospf | include ID** command on router GW2, and find out that 10.0.1.11 is indeed GW2's OSPF router ID. This proves that the problem is reported correctly. Our job is to discover why the neighbor relationship between routers GW1 and R1 is down, and fix that problem.

Example 7-18 *Verify the Problem: Check Whether GW1 Has Only One OSPF Neighbor*

```
GW1# show ip ospf neighbor


Neighbor ID     Pri   State        Dead Time    Address       Interface
10.0.1.11         1   FULL/DR      00:00:37     10.0.10.34    Ethernet0/0
GW1#




GW2# show ip ospf | include ID
 Routing Process "ospf 1" with ID 10.0.1.11
GW2#
```

We can take the bottom-up approach, focusing on the link between GW1 and R1 and work our way up.

Gathering Information

As the first step in the bottom-up troubleshooting approach, we check the status of interface Ethernet 0/3 on routers GW1 and R1; these routers are connected to each other through this interface. Also, using **show ip interface brief**, we find that the IP addresses of these interfaces on both routers are configured correctly. Example 7-19 shows these results.

Example 7-19   *Checking the Status of Interfaces Connecting GW1 and R1*

```
GW1# show interfaces ethernet 0/3
Ethernet0/3 is up, line protocol is up
< ...output omitted... >
GW1# show ip interface brief
Interface              IP-Address     OK? Method Status                 Protocol
Ethernet0/0            10.0.10.33     YES NVRAM  up                     up
Ethernet0/1            209.165.200.1  YES NVRAM  up                     up
Ethernet0/2            unassigned     YES NVRAM  administratively down  down
Ethernet0/3            10.0.10.26     YES NVRAM  up                     up
Loopback0              10.0.1.10      YES NVRAM  up                     up
NVI0                   10.0.10.33     YES unset  up                     up
GW1#



R1# show interfaces ethernet 0/3
Ethernet0/3 is up, line protocol is up
< ...output omitted... >
R1# show ip int brief
Interface              IP-Address     OK? Method Status                 Protocol
Ethernet0/0            10.0.10.21     YES NVRAM  up                     up
Ethernet0/1            unassigned     YES NVRAM  administratively down  down
Ethernet0/2            unassigned     YES NVRAM  administratively down  down
Ethernet0/3            10.0.10.25     YES NVRAM  up                     up
Ethernet1/0            unassigned     YES NVRAM  up                     up
Ethernet1/0.11         10.0.11.2      YES NVRAM  up                     up
Ethernet1/0.22         10.0.22.2      YES NVRAM  up                     up
Ethernet1/1            10.0.33.2      YES NVRAM  up                     up
Ethernet1/2            10.0.44.2      YES NVRAM  up                     up
Ethernet1/3            unassigned     YES NVRAM  administratively down  down
Loopback0              10.0.1.8       YES NVRAM  up                     up
R1#
```

We must now check the OSPF configuration on routers GW1 and R1. We can look at
the OSPF section within the running-config and also make use of the **show ip ospf** command on both routers for any clues that can help our troubleshooting effort. The output
of these commands is shown in Example 7-20. Both routers have activated all interfaces
within network 10.0.0.0 for backbone area 0. GW1 has OSPF active on four interfaces,
and R1 has it active on seven interfaces.

Example 7-20   *Information Gathering: OSPF Configuration on GW1 and R1*

```
GW1# show running-config | section router ospf
router ospf 1
 network 10.0.0.0 0.255.255.255 area 0
 default-information originate
GW1# show ip ospf
 Routing Process "ospf 1" with ID 10.0.1.10
< ...output omitted... >
  Reference bandwidth unit is 100 mbps
    Area BACKBONE(0)
        Number of interfaces in this area is 4 (1 loopback)
        Area has no authentication
        SPF algorithm last executed 00:00:49.696 ago
        SPF algorithm executed 2 times
        Area ranges are
        Number of LSA 11. Checksum Sum 0x05FED4
        Number of opaque link LSA 0. Checksum Sum 0x000000
        Number of DCbitless LSA 0
        Number of indication LSA 0
        Number of DoNotAge LSA 0
        Flood list length 0
GW1#


R1# show running-config | section router ospf
router ospf 1
 network 10.0.0.0 0.255.255.255 area 0
R1# show ip ospf
 Routing Process "ospf 1" with ID 10.0.1.8
< ...output omitted... >
    Area BACKBONE(0)
        Number of interfaces in this area is 7 (1 loopback)
        Area has no authentication
        SPF algorithm last executed 00:00:08.390 ago
        SPF algorithm executed 4 times
        Area ranges are
        Number of LSA 9. Checksum Sum 0x0435EC
        Number of opaque link LSA 0. Checksum Sum 0x000000
        Number of DCbitless LSA 0
        Number of indication LSA 0
        Number of DoNotAge LSA 0
        Flood list length 0
 R1#
```

Because the configurations we have seen so far look correct, we can try the **debug ip ospf hello** option to see whether we can gather any clues about the root of the problem. We enabled this debug option on both routers, and Example 7-21 shows the results. The debug output for R1 includes a line within which mismatched hello parameters from 10.0.10.26 (GW1's IP address on Ethernet 0/3) are reported.

Example 7-21 *Information Gathering: Debug Results for IP OSPF Hello*

```
GW1# debug ip ospf hello
*Aug 22 23:29:03.999: OSPF-1 HELLO Et0/0: Rcv hello from 10.0.1.11 area 0 10.0.10.34
*Aug 22 23:29:04.599: OSPF-1 HELLO NV0: Send hello to 224.0.0.5 area 0 from 0.0.0.0
GW1#
*Aug 22 23:29:10.282: OSPF-1 HELLO Et0/0: Send hello to 224.0.0.5 area 0 from
  10.0.10.33
*Aug 22 23:29:10.320: OSPF-1 HELLO Et0/3: Send hello to 224.0.0.5 area 0 from
  10.0.10.26
GW1#
*Aug 22 23:29:13.611: OSPF-1 HELLO Et0/0: Rcv hello from 10.0.1.11 area 0 10.0.10.34
*Aug 22 23:29:13.882: OSPF-1 HELLO NV0: Send hello to 224.0.0.5 area 0 from 0.0.0.0
GW1#


R1# debug ip ospf hello
OSPF hello debugging is on
R1#
*Aug 22 23:29:47.878: OSPF-1 HELLO Et1/2: Rcv hello from 10.0.1.9 area 0 10.0.44.3
*Aug 22 23:29:48.581: OSPF-1 HELLO Et0/0: Send hello to 224.0.0.5 area 0 from
  10.0.10.21
*Aug 22 23:29:48.916: OSPF-1 HELLO Et0/3: Rcv hello from 10.0.1.10 area 0 10.0.10.26
*Aug 22 23:29:48.916: OSPF-1 HELLO Et0/3: Mismatched hello parameters from 10.0.10.26
*Aug 22 23:29:48.916: OSPF-1 HELLO Et0/3: Dead R 40 C 120, Hello R 10 C 30 Mask R
  255.255.255.252 C 255.255.255.252
R1#
*Aug 22 23:29:48.948: OSPF-1 HELLO Et1/0.11: Send hello to 224.0.0.5 area 0 from
  10.0.11.2
*Aug 22 23:29:49.336: OSPF-1 HELLO Et1/0.22: Rcv hello from 10.0.1.9 area 0 10.0.22.3
R1# n
*Aug 22 23:29:50.926: OSPF-1 HELLO Et1/0.22: Send hello to 224.0.0.5 area 0 from
  10.0.22.2
R1#
```

Because of the "Mismatched hello parameters from 10.10.10.26" message we see in the debug output produced on R1, we must check interface specific configurations of OSPF on the interface Ethernet 0/3 for both routers. We used **show ip ospf interface ethernet 0/3** on both routers, and Example 7-22 shows the results.

Example 7-22   *Information Gathering: OSPF Configuration on Ethernet 0/3 Interface*

```
GW1# show ip ospf int eth 0/3
Ethernet0/3 is up, line protocol is up
  Internet Address 10.0.10.26/30, Area 0, Attached via Network Statement
  Process ID 1, Router ID 10.0.1.10, Network Type BROADCAST, Cost: 10
  Topology-MTID    Cost    Disabled    Shutdown    Topology Name
       0            10         no          no          Base
  Transmit Delay is 1 sec, State DR, Priority 1
  Designated Router (ID) 10.0.1.10, Interface address 10.0.10.26
  No backup designated router on this network
  Timer intervals configured, Hello 10, Dead 40, Wait 40, Retransmit 5
    oob-resync timeout 40
    Hello due in 00:00:00
  Supports Link-local Signaling (LLS)
  Cisco NSF helper support enabled
  IETF NSF helper support enabled
  Index 2/2, flood queue length 0
  Next 0x0(0)/0x0(0)
  Last flood scan length is 0, maximum is 0
  Last flood scan time is 0 msec, maximum is 0 msec
  Neighbor Count is 0, Adjacent neighbor count is 0
  Suppress hello for 0 neighbor(s)
GW1#



R1# show ip ospf int eth 0/3
Ethernet0/3 is up, line protocol is up
  Internet Address 10.0.10.25/30, Area 0, Attached via Network Statement
  Process ID 1, Router ID 10.0.1.8, Network Type NON_BROADCAST, Cost: 10
  Topology-MTID    Cost    Disabled    Shutdown    Topology Name
       0            10         no          no          Base
  Transmit Delay is 1 sec, State DR, Priority 1
  Designated Router (ID) 10.0.1.8, Interface address 10.0.10.25
  No backup designated router on this network
  Timer intervals configured, Hello 30, Dead 120, Wait 120, Retransmit 5
    oob-resync timeout 120
    Hello due in 00:00:10
  Supports Link-local Signaling (LLS)
  Cisco NSF helper support enabled
  IETF NSF helper support enabled
  Index 2/2, flood queue length 0
  Next 0x0(0)/0x0(0)
  Last flood scan length is 0, maximum is 0
  Last flood scan time is 0 msec, maximum is 0 msec
```

```
  Neighbor Count is 0, Adjacent neighbor count is 0
  Suppress hello for 0 neighbor(s)
R1#
```

Based on the output shown in Example 7-22, on router GW1, the OSPF network type on interface Ethernet 0/3 is shown as BROADCAST, which is the default. The OSPF Hello and Dead timers over the broadcast network are 10 and 40 seconds by default. However, on router R1, the OSPF network type on interface Ethernet 0/3 is shown as NON_BROADCAST. The OSPF Hello and Dead timers over the NON_BROADCAST network are 30 and 120 seconds by default.

Analyzing Information, Eliminating Possibilities, and Proposing a Hypothesis

When OSPF neighbors receive each other's Hello messages, they expect to be in agreement about the network address, area number, Hello and Dead timers, area type, and authentication parameters. The mismatched Hello parameters that we have discovered are the Hello and Dead timers, and the reason is that R1 has interface Ethernet 0/3 configured as a NON_BROADCAST OSPF network type. We can, for now, eliminate other causes for the neighbor relationship problem between GW1 and R1, and propose the NON_BROADCAST network type configured on router R1's interface Ethernet 0/3 as the problem's cause.

Testing the Hypothesis and Solving the Problem

To test our hypothesis, as shown in Example 7-23, we display the interface Ethernet 0/3 section of router R1's running-config and then remove the **ip ospf network non-broadcast** command. We check the result of our work by using the **show ip ospf interface ethernet 0/3** command, and the network type is correctly shown as BROADCAST.

Example 7-23 *Testing the Hypothesis: Correct the OSPF Network Type on R1*

```
R1# show running-config interface ethernet 0/3
Building configuration...

Current configuration : 99 bytes
!
interface Ethernet0/3
 ip address 10.0.10.25 255.255.255.252
 ip ospf network non-broadcast
end

R1# conf term
Enter configuration commands, one per line.  End with CNTL/Z.
R1(config)# interface ethernet 0/3
R1(config-if)# no ip ospf network non-broadcast
R1(config-if)# end
```

```
R1#
*Aug 22 23:32:58.432: %SYS-5-CONFIG_I: Configured from console by console
*Aug 22 23:32:59.275: %OSPF-5-ADJCHG: Process 1, Nbr 10.0.1.10 on Ethernet0/3 from
  LOADING to FULL, Loading Done
R1#

R1# show ip ospf interface ethernet 0/3
Ethernet0/3 is up, line protocol is up
  Internet Address 10.0.10.25/30, Area 0, Attached via Network Statement
  Process ID 1, Router ID 10.0.1.8, Network Type BROADCAST, Cost: 10
  Topology-MTID    Cost    Disabled    Shutdown      Topology Name
       0            10        no          no            Base
  Transmit Delay is 1 sec, State BDR, Priority 1
  Designated Router (ID) 10.0.1.10, Interface address 10.0.10.26
  Backup Designated router (ID) 10.0.1.8, Interface address 10.0.10.25
  Timer intervals configured, Hello 10, Dead 40, Wait 40, Retransmit 5
    oob-resync timeout 40
    Hello due in 00:00:02
< ...output omitted... >
R1#
```

We must now see whether GW1 and R1 routers have formed a neighbor relationship.
Example 7-24 shows the result of the **show ip ospf neighbor** command on both routers.
As shown, router GW1 has 10.0.1.8 (R1) as a neighbor through interface Ethernet 0/3,
and router R1 has 10.0.1.10 (GW1) as a neighbor through interface Ethernet 0/3 as well.

Example 7-24   *Verify the Solution: GW1 and R1 Form Neighbor Relation*

```
R1# show ip ospf neighbor

Neighbor ID    Pri    State       Dead Time    Address        Interface
10.0.1.9        1     FULL/DR     00:00:35     10.0.44.3      Ethernet1/2
10.0.1.9        1     FULL/DR     00:00:32     10.0.33.3      Ethernet1/1
10.0.1.9        1     FULL/DR     00:00:37     10.0.22.3      Ethernet1/0.22
10.0.1.9        1     FULL/DR     00:00:35     10.0.11.3      Ethernet1/0.11
10.0.1.10       1     FULL/DR     00:00:30     10.0.10.26     Ethernet0/3
10.0.1.9        1     FULL/DR     00:00:37     10.0.10.22     Ethernet0/0
R1#



GW1# show ip ospf neighbor

Neighbor ID    Pri    State       Dead Time    Address        Interface
10.0.1.8        1     FULL/BDR    00:00:32     10.0.10.25     Ethernet0/3
10.0.1.11       1     FULL/DR     00:00:38     10.0.10.34     Ethernet0/0
GW1#
```

The neighbor relationship problem between routers GW1 and R1 is solved. We must now document our work and notify Donovan that the problem is solved.

Troubleshooting OSPF Adjacency

Before they can exchange routing information, OSPF neighbors must form adjacency. To form adjacency, the OSPF neighbor relationship transitions through several phases. Depending on the network type, neighbors will finally transition to either Full or 2Way states. Please note that on a multi-access network, the state of OSPF neighbor adjacency between two DRother routers will be 2Way. To check the state of the neighbor relationship, use the **show ip ospf neighbor** command. If the output of this command does not list a neighbor you expect, use the following guidelines:

■ Verify the interface status with the **show interface** command. The interface to the neighbor must be in the up/up state.

■ Check the IP connectivity to the neighbor with the **ping** command. Ping the IP address of the neighbor and multicast IP address 224.0.0.5, which is the destination address for Hello messages.

■ Check to see whether any access list is applied to the interface by using the **show ip interface** command.

■ Check the OSPF status on the interface with the **show ip ospf interface** command. The command reveals all the interfaces where OSPF is enabled.

■ Check whether the interface is configured as passive. You can use **show ip ospf interface** as well. Active OSPF interfaces should display a remaining time to the next Hello message.

■ Verify that the router ID of the routers is not the same. If the router receives a Hello packet with the same router ID, the router will ignore this Hello packet. Use the **show ip ospf** command to verify the OSPF router ID.

■ Verify that the Hello parameters match between neighbors. Several parameters must match to establish the full adjacency:

  ■ **OSPF area number:** You can verify this using the **show ip ospf interface** command.

  ■ **OSPF area type (such as stub or NSSA):** Use the **show ip ospf** command to discover the area type.

  ■ **Subnet and subnet mask:** Check the IP address and the mask with the **show ip interface** command.

  ■ **OSPF Hello and Dead timers:** The **show ip ospf interface** command reveals the OSPF timers.

If the state of a router's OSPF neighbor is shown as (and stuck in) Down state, Init state, or Exstart/Exchange state, you need to investigate and discover the reason.

A dynamically discovered neighbor could be in Down state when the OSPF process does not receive the Hello packet from that neighbor for a time period longer than the Dead timer interval. The Down state is transient, which means that the neighbor will either advance to other states or it will be deleted from the OSPF neighbor table. The neighbor could also be seen as Down when it is manually configured using the **neighbor** command. A manually configured neighbor is always kept in the OSPF neighbor table; however, when the neighbor is shown in Down state, it usually means that no Hello message was received from it or that the Dead timer expired. A manually configured neighbor can only be configured in non-broadcast multi-access (NBMA) networks or nonbroadcast point-to-multipoint networks. To troubleshoot the Down state, follow the same procedure as if the neighbor did not show up in the OSPF neighbor table at all.

When a neighbor is stuck in the Init state, it indicates that the router has seen the Hello packets from the neighbor, but the Hello message did not include the local router-id in the list of neighbors. Check that the routers have reachability, no access-list blocks their communication, and that there are no authentication mismatches between them.

When the neighbor relationship is stuck in Exstart/Exchange state, verify that it is not due to maximum transmission unit (MTU) mismatch between routers. The MTU mismatch problem happens when the router on one side sends an OSPF message larger than the MTU configured on the other router. The larger message is ignored by the receiving router, and the relationship stays in the Exstart/Exchange state. To check MTU settings on an OSPF router, use the **show running-config** command. You can use the **ip ospf mtu-ignore** interface configuration mode command to disable MTU mismatch detection on an interface. By default, OSPF checks whether neighbors are using the same MTU on a common interface. If the receiving MTU is higher than the IP MTU configured on the incoming interface, OSPF does not establish adjacencies. Use the **ip ospf mtu-ignore** command to disable this check and allow adjacencies when the MTU value differs between OSPF neighbors.

Troubleshooting Secure Shell Version 2 Access to Router R2 from PC4

According to Donovan's e-mail, all the routers in the TINC Garbage Disposal network are configured with remote access via SSH Version 2. However, for an unknown reason, PC4 cannot access R2, even though it can access GW1, GW2, and R1. Our troubleshooting task is to fix this, but we must first verify the problem.

Verifying the Problem

To verify the problem as reported by Donovan, we try SSHv2 to access routers GW1, GW2, R1, and R2 from PC4. Example 7-25 shows the results.

Example 7-25   *Verify the Problem: SSHv2 from PC4 to All Routers*

```
PC4# ssh -v 2 -l admin 10.0.1.10
Password:
GW1> exit
[Connection to 10.0.1.10 closed by foreign host]


PC4# ssh -v 2 -l admin 10.0.1.11
Password:
GW2> exit
[Connection to 10.0.1.11 closed by foreign host]


PC4# ssh -v 2 -l admin 10.0.1.8
Password:
R1> exit
[Connection to 10.0.1.8 closed by foreign host]


PC4# ssh -v 2 -l admin 10.0.1.9
[Connection to 10.0.1.9 aborted: error status 0]
PC4#
```

Based on the results shown in Example 7-25, all routers except R2 can be accessed from PC4 using SSHv2. The problem was correctly reported. It is time to do some information gathering.

Gathering Information

As the first step in information gathering, we tried SSH again from PC4, but this time with Version 1. The success of this attempt, shown in Example 7-26, helped us immediately eliminate many possible causes and focus on the SSH version.

Example 7-26   *Information Gathering: Try SSH Version 1 from PC4 to Router R1*

```
PC4#
PC4# ssh -l admin 10.0.1.9
Password:
R2>
```

Because R1 can be accessed through SSHv2 from PC4, but R2 can only be accessed using SSHv1 from the same device (PC4), we can use the spot-the-differences technique. We used the **show ip ssh** command on routers R1 and R2. As shown in Example 7-27, SSH is enabled on R1, and the version is displayed as 1.99. On R2, though, the SSH is enabled, and the version is displayed as 1.5. We then look at the running-config on R2, and as shown in Example 7-27, R2 is configured with the **ip ssh version 1** command.

Example 7-27 *Information Gathering: Compare R1 and R2 SSH Settings*

```
R1#
R1# show ip ssh
SSH Enabled - version 1.99
Authentication timeout: 120 secs; Authentication retries: 3
Minimum expected Diffie Hellman key size : 1024 bits
IOS Keys in SECSH format(ssh-rsa, base64 encoded):
ssh-rsa AAAAB3NzaC1yc2EAAAADAQABAAAAgQDP0MHXQTmy0xA0yTH65tOi3ry6q+tyrUkmt2zw+GlP
DfGDfNzAy0x3b4ySB06VxWsUpzpjDan6TLg8TgVRgydm3eDH8N6ShQq1VmFZSLj0/Eb+4TdlJ+FoCFjZc7Vk
K3KOSR16/7dsRmK4dOst9MNnQ0XV3qhaLUeyz+0MHHRcjQ==
R1#


R2#
R2# show ip ssh
SSH Enabled - version 1.5
Authentication timeout: 120 secs; Authentication retries: 3
Minimum expected Diffie Hellman key size : 1024 bits
IOS Keys in SECSH format(ssh-rsa, base64 encoded):
ssh-rsa AAAAB3NzaC1yc2EAAAADAQABAAAAQQCpX9dE4K/BMKTG9GdSa72+hk5Afa8rRIiQL/LzcuuC
QoKolHe8DGK6thseXiu9WHfIvEX+N4vPa0yATb9+8JiP
R2#
R2# show running-config | include ip ssh
ip ssh version 1
R2#
```

Proposing a Hypothesis and Testing the Hypothesis

Knowing that SSHv2 is the default version on Cisco IOS, we can propose with confidence that we need to remove the **ip ssh version 1** command from R2's running-config.

The output from the **show ip ssh** command in Example 7-28 shows that we removed the offending command from R2's running-config and verified that the SSH version indeed changed to 2. However, as shown in Example 7-28, when we retried SSHv2 from PC4, we received an error message indicating that the server's configured key size is below the mandatory size of 768 bits.

Example 7-28 *Testing the Hypothesis: R2's Existing Key Is Not Long Enough for SSH Version 2*

```
R2#
R2# conf term
Enter configuration commands, one per line.  End with CNTL/Z.
R2(config)# no ip ssh ver 1
R2(config)# end
R2#
```

```
*Aug 26 00:27:23.671: %SYS-5-CONFIG_I: Configured from console by console
R2# show ip ssh
SSH Enabled - version 1.99
Authentication timeout: 120 secs; Authentication retries: 3
Minimum expected Diffie Hellman key size : 1024 bits
IOS Keys in SECSH format(ssh-rsa, base64 encoded):
ssh-rsa AAAAB3NzaC1yc2EAAAADAQABAAAAQQCpX9dE4K/BMKTG9GdSa72+hk5Afa8rRIiQL/LzcuuC
QoKolHe8DGK6thseXiu9WHfIvEX+N4vPa0yATb9+8JiP
R2#



PC4# ssh -v 2 -l admin 10.0.1.9
[Connection to 10.0.1.9 aborted: error status 0]
Server's public key below the mandatory size of 768 bits!
PC4#
*Aug 26 00:28:48.111: %SSH-3-RSA_SIGN_FAIL: Signature verification failed, status 8
PC4#
```

Solving the Problem

Note that we could use the **show crypto key mypubkey rsa** command to display
the RSA key pair that SSH uses, but the output does not specify the size of the key.
Concluding that to use SSHv2 R2 needs to regenerate a new key that is 768 bits or longer, we used the **crypto key generate rsa modulus 1024** command to generate a 1024-
bit RSA key pair on R2. With the new key pair on R2, the SSHv2 attempt from PC4 to
R2 was successful (see Example 7-29); the problem is solved.

Example 7-29   *Solving the Problem: SSHv2 from PC4 to R2 Is Successful*

```
R2# conf term
Enter configuration commands, one per line.  End with CNTL/Z.
R2(config)# crypto key generate rsa modulus 1024
% You already have RSA keys defined named R2.cisco.com.
% They will be replaced.
% The key modulus size is 1024 bits
% Generating 1024 bit RSA keys, keys will be non-exportable...
[OK] (elapsed time was 1 seconds)
R2(config)#
*Aug 26 00:30:02.958: %SSH-5-DISABLED: SSH 1.99 has been disabled
*Aug 26 00:30:03.574: %SSH-5-ENABLED: SSH 1.99 has been enabled
R2(config)# end
R2# wr
Building configuration...
[OK]
R2#
```

```
*Aug 26 00:30:12.390: %SYS-5-CONFIG_I: Configured from console by console
R2#


PC4# ssh -v 2 -l admin 10.0.1.9
Password:
R2>
```

We must document our work and notify Donovan that the SSHv2 from PC4 to R2 is now working.

Troubleshooting SSH and Telnet

The Telnet protocol is a much simpler protocol than SSH, but its use is not recommended because it sends commands in plain text, including passwords. Therefore, you should use Telnet only in lab or test environments. Common causes of SSH/Telnet problems include the following:

■ **Access lists:** It is a good practice to limit Telnet/SSH access to network devices to authorized IP addresses only; you can do this by applying access lists to the vty lines. If Telnet or SSH connections to a device are refused, check whether access lists are applied to vty lines or interfaces.

■ **Telnet/SSH not enabled on the vty line:** By default, all protocols are enabled on the vty lines. You can limit the protocols by using the **transport input** command. To check the enabled protocols, you can use the **show line** command.

■ **Authentication:** To authenticate Telnet/SSH access to a device, several authentication methods are available. For example, you can use local authentication, or you can use centralized authentication using RADIUS, TACACS+, or LDAP protocols and servers. You should check the running configuration to find out the AAA (authentication, authorization, and accounting) mechanisms that are used. The **debug radius** and the **debug tacacs** commands are also useful for troubleshooting RADIUS and TACACS+ protocols.

■ **All vty lines are busy:** A limited number of vty lines are available to manage network devices. Vty lines are identified by numbers, starting with 0. Though it happens rarely, eventually all the vty lines can become busy if clients do not close connections when done. Vty lines are cleared when the connection timeout expires. To check all the connections to the vty lines, use the **show line** command. To clear some of the vty lines, use the **clear line** command.

■ **SSH version:** Make sure that the correct SSH version and key size are configured.

Troubleshooting Duplicate Address Problem Discovered Through R1 and R2's Log Messages

The last item on Donovan's e-mail was that routers R1 and R2 keep generating log messages indicating duplicate IP addresses. We must verify this problem and, if true, identify the source of this address conflict and eliminate it.

Verifying the Problem

Soon after logging in to routers R1 and R2, we notice the log message from both routers about duplicate address 10.0.33.1 on interface Ethernet 1/1. According to the output shown in Example 7-30, router R1 states that the duplicate address is sourced from the MAC address 0000.0c07.ac03. However, R2 states that the duplicate address is sourced from the MAC address 0000.0c07.ac21.

Example 7-30 *Log Messages from R1 and R2 Indicate Duplicate IP Address*

```
R1#
*Aug 27 01:50:15.817: %IP-4-DUPADDR: Duplicate address 10.0.33.1 on Ethernet1/1,
   sourced by 0000.0c07.ac03
R1#


R2#
*Aug 27 01:51:16.395: %IP-4-DUPADDR: Duplicate address 10.0.33.1 on Ethernet1/1,
   sourced by 0000.0c07.ac21
R2#
```

We not only verified that the reported problem is true, we also have gained a substantial amount of information. We know the actual duplicated IP address, and we also know the two MAC addresses claiming this IP address. Before we decide how to approach this troubleshooting task, we must determine which devices own these MAC addresses and have been configured with this IP address.

Gathering Information

The duplicate IP address 10.0.33.1 belongs to subnet 10.0.33.0. According to TINC's documentation, this subnet maps to VLAN 33, which exists only on switch ASW2. As shown in Example 7-31, we examined the MAC address table on ASW2 and found that MAC addresses 0000.0c07.ac03 and 0000.0c07.ac21 have been learned through interfaces Ethernet 0/0 and Ethernet 0/1.

Example 7-31 *Information Gathering: Examine ASW2's MAC Address Table*

```
SW2# show mac address-table | include 0000.0c07.ac03
  33    0000.0c07.ac03    DYNAMIC    Et0/1
SW2#
SW2# show mac address-table | include 0000.0c07.ac21
```

```
   33    0000.0c07.ac21    DYNAMIC       Et0/0
SW2#

SW2# show cdp neighbors
Capability Codes: R - Router, T - Trans Bridge, B - Source Route Bridge
                  S - Switch, H - Host, I - IGMP, r - Repeater, P - Phone,
                  D - Remote, C - CVTA, M - Two-port Mac Relay


Device ID          Local Intrfce      Holdtme   Capability  Platform     Port ID
R2.cisco.com       Eth 0/1            154                R  Linux Uni    Eth 1/1
R1.cisco.com       Eth 0/0            160                R  Linux Uni    Eth 1/1
SW2#
```

Example 7-31 also shows the output of the **show cdp neighbors** command we tried on the ASW2 switch. Router R2 connects to ASW2's Ethernet 0/1, and router R1 connects to ASW2's Ethernet 0/0 interface. We conclude that the aforementioned MAC addresses, claiming the duplicate IP address, belong to routers R2 and R1. According to CDP, both routers are connected to the ASW2 switch through their Ethernet 1/1 interfaces.

As the next step in troubleshooting, we can display the configuration of Ethernet 1/1 interface on routers R1 and R2. Example 7-32 shows that routers R1 and R2 are configured with Hot Standby Router Protocol (HSRP) on these interfaces, but there seems to be some HSRP configuration discrepancies.

Example 7-32   *Information Gathering: Examine the Configuration on R1 and R2*

```
R1# show running-config interface ethernet 1/1
Building configuration...


Current configuration : 154 bytes
!
interface Ethernet1/1
 ip address 10.0.33.2 255.255.255.0
 standby 3 preempt
 standby 33 ip 10.0.33.1
 standby 33 priority 110
 standby 33 preempt
end


R1#



R2# show running-config interface ethernet 1/1
Building configuration...


Current configuration : 131 bytes
!
```

```
interface Ethernet1/1
 ip address 10.0.33.3 255.255.255.0
 standby 3 ip 10.0.33.1
 standby 3 priority 90
 standby 3 preempt
end

R2#
```

We need to gather more information about HSRP on routers R1 and R2. So, we use the **show standby** command on routers R1 and R2. The output shown in Example 7-33 reveals that the HSRP virtual MAC address for the standby group 33 on R1 is 0000.0c07.ac21, and the HSRP virtual MAC address for the standby group 3 on R2 is 0000.0c07.ac03. These are the two MAC addresses that claimed the duplicate IP address under our investigation. HSRP Version 1's virtual MAC address is 0000.0c07.acXX, where XX is the hexadecimal equivalent to the HSRP group number in decimal.

Example 7-33 *Information Gathering: Further Investigate HSRP on R1 and R2*

```
R1# show standby
< ...Output Omitted... >
Ethernet1/1 - Group 33
  State is Active
    2 state changes, last state change 00:08:43
  Virtual IP address is 10.0.33.1
  Active virtual MAC address is 0000.0c07.ac21
    Local virtual MAC address is 0000.0c07.ac21 (v1 default)
  Hello time 3 sec, hold time 10 sec
    Next hello sent in 1.776 secs
  Preemption enabled
  Active router is local
  Standby router is unknown
  Priority 110 (configured 110)
  Group name is "hsrp-Et1/1-33" (default)
< ...Output Omitted... >
R1#



R2# show standby
< ...Output Omitted... >
Ethernet1/1 - Group 3
  State is Active
    2 state changes, last state change 00:10:12
  Virtual IP address is 10.0.33.1
  Active virtual MAC address is 0000.0c07.ac03
    Local virtual MAC address is 0000.0c07.ac03 (v1 default)
```

```
  Hello time 3 sec, hold time 10 sec
    Next hello sent in 2.480 secs
  Preemption enabled
  Active router is local
  Standby router is unknown
  Priority 90 (configured 90)
  Group name is "hsrp-Et1/1-3" (default)
< ...Output Omitted... >
R2#
```

Analyzing the Information and Proposing a Hypothesis

The configuration of HSRP on the Ethernet 1/1 interface of routers R1 and R2 (shown in Example 7-32) revealed that the HSRP group number on R1 is 33, but the HSRP group number on R2 is 3. The routers are not participating in the same HSRP group; therefore, they cannot use the same virtual IP address (10.0.33.1). If they are meant to belong to the same HSRP group, we need to change the group number on one of the routers. Because the IP address 10.0.33.1 belongs to VLAN 33, keeping the group 33 on R1 (and deleting a reference to group 3 on it) and changing the group 3 to 33 on R2 forms our proposed hypothesis. Note that the HSRP group number does not have to match the VLAN number, but it is a good practice.

Testing the Hypothesis and Solving the Problem

As shown in Example 7-34, we first delete the line in router R1's Ethernet 1/1 configuration that makes a reference to HSRP standby group 3. Next, we delete all references to standby group 3 on router R2's Ethernet 1/1 configuration and replace them all with standby group 33.

Example 7-34 *Testing the Hypothesis: Correct the HSRP Configuration*

```
R1# conf term
Enter configuration commands, one per line.  End with CNTL/Z.
R1(config)# interface ethernet 1/1
R1(config-if)# no standby 3 preempt
R1(config-if)#
*Aug 27 02:01:54.440: %IP-4-DUPADDR: Duplicate address 10.0.33.1 on Ethernet1/1,
sourced by 0000.0c07.ac03
R1(config-if)# end
R1# wr
Building configuration...
[OK]
R1# show running-config  interface ethernet 1/1
Building configuration...

Current configuration : 135 bytes
```

```
!
interface Ethernet1/1
 ip address 10.0.33.2 255.255.255.0
 standby 33 ip 10.0.33.1
 standby 33 priority 110
 standby 33 preempt
end


R1#



R2# conf term
Enter configuration commands, one per line.  End with CNTL/Z.
R2(config)# interface ethernet 1/1
R2(config-if)# no standby 3 ip 10.0.33.1
R2(config-if)# no standby 3 priority 90
R2(config-if)# no standby 3 preempt
R2(config-if)# standby 33 ip 10.0.33.1
R2(config-if)# standby 33 priority 90
R2(config-if)# standby 33 preempt
R2(config-if)# end
*Aug 27 02:05:09.796: %SYS-5-CONFIG_I: Configured from console by console
R2# wr
Building configuration...
[OK]
R2#
```

After the corrections were made in routers R1 and R2, the duplicate IP address messages never appeared again, and the problem seems to be correctly diagnosed and resolved. We can now document our findings and corrections and notify Donovan of our work and results.

Troubleshooting HSRP

The following are some possible configuration errors with respect to HSRP:

- Error in HSRP group configuration leads to the duplicate IP address problem, as demonstrated in the preceding troubleshooting ticket.

- If HSRP virtual IP addresses are configured differently, you will receive appropriate log messages. With such configuration, when the active router fails, the standby router takes over with a virtual IP address that differs from the default gateway address configured on end devices.

- HSRP authentication can ensure that there is no rogue HSRP router in the network. Incorrect configuration of the HSRP authentication is also informed through log messages.

- HSRP for IPv4 has Versions 1 and 2. If there is a version mismatch, both routers will become active. This results in duplicate IP addresses, too.

- If a wrong HSRP group is configured on the peers, both peers become active. This will also manifest as a duplicate IP address problem.

- HSRP Versions 1 and 2 are not compatible.

You can solve most of the HSRP configuration problems by checking the output of the **show standby** command. In the output, you can view the active IP and the MAC address, timers, the active router, and several other parameters. HSRP messages are sent to multicast IP address 224.0.0.2 and UDP port 1985 in Version 1 and multicast IP address 224.0.0.10 and UDP port 1985 in Version 2. These IP addresses and ports need to be permitted by access lists. If the packets are blocked, the peers will not receive each other's messages, and there will be no HSRP redundancy. Besides configuration errors, the duplicate IP address problem can be the result of STP loops, EtherChannel configuration errors, or duplicated frames. Constant HSRP state changes could be the result of network performance problems, application timeouts, connectivity disruption, link flapping, and hardware issues. In some cases, Hello and the Hold timer adjustment alleviates the problems.

TINC Garbage Disposal Trouble Ticket 3

TINC Garbage Disposal has recently made some changes to their network. They have contacted SECHNIK Networking to seek assistance with certain network problems they have been experiencing ever since those changes. Their list mentions three specific items:

- Users of PC1 and PC2 can only access the Internet sporadically. Most of the pings from these PCs fail. This issue needs to be resolved as soon as possible. Use the IP address 209.165.201.225 to test Internet connectivity.

- Donovan, the network engineer, was assigned to migrate the network's first-hop redundancy protocol from Cisco proprietary HSRP to the industry-standard Virtual Router Redundancy Protocol (VRRP). Donovan believes that the job is complete, but he needs help finding out why both routers R1 and R2 are in Master state within VLAN 33.

- Donovan connected a new switch (ASW4) to ASW3. Because a lot of traffic is expected to go between the two switches, Donovan decided to make use of two links and bundle them using the EtherChannel technology, but the EtherChannel bundle is not functioning. For some undisclosed reasons, the ASW4 switch is not accessible to us.

Troubleshooting Sporadic Internet Connectivity Problem Experienced by Users of PC1 and PC2

It has been reported to us that users of PC1 and PC2 have sporadic access to the Internet. We have been asked to resolve this issue so that Internet access is solid and reliable (with redundancy). We need to verify the problem, define the problem, and make a trouble-shooting plan to fix the problem.

Verifying and Defining the Problem

As the first step, we accessed PC1 and PC2, and tried to ping to the Internet server address (209.165.201.225) that we were given. As Example 7-35 shows, the ping is unsuccessful from both PCs. Note that half of the echo requests timed out ("." is a ping timeout) and the other half are unreachable ("U" is ping *unreachable*).

Example 7-35 *Verifying the Problem: Try Internet Access from PC1 and PC2*

```
PC1> ping 209.165.201.225
Type escape sequence to abort.
Sending 5, 100-byte ICMP Echos to 209.165.201.225, timeout is 2 seconds:
.U.U.
Success rate is 0 percent (0/5)
PC1>


PC2> ping 209.165.201.225
Type escape sequence to abort.
Sending 5, 100-byte ICMP Echos to 209.165.201.225, timeout is 2 seconds:
U.U.U
Success rate is 0 percent (0/5)
PC2>
```

Based on the observation that half of the echo requests sent from PC1 and PC2 time out and the other half are unreachable, it is logical to consider that the packets are taking different paths; nevertheless, both paths are dysfunctional. Before we define the problem, we need to determine whether other PCs can reach the Internet. This is a swap-the-component technique that can shed some light on the situation at hand. We tried to ping the same server from PC3 and PC4, and to our surprise, the results were identical to the results we had with PC1 and PC2. We now know that the problem is more general than first thought; the Internet is not reachable from any PC within the TINC network. The problem is defined, and accordingly, we can take the follow-the-path approach to narrow down where the path of the packet to the Internet fails.

Gathering Information

Because routers R1 and R2 are considered the redundant gateways for the PCs within TINC's network, we start our information gathering on those routers.

Example 7-36 shows that pinging 206.165.201.225 from R1 fails also. R1's routing table shows the default route with two paths, both learned through OSPF (E2). Of the two paths, one has 10.0.11.111 as the next hop reachable out of interface Ethernet 1/0.11 (VLAN 11), and the other has 10.0.10.26 as the next hop reachable out of interface Ethernet 0/3. The address 10.0.10.26 belongs to GW1, but the address 10.0.11.111 is unknown (in VLAN 11) and is reachable out of Ethernet 1/0.11 toward access switch ASW1.

Example 7-36   *Information Gathering: Examining R1's Routing Table*

```
R1# ping 209.165.201.225
Type escape sequence to abort.
Sending 5, 100-byte ICMP Echos to 209.165.201.225, timeout is 2 seconds:
U.U.U
Success rate is 0 percent (0/5)
R1#
R1# show ip route
< ...output omitted... >
Gateway of last resort is 10.0.11.111 to network 0.0.0.0

O*E2  0.0.0.0/0 [110/1] via 10.0.11.111, 00:04:45, Ethernet1/0.11
                  [110/1] via 10.0.10.26, 00:04:45, Ethernet0/3
< ...output omitted... >
R1#
```

Example 7-37 shows R2's routing table, and it, too, shows the default route with two paths, both learned through OSPF (E2). We do not expect two default route paths. Of the two paths, one has 10.0.11.111 as the next hop reachable out of interface Ethernet 1/0.11 (VLAN 11), and the other has 10.0.10.30 as the next hop reachable out of interface Ethernet 0/3. The address 10.0.10.30 belongs to GW2, but the address 10.0.11.111 is unknown (in VLAN 11) and is reachable out of Ethernet 1/0.11 toward access switch ASW1.

Example 7-37   *Information Gathering: Examining R2's Routing Table*

```
R2# show ip route
< ...output omitted... >

Gateway of last resort is 10.0.11.111 to network 0.0.0.0

O*E2  0.0.0.0/0 [110/1] via 10.0.11.111, 00:38:37, Ethernet1/0.11
                  [110/1] via 10.0.10.30, 00:37:15, Ethernet0/3
< ...output omitted... >
R2#
```

Next, we try traceroute from R1 and R2 to the 209.165.201.225 address to confirm usage of the two default route paths in the routing table. As shown in Example 7-38, packets that are sent from R1 to 10.0.10.26 (GW1) arrive at their destination in two hops, but the packets sent from R1 to 10.0.11.111 (unknown) have the letter H (indicating host unreachable). Example 7-38 shows the results for R1; the results for R2 are similar to R1.

Example 7-38   *Information Gathering: Traceroute from R1 to 209.165.201.225*

```
R1# trace 209.165.201.225
Type escape sequence to abort.
Tracing the route to 209.165.201.225
VRF info: (vrf in name/id, vrf out name/id)
  1 10.0.10.26 1 msec
    10.0.11.111 1 msec
    10.0.10.26 1 msec
  2 10.0.11.111 !H
    209.165.200.2 1 msec
    10.0.11.111 !H
R1#


R2# trace 209.165.201.225
Type escape sequence to abort.
Tracing the route to 209.165.201.225
VRF info: (vrf in name/id, vrf out name/id)
  1 10.0.10.30 0 msec
    10.0.11.111 1 msec
    10.0.10.30 0 msec
  2 10.0.11.111 !H
    209.165.201.6 1 msec
    10.0.11.111 !H
R2#
```

Analyzing Information and Proposing a Hypothesis

Based on the information we have gathered so far, routers R1 and R2 have two default route paths. The path to GW1 from R1 and the path to GW2 from R2 are legitimate, expected, and operational, but the second path for the default route using 10.0.11.111 is unexpected. Packets that take this second path are dropped and cannot reach the Internet.

We can propose the hypothesis that the second path for the default route is not legitimate and it is probably sourced by a rogue device. However, we must first identify the rogue device and find out where in our network it resides and what it connects to.

As shown in Example 7-39, we use the **show ip ospf neighbor** command on R1 and see a neighbor with the OSPF router ID 172.16.0.1 that we do not recognize. This device owns the address 10.0.11.111 and has formed a neighbor relationship with R1 through R1's Ethernet 1/0.11 interface.

Example 7-39   *Information Gathering: Discovering the Rogue OSPF Device*

```
R1# show ip ospf neighbor


Neighbor ID    Pri    State         Dead Time    Address        Interface
10.0.1.9        1     FULL/DR       00:00:39     10.0.44.3      Ethernet1/2
10.0.1.9        1     FULL/DR       00:00:39     10.0.33.3      Ethernet1/1
10.0.1.9        1     FULL/DR       00:00:37     10.0.22.3      Ethernet1/0.22
10.0.1.9        1     FULL/BDR      00:00:35     10.0.11.3      Ethernet1/0.11
172.16.0.1      1     FULL/DR       00:00:35     10.0.11.111    Ethernet1/0.11
10.0.1.10       1     FULL/BDR      00:00:31     10.0.10.26     Ethernet0/3
10.0.1.9        1     FULL/DR       00:00:32     10.0.10.22     Ethernet0/0
R1# ping 10.0.11.111
Type escape sequence to abort.
Sending 5, 100-byte ICMP Echos to 10.0.11.111, timeout is 2 seconds:
!!!!!
Success rate is 100 percent (5/5), round-trip min/avg/max = 1/1/1 ms
```

Next, we ping the address 10.0.11.111 of the rogue device from R1 and immediately display R1's Address Resolution Protocol (ARP) table to discover the MAC address corresponding to 10.0.11.111. The MAC address is aabb.cc00.a600. As you see in Example 7-40, we then examine ASW1's MAC address table to find out which interface on ASW1 the rogue device is plugged into. The MAC address aabb.cc00.a600 is learned on interface Ethernet 2/0.

Example 7-40   *Information Gathering: Discovering the Rogue OSPF Device*

```
R1# ping 10.0.11.111
Type escape sequence to abort.
Sending 5, 100-byte ICMP Echos to 10.0.11.111, timeout is 2 seconds:
!!!!!
Success rate is 100 percent (5/5), round-trip min/avg/max = 1/1/1 ms
R1#
R1# show arp
Protocol  Address          Age (min)  Hardware Addr   Type    Interface
< ...output omitted... >
Internet  10.0.11.3            51     aabb.cc00.a101  ARPA    Ethernet1/0.11
Internet  10.0.11.111          49     aabb.cc00.a600  ARPA    Ethernet1/0.11
Internet  10.0.11.128          49     aabb.cc00.5200  ARPA    Ethernet1/0.11
< ...output omitted... >
R1#



SW1# show mac address-table
         Mac Address Table
-------------------------------------------
```

```
  Vlan    Mac Address       Type        Ports
  ----    -----------       --------    -----
    11    0000.5e00.0101    DYNAMIC     Et0/0
    11    aabb.cc00.5200    DYNAMIC     Et0/2
    11    aabb.cc00.9e01    DYNAMIC     Et0/0
    11    aabb.cc00.a101    DYNAMIC     Et0/1
    11    aabb.cc00.a600    DYNAMIC     Et2/0
    22    0000.5e00.0102    DYNAMIC     Et0/0
    22    aabb.cc00.8f00    DYNAMIC     Et0/3
    22    aabb.cc00.9e01    DYNAMIC     Et0/0
    22    aabb.cc00.a101    DYNAMIC     Et0/1
     1    aabb.cc00.9e01    DYNAMIC     Et0/0
     1    aabb.cc00.a101    DYNAMIC     Et0/1
Total Mac Addresses for this criterion: 11
SW1#
```

Testing the Hypothesis and Solving the Problem

Based on our hypothesis, if we shut down the interface Ethernet 2/0 of ASW1, the rogue device is shut out of the network and will not be able to inject invalid OSPF routes into the network any more. As shown in Example 7-41, after we shut down interface Ethernet 2/0 of switch ASW1, the second path for the default route disappeared from the R1 routing table.

Example 7-41   *Testing the Hypothesis: Shut Down Interface Ethernet 2/0 on ASW1*

```
SW1#
SW1# conf term
Enter configuration commands, one per line.  End with CNTL/Z.
SW1(config)# int ethernet 2/0
SW1(config-if)# shut
SW1(config-if)# end
SW1#



R1# show ip route
< ...output omitted... >


Gateway of last resort is 10.0.10.26 to network 0.0.0.0

O*E2  0.0.0.0/0 [110/1] via 10.0.10.26, 00:25:10, Ethernet0/3
      10.0.0.0/8 is variably subnetted, 18 subnets, 3 masks
C         10.0.1.8/32 is directly connected, Loopback0

< ...output omitted... >


R1#
```

We can now test Internet reachability from PC1 and PC2. Example 7-42 shows that we can successfully ping the address 209.165.201.225. The problem is solved.

Example 7-42   *Solving the Problem: PC1 and PC2 Can Reach the Internet Now*

```
PC1# ping 209.165.201.225
Type escape sequence to abort.
Sending 5, 100-byte ICMP Echos to 209.165.201.225, timeout is 2 seconds:
!!!!!
Success rate is 100 percent (5/5), round-trip min/avg/max = 1/1/1 ms
PC1#


PC2# ping 209.165.201.225
Type escape sequence to abort.
Sending 5, 100-byte ICMP Echos to 209.165.201.225, timeout is 2 seconds:
!!!!!
Success rate is 100 percent (5/5), round-trip min/avg/max = 1/1/1 ms
PC2#
```

Even though we solved the problem, it is important to learn the following from this experience and make appropriate recommendations to TINC Garbage Disposal:

- Unused interfaces on access switches must be shut down. This stops rogue devices plugged into available jacks from connecting to your network and causing damage.

- Make use of authentication for control plane protocols such as OSPF. This stops rogue devices from forming relationships with your network devices and injecting routes into your network.

- Routing protocols should be put in Passive state on interfaces where neighbors are not expected.

We must now complete the documentation and inform Donovan at TINC Garbage Disposal and any other party involved that the problem is solved.

Troubleshooting Erroneous Routing Information

Building accurate routing and forwarding tables depends on the exchange of routing information, sourced by routing devices in the network. If those devices are compromised or configured incorrectly, they can negatively affect or disrupt the network operation. Any unauthorized participation in the routing process should be prevented; it is essential to know and control the sources of routing information. Incorrect routing information can be sourced from

- Illegitimate devices participating in the process

- Legitimate devices sourcing incorrect information

Securing the network infrastructure as a whole entails securing all layers and devices within the network. Physical access limitations should be in place. On access devices such as switches, all unused interfaces should be shut down and removed from the default VLAN 1; preferably, unused interfaces should be assigned to an unused VLAN that is in Showdown state (also called Suspended).

Additional security configuration such as port security should be enabled on access switch edge interfaces. Access to management functions of all devices should always be restricted. In addition to these measures, the routing functions and protocols (control plane) should also be secured. It is possible to restrict the peer relations only to trusted sources, control the extent of the message exchange, and verify the integrity of the information exchanged.

Most routing protocols require the establishment of specific relationships or sessions before exchange of routing information. Peer discovery mechanisms are automatic by default (except for BGP) and operate under the assumption that the peers are legitimate/trusted devices. Manual neighbor configuration and neighbor authentication help avoidance of unwanted peers.

Explicit configuration of routing peers is an option with some routing protocols, but it is mandatory with BGP. (Dynamic BGP neighbor discovery is possible, but it is rarely allowed or used.) If you want to have strict control over peering relations, disable the automatic peer discovery mechanisms. All the neighbors of the device should then be explicitly configured. In the case of OSPF and EIGRP, the protocols behave differently when the peer is configured manually. For example, when the neighbor is configured manually, EIGRP messages are exchanged using unicast packets, and packets are accepted only from manually configured neighbors. This does not hold true for OSPF.

Neighbor authentication is supported for BGP, Intermediate System-to-Intermediate System (IS-IS) Protocol, OSPF, RIPv2, and EIGRP. Neighbor authentication provides for source authentication and message integrity checks. It is applied to the peer establishment and routing update messages. Most routing protocols support two types of authentication: plain-text and message digest 5 (MD5) authentication. Because MD5 is more secure, it is recommended as the preferred authentication method. The following are the authentication options for currently used IPv4 routing protocols:

- **OSPF:** Authentication can be enabled for the whole OSPF area, or on an interface-by-interface basis.

- **EIGRP and RIPv2:** Authentication is enabled in interface configuration mode. Cisco EIGRP makes use of a key chain for authentication.

- **BGP:** Neighbor authentication is configured in the router configuration mode for each neighbor individually. It is possible to use the same pre-shared key for all neighbors or to configure a different key for each neighbor

Routing information exchange should be limited only to the network segments where legitimate peers are expected. To exclude segments from routing information exchange, in the router configuration mode make use of the **passive-interface** command. You can also issue the **passive-interface default** command. This command treats all the interfaces that are configured to participate in the routing process as passive. Therefore, interfaces that are supposed to exchange routing information should be explicitly configured to do so using the **no passive-interface** command. Both commands are used in the router configuration mode.

Troubleshooting Multiple Masters within a VRRP

Donovan, at TINC, believes that he has successfully migrated his first-hop gateways (routers R1 and R2) from HSRP to VRRP on all VLANs. However, he needs help with VLAN 33 (IP subnet 10.0.33.0/24), where he says that both routers are in Master state.

Verifying and Defining the Problem

Using the **show vrrp brief** command on routers R1 and R2, as shown in Example 7-43, we see that with respect to VRRP group 3 both R1 and R2 are in Master state. This verifies that the problem exists and it needs to be corrected.

Example 7-43 *Verifying the Problem: R1 and R2 Are Both in Master State*

```
R1# show vrrp brief
Interface      Grp  Pri  Time  Own Pre State   Master addr    Group addr
Et1/0.11        1   100  3609   Y  Master    10.0.11.2      10.0.11.1
Et1/0.22        2   110  3570   Y  Master    10.0.22.2      10.0.22.1
Et1/1           3   110  3570   Y  Master    10.0.33.2      10.0.33.1
Et1/2           4   110  3570   Y  Master    10.0.44.2      10.0.44.1
R1#



R2# show vrrp brief
Interface      Grp Pri  Time  Own Pre State   Master addr    Group addr
Et1/0.11        1   90  3648   Y  Backup    10.0.11.2      10.0.11.1
Et1/0.22        2   90  3648   Y  Backup    10.0.22.2      10.0.22.1
Et1/1           3   90  3648   Y  Master    10.0.33.3      10.0.33.1
Et1/2           4   90  3648   Y  Backup    10.0.44.2      10.0.44.1
R2#
```

The problem definition is simple: Routers R1 and R2, through their Ethernet 1/1 interfaces, are configured for VRRP group 3 on VLAN 33 (IP subnet 10.0.33.0/24). Even though only one of the two routers is supposed to take on the Master role in the group, they both show as Master on the output of the **show vrrp brief** command.

In this case, the problem is already narrowed down for us; therefore, we can start information gathering about VRRP configuration on R1 and R2 routers right away. Moreover, because VRRP is configured in other subnets (VLANS), where it appears to be functioning properly, it makes sense for us to make use of the spot-the-difference technique.

Gathering Information

We can start information gathering on routers R1 and R2 using the **show vrrp interface ethernet 1/1** command. Example 7-44 shows the output of this command on both routers. The output shows that the routers R1 and R2 are configured differently for authentication within VRRP group 3 on interface Ethernet 1/1. R1 is configured for clear text, and R2 is configured for MD5 authentication.

Example 7-44 *Information Gathering: Obtain VRRP Information on Ethernet 1/1*

```
R1# show vrrp interface ethernet 1/1
Ethernet1/1 - Group 3
  State is Master
  Virtual IP address is 10.0.33.1
  Virtual MAC address is 0000.5e00.0103
  Advertisement interval is 1.000 sec
  Preemption enabled
  Priority is 110
  Authentication text, string "c1sc0"
  Master Router is 10.0.33.2 (local), priority is 110
  Master Advertisement interval is 1.000 sec
  Master Down interval is 3.570 sec
R1#


R2# show vrrp interface ethernet 1/1
Ethernet1/1 - Group 3
  State is Master
  Virtual IP address is 10.0.33.1
  Virtual MAC address is 0000.5e00.0103
  Advertisement interval is 1.000 sec
  Preemption enabled
  Priority is 90
  Authentication MD5, key-string
  Master Router is 10.0.33.3 (local), priority is 90
  Master Advertisement interval is 1.000 sec
  Master Down interval is 3.648 sec
R2#
```

Routers R1 and R2 cannot engage in the election process while they cannot authenticate each other's messages. Therefore, it is best to make use of the spot-the-difference technique, and inspect their configurations on the other VRRG groups. Example 7-45 shows the output of the **show vrrp** command we tried on router R1. As you can see, R1 is configured for MD5 authentication in all VRRP groups, except for VRRP group 3.

Example 7-45 *Information Gathering: Inspect Other VRRP Group Authentication Methods*

```
R1# show vrrp
Ethernet1/0.11 - Group 1
< ...output omitted... >
  Authentication MD5, key-string
< ...output omitted... >
Ethernet1/0.22 - Group 2
< ...output omitted... >
  Authentication MD5, key-string
< ...output omitted... >
Ethernet1/1 - Group 3
< ...output omitted... >
  Authentication text, string "c1sc0"
< ...output omitted... >
  Ethernet1/2 - Group 4
< ...output omitted... >
  Authentication MD5, key-string
< ...output omitted... >
R1#
```

Analyzing the Information and Proposing a Hypothesis

R1 and R2 are configured with MD5 authentication for all VRRP groups; the exception is that R1 is configured for clear-text authentication for VRRP group 3. Within VRRP group 3, because R1 and R2 cannot authenticate each other's messages, they both assume the VRRP Master role.

Based on the information gathered, it appears that R1's clear-text authentication for VRRP group 3 is an error. After verifying that this assumption is indeed true, we can propose that modifying R1's authentication (to MD5) for VRRP group 3 will fix the problem.

Testing the Hypothesis, and Solving the Problem

Example 7-46 shows that we first removed authentication for VRRP group 3 from the Ethernet 1/1 interface on both routers (R1 and R2). We then enabled MD5 authentication on the Ethernet 1/1 interfaces of both routers with a common pre-shared key.

Example 7-46 *Testing a Hypothesis: Modify Authentication Method to MD5*

```
R1# config term
Enter configuration commands, one per line.  End with CNTL/Z.
R1(config)# interface ethernet 1/1
R1(config-if)# no vrrp 3 authentication
```

```
R1(config-if)# vrrp 3 authentication md5 key-string C1sc0ROX
R1(config-if)# end
R1# wr
Building configuration...
[OK]
R1#


R2# config term
Enter configuration commands, one per line.  End with CNTL/Z.
R2(config)# interface ethernet 1/1
R2(config-if)# no vrrp 3 authentication
R2(config-if)# vrrp 3 authentication md5 key-string C1sc0ROX
R2(config-if)# end
R2# wr
Building configuration...
[OK]
R2#
```

Following implementation of the proposed hypothesis, we display the status of all VRRP groups on routers R1 and R2. The results, as shown in Example 7-47, are positive. R1, because of its higher priority of 110, is elected as the Master; R2, with its VRRP priority of 90, is acting as Backup within VRRP group 3. The problem seems to be solved.

Example 7-47 *Solving the Problem: Only the Router with Higher VRRP Priority Is Elected as Master*

```
R1# show vrrp brief
Interface        Grp Pri Time    Own Pre State   Master addr     Group addr
Et1/0.11         1   100 3609    Y   Master      10.0.11.2       10.0.11.1
Et1/0.22         2   110 3570    Y   Master      10.0.22.2       10.0.22.1
Et1/1            3   110 3570    Y   Master      10.0.33.2       10.0.33.1
Et1/2            4   110 3570    Y   Master      10.0.44.2       10.0.44.1
R1#


R2# show vrrp brief
Interface        Grp Pri Time    Own Pre State   Master addr     Group addr
Et1/0.11         1   90  3648    Y   Backup      10.0.11.2       10.0.11.1
Et1/0.22         2   90  3648    Y   Backup      10.0.22.2       10.0.22.1
Et1/1            3   90  3648    Y   Backup      10.0.33.2       10.0.33.1
Et1/2            4   90  3648    Y   Backup      10.0.44.2       10.0.44.1
R2#
```

We must document our work and notify Donovan and any other party involved that the problem is solved.

Troubleshooting VRRP

When troubleshooting VRRP, consider the following configuration errors:

- The VRRP group virtual IP address may be configured incorrectly.

- The VRRP group number may be configured incorrectly.

- The VRRP group members may have authentication discrepancies.

- The VRRP group members may have advertisement timer discrepancies.

- The VRRP messages may be erroneously blocked by ACLs.

The following commands can prove useful in diagnosing VRRP-related issues:

- Use the **show vrrp brief** command to get a concise overview of the VRRP groups and their basic parameters.

- Use the **show vrrp interface** command to view VRRP groups on a specific interface.

- Use the **debug vrrp all** command to display debugging messages for VRRP errors, events, and state transitions.

- Use the **debug vrrp authentication**, **debug vrrp error**, and **debug vrrp state** commands to see debug messages specifically related to MD5 authentication, error conditions, and status transitions.

- Use the **debug vrrp packets** and **debug vrrp events** commands to view summary information about the sent and the received packets and VRRP events.

Troubleshooting EtherChannel Between ASW4 and ASW3

Donovan has reported to us that he has tried to set up an EtherChannel connection between switch ASW3 and a new switch ASW4 (not in the TINC network diagram). According to Donovan, the EtherChannel he tried to set up is not functioning properly, and he needs assistance. Unfortunately, we (employees of SECHNIK Networking) have no access to the new access switch ASW4.

Verifying the Problem

Because we do not have access to switch ASW4, we can verify the problem by examining switch ASW3 only. As shown in Example 7-48, we tried the **show etherchannel summary** command on switch ASW3. The output displays two interfaces (Eth2/0 and Eth2/1) as the members (ports) of this EtherChannel group. However, the interface Eth2/0 is reported as suspended (see small letter *s* in parentheses). Example 7-48 also shows no protocol for EtherChannel; this means that neither Port Aggregation Protocol (PAgP) nor Link Aggregation Control Protocol (LACP) is in use.

Example 7-48 *Verifying the Problem: Assess the EtherChannel Status on ASW3*

```
SW3# show etherchannel summary
Flags:  D - down        P - bundled in port-channel
        I - stand-alone s - suspended
        H - Hot-standby (LACP only)
        R - Layer3       S - Layer2
        U - in use       N - not in use, no aggregation
        f - failed to allocate aggregator

        M - not in use, no aggregation due to minimum links not met
        m - not in use, port not aggregated due to minimum links not met
        u - unsuitable for bundling
        d - default port

        w - waiting to be aggregated
Number of channel-groups in use: 1
Number of aggregators:           1


Group  Port-channel  Protocol    Ports
------+-------------+-----------+---------------------------------------------
1      Po1(SU)          -        Et2/0(s)       Et2/1(P)

SW3#
```

Defining the Problem

In addition to verifying the problem, we have also learned that the interface Ethernet 2/0 is suspended. This means that some characteristics of this interface do not match to that of other interfaces in the EtherChannel bundle. We can define the problem as EtherChannel connection between switches ASW3 and ASW4 down due to configuration mismatch between ASW3 Ethernet 2/0 and Ethernet 2/1 interfaces.

Gathering Information

Now that the problem is well defined, we must gather information directly about the EtherChannel configuration on ASW3. Example 7-49 shows the output of the **show etherchannel 1** command on switch ASW3. The output notifies us that the probable reason for interface Ethernet 2/0 being suspended is that DTP (Dynamic Trunking Protocol) mode is off but Ethernet 2/1's DTP mode is on.

Example 7-49   *Gathering Information: Discover the Reason for Interface Ethernet 2/0 Being Suspended*

```
SW3# show etherchannel 1 detail
Group state = L2
Ports: 2    Maxports = 8
Port-channels: 1 Max Port-channels = 1
Protocol:     -
Minimum Links: 0
                Ports in the group:
                -------------------
Port: Et2/0
------------

Port state      = Up Cnt-bndl Suspend Not-in-Bndl
Channel group = 1              Mode = On      Gcchange = -
Port-channel  = null           GC    =    -      Pseudo port-channel = Po1
Port index    = 0              Load = 0x00     Protocol =     -
Age of the port in the current state: 0d:00h:02m:39s
Probable reason: dtp mode of Et2/0 is off, Et2/1 is on


Port: Et2/1
------------

Port state      = Up Mstr In-Bndl
Channel group = 1              Mode = On      Gcchange = -
Port-channel  = Po1            GC    =    -      Pseudo port-channel = Po1
Port index    = 0              Load = 0x00     Protocol =     -
Age of the port in the current state: 0d:00h:02m:35s


< ...output omitted...>

SW3#
```

To confirm the information about the DTP mode mismatch between Ethernet 2/0 and Ethernet 2/1 interfaces, we tried the **show interface** command (with the **switchport** option) on these interfaces. Example 7-50 shows the output, which reveals that Ethernet 2/0 is administratively and operationally configured for static access mode. In contrast, Ethernet 2/1 is administratively and operationally configured for 802.1Q trunking with all VLANs allowed and VLAN 1 as the native VLAN.

Example 7-50   *Gathering Information: Confirm Configuration Discrepancy Between the EtherChannel Bundle Members*

```
SW3# show interface ethernet 2/0 switchport
Name: Et2/0
Switchport: Enabled
Administrative Mode: static access
```

```
Operational Mode: static access (suspended member of bundle Po1)


< ...output omitted... >


SW3#



SW3# show interface ethernet 2/1 switchport
Name: Et2/1
Switchport: Enabled
Administrative Mode: trunk
Operational Mode: trunk (member of bundle Po1)


< ...output omitted... >


SW3#
```

Proposing a Hypothesis and Testing the Hypothesis

Because Donovan requires the EtherChannel link between switches ASW3 and ASW4 to be trunking, our proposed hypothesis is to change the configuration on ASW3's Ethernet 2/0 interface to **switchport mode trunk**. This change, shown in Example 7-51, would make this interface consistent with interface Ethernet 2/1. As you can see, we shut down both interfaces and configured them both with the required commands before doing **no shutdown** to bring them up together.

Example 7-51 *Testing the Hypothesis: Configuring Ethernet 2/0 for Trunking*

```
SW3# conf term
Enter configuration commands, one per line.  End with CNTL/Z.
SW3(config)# interface range ethernet 2/0-1
SW3(config-if-range)# shutdown

*Aug 31 21:57:01.891: %LINK-3-UPDOWN: Interface Port-channel1, changed state to down
*Aug 31 21:57:01.899: %LINEPROTO-5-UPDOWN: Line protocol on Interface Port-channel1,
  changed state to down
*Aug 31 21:57:03.875: %LINK-5-CHANGED: Interface Ethernet2/0, changed state to
  administratively down
*Aug 31 21:57:03.875: %LINK-5-CHANGED: Interface Ethernet2/1, changed state to
  administratively down
*Aug 31 21:57:04.879: %LINEPROTO-5-UPDOWN: Line protocol on Interface Ethernet2/0,
  changed state to down
*Aug 31 21:57:04.879: %LINEPROTO-5-UPDOWN: Line protocol on Interface Ethernet2/1,
  changed state to down

SW3(config-if-range)# switchport mode trunk
SW3(config-if-range)# switchport trunk encap dot1q
```

```
SW3(config-if-range)# channel-group 1 mode on
SW3(config-if-range)# no shutdown
SW3(config-if-range)# end


*Aug 31 21:59:14.203: %SYS-5-CONFIG_I: Configured from console by console
SW3# wr
Building configuration...


*Aug 31 21:59:14.367: %LINK-3-UPDOWN: Interface Ethernet2/0, changed state to up
*Aug 31 21:59:14.371: %LINK-3-UPDOWN: Interface Ethernet2/1, changed state to up
*Aug 31 21:59:15.371: %LINEPROTO-5-UPDOWN: Line protocol on Interface Ethernet2/0,
  changed state to up
*Aug 31 21:59:15.387: %LINK-3-UPDOWN: Interface Port-channel1, changed state to up
*Aug 31 21:59:15.391: %LINEPROTO-5-UPDOWN: Line protocol on Interface Port-channel1,
  changed state to up[OK]
*Aug 31 21:59:16.379: %LINEPROTO-5-UPDOWN: Line protocol on Interface Ethernet2/1,
  changed state to up


SW3#
```

Solving the Problem

After implementing the proposed change, we checked the status of the EtherChannel using the **show etherchannel summary** command. Example 7-52 shows the result with the PO1 (port channel 1) interface as switch port/up (SU) and both member interfaces successfully bundled in the port channel (P).

Example 7-52   *Solve the Problem:* **show etherchannel summary** *Reveals the Port Channel Interface Is In Operational State with Both Member Interfaces*

```
SW3# show etherchannel summary
Flags:  D - down        P - bundled in port-channel
        I - stand-alone s - suspended
        H - Hot-standby (LACP only)
        R - Layer3       S - Layer2
        U - in use       N - not in use, no aggregation
        f - failed to allocate aggregator

        M - not in use, no aggregation due to minimum links not met
        m - not in use, port not aggregated due to minimum links not met
        u - unsuitable for bundling
        d - default port

        w - waiting to be aggregated
Number of channel-groups in use: 1
Number of aggregators:           1
```

```
Group  Port-channel  Protocol    Ports
-------+-------------+-----------+----------------------------
1          Po1(SU)        -            Et2/0(P)      Et2/1(P)

SW3#
```

We must document our work and notify Donovan and any other party involved that the EtherChannel problem between ASW3 and the new switch AS4 is now fixed.

Troubleshooting EtherChannel

EtherChannel is a technology that bundles multiple physical Ethernet links (100 Mbps, 1 Gbps, 10 Gbps) into a single logical link and distributes the traffic across these links. This logical link is represented in Cisco IOS syntax as a port channel (PO) interface. Control protocols such as spanning tree or routing protocols interact only with this single port channel interface and not with the associated physical interfaces. Packets and frames are routed or switched to the port channel interface, and then a hashing mechanism determines which physical link will be used to transmit them.

The following characteristics must match among the interfaces that are members of an EtherChannel bundle:

- **Interface speed and duplex:** Use the **show interface** command to verify the interface speed and duplex.

- **Interface trunking mode and related VLANs:** Use the **show interface** command with the **switchport** option or **show running-config interface** *type number* command to verify trunking mode of an interface. The following must match: mode (access or trunk), VLAN number (for access interfaces), native VLAN, allowed VLANs, and encapsulation (for trunk interfaces).

- **switchport (Layer 2 interface) or no switchport (Layer 3 interface):** All the physical interfaces must be acting in the same layer; otherwise, EtherChannel will not form.

To achieve configuration consistency among the member interfaces, take advantage of the **interface range** command. Always verify the operational (that is, the negotiated) characteristics of the interfaces, and remind yourself that there are two sides to the link. The operational parameters of a port channel interface depend on the configurations of both sides. For example, it is possible for a link to be connected (up, up) even if there are duplex mismatches. Duplex mismatches on an operational link can be noted in the output of **show interface** *type number* and are indicated by a high number of packet errors. Once the EtherChannel is established, logical interface port channel is automatically created. Member interfaces can be further configured by using the logical interface configuration mode; configuration will apply to all physical interfaces in the channel. Therefore, using the port channel configuration mode makes it simpler to achieve VLAN consistency and configuration over the members of the aggregated link.

To check the status of the member interfaces and the logical channel interface, use the **show etherchannel summary** and **show etherchannel** *groupnumber* **detail** commands. In the output of the **show etherchannel summary** command, operational links are marked with the capital letter *P*, which stands for passive and signifies that the link is bundled to the port channel. Suspended links are marked with a small letter *s* in the output of the **show etherchannel summary** command or with the suspended port state in the output of the **show etherchannel** *groupnumber* **detail** command.

If one of the physical links changes its operational status in such a way that a mismatch with other physical links is created, this link will be suspended and removed from the EtherChannel bundle until consistency is restored. To check which distribution algorithm is configured for the channels, use the **show etherchannel load-balance** command, and for traffic statistics, use the **show etherchannel traffic** command. Finally, EtherChannel negotiation protocol must be the same for all the interfaces in the bundle. You cannot run two EtherChannel protocols in one EtherChannel bundle. You can configure the switch interface using one of the following three channel-establishment options:

- **Manual:** No protocol, statically configured channel

- **PAgP:** Port Aggregation Protocol, a Cisco proprietary link aggregation protocol

- **LACP:** Link Aggregation Control Protocol (standards based)

Use the **show etherchannel summary** or **show etherchannel** *group_number* **detail** command to verify the status of the channel and protocol of choice. In the output, under the column with the Protocol heading, dash (-) means manually set. Check the protocol mode of operation on all interfaces and on both devices. Only the following combinations of port channel modes make the port channel form successfully:

- **LACP:** Active-active and active-passive

- **PAgP:** Desirable-desirable and desirable-passive

- **With no protocol:** On-on

The on mode means that EtherChannel is established immediately, provided that all the physical interfaces have the same characteristics. There is no message exchange with the other side of the link. That means that the channel forms even if the other side is not configured to aggregate ports. In such situations, the other nonconfigured (mismatched) side considers physical interfaces as individual interfaces, and STP detects a loop and consequently brings the interface down, placing it in Err-Disabled state.

To check for misconfigurations use the **show etherchannel summary** command. Under Port-Channel, if you see the letter *D* (meaning down), the channel has not formed. Under the Ports column, the following letters can appear and have specific meanings:

- **I:** Means individual. When there is a protocol mismatch, a link is treated as an individual link and it does not join the channel group.

- **D:** Interfaces are disabled manually or by software.

It is a common misconception that the load sharing among the elements of an EtherChannel is balanced; that is not necessarily the case at all times. Frame and packet header fields such as destination MAC address, source MAC address, destination IP address, source IP address, and IP header protocol fields are used by the default EtherChannel load-sharing algorithm to calculate a hash value. In simple terms, modulo *n* of the hash value is then computed (where *n* is the number of elements in the EtherChannel bundle). The result assigns the frame to one of the physical elements of the EtherChannel bundle. The result is that frames that belong to the same flow are all assigned to the same element. However, we have no guarantee that flows will distribute between the elements evenly. To achieve better load balancing, consider experimenting with the slightly different options you have for EtherChannel load sharing. To check the distribution algorithm configured for the channels, use the **show etherchannel load-balance** command, and for traffic statistics, use the **show etherchannel traffic** command.

TINC Garbage Disposal Trouble Ticket 4

Donovan, the network support engineer at TINC Garbage Disposal, has contacted us (SECHNIK Networking) about a few new problems at their computer network. Three specific items readily need attention:

■ Donovan attended a networking technologies workshop and learned about benefits of Gateway Load Balancing Protocol (GLBP) over other first-hop redundancy protocols (FHRPs). With the goal of better utilizing the gateways uplinks, Donovan has migrated the FHRP on R1 and R2 from VRRP to GLBP. GLBP is working well on VLANs 33 and 44, but on VLAN 11, ever since the migration, clients report inconsistent and sporadic Internet connectivity from their workstations (PC1 and PC2).

■ Donovan is puzzled by a problem PC4 is experiencing. PC4 loses its IP connectivity at times; renewing its IP address lease seems to solve the problem. He wants to find a permanent solution for this problem.

■ Donovan reports that GW2 does not accept SSH sessions from PC4. GW2 is supposed to accept SSH sessions from PC4 and no other device. Donovan cannot identify the cause of this issue and needs assistance.

Donovan has given us permission to perform disruptive testing if necessary, and has asked us to test for Internet reachability using the IP address 209.165.201.255.

Troubleshooting Inconsistent and Sporadic Internet Connectivity Problem Experienced By Users of PC1 and PC2

Sporadic lack of Internet connectivity reported by users of PC1 and PC2 has apparently started ever since Donovan migrated the FHRP on routers R1 and R2 from VRRP to GLBP. However, there have been no complaints by the PC users that operate within VLANs 33 and 44.

Verifying and Defining the Problem

To verify the problem, we use PC1 and PC2 to ping the given IP address (209.165.201.225) on the Internet. As shown in Example 7-53, the ping from PC1 is successful, but it failed when tried from PC2.

Example 7-53   *Verifying the Problem: PC1 and PC2 Have Inconsistent and Sporadic Internet Connectivity*

```
PC1# ping 209.165.201.225
Type escape sequence to abort.
Sending 5, 100-byte ICMP Echos to 209.165.201.225, timeout is 2 seconds:
!!!!!
Success rate is 100 percent (5/5), round-trip min/avg/max = 1/202/1007 ms
PC1#


PC2# ping 209.165.201.225
Type escape sequence to abort.
Sending 5, 100-byte ICMP Echos to 209.165.201.225, timeout is 2 seconds:
.....
Success rate is 0 percent (0/5)
PC2#
```

Before confirming the problem and defining it, we decided to check the default gateway address on each PC and ping that address. Both PCs, as shown in Example 7-54, have the IP address 10.0.11.1 as their default gateway. However, although PC1 can successfully ping this address, PC2 has 0 percent success rate with the same task. When we displayed the ARP table on each PC, for the IP address 10.0.11.1 PC1 has 0007.b400.0102, whereas PC2 has 0007.b400.0101 in the ARP table. Both of these addresses are GLBP virtual MAC addresses for GLBP group 001. Note that the GLBP virtual MAC address has the format 0007.b40x.xxyy, where xxx is the GLBP group number and yy indicates the active virtual forwarder (AVF) number.

Example 7-54   *Verifying the Problem: PC1 Can Ping Its Default Gateway IP Address, but PC2 Cannot*

```
PC1#
PC1# show ip route
Default gateway is 10.0.11.1
Host              Gateway          Last Use   Total Uses  Interface
ICMP redirect cache is empty
PC1# ping 10.0.11.1
Type escape sequence to abort.
Sending 5, 100-byte ICMP Echos to 10.0.11.1, timeout is 2 seconds:
!!!!!
Success rate is 100 percent (5/5), round-trip min/avg/max = 1/1/1 ms
```

```
PC1#
PC1# show arp
Protocol  Address           Age (min)    Hardware Addr    Type    Interface
Internet  10.0.11.1          0            0007.b400.0102   ARPA    Ethernet0/0
Internet  10.0.11.129        -            aabb.cc00.1000   ARPA    Ethernet0/0
PC1#


PC2# show ip route
Default gateway is 10.0.11.1
Host             Gateway          Last Use    Total Uses  Interface
ICMP redirect cache is empty
PC2# ping 10.0.11.1
Type escape sequence to abort.
Sending 5, 100-byte ICMP Echos to 10.0.11.1, timeout is 2 seconds:
.....
Success rate is 0 percent (0/5)
PC2#
PC2# show arp
Protocol  Address           Age (min)    Hardware Addr    Type    Interface
Internet  10.0.11.1          0            0007.b400.0101   ARPA    Ethernet0/0
Internet  10.0.11.11         -            aabb.cc00.3200   ARPA    Ethernet0/0
PC2#
```

We can now define the problem. PC1 and PC2 in VLAN 11 (mapping to IP subnet 10.0.11.0/24) have sporadic Internet connectivity problems. Both PCs have the correct default gateway address, and their ARP tables show that each has a GLBP virtual MAC address mapping to the default gateway IP address. On the last test, PC1 was 100 percent successful at pinging the test Internet IP address, but PC2 could not ping either that address or even its configured default gateway IP address.

Gathering Information

Based on the information Donovan supplied with respect to the recent migration to GLBP from VRRP, it is best to start gathering information about GLBP on routers R1 and R2. These routers are the first-hop gateways for the PCs and should provide reliable redundancy for the PCs to reach devices outside their subnets.

Example 7-55 shows the output of the **show glbp brief** command on routers R1 and R2. Focusing on GLBP group 1, you can see that R1 (10.0.11.2) with the priority of 100 has the active virtual gateway (AVG) role, and R2 (10.0.11.3) is in Standby state for the AVG role. AVG is responsible to respond to ARP requests for the virtual IP address of the GLBP group. However, you can also see that the virtual IP address on R1 for GLBP group 1 is correctly shown as 10.0.11.1, whereas the virtual IP address on R2 for GLBP group 1 is shown as 10.0.11.11 instead! Nevertheless, R1 (AVG) has assigned the virtual MAC address 0007.b400.0101 to R2 and has picked up the virtual MAC address 0007.b400.0102 for itself within the GLBP group 1.

Example 7-55 *Information Gathering: Examining GLBP Status on R1 and R2*

```
R1# show glbp brief
Interface   Grp  Fwd  Pri  State     Address          Active router    Standby router
Et1/0.11    1    -    100  Active    10.0.11.1        local            10.0.11.3
Et1/0.11    1    1    -    Listen    0007.b400.0101   10.0.11.3        -
Et1/0.11    1    2    -    Active    0007.b400.0102   local            -
< ...output omitted... >
R1#



R2# show glbp brief
Interface   Grp  Fwd  Pri  State  Address     Active router    Standby router
Et1/0.11    1    -    90   Standby 10.0.11.11  10.0.11.2        local
Et1/0.11    1    1    -    Active  0007.b400.0101  local        -
Et1/0.11    1    2    -    Listen  0007.b400.0102  10.0.11.2    -
< ...output omitted... >
R2#
```

The seemingly incorrect virtual IP address for GLBP group 1 on R2 makes us continue
information gathering by shutting down the Ethernet 1/0.11 on router R1. If our observation about the incorrect virtual IP address is correct, neither PC1 nor PC2 should be
able to ping the IP address 209.165.201.225 at all. Example 7-56 shows the results of
this work. After shutting down the Ethernet 1/0.11 interface on R1, we cleared the ARP
table on PC1 and attempted to ping the IP address 209.165.201.225. Unlike last time,
the ping to 209.165.201.225 failed this time.

Example 7-56 *Information Gathering: Try Internet Access After Shutting Down R1
Interface Ethernet 1/0.11*

```
R1# conf term
Enter configuration commands, one per line.  End with CNTL/Z.
R1(config)# interface ethernet 1/0.11
R1(config-subif)# shutdown
R1(config-subif)#



PC1# clear ip arp 10.0.11.1
PC1# ping 209.165.201.225
Type escape sequence to abort.
Sending 5, 100-byte ICMP Echos to 209.165.201.225, timeout is 2 seconds:
.....
Success rate is 0 percent (0/5)
PC1#
PC1# show arp
Protocol  Address           Age (min)  Hardware Addr   Type   Interface
```

```
Internet   10.0.11.1                0          Incomplete        ARPA
Internet   10.0.11.129              -          aabb.cc00.1000    ARPA Ethernet0/0
PC1#
```

Analyzing Information and Proposing a Hypothesis

Based on the gathered information so far, R2 is not backing R1 within GLBP group 1
that is set up for VLAN 11. This confirms that our earlier observation that R2's configured virtual IP address for GLBP group 1 is incorrect, and so this is now our proposed
hypothesis. This hypothesis also explains why R2 does not reply to ARP requests for the
IP address 10.0.11.1, which is the correct virtual IP address for the GLBP group 1.

Testing the Hypotheses

To test our hypothesis, we first bring up the Ethernet 1/0.11 interface on R1 using the
no shutdown command. Next, we remove the existing virtual IP address 10.0.11.11
and add the correct virtual IP address 10.0.11.1 to the configuration of R2, as shown in
Example 7-57.

Example 7-57   *Testing the Hypothesis: Correct the Virtual IP Address on R2*

```
R2# show run interface ethernet 1/0.11
Building configuration...

Current configuration : 235 bytes
!
interface Ethernet1/0.11
 encapsulation dot1Q 11
 ip address 10.0.11.3 255.255.255.0
 glbp 1 ip 10.0.11.11
 glbp 1 priority 90
 glbp 1 preempt
 glbp 1 load-balancing weighted
 glbp 1 authentication md5 key-string 7 00074215070B
end


R2# conf term
Enter configuration commands, one per line.  End with CNTL/Z.
R2(config)# interface ethernet 1/0.11
R2(config-subif)# no glbp 1 ip 10.0.11.11
R2(config-subif)# glbp 1 ip 10.0.11.1
R2(config-subif)# end
R2# wr
Building configuration...
 [OK]
R2#
```

To check the validity of our hypothesis, we perform two tests from PC1 and PC2. First, from each PC we ping their default gateway IP address 10.0.11.1, which is the virtual IP address for the GLBP group 1. The second test is pinging the IP address 209.165.201.225, which we are supposed to use for Internet reachability. As shown in Example 7-58, both tests from both PCs are 100 percent successful.

Example 7-58 *Testing the Hypothesis: Reaching the Internet from Both PCs*

```
PC1# ping 10.0.11.1
Type escape sequence to abort.
Sending 5, 100-byte ICMP Echos to 10.0.11.1, timeout is 2 seconds:
!!!!!
Success rate is 100 percent (5/5), round-trip min/avg/max = 1/1/1 ms
PC1# ping 209.165.201.225
Type escape sequence to abort.
Sending 5, 100-byte ICMP Echos to 209.165.201.225, timeout is 2 seconds:
!!!!!
Success rate is 100 percent (5/5), round-trip min/avg/max = 1/1/1 ms
PC1#


PC2# ping 10.0.11.1
Type escape sequence to abort.
Sending 5, 100-byte ICMP Echos to 10.0.11.1, timeout is 2 seconds:
!!!!!
Success rate is 100 percent (5/5), round-trip min/avg/max = 1/1/1 ms
PC2# ping 209.165.201.225
Type escape sequence to abort.
Sending 5, 100-byte ICMP Echos to 209.165.201.225, timeout is 2 seconds:
!!!!!
Success rate is 100 percent (5/5), round-trip min/avg/max = 1/1/1 ms
PC2#
```

We cannot claim the problem solved unless both PCs have Internet reachability while one of the two GLBP routers (either R1 or R2) is not available. As shown in Example 7-59, we once again shut down the Ethernet 1/0.11 on router R1 to simulate a failure. Next, we check the GLBP status on router R2 and see that R2 is now in the Active state with the correct virtual IP address 10.0.11.1. Finally, from both PCs, we ping the default gateway (10.0.11.1) and the IP address 209.165.201.225 and observe 100 percent success. At this moment, when we displayed the content of the access switch (ASW1) MAC address table for VLAN 1, we notice that both of the GLBP virtual MAC addresses 0007.b400.0101 and 0007.b400.0102 are learned through interface Ethernet 0/1 interface. When we display the content of the Cisco Discovery Protocol (CDP) table, we confirm that the neighbor connected to this interface is indeed router R2. This confirms that when we shut down R1's Ethernet 1/0.11 interface, R2 has taken responsibility for both of the GLBP virtual MAC addresses.

Example 7-59 *Solving the Problem: GLBP Operation During Failure Period*

```
R1# conf term
Enter configuration commands, one per line.   End with CNTL/Z.
R1(config)# interface eth 1/0.11
R1(config-subif)# shutdown
R1(config-subif)#



R2# show glbp ethernet 1/0.11
Ethernet1/0.11 - Group 1
  State is Active
    12 state changes, last state change 00:00:30
  Virtual IP address is 10.0.11.1
   Hello time 3 sec, hold time 10 sec
     Next hello sent in 1.472 secs
   Redirect time 600 sec, forwarder timeout 14400 sec
   Authentication MD5, key-string
   Preemption enabled, min delay 0 sec
   Active is local
  Standby is unknown
   Priority 90 (configured)
   Weighting 100 (default 100), thresholds: lower 1, upper 100
   Load balancing: weighted
   Group members:
     aabb.cc00.6101 (10.0.11.3) local
   There are 2 forwarders (2 active)
   Forwarder 1
     State is Active
       5 state changes, last state change 00:02:38
     MAC address is 0007.b400.0101 (default)
     Owner ID is aabb.cc00.6101
     Redirection enabled
     Preemption enabled, min delay 30 sec
     Active is local, weighting 100
     Client selection count: 158
   Forwarder 2
     State is Active
       5 state changes, last state change 00:00:29
     MAC address is 0007.b400.0102 (learnt)
     Owner ID is aabb.cc00.5f01
     Redirection enabled, 558.912 sec remaining (maximum 600 sec)
     Time to live: 14358.912 sec (maximum 14400 sec)
     Preemption enabled, min delay 30 sec
     Active is local, weighting 100
     Client selection count: 158
R2#
```

```
PC1# ping 10.0.11.1
Type escape sequence to abort.
Sending 5, 100-byte ICMP Echos to 10.0.11.1, timeout is 2 seconds:
!!!!!
Success rate is 100 percent (5/5), round-trip min/avg/max = 1/1/1 ms
PC1#
PC1# ping 209.165.201.225
Type escape sequence to abort.
Sending 5, 100-byte ICMP Echos to 209.165.201.225, timeout is 2 seconds:
!!!!!
Success rate is 100 percent (5/5), round-trip min/avg/max = 1/1/1 ms
PC1#


PC2# ping 10.0.11.1
Type escape sequence to abort.
Sending 5, 100-byte ICMP Echos to 10.0.11.1, timeout is 2 seconds:
!!!!!
Success rate is 100 percent (5/5), round-trip min/avg/max = 1/1/1 ms
PC2#
PC2# ping 209.165.201.225
Type escape sequence to abort.
Sending 5, 100-byte ICMP Echos to 209.165.201.225, timeout is 2 seconds:
!!!!!
Success rate is 100 percent (5/5), round-trip min/avg/max = 1/1/1 ms
PC2#


SW1# show mac address-table vlan 11
          Mac Address Table
-------------------------------------------

Vlan    Mac Address      Type       Ports
----    -----------      -------    -------
 11     0007.b400.0101   DYNAMIC     Et0/1
 11     0007.b400.0102   DYNAMIC     Et0/1
 11     aabb.cc00.1000   DYNAMIC     Et0/2
 11     aabb.cc00.3200   DYNAMIC     Et0/3
 11     aabb.cc00.5f01   DYNAMIC     Et0/0
 11     aabb.cc00.6101   DYNAMIC     Et0/1
Total Mac Addresses for this criterion: 6
SW1#
SW1# show cdp neighbors
Capability Codes: R - Router, T - Trans Bridge, B - Source Route Bridge
                  S - Switch, H - Host, I - IGMP, r - Repeater, P - Phone,
                  D - Remote, C - CVTA, M - Two-port Mac Relay
```

```
Device ID        Local Intrfce    Holdtme    Capability  Platform    Port ID
R2.cisco.com     Eth 0/1          148             R      Linux Uni   Eth 1/0
R1.cisco.com     Eth 0/0          163             R      Linux Uni   Eth 1/0
SW1#
```

Solving the Problem

We can now bring router R1's Ethernet 1/0.11 interface up and, because of its higher GLBP priority and the preempt option, see it become the AVG for GLBP group 1. Example 7-60 shows that this indeed is the case. Furthermore, as shown in Example 7-60, both PC1 and PC2 are able to ping their default gateway IP address (10.0.11.1) and the Internet server at 209.165.201.225.

Example 7-60 *Solving the Problem: GLBP Operation While Both Routers Are Up*

```
R1# config term
R1(config)# interface Ethernet 1/0.11
R1(config-subif)# no shut
R1(config-subif)# end

R1# show glbp eth 1/0.11
Ethernet1/0.11 - Group 1
  State is Active
    7 state changes, last state change 00:00:21
  Virtual IP address is 10.0.11.1
  Hello time 3 sec, hold time 10 sec
    Next hello sent in 2.304 secs
  Redirect time 600 sec, forwarder timeout 14400 sec
  Authentication MD5, key-string
  Preemption enabled, min delay 0 sec
  Active is local
  Standby is 10.0.11.3, priority 90 (expires in 8.480 sec)
  Priority 100 (default)
  Weighting 100 (default 100), thresholds: lower 1, upper 100
  Load balancing: weighted
  Group members:
    aabb.cc00.5f01 (10.0.11.2) local
    aabb.cc00.6101 (10.0.11.3) authenticated
  There are 2 forwarders (0 active)
  Forwarder 1
    State is Listen
      4 state changes, last state change 00:06:51
    MAC address is 0007.b400.0101 (learnt)
    Owner ID is aabb.cc00.6101
      Redirection enabled, 598.496 sec remaining (maximum 600 sec)
```

```
        Time to live: 14398.496 sec (maximum 14400 sec)
        Preemption enabled, min delay 30 sec
        Active is 10.0.11.3 (primary), weighting 100 (expires in 10.304 sec)
        Client selection count: 8
     Forwarder 2
        State is Listen
          6 state changes, last state change 00:04:51
        MAC address is 0007.b400.0102 (default)
        Owner ID is aabb.cc00.5f01
        Redirection enabled
        Preemption enabled, min delay 30 sec (5 secs remaining)
        Active is 10.0.11.3 (secondary), weighting 100 (expires in 10.048 sec)
        Client selection count: 7
R1#
R1# wr
Building configuration...
[OK]
R1#


PC1# ping 10.0.11.1
Type escape sequence to abort.
Sending 5, 100-byte ICMP Echos to 10.0.11.1, timeout is 2 seconds:
!!!!! .
Success rate is 100 percent (5/5), round-trip min/avg/max = 1/1/1 ms
PC1#
PC1# ping 209.165.201.225
Type escape sequence to abort.
Sending 5, 100-byte ICMP Echos to 209.165.201.225, timeout is 2 seconds:
!!!!!
Success rate is 100 percent (5/5), round-trip min/avg/max = 1/1/1 ms
PC1#


PC2# ping 10.0.11.1
Type escape sequence to abort.
Sending 5, 100-byte ICMP Echos to 10.0.11.1, timeout is 2 seconds:
!!!!!
Success rate is 100 percent (5/5), round-trip min/avg/max = 1/1/1 ms
PC2# ping 209.165.201.225
Type escape sequence to abort.
Sending 5, 100-byte ICMP Echos to 209.165.201.225, timeout is 2 seconds:
!!!!!
Success rate is 100 percent (5/5), round-trip min/avg/max = 1/1/1 ms
PC2#
```

It is now evident that routers R1 and R2 are now operating correctly within VLAN 11 providing GLBP group 1 service. GLBP offers first-hop redundancy while it also provides load sharing among the GLBP group members.

We must now complete the documentation and inform Donovan at TINC Garbage Disposal and any other party involved that the GLBP problem within VLAN 11 is solved and that PC1 and PC2 can reliably access the Internet.

Troubleshooting FHRPs

GLBP, in addition to HSRP, is a Cisco proprietary FHRP. The advantages of GLBP over HSRP are its built-in support for load sharing and that up to four routers can participate in every GLBP group as active forwarders.

The following is a list of common GLBP misconfigurations:

- Virtual IP address configured incorrectly on one or more of the GLBP group members.
- GLBP group number discrepancy among GLBP group members.
- Authentication method or key mismatch among GLBP group members.
- Preempt option missing or configured on one router only.
- Access lists or firewalls blocking GLBP messages (GLBP messages are sent to the IP multicast address 224.0.0.102, and GLBP's UDP port number is 3222).

The following is a list of useful GLBP diagnostic commands:

- **show glbp brief**
- **show glbp interface** *type number* **[brief]**
- **debug glbp [packets | events | terse | error | all]**

The following are some significant facts about FHRPs:

- HSRP and GLBP do not allow the group virtual IP address to be assigned to either of the routers participating in the group. VRRP, however, does allow you to assign the virtual IP address to one of the routers within the group. The router whose address is used as the virtual IP address will be the Master router for that VRRP group, even if another router has a higher priority.
- VRRP is an IETF standard (RFC 5798); this makes VRRP the only FHRP suitable for multivendor environments.
- HSRP and GLBP do not have the preempt option enabled by default; VRRP does. If you do not want the preempt option with VRRP, you can disable it.
- GLBP's main feature is that up to four routers belonging to the same group forward traffic and exercise load sharing for a single virtual IP address.
- The default Hello and Hold timers for HSRP and GLBP are 3 seconds and 10 seconds; the default Hello and Hold timers for VRRP are 1 second and 3 seconds.

Troubleshooting Sporadic Loss of Connectivity on PC4

Donovan has reported this problem as a very confusing one. The problem is specific to PC4. This PC has unreliable network connectivity. He has also reported that PC4 can renew its IP address lease (through DHCP) successfully, and he reminded us that PC4 resides in VLAN 44, which maps to IP subnet 10.0.44.0/24

Verifying the Problem and Making a Troubleshooting Plan

After getting access to PC4, we decided to simply ping the IP address 10.0.44.1 from there. This address is the designated default gateway address within VLAN 44. This VLAN matches the IP subnet 10.0.44.0/24. As shown in Example 7-61, PC4 had a 0 percent success rate when we tried to ping the designated default gateway address 10.0.44.1.

Example 7-61 *Verifying the Problem: PC4 Cannot Ping Its Own Default Gateway*

```
PC4# ping 10.0.44.1
Type escape sequence to abort.
Sending 5, 100-byte ICMP Echos to 10.0.44.1, timeout is 2 seconds:
.....
Success rate is 0 percent (0/5)
PC4#
```

Now that the problem has been verified, we can take the bottom-up troubleshooting approach and the follow-the-path technique to first make sure that PC4 reaches its default gateway. For now, we can define the problem as this: PC4 cannot reach its default gateway. Once that problem is fixed, we can then investigate whether PC4's IP connectivity problems are all resolved or if further troubleshooting is necessary.

Gathering Information

Because we decided to take the bottom-up approach, we can check the status of PC4's Ethernet interface first. Example 7-62 shows the result. PC4's Ethernet interface is up, and it has an IP address, but the IP address does not belong to the IP subnet 10.0.44.0/24 (VLAN 44).

Example 7-62 *Information Gathering: Check PC4's Ethernet Interface Status*

```
PC4# show ip int brief
Interface              IP-Address      OK? Method Status            Protocol
Ethernet0/0            10.0.0.7        YES DHCP   up                up
< ...output omitted... >
PC4#
```

We must readily check whether the interface Ethernet 0/2 on the access switch (ASW3) is properly assigned to VLAN 44. As shown in Example 7-63, we first discover PC4's

MAC address, then we search for PC4's MAC address table in access switch ASW3's MAC address table. The output shows that PC4's MAC address was learned through switch interface Ethernet 0/2 and that it is assigned to VLAN 44.

Example 7-63 *Information Gathering: Check VLAN Number on the Access Switch Interface (for PC4)*

```
PC4#
PC4# show int ethernet 0/0 | include Hardware
  Hardware is AmdP2, address is aabb.cc00.bf00 (bia aabb.cc00.bf00)
PC4#


SW3# show mac address-table | include aabb.cc00.bf00
   44     aabb.cc00.bf00     DYNAMIC     Et0/2
SW3#
```

Now that we know that PC4 has no physical or data link layer problems, its MAC address is learned on the proper access switch interface, and that it belongs to the correct VLAN, we need to find out why it is offered an improper IP address (through DHCP). The first-hop gateways, R1 and R2, act as redundant DHCP servers, so we need to examine their configuration for VLAN 44 (IP subnet 10.0.44.0/24). Example 7-64 shows the DHCP-related configuration commands on R1 and R2. Both configurations look correct.

Example 7-64 *Information Gathering: Check the DHCP Configuration for VLAN 44 on the Redundant First-Hop Routers (R1 and R2)*

```
R1# show run | section dhcp
< ...output omitted... >
ip dhcp pool VLAN44_CLIENTS
 network 10.0.44.0 255.255.255.0
 default-router 10.0.44.1
R1#


R2# show run | section dhcp
< ...output omitted... >
ip dhcp pool VLAN44_CLIENTS
 network 10.0.44.0 255.255.255.0
 default-router 10.0.44.1
R2#
```

Because PC4 is properly connected to the network within VLAN 44, and the DHCP servers are configured correctly for this VLAN (IP subnet 10.0.44.0/24), we need to investigate to determine from where (which DHCP server) PC4 is getting its invalid IP address.

Therefore, we enable DHCP debugging on PC4 and release and renew its IP address lease. The results, as shown in Example 7-65, reveal that PC4 is obtaining its IP address from a server with IP address 10.0.0.1.

Example 7-65   *Information Gathering: Discover Which DHCP Server Is Serving PC4 Its Invalid IP Address*

```
PC4# debug dhcp
DHCP client activity debugging in on

PC4# release  dhcp ethernet 0/0
< ...output omitted... >
PC4# renew  dhcp ethernet 0/0
PC4#
< ...output omitted... >
*Sep  2 15:40:08.071: DHCP: Received a BOOTREP pkt
*Sep  2 15:40:08.071: DHCP: offer received from 10.0.0.1
*Sep  2 15:40:08.071: DHCP: SRequest attempt # 1 for entry:
*Sep  2 15:40:08.071: DHCP: SRequest- Server ID option: 10.0.0.1
*Sep  2 15:40:08.071: DHCP: SRequest- Requested IP addr option: 10.0.0.7
*Sep  2 15:40:08.071: DHCP: SRequest: 304 bytes
*Sep  2 15:40:08.071: DHCP: SRequest: 304 bytes
*Sep  2 15:40:08.071:                 B'cast on Ethernet0/0 interface from 0.0.0.0
*Sep  2 15:40:08.072: DHCP: Received a BOOTREP pkt
*Sep  2 15:40:12.088: DHCP: Sending notification of ASSIGNMENT:
*Sep  2 15:40:12.088:    Address 10.0.0.7 mask 255.0.0.0
*Sep  2 15:40:12.088: DHCP Client Pooling: ***Allocated IP address: 10.0.0.7
*Sep  2 15:40:12.109: Allocated IP address = 10.0.0.7  255.0.0.0
*Sep  2 15:40:12.109: %DHCP-6-ADDRESS_ASSIGN: Interface Ethernet0/0 assigned DHCP
   address 10.0.0.7, mask 255.0.0.0, hostname PC4

PC4#
```

Analyzing the Information and Gathering Further Information

The DHCP server with the IP address 10.0.0.1 is unknown; in other words, it is a rogue DHCP server within the network. To locate this rogue DHCP server, we ping its IP address (from PC4) and immediately display PC4's ARP table to discover the rogue DHCP server's MAC address. As shown in Example 7-66, the MAC address of the rogue DHCP server is aabb.cc00.ce00. When we display the MAC address table of the access switch ASW3 (specifying this MAC address), we notice that the rogue server is connected to the access switch ASW3 interface Ethernet 2/0 within VLAN 44 (see Example 7-66).

Example 7-66 *Information Gathering: Discover Which Access Switch Interface the Rogue DHCP Server Is Connected To*

```
PC4# ping 10.0.0.1
Type escape sequence to abort.
Sending 5, 100-byte ICMP Echos to 10.0.0.1, timeout is 2 seconds:
!!!!!
Success rate is 100 percent (5/5), round-trip min/avg/max = 1/202/1006 ms
PC4#
PC4# show arp
Protocol  Address          Age (min)  Hardware Addr   Type   Interface
Internet  10.0.0.1                 0  aabb.cc00.ce00  ARPA   Ethernet0/0
Internet  10.0.0.7                 -  aabb.cc00.bf00  ARPA   Ethernet0/0
PC4#



SW3# show mac address-table | include aabb.cc00.ce00
   44    aabb.cc00.ce00   DYNAMIC     Et2/0
SW3#
```

Proposing a Hypothesis and Testing the Hypothesis

We can now propose that a rogue DHCP server connected to access switch ASW3 interface Ethernet 2/0 is assigning the invalid IP address to PC4 on VLAN 44.

An excellent mitigation tool against rogue DHCP servers is the Cisco IOS DHCP snooping feature. When you enable this feature on a switch, you must also specify the VLAN you want the feature to be applied to. No interface that belongs to that VLAN will accept DHCP server messages (OFFER and ACKNOWLEDGE) any more. The interfaces that connect to or lead toward the legitimate DHCP servers must then be configured as "trusted" so that DHCP servers from those particular interfaces are accepted and forwarded.

As you can see in Example 7-67, the output of the **show cdp neighbors** command on access switch ASW3 indicates that routers R1 and R2 (the legitimate DHCP servers) are connected to interfaces Ethernet 0/0 and Ethernet 0/1. As a result, after we enable **ip dhcp snooping** globally, in addition to enabling it on VLAN 44, we configure those interfaces with the **ip dhcp snooping trust** command. Finally, Example 7-67 shows the output of the **show ip dhcp snooping** command on access switch ASW3, confirming our configuration efforts.

Example 7-67 *Testing a Hypothesis: Implement DHCP Snooping and Apply It to VLAN 44*

```
SW3# show cdp neighbors
Capability Codes: R - Router, T - Trans Bridge, B - Source Route Bridge
                  S - Switch, H - Host, I - IGMP, r - Repeater, P - Phone,
                  D - Remote, C - CVTA, M - Two-port Mac Relay
```

```
Device ID          Local Intrfce     Holdtme    Capability  Platform  Port ID
R2.cisco.com       Eth 0/1           136                R   Linux Uni Eth 1/2
R1.cisco.com       Eth 0/0           148                R   Linux Uni Eth 1/2
SW3#
SW3# config term
Enter configuration commands, one per line.  End with CNTL/Z.
SW3(config)# ip dhcp snooping
SW3(config)# ip dhcp snooping vlan 44
SW3(config)# interface range ethernet 0/0-1
SW3(config-if-range)# ip dhcp snooping trust
SW3(config-if-range)# end
SW3# wr
Building configuration...
[OK]
SW3#
*Sep  2 16:06:32.727: %SYS-5-CONFIG_I: Configured from console by console
SW3# show ip dhcp snooping
Switch DHCP snooping is enabled
DHCP snooping is configured on following VLANs:
44
DHCP snooping is operational on following VLANs:
44
DHCP snooping is configured on the following L3 Interfaces:

Insertion of option 82 is enabled
Option 82 on untrusted port is not allowed
Verification of hwaddr field is enabled
Verification of giaddr field is enabled
DHCP snooping trust/rate is configured on the following Interfaces:

Interface                Trusted     Rate limit (pps)
------------------------  -------    ----------------
Ethernet0/0                 yes       unlimited
Ethernet0/1                 yes       unlimited
SW3#
```

Solving the Problem

We can now return to PC4, release and renew its IP address lease, and observe whether it obtains its address from a legitimate DHCP server only. Example 7-68 shows the **debug dhcp** results on PC4 while we released and renewed its IP address lease. Example 7-68 also shows that we can ping the IP address 209.165.201.225 (on the Internet) successfully; this shows that PC4 now has good IP connectivity.

Example 7-68 *Solving the Problem: PC4 Does Not Obtain an Invalid IP Address Lease from a Rogue DHCP Server Any Longer*

```
PC4# debug dhcp
DHCP client activity debugging is on
PC4# release dhcp ethernet 0/0
< ...output omitted... >
*Sep  2 16:09:26.828: DHCP: offer received from 10.0.44.3
*Sep  2 16:09:26.828: DHCP: SRequest attempt # 1 for entry:
*Sep  2 16:09:26.828: DHCP: SRequest- Server ID option: 10.0.44.3
*Sep  2 16:09:26.828: DHCP: SRequest- Requested IP addr option: 10.0.44.132
*Sep  2 16:09:26.828: DHCP: SRequest: 304 bytes
*Sep  2 16:09:26.828: DHCP: SRequest: 304 bytes
*Sep  2 16:09:26.828:              B'cast on Ethernet0/0 interface from 0.0.0.0
*Sep  2 16:09:26.829: DHCP: Received a BOOTREP pkt
PC4#
*Sep  2 16:09:30.844: DHCP: Sending notification of ASSIGNMENT:
*Sep  2 16:09:30.844:   Address 10.0.44.132 mask 255.255.255.0
*Sep  2 16:09:30.844: DHCP Client Pooling: ***Allocated IP address: 10.0.44.132
*Sep  2 16:09:30.956: Allocated IP address = 10.0.44.132   255.255.255.0


PC4#
*Sep  2 16:09:30.956: %DHCP-6-ADDRESS_ASSIGN: Interface Ethernet0/0 assigned DHCP
 address 10.0.44.132, mask 255.255.255.0, hostname PC4
*Sep  2 16:09:36.872: DHCP: Client socket is closed
PC4# no debug dhcp
DHCP client activity debugging is off
PC4#
PC4# sho ip int brief
Interface             IP-Address      OK? Method Status          Protocol
Ethernet0/0           10.0.44.132     YES DHCP   up               up
< ...output omitted...>
PC4# ping 209.165.201.225
Type escape sequence to abort.
Sending 5, 100-byte ICMP Echos to 209.165.201.225, timeout is 2 seconds:
!!!!!
Success rate is 100 percent (5/5), round-trip min/avg/max = 1/201/1004 ms
PC4#
```

We have solved the rogue DHCP problem on VLAN 44 using the DHCP snooping feature. However, we must warn Donovan at TINC Garbage Disposal that the same danger exists for VLANs 11 and 22 and that we recommend implementing DHCP snooping on all user VLANs. We also tested that PC4 has good IP connectivity. We must now document our work, notify Donovan that this problem is solved, and provide him with our recommendations.

The Cisco IOS DHCP Snooping Feature

DHCP snooping is a Layer 2 security feature that acts like a firewall between untrusted hosts and trusted DHCP servers. The primary function of the DHCP snooping is to prevent rogue DHCP servers in the network. DHCP snooping is enabled on switches on a per-VLAN basis. Interfaces of a LAN switch are configured as trusted or untrusted. Trusted interfaces allow all types of DHCP messages through, whereas only DISCOVER and REQUEST messages are allowed on untrusted interfaces. Trusted interfaces are interfaces that connect to a DHCP server or are uplinks toward the DHCP server. With DHCP snooping enabled, the switch also builds a DHCP snooping binding database. Each entry in the database includes the MAC address of the host, the leased IP address, the lease time, the binding type, the VLAN number, and interface information associated with the host. The DHCP snooping binding database can be used by other security features such as dynamic ARP inspection (DAI). DHCP snooping may also be used to limit the rate of DHCP messages (ADDRESS REQUEST). This option is configured per switch interface.

To configure DHCP snooping on a Cisco LAN switch, follow these steps:

Step 1.   Enable DHCP snooping globally using the command **ip dhcp snooping**.

Step 2.   Apply DHCP snooping to a particular VLAN using the command ip **dhcp snooping** *vlan-number*.

Step 3.   Configure interfaces that connect to the DHCP server or lead toward the legitimate DHCP servers as trusted, using the **ip dhcp snooping trust** command.

Step 4.   Optionally, you can enable rate limiting on the DHCP snooping untrusted interfaces. Rate is configured as DHCP packets per second. This is accomplished using the interface configuration mode command **ip dhcp snooping limit rate** *rate*.

Step 5.   To verify the DHCP snooping configuration, use the **show ip dhcp snooping** command. You can display the DHCP snooping binding database using the **show ip dhcp snooping binding** command.

Cisco Technical Assistance Center

When you have a technical problem associated with the device configuration process or have identified a failure in the Cisco software or in the network that you are unable to fix, if you cannot find the answer to your questions on the Cisco Support website, you can contact the Cisco Technical Assistance Center (TAC). Cisco TAC provides 24-hour-a-day technical assistance to all those who hold valid Cisco service contracts.

Depending on the priority of your problem, you have two options for opening a case with Cisco TAC:

- Using the Support Case Manager website or e-mail for lower-priority incidents

  - **Priority 4:** Additional information or assistance with Cisco product capabilities, installation, or configuration is required. There is little or no effect on business operations.

- **Priority 3:** Operational performance of the network is impaired, while most business operations remain functional.

- By telephone for higher priority incidents

   - **Priority 2:** Operation of an existing network is severely degraded, or significant aspects of business operation are negatively affected by inadequate performance of Cisco products.

   - **Priority 1:** The network is down, or there is a critical impact on business operations.

When using the website, the TAC Service Request Tool automatically provides the recommended solutions. If this does not solve your problem, the case is then assigned to a Cisco TAC engineer.

When you open a case with the Cisco TAC, you must provide preliminary information to better explain the issue. The following information is necessary:

- **Cisco service contract number and device serial number**

- **Network layout:** Provide a detailed description of the physical and logical setup, in addition to all the network elements involved and their software versions.

- **Problem description:** Provide step-by-step detail of actions taken when the problem incident occurs. Include the information about expected behavior and all the observed behavior.

- **General information:** Information such as whether this is a new installation, what changes were recently made to the system, is the issue reproducible, what are the affected devices, how did you try to troubleshoot, relevant syslog/TAC logs before the issue occurred, and so on.

You have the option to check the status of your opened case at any time using your case reference number. There is also an applet available that allows you and your Cisco TAC engineer to work together more effectively by using Collaborative Web Browsing, whiteboard, Telnet, and clipboard tools.

Troubleshooting SSH Connection from PC4 to Router GW2

Donovan, from TINC Garbage Disposal, has informed us that PC4, and only PC4, must be able to build an SSH session to all Layer 3 devices within the TINC computer network. Donovan cannot figure out why PC4 is not able to build an SSH session to router GW2 and needs assistance with this matter.

Verifying the Problem and Making a Troubleshooting Plan

As the first step in the troubleshooting exercise, we must verify that PC4 indeed cannot access router GW2 using SSH. Example 7-69 shows that our attempt to build an SSH session from PC4 to GW2 receives a "connection refused by remote host" message and fails.

Example 7-69 *Verifying the Problem: PC4 Cannot Build an SSH Session to GW2*

```
PC4#
PC4# ssh -1 admin 10.0.1.11

% Connection refused by remote host

PC4#
```

Now that the problem is verified, we can decide on the troubleshooting method. Because SSH is an application layer protocol, we can take the divide-and-conquer approach and start by testing basic reachability between PC4 and GW2 using ping or trace utilities. Based on the results, we can then shift our focus to the lower or upper protocol layers accordingly.

Gathering Information

As planned, we first tried to ping the GW2 router from PC4 and, as shown in Example 7-70, the ping is 100 percent successful. This leads us to believe that no basic connectivity issues exist between PC4 and GW2 and that we can focus on upper-layer protocol matters.

Example 7-70 *Information Gathering: Ping from PC4 to GW2 Is Successful*

```
PC4# ping 10.0.1.11
Type escape sequence to abort.
Sending 5, 100-byte ICMP Echos to 10.0.1.11, timeout is 2 seconds:
!!!!!
Success rate is 100 percent (5/5), round-trip min/avg/max = 1/1/1 ms
PC4#
```

We can now examine GW2 and gather information about SSH on GW2. As shown in Example 7-71, the **show ip ssh** command on GW2 reveals that GW2 is set up for SSHv2 only. Therefore, we immediately attempt an SSH version session from PC4 to GW2; however, SSHv2 also returns the same response message ("Connection refused by remote host").

Example 7-71 *Information Gathering: Reattempt with SSHv2*

```
GW2# show ip ssh
SSH Enabled - version 2.0
Authentication timeout: 120 secs; Authentication retries: 3
Minimum expected Diffie Hellman key size : 1024 bits
IOS Keys in SECSH format(ssh-rsa, base64 encoded):
ssh-rsa AAAAB3NzaC1yc2EAAAADAQABAAAAgQCb9WWBhdHqK4aHjdrKDqq490b8AYSrDWEHMKujaI9N
9yieVXF/pVIpxk16YdxsyTdG2psT7QoQWRUZai3i68ev7dvX2dz0Q36O8p2s/Kz82USErGRxi2yqriP6
EAR4DN7ahp1dxWAxdCw/DiiDl325NoBhPkbNKs3iz7xPXp1d8Q==
```

```
GW2#


PC4# ssh -v 2 -l admin 10.0.1.11
% Connection refused by remote host

PC4#
```

Based on the message received when we attempt both SSH versions from PC4, it is reasonable to suspect a security or management control mechanism as the culprit. Therefore, we can first inspect the vty line configuration on GW2. Example 7-72 shows the corresponding section of GW2's running-config. As you can see, ACL 22 is applied to vty lines 0 through 4 in the inbound direction. The output of the **show access-list 22** command that we tried next shows that this ACL only permits packets whose source IP addresses get a 24-bit match to 10.0.33.0.

Example 7-72   *Information Gathering: Examine the vty Configuration on GW2*

```
GW2# show run | section line
line con 0
 logging synchronous
line aux 0
line vty 0 4
 access-class 22 in
 transport input ssh
GW2#
GW2# show access-lists 22
Standard IP access list 22
    10 permit 10.0.33.0, wildcard bits 0.0.0.255
GW2#
```

Proposing a Hypothesis and Testing the Hypothesis

The ACL 22 that is currently applied to the vty lines of GW2 in the inbound direction would clearly deny PC4 access to GW2's vty line through SSHv1, SSHv2, or Telnet. Because Donovan has insisted that PC4 (only from VLAN 44) must have management access to the Layer 3 devices, we propose modifying the ACL so that it only permits access from network 10.0.44.0/24 (VLAN 44), which is considered the management VLAN, and it is where PC4 resides. Example 7-73 shows our work deleting the existing ACL 22 and re-creating it with the proper address and wildcard mask.

Example 7-73   *Hypothesis: Modify the ACL Applied to GW2's vty Lines*

```
GW2# conf term
Enter configuration commands, one per line.  End with CNTL/Z.
GW2(config)# no access-list 22
```

```
GW2(config)# access-list 22 permit 10.0.44.0 0.0.0.255
GW2(config)# do show access-list 22
Standard IP access list 22
    10 permit 10.0.44.0, wildcard bits 0.0.0.255
GW2(config)# end
GW2#
*Sep  2 21:17:04.269: %SYS-5-CONFIG_I: Configured from console by console
GW2# wr
Building configuration...
[OK]
GW2#
```

Solving the Problem

Following the modification we proposed to the ACL applied to GW2's vty lines, we must access PC4 to ascertain that it can access GW2 using SSH. Example 7-74 shows that PC4 can now successfully build an SSHv2 session with GW2, and so the problem is solved.

Example 7-74   *Solve the Problem: SSHv2 from PC4 to GW2 Works*

```
PC4# ssh -v 2 -l admin 10.0.1.11
Password:

GW2>
```

We must now document our work and notify Donovan that the last problem he reported is now fixed.

Summary

This chapter presented four troubleshooting tickets at TINC Garbage Disposal, a fictitious company, based on the topology shown in Figure 7-2.

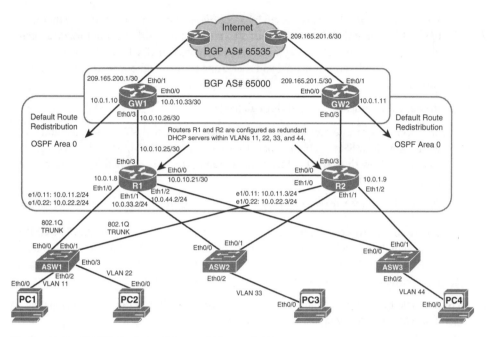

Figure 7-2 *TINC Garbage Disposal Network Diagram*

Trouble ticket 1: Donovan, the network engineer from TINC Garbage Disposal, reported the following network problems and asked for help:

1. GW2 does not serve as the backup gateway to the Internet; Internet connectivity is solely through GW1.

   Solution: This problem was caused by the fact that GW2 had the wrong autonomous system number configured for its eBGP neighbor (ISP) and that the BGP relationship never established. Therefore, GSW2 did not receive a default route from its eBGP neighbor and did not redistribute it into OSPF.

2. PC1 does not have Internet connectivity.

   Solution: This problem was caused by the fact that ASW1 was configured with port security on Interface Ethernet 0/2, but the wrong MAC address was hard-coded, and PC1 could not use this interface and get connected.

3. PC2 does not have Internet connectivity.

   Solution: This problem was caused by the fact that VLAN 22 did not exist on ASW1. Traffic from PC2 on VLAN 22 was dropped on ASW1.

Trouble ticket 2: Donovan, the network engineer from TINC Garbage Disposal, sent us an e-mail asking for help with the following problems:

1. GW1 has only one OSPF neighbor (GW1), and it does not have a neighbor relationship (adjacency) with R1.

Solution: This problem was caused by a configuration error on interface Ethernet 0/3 of R1, where OSPF was configured to treat the network as a nonbroadcast network. As a result of network type discrepancy between GW1 and R1, their timers (Hello and Hold) did not match, and that stopped the neighbor relationship from forming.

2. Router R2 cannot be accessed through SSHv2.

Solution: This problem was caused by the fact that R2 had SSHv1 enabled and would not allow SSHv2 connections. However, after SSHv1 was disabled on this router (to allow the SSHv2, which is the default), the SSH key had to be regenerated (to at least 768 bits).

3. Routers R1 and R2 keep generating duplicate IP address on Ethernet 1/1 messages.

Solution: This was caused by an HSRP group configuration error on R2. The HSRP group number on R1 was correctly configured as 33, but the HSRP group number on R2 was configured as 3. The two groups configured on R1 and R2 were using the same virtual IP address, causing duplicate IP address error.

Trouble ticket 3: After implementing some changes at TINC's network, Donovan contacted us with the following list of issues he needed help with:

1. PC1 and PC2 have sporadic Internet connectivity.

Solution: A rogue OSPF device injecting an invalid default route into the network caused this problem. When we shut down the unused interfaces on switch 1, the rogue device lost its connectivity to the network, and the invalid default routes were removed.

After migrating from HSRP to VRRP, on VLAN 33 only, both R1 and R2 claim the Master role. Different authentication methods configured on R1 and R3 for VRRP group 3 caused the two routers to ignore each other's messages and assume the Master role within VRRP group 3.

2. The EtherChannel Donovan set up between switch 3 and the new switch 4 is not functioning.

Solution: The Ethernet 2/0 and Ethernet 2/1 interfaces on switch 4 were supposed to be the elements of the EtherChannel bundle between switch 3 and switch 4. However, the Ethernet 2/0 was configured as an access port, unlike the other interfaces (which were configured for trunking), causing this interface to be suspended and out of the bundle.

Trouble ticket 4: Donovan presented us with three more problems that he needed help with:

1. Donovan, who learned about Cisco GLBP in a workshop, migrated R1 and R2 from VRRP to GLBP on all VLANs (11, 33, and 44). However, he discovered that GLBP was not functioning well on VLAN 11; PC1 and PC2 both had difficulty connecting to the Internet. Also, R2 was not providing gateway services in R1's absence.

Solution: This problem was caused by a configuration error on R2. The virtual IP address for GLBP group 1 on R2 was configured as 10.0.11.11 instead of 10.0.11.1.

2. PC4, in VLAN 44, Donovan claimed, had unpredictable Internet connectivity and he needed help with it.

Solution: We discovered that a rogue DHCP server in VLAN 44 supplying invalid IP addresses to DHCP clients was causing this problem. The DHCP snooping feature was used to mitigate this problem. Only devices in VLAN 44 (which was PC4 at the moment) were supposed to have management access (SSH/Telnet) to Layer 3 devices. However, PC4 could not access GW2. This problem was caused by an erroneous ACL that was applied to the vty lines in GW2.

Review Questions

1. Which statement correctly describes the "protect" violation mode?

   a. The interface is error-disabled when a security violation occurs.
   b. A security violation sends a trap to the network management station.
   c. Drops packets with unknown source addresses or when maximum number of MAC addresses is reached.
   d. The interface clears all dynamic MAC addresses when a security violation occurs.

2. Specify the BGP neighbor state (Connect, Open Confirm, Idle, Active) for each of the listed descriptions.

   a. Router is trying to build the TCP three-way handshake with its counterpart. _____
   b. Router is searching its forwarding table for a path to reach its counterpart. _____
   c. Router found a route to its counterpart and has completed the TCP three-way handshake. _____
   d. Router received agreement on the parameters for establishing a BGP session. _____

3. In what state will the OSPF neighbor relationship be stuck in the following cases?

   a. Neighbor is manually configured, and an ACL is blocking OSPF packets. _____
   b. OSPF authentication discrepancy exists between two routers. _____
   c. Hello parameters are mismatched. _____
   d. There is an MTU mismatch between the routers. _____

4. In the output of the **show ip ssh** command, what does version 1.99 indicate?

   a. Only SSHv1 is enabled.
   b. Only SSHv2 is enabled, but the key size is 512 bits.
   c. SSHv2 is enabled, but the server also supports SSHv1 for backward compatibility.
   d. The Cisco proprietary SSH version is enabled.

5. Which multicast address must be allowed in the inbound access list when using HSRP? (Choose two.)

   a. 224.0.0.2 when using HSRPv1

   b. 224.0.0.10 when using HSRPv1

   c. 224.0.0.2 when using HSRPv2

   d. 224.0.0.10 when using HSRPv2

6. Two routers, R1 and R2, are configured as part of VRRP group 1. They are incorrectly configured with different virtual addresses. R1's virtual IP address is configured as 10.0.1.1. R2's virtual address is configured as 10.0.1.2. What MAC address will each router send in response to an ARP request for its configured virtual IP address?

   a. R1 = 0000.5e00.0101, R2 = 0000.5e00.0102

   b. R1 = 0000.5e00.0101, R2 = 0000.5e00.0101

   c. Its own MAC address

   d. R1 = its own MAC address, R2 = 0000.5e00.0101

7. Review the following partial output of the DHCP snooping configuration. Which of the DHCP messages are allowed on the interface Fast Ethernet 0/2? (Choose two.)

```
!
ip dhcp snooping
ip dhcp snooping vlan 10
!
interface FastEthernet0/1
 switchport mode access
 switchport access vlan 10
 ip dhcp snooping trust
!
interface FastEthernet0/2
 switchport mode access
 switchport access vlan 10
!
```

   a. DHCP DISCOVER

   b. DHCP OFFER

   c. DHCP REQUEST

   d. DHCP ACK

8. Which of the following commands enables you to apply an ACL to vty lines?

   a. ip access-group

   b. access-group

   c. access-class

   d. ip access-class

Troubleshooting Case Study: PILE Forensic Accounting

This chapter presents five troubleshooting cases at PILE Forensic Accounting, a fictitious company, based on the topology shown in Figure 8-1. PILE has hired SECHNIK Networking for technical support; as employees of SECHNIK, we need to solve all problems reported by the customer and document them. Each troubleshooting case includes a few configuration errors. Configuration errors will be dealt with as real-world troubleshooting scenarios. Certain technologies are explained briefly to refresh your memory.

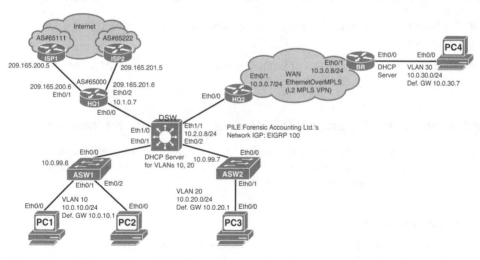

Figure 8-1 *PILE Forensic Accounting Network Diagram*

We have the following list of notes that Carrie, the resident network engineer at PILE Forensic Accounting, has provided us:

- For the Internet connectivity test, use the IP address 209.165.200.129.

- We are allowed to perform intrusive and disruptive testing during our troubleshooting efforts.

- Because we operate from the headquarters, we do not have access to the branch routers console; we can use Telnet to access the branch router.

- Telnet and enable passwords on all devices are C1sc0.

Note   The networks presented in this and the following chapters use Cisco routers to simulate the servers and personal computers (PCs); keep that in mind as you observe the output shown in the examples presented.

PILE Forensic Accounting Trouble Ticket 1

We work for SECHNIK Networking, and PILE Forensic Accounting is a valuable customer of ours. One of our staff, Peter, has made a few improvements at PILE's network over the weekend. On Monday, Carrie, who works for PILE as a resident network engineer, was made aware of the following two problems that we need to solve immediately:

- The branch office at PILE has lost connectivity to the headquarters and thus from the Internet.

- When ISP1's connection is lost or brought down, the connection to ISP2 does not provide Internet connectivity as backup.

Troubleshooting PILE's Branch Connectivity to HQ and the Internet

According to Carrie, the branch site of PILE has lost connectivity to the headquarters. Because the branch site has Internet connectivity through the headquarters, they are also suffering from lack of Internet connectivity.

Verifying and Defining the Problem

While at PILE's headquarters, we have no direct access to the branch router's console line. Therefore, to verify the problems as explained to us, we decide to telnet from headquarter's HQ1 router into the branch router. The branch router's IP address is 10.3.0.8. Example 8-1 shows our Telnet attempt to the branch router from HQ1 failing; it also shows that a ping to the same address failed every time (0 percent success rate).

Example 8-1 *Verifying the Problem: Telnet and Ping from HQ1 to Branch Fail*

```
PC1# telnet 10.3.0.8
Trying 10.3.0.8 ...
% Connection timed out; remote host not responding

PC1# ping 10.3.0.8
Type escape sequence to abort.
Sending 5, 100-byte ICMP Echos to 10.3.0.8, timeout is 2 seconds:
.....
Success rate is 0 percent (0/5)
PC1#




HQ2# telnet 10.3.0.8
Trying 10.3.0.8 ... Open

User Access Verification
Password:
BR> exit

[Connection to 10.3.0.8 closed by foreign host]
HQ2#
```

Carrie, PILE's network engineer, accesses the branch router from her PC (PC1) in the headquarters on a regular basis. However, this lack of connectivity has been reported following the changes that our colleague Peter has made over the weekend.

We decided to try our next attempt to access the branch router from the HQ2 router, which has a more direct connection to it over the WAN service. As shown in the second part of Example 8-1, a Telnet from HQ2 to BR (branch router) was successful. This proves that the WAN service is working properly.

Next, from the branch router (BR), we tried an extended ping to the distribution switch (DSW) at the headquarters (10.2.0.8) and the IP address given to us for the Internet connectivity test (209.165.200.129), using Ethernet 0/0's IP as the source. BR's Ethernet 0/0 with the IP address 10.0.30.7 belongs to the branch LAN IP subnet. Example 8-2 shows the result of both extended pings. As you can see, both pings failed (again, 0 percent success rate).

Example 8-2 *Verifying the Problem: Ping from BR to HQ and Internet Failed*

```
BR# ping
Protocol [ip]:
Target IP address: 10.2.0.8
Repeat count [5]:
```

```
Datagram size [100]:
Timeout in seconds [2]:
Extended commands [n]: y
Source address or interface: 10.0.30.7
< ...output omitted... >
Sending 5, 100-byte ICMP Echos to 10.2.0.8, timeout is 2 seconds:
Packet sent with a source address of 10.0.30.7
.....
Success rate is 0 percent (0/5)
BR#
BR# ping
Protocol [ip]:
Target IP address: 209.165.200.129
Repeat count [5]:
Datagram size [100]:
Timeout in seconds [2]:
Extended commands [n]: y
Source address or interface: 10.0.30.7
< ...output omitted... >
Sending 5, 100-byte ICMP Echos to 209.165.200.129, timeout is 2 seconds:
Packet sent with a source address of 10.0.30.7
.....
Success rate is 0 percent (0/5)
BR#
```

Now that we verified the problem on our own, we can define it as a branch site IP reachability problem to the headquarters and, consequently, to the Internet. Because the devices in the headquarters have no Internet connectivity problems and the direct WAN connection between HQ2 and BR routers is in working order, we can try the shooting-from-the-hip approach and jump straight into Interior Gateway Protocol (IGP) troubleshooting.

Gathering Information

DSW is a Layer 3 switch within the headquarters site, and it is a focal point of PILE's network. Therefore, we decided to start our information gathering from DSW. As shown in Example 8-3, DSW has no routing information for the 10.0.30.0/24 network (the branch LAN network address); DSW does, however, have an entry for the 10.0.10.0/24 network (where PC1 resides) in its routing table.

Example 8-3 *Information Gathering: Examine DSW's Routing Table*

```
DSW# show ip route
< ...output omitted... >
Gateway of last resort is 10.1.0.7 to network 0.0.0.0

D*    0.0.0.0/0 [90/281600] via 10.1.0.7, 00:04:48, Ethernet1/0
```

```
            10.0.0.0/8 is variably subnetted, 12 subnets, 3 masks
D           10.0.0.0/8 [90/281600] via 10.1.0.7, 00:04:48, Ethernet1/0
C           10.0.10.0/24 is directly connected, Vlan10
L           10.0.10.1/32 is directly connected, Vlan10
C           10.0.20.0/24 is directly connected, Vlan20
L           10.0.20.1/32 is directly connected, Vlan20
C           10.0.99.0/24 is directly connected, Vlan99
L           10.0.99.1/32 is directly connected, Vlan99
C           10.1.0.0/24 is directly connected, Ethernet1/0
L           10.1.0.8/32 is directly connected, Ethernet1/0
C           10.2.0.0/24 is directly connected, Ethernet1/1
L           10.2.0.8/32 is directly connected, Ethernet1/1
D           10.3.0.0/24 [90/307200] via 10.2.0.7, 00:05:52, Ethernet1/1
            209.165.200.0/24 is variably subnetted, 2 subnets, 2 masks
D           209.165.200.4/30 [90/307200] via 10.1.0.7, 00:04:48, Ethernet1/0
D           209.165.200.248/29 [90/281600] via 10.1.0.7, 00:04:48, Ethernet1/0
            209.165.201.0/30 is subnetted, 1 subnets
D           209.165.201.4 [90/307200] via 10.1.0.7, 00:04:48, Ethernet1/0
DSW# show ip route 10.30.0.0
Routing entry for 10.0.0.0/8
  Known via "eigrp 100", distance 90, metric 281600, type internal
  Redistributing via eigrp 100
  Last update from 10.1.0.7 on Ethernet1/0, 00:05:22 ago
  Routing Descriptor Blocks:
  * 10.1.0.7, from 10.1.0.7, 00:05:22 ago, via Ethernet1/0
      Route metric is 281600, traffic share count is 1
      Total delay is 1000 microseconds, minimum bandwidth is 10000 Kbit
      Reliability 0/255, minimum MTU 1500 bytes
      Loading 1/255, Hops 1
DSW#
```

So far, we have gathered a significant piece of information: DSW is not receiving reachability information toward the branch site from the HQ2 router through IGP. Naturally, it is a good idea to examine HQ2's routing table next. HQ2 is supposed to receive reachability information toward 10.0.30.0/24 from BR through Enhanced Interior Gateway Routing Protocol (EIGRP) 100 over the WAN link. However, as Example 8-4 shows, HQ2 does not have this network in its routing table; in other words, it has not received it through EIGRP 100.

Example 8-4 *Information Gathering: Examine HQ2's Routing Table*

```
HQ2# show ip route
< ...output omitted... >
Gateway of last resort is 10.2.0.8 to network 0.0.0.0

D*    0.0.0.0/0 [90/307200] via 10.2.0.8, 00:07:13, Ethernet0/0
```

```
        10.0.0.0/8 is variably subnetted, 9 subnets, 3 masks
D         10.0.0.0/8 [90/307200] via 10.2.0.8, 00:07:13, Ethernet0/0
D         10.0.10.0/24 [90/281856] via 10.2.0.8, 00:07:51, Ethernet0/0
D         10.0.20.0/24 [90/281856] via 10.2.0.8, 00:07:51, Ethernet0/0
D         10.0.99.0/24 [90/281856] via 10.2.0.8, 00:07:51, Ethernet0/0
D         10.1.0.0/24 [90/307200] via 10.2.0.8, 00:08:17, Ethernet0/0
C         10.2.0.0/24 is directly connected, Ethernet0/0
L         10.2.0.7/32 is directly connected, Ethernet0/0
C         10.3.0.0/24 is directly connected, Ethernet0/1
L         10.3.0.7/32 is directly connected, Ethernet0/1
        209.165.200.0/24 is variably subnetted, 2 subnets, 2 masks
D         209.165.200.4/30 [90/332800] via 10.2.0.8, 00:07:13, Ethernet0/0
D         209.165.200.248/29 [90/307200] via 10.2.0.8, 00:07:13, Ethernet0/0
        209.165.201.0/30 is subnetted, 1 subnets
D         209.165.201.4 [90/332800] via 10.2.0.8, 00:07:13, Ethernet0/0
HQ2#
```

In our next information gathering attempt, it is best to use the **show ip protocols** command on the HQ2 router. Example 8-5 shows the output of this command, which allows us to examine HQ2's IP routing configuration parameters and neighbor adjacencies. As you can see, HQ2 has EIGRP activated on correct networks, but it only has one gateway (10.2.0.8) listed as a routing information source, which is DSW.

Example 8-5   *Information Gathering: Output of the Show IP Protocols on HQ2*

```
HQ2# show ip protocols
*** IP Routing is NSF aware ***

Routing Protocol is "eigrp 100"
  Outgoing update filter list for all interfaces is not set
  Incoming update filter list for all interfaces is not set
  Default networks flagged in outgoing updates
  Default networks accepted from incoming updates
  EIGRP-IPv4 Protocol for AS(100)
    Metric weight K1=1, K2=0, K3=1, K4=0, K5=0
    NSF-aware route hold timer is 240
    Router-ID: 10.3.0.7
    Topology : 0 (base)
      Active Timer: 3 min
      Distance: internal 90 external 170
      Maximum path: 4
      Maximum hopcount 100
      Maximum metric variance 1

  Automatic Summarization: disabled
  Maximum path: 4
```

```
 Routing for Networks:
   10.2.0.0/24
   10.3.0.0/24
 Routing Information Sources:
   Gateway          Distance       Last Update
   10.2.0.8              90         00:07:52
 Distance: internal 90 external 170
HQ2#
```

To gather information about the lack of neighbor adjacency between HQ2 and the BR over the WAN, we can use **debug eigrp packets**. Example 8-6 shows the output of this command. The EIGRP process on HQ2 is sending hello packets out of Eth0/0 toward DSW and out of Eth0/1 over the WAN link. However, HQ2 is only receiving hello packets from DSW over the Eth0/0 interface. HQ2 is not receiving hello packets on Eth0/1 over the WAN link.

Example 8-6 *Information Gathering: EIGRP Debug Output*

```
HQ2# debug eigrp packets
    (UPDATE, REQUEST, QUERY, REPLY, HELLO, IPXSAP, PROBE, ACK, STUB, SIAQUERY,
SIAREPLY)
EIGRP Packet debugging is on
HQ2#
*Sep  4 16:20:25.843: EIGRP: Sending HELLO on Et0/0 - paklen 20
< ...output omitted... >
*Sep  4 16:20:29.305: EIGRP: Sending HELLO on Et0/1 - paklen 20
< ...output omitted... >
*Sep  4 16:20:30.293: EIGRP: Received HELLO on Et0/0 - paklen 20 nbr 10.2.0.8
< ...output omitted... >
*Sep  4 16:20:30.459: EIGRP: Sending HELLO on Et0/0 - paklen 20
< ...output omitted... >
*Sep  4 16:20:33.680: EIGRP: Sending HELLO on Et0/1 - paklen 20
< ...output omitted... >
*Sep  4 16:20:35.285: EIGRP: Received HELLO on Et0/0 - paklen 20 nbr 10.2.0.8
< ...output omitted... >
HQ2# no debug all
All possible debugging has been turned off
HQ2#
```

To find out why BR is not sending EIGRP hello packets on the WAN link toward HQ2, we use **show ip protocols** again, this time on the BR router. As shown in Example 8-7, BR has EIGRP correctly activated on Eth0/0 connected to the branch LAN (10.0.30.0/24); however, the second network shown for EIGRP is 10.3.0.0/32.

Example 8-7   *Information Gathering: Output of the Show IP Protocols on BR*

```
BR# show ip protocols
*** IP Routing is NSF aware ***

Routing Protocol is "eigrp 100"
  Outgoing update filter list for all interfaces is not set
  Incoming update filter list for all interfaces is not set
  Default networks flagged in outgoing updates
  Default networks accepted from incoming updates
  EIGRP-IPv4 Protocol for AS(100)
    Metric weight K1=1, K2=0, K3=1, K4=0, K5=0
    NSF-aware route hold timer is 240
    Router-ID: 10.3.0.8
    Topology : 0 (base)
      Active Timer: 3 min
      Distance: internal 90 external 170
      Maximum path: 4
      Maximum hopcount 100
      Maximum metric variance 1

  Automatic Summarization: disabled
  Maximum path: 4
  Routing for Networks:
    10.0.30.0/24
    10.3.0.0/32
  Routing Information Sources:
    Gateway         Distance      Last Update
  Distance: internal 90 external 170
BR#
```

Analyzing Information

The information gathered from the output of the **show ip protocols** command on the BR router revealed that EIGRP is not activated on BR's Eth0/1 interface facing the WAN. The reason is that the mask used (/32) with the network 10.3.0.0 causes the routing process to only get activated on an interface that gets a 32-bit match to 10.3.0.0. The interface Eth0/1 (with the IP address 10.3.0.8/24) gets a 24-bit match to 10.3.0.0, but not a 32-bit match.

Proposing a Hypothesis and Testing the Hypothesis

Our proposed hypothesis is to modify the second **network** statement to 10.3.0.8/32 so that it will have a 32-bit match to BR's Eth0/1 interface IP address and go active on the WAN circuit toward HQ2. Example 8-8 shows our work on the BR router, modifying the EIGRP configuration according to the proposed hypothesis.

Example 8-8 *Proposing a Hypothesis: Modify EIGRP* network *Statement on BR*

```
BR# show run | section router eigrp 100
router eigrp 100
 network 10.0.30.0 0.0.0.255
 network 10.3.0.0 0.0.0.0
BR# conf term
Enter configuration commands, one per line.  End with CNTL/Z.
BR(config)# router eigrp 100
BR(config-router)# no network 10.3.0.0 0.0.0.0
BR(config-router)# network 10.3.0.8 0.0.0.0
BR(config-router)# end
*Sep  4 16:23:42.533: %DUAL-5-NBRCHANGE: EIGRP-IPv4 100: Neighbor 10.3.0.8
(Ethernet0/1) is up: new adjacency
BR# wr
Building configuration...
[OK]
BR#
```

Now we can test our hypothesis; first we use the **show ip eigrp neighbor** command on the BR router. Example 8-9 shows the output of this command; as you can see, HQ2 is now listed as an EIGRP neighbor through BR's interface Eth0/1.

Example 8-9 *Testing a Hypothesis: The BR and HQ2 Routers Form an EIGRP Neighbor Relationship over the WAN Connection*

```
BR# show ip eigrp neighbors
EIGRP-IPv4 Neighbors for AS(100)
H   Address                 Interface       Hold Uptime   SRTT   RTO  Q  Seq
                                            (sec)         (ms)        Cnt Num
0   10.3.0.7                Et0/1           14 00:00:15   13     100  0  9
BR#
```

Solving the Problem

Finally, we try extended ping from BR (using Eth0/0 as the source interface), first to DSW (10.2.0.8), and next to the Internet (209.165.200.129). Example 8-10 shows that both of these pings are 100 percent successful and that the problem is solved. PILE's branch site is now connected to the Internet through PILE's headquarters site over the WAN.

Example 8-10 *Solving the Problem: Branch Site Internet Connectivity Is Restored*

```
BR# ping
Protocol [ip]:
Target IP address: 10.2.0.8
Repeat count [5]:
```

```
Datagram size [100]:
Timeout in seconds [2]:
Extended commands [n]: y
Source address or interface: 10.0.30.7
< ...output omitted... >
Type escape sequence to abort.
Sending 5, 100-byte ICMP Echos to 10.2.0.8, timeout is 2 seconds:
Packet sent with a source address of 10.0.30.7
!!!!!
Success rate is 100 percent (5/5), round-trip min/avg/max = 1/1/5 ms
BR#
BR# ping
Protocol [ip]:
Target IP address: 209.165.200.129
Repeat count [5]:
Datagram size [100]:
Timeout in seconds [2]:
Extended commands [n]: y
Source address or interface: 10.0.30.7
< ...output omitted... >
Type escape sequence to abort.
Sending 5, 100-byte ICMP Echos to 209.165.200.129, timeout is 2 seconds:
Packet sent with a source address of 10.0.30.7
!!!!!
Success rate is 100 percent (5/5), round-trip min/avg/max = 1/2/7 ms
BR#
```

We must now document our work and notify Carrie that the problem is solved.

Troubleshooting EIGRP Adjacency

The following are some of the possible causes for EIGRP neighbor relationship problems:

- Circuit (physical or data link layer) malfunction between EIGRP adjacent neighbors.

- Incorrect IP address/subnet mask on either neighbor.

- Autonomous system number (ASN) mismatch between neighbors.

- EIGRP metric's K values not matching between neighbors. K1 and K3 equal 1 by default; and K2, K4, and K5 equal 0 by default. Modifying K values affects incorporation of bandwidth, delay, reliability, and load in the EIGRP metric calculation.

- Erroneous **network** statement on either neighbor.

- EIGRP may be configured as passive on an interface where it is supposed be active and form adjacency.

- EIGRP authentication configuration mismatch between neighbors (authentication mode or key).

- ACLs/firewalls can stop EIGRP messages from being exchanged between adjacent neighbors.

The Cisco IOS **show ip protocols** command output displays the configured ASN, K values, and networks, plus any discovered gateways (neighbors). Useful EIGRP-specific troubleshooting commands include the following:

- **show ip eigrp neighbors:** Use this command to display the current EIGRP adjacencies.

- **show ip eigrp interfaces:** Use this command to display the list of interfaces where EIGRP is active.

- **debug ip eigrp packets:** Use this command to see the EIGRP packets as they are sent or received on the local router.

Troubleshooting PILE's Secondary Internet Connection Through ISP2

According to Carrie, when PILE's connection to ISP1 fails or it is brought down for testing, the secondary Internet connection through ISP2 does not act as backup, and Internet connectivity is lost altogether. This is considered a critical issue, and they need a permanent solution.

Verifying and Defining the Problem

To verify the problem, we first tried to ping the Internet address 209.165.200.129 from PC1, and as you can see in Example 8-11, it was 100 percent successful. Then, with Carrie's permission, we shut down HQ1's interface Eth0/1, which connects to ISP1. Pinging from PC1 was no longer successful after the connection to ISP1 had been shut down. This verifies the problem as Carrie described it.

Example 8-11 *Verifying the Problem: Testing PILE's Internet Connectivity With and Without ISP1*

```
PC1> ping 209.165.200.129
Type escape sequence to abort.
Sending 5, 100-byte ICMP Echos to 209.165.200.129, timeout is 2 seconds:
!!!!!
Success rate is 100 percent (5/5), round-trip min/avg/max = 1/201/1004 ms
PC1>

HQ1# conf term
Enter configuration commands, one per line.  End with CNTL/Z.
HQ1(config)# int eth0/1
HQ1(config-if)# shut
HQ1(config-if)#
```

```
*Sep  5 15:56:53.852: %BGP-5-ADJCHANGE: neighbor 209.165.200.5 Down Interface flap
*Sep  5 15:56:53.852: %BGP_SESSION-5-ADJCHANGE: neighbor 209.165.200.5 IPv4 Unicast
  topology base removed from session  Interface flap
*Sep  5 15:56:55.852: %LINK-5-CHANGED: Interface Ethernet0/1, changed state to
  administratively down
*Sep  5 15:56:56.852: %LINEPROTO-5-UPDOWN: Line protocol on Interface Ethernet0/1,
  changed state to down
HQ1(config-if)#


PC1> ping 209.165.200.129
Type escape sequence to abort.
Sending 5, 100-byte ICMP Echos to 209.165.200.129, timeout is 2 seconds:
U.U.U

Success rate is 0 percent (0/5)
PC1>
```

We can define the problem as follows: PILE Forensic Accounting has two Internet connections through ISP1 and ISP2. The policy at PILE is that Internet connectivity must survive in case the connection to either ISP fails. We have verified that Internet connection through ISP2 does not function and that PILE's Internet connectivity is lost when the connection to ISP1 is down.

Gathering Information

Based on the fact that the Internet connection to ISP1 is working well from the HQ1 router, yet the Internet connection to ISP2 is not working from the same router (HQ1), we can use the spot-the-differences approach. We will start by looking at HQ1 router's configuration toward ISP1 and ISP2.

Example 8-12 shows the output of the **show ip protocols** command on router HQ1. As you can see, HQ1 is running Border Gateway Protocol (BGP) 65000 and has two neighbors (209.165.200.5 and 209.165.201.5) configured. However, only one neighbor (209.165.200.5) seems to be operational. Neighbor 209.165.200.5 is ISP1's router. We need to find out why the relationship with 209.165.201.5, which is ISP2's router, is not operational.

Example 8-12 *Information Gathering: Examine HQ's External Routing Status*

```
HQ1# show ip protocols | section bgp
Routing Protocol is "bgp 65000"
  Outgoing update filter list for all interfaces is not set
  Incoming update filter list for all interfaces is not set
  IGP synchronization is disabled
  Automatic route summarization is disabled
  Neighbor(s):
    Address       FiltIn FiltOut DistIn DistOut Weight RouteMap
```

```
     209.165.200.5                        RouteOu
     209.165.201.5                        RouteOu
  Maximum path: 1
  Routing Information Sources:
     Gateway          Distance       Last Update
     209.165.200.5         20        00:00:00
  Distance: external 20 internal 200 local 200
HQ1#
```

To gather more information about the status of HQ1's BGP relationship with its neighbors (ISP1 and ISP2), we can use the **show ip bgp summary** command. As shown in Example 8-13, the state of the BGP relationship with ISP1 (neighbor 209.165.200.5) is established with seven prefixes received, and the state of the BGP relationship with neighbor 209.165.201.5 (ISP2) is active. The active state means that a culprit is stopping the TCP three-way handshake from completing between HQ1 and ISP2's BGP speaker.

Example 8-13 *Information Gathering: Examine HQ1's BGP Neighbor Status*

```
HQ1# show ip bgp summary
BGP router identifier 10.10.10.10, local AS number 65000
BGP table version is 9, main routing table version 9
8 network entries using 1184 bytes of memory
8 path entries using 512 bytes of memory
8/8 BGP path/bestpath attribute entries using 1088 bytes of memory
7 BGP AS-PATH entries using 268 bytes of memory
0 BGP route-map cache entries using 0 bytes of memory
0 BGP filter-list cache entries using 0 bytes of memory
BGP using 3052 total bytes of memory
BGP activity 8/0 prefixes, 8/0 paths, scan interval 60 secs

Neighbor        V    AS MsgRcvd MsgSent   TblVer  InQ OutQ Up/Down  State/PfxRcd
209.165.200.5   4    65111      12        4       9   0    0        00:01:39            7
209.165.201.5   4    65222      0         0       1   0    0        never      Active
HQ1#
```

It is best to first determine whether neighbor 209.165.201.5 is reachable. Example 8-14 shows that a ping to this address is successful. Note that network 209.165.201.0/24 is connected through HQ1's interface Eth0/2.

Example 8-14 *Information Gathering: On HQ1, Check for Neighbor Reachability*

```
HQ1# ping 209.165.201.5
Type escape sequence to abort.
Sending 5, 100-byte ICMP Echos to 209.165.201.5, timeout is 2 seconds:
!!!!!
Success rate is 100 percent (5/5), round-trip min/avg/max = 1/1/1 ms
HQ1#
```

Next, we can check whether any access control list is blocking the TCP three-way handshake between HQ1 and ISP2's router. Example 8-15 shows HQ1's running-config, where you can see that access list 100 is applied to both interfaces Eth0/1 and Eth0/2 in the inbound direction. Example 8-15 also shows the output of the **show access-list 100** command, which reveals the contents of this access control list (ACL).

Example 8-15 *Information Gathering: Is an ACL Blocking TCP's Handshake?*

```
HQ1# show running-config | section interface
< ...output omitted... >
interface Ethernet0/1
 description ISP1
 ip address 209.165.200.6 255.255.255.252
 ip access-group 100 in
 ip nat outside
 ip inspect INSPECT out
 ip virtual-reassembly in
interface Ethernet0/2
 description ISP2
 ip address 209.165.201.6 255.255.255.252
 ip access-group 100 in
 ip nat outside
 ip inspect INSPECT out
 ip virtual-reassembly in
< ...output omitted... >
HQ1#
HQ1# show access-list 100
Extended IP access list 100
    10 permit tcp host 209.165.200.5 host 209.165.200.6 eq bgp
    20 permit tcp host 209.165.200.5 eq bgp host 209.165.200.6 (19 matches)
    30 permit tcp host 209.165.201.6 eq bgp host 209.165.201.5
    40 permit tcp host 209.165.201.6 host 209.165.201.5 eq bgp
    50 permit icmp any any echo-reply (5 matches)
HQ1#
```

Analyzing Information and Proposing a Hypothesis

We can now analyze the content of ACL 100, which is applied (inbound) to both Eth0/1 (connecting to ISP1) and to Eth0/2 (connecting to ISP2). The first two lines of this ACL permit TCP traffic from 209.165.200.5 (ISP1) to HQ1. The first line has the destination port number listed as BGP (179), and the second line has the source port number listed as BGP (179). The first two lines are correct, considering that the ACL is applied in the inbound direction. The third line in the ACL permits TCP packets from the source IP address 209.165.201.6 (with BGP as the source port) to destination IP address 209.165.201.5. This line is incorrect because 209.165.201.6 is HQ1's Eth0/2 IP address, so we would never receive a packet from this address. The source and destination addresses on this line are mistakenly swapped. The same is true for the fourth line. The fifth line in the ACL permits Internet Control Message Protocol (ICMP) echo-reply messages.

Our hypothesis is to correct ACL 100's third and fourth lines so that the TCP three-way handshake between HQ1 and ISP2's router can complete and so that the BGP relationship between these routers can be established. Note that after ACL 100's third and fourth lines are corrected, we can expect the BGP relationship between HQ1 and ISP2, in addition to the relationship between HQ1 and ISP1, to get established. However, because of the implicit deny on the ACL, no other traffic (except ICMP echo-reply) will be allowed to enter the HQ1 router through either Eth0/1 or Eth0/2 interfaces. We need to consult with Carrie, from PILE, to add appropriate additional **permit** statements to ACL 100; for now, though, we will focus on fixing the BGP neighbor problem.

Testing the Hypothesis

Example 8-16 shows us shutting down both Eth0/1 and Eth0/2 interfaces of router HQ1 and correcting ACL 100's erroneous third and fourth lines. Note that we are going to leave further corrections needed on ACL 100 (to allow traffic other than BGP and ICMP echo-reply) up to Carrie at PILE.

Example 8-16   *Testing the Hypothesis: Correcting ACL 100's Statements*

```
HQ1# conf t
Enter configuration commands, one per line.  End with CNTL/Z.
HQ1(config)# int range ether0/1-2
HQ1(config-if-range)# shut
HQ1(config-if-range)# end
< ...output omitted... >
HQ1#
HQ1# show access-list 100
Extended IP access list 100
    10 permit tcp host 209.165.200.5 host 209.165.200.6 eq bgp
    20 permit tcp host 209.165.200.5 eq bgp host 209.165.200.6 (19 matches)
    30 permit tcp host 209.165.201.6 eq bgp host 209.165.201.5
    40 permit tcp host 209.165.201.6 host 209.165.201.5 eq bgp
    50 permit icmp any any echo-reply (5 matches)
HQ1#
HQ1# conf term
Enter configuration commands, one per line.  End with CNTL/Z.
HQ1(config)# ip access-list extended 100
HQ1(config-ext-nacl)# no 30
HQ1(config-ext-nacl)# no 40
HQ1(config-ext-nacl)# permit tcp host 209.165.201.5 host 209.165.201.6 eq bgp
HQ1(config-ext-nacl)# permit tcp host 209.165.201.5 eq bgp host 209.165.201.6
```

```
HQ1(config-ext-nacl)# do show access-list 100
Extended IP access list 100
    10 permit tcp host 209.165.200.5 host 209.165.200.6 eq bgp
    20 permit tcp host 209.165.200.5 eq bgp host 209.165.200.6
    50 permit icmp any any echo-reply
    60 permit tcp host 209.165.201.5 host 209.165.201.6 eq bgp
    70 permit tcp host 209.165.201.5 eq bgp host 209.165.201.6
HQ1(config-ext-nacl)# no 50
HQ1(config-ext-nacl)# permit icmp any any echo-reply
HQ1(config-ext-nacl)# end
*Sep  5 16:41:43.159: %SYS-5-CONFIG_I: Configured from console by console
HQ1# conf t
Enter configuration commands, one per line.  End with CNTL/Z.
HQ1(config)# int range eth 0/1-2
HQ1(config-if-range)# no shut
HQ1(config-if-range)# end
< ...output omitted... >
*Sep  5 16:57:16.388: %BGP-5-ADJCHANGE: neighbor 209.165.201.5 Up
*Sep  5 16:57:27.747: %BGP-5-ADJCHANGE: neighbor 209.165.200.5 Up
HQ1#
HQ1# wr
Building configuration...
[OK]
HQ1#
```

After we corrected ACL 100's statements and brought up the two interfaces (Eth0/1 and Eth0/2) of the HQ1 router, as shown in Example 8-16, IOS console logging messages indicated that the BGP sessions with both ISPs were established. Yet, we still entered the **show ip bgp summary** command on HQ1 again. As shown in Example 8-17, both neighbors are listed, and a BGP relationship with both is established, with seven prefixes received from 209.165.200.5 and eight prefixes received from 209.165.201.5.

Example 8-17   *Testing the Hypothesis: Examining BGP Neighbor Relationships*

```
HQ1# show ip bgp summary
BGP router identifier 10.10.10.10, local AS number 65000
BGP table version is 38, main routing table version 38
9 network entries using 1332 bytes of memory
16 path entries using 1024 bytes of memory
15/8 BGP path/bestpath attribute entries using 2040 bytes of memory
14 BGP AS-PATH entries using 536 bytes of memory
0 BGP route-map cache entries using 0 bytes of memory
0 BGP filter-list cache entries using 0 bytes of memory
BGP using 4932 total bytes of memory
BGP activity 23/14 prefixes, 30/14 paths, scan interval 60 secs
```

Neighbor	V	AS	MsgRcvd	MsgSent	TblVer	InQ	OutQ	Up/Down	State/PfxRcd
209.165.200.5	4	65111	12	4	38	0	0	00:00:55	7
209.165.201.5	4	65222	15	6	38	0	0	00:01:07	8
HQ1#									

Solving the Problem

We can now test whether PILE's Internet connectivity survives in case connectivity to ISP1 is lost. As shown in Example 8-18, we can ping the IP address 209.165.200.129 while both Eth0/1 and Eth0/2 interfaces of HQ1 are up. Next, we shut down HQ1's Eth0/1 interface (connected to ISP1) and repeat the ping test; ping is 100 percent successful. It is evident that PILE's redundant Internet connection is now operational.

Example 8-18   *Solving the Problem: PILE's Redundant Internet Connectivity Test*

```
PC1> ping 209.165.200.129
Type escape sequence to abort.
Sending 5, 100-byte ICMP Echos to 209.165.200.129, timeout is 2 seconds:
!!!!!
Success rate is 100 percent (5/5), round-trip min/avg/max = 1/202/1005 ms
PC1>



HQ1# conf t
Enter configuration commands, one per line.  End with CNTL/Z.
HQ1(config)# int eth 0/1
HQ1(config-if)# shut
HQ1(config-if)#
*Sep  5 17:02:37.200: %BGP-5-ADJCHANGE: neighbor 209.165.200.5 Down Interface flap
*Sep  5 17:02:37.200: %BGP_SESSION-5-ADJCHANGE: neighbor 209.165.200.5 IPv4 Unicast
  topology base removed from session  Interface flap
HQ1(config-if)#
*Sep  5 17:02:39.200: %LINK-5-CHANGED: Interface Ethernet0/1, changed state to
  administratively down
*Sep  5 17:02:40.204: %LINEPROTO-5-UPDOWN: Line protocol on Interface Ethernet0/1,
  changed state to down
HQ1(config-if)# end
HQ1#



PC1> ping 209.165.200.129
Type escape sequence to abort.
Sending 5, 100-byte ICMP Echos to 209.165.200.129, timeout is 2 seconds:
!!!!!
Success rate is 100 percent (5/5), round-trip min/avg/max = 1/1/1 ms
PC1>
```

```
HQ1# conf t
Enter configuration commands, one per line.  End with CNTL/Z.
HQ1(config)# int eth 0/1
HQ1(config-if)# no shut
HQ1(config-if)# end
HQ1# wr
```

We must now document our work and notify Carrie that the problem is solved. Carrie will have to further modify ACL 100 or ask us to do it; otherwise, no traffic other than BGP and ICMP echo-reply is allowed by this ACL.

PILE Forensic Accounting Trouble Ticket 2

This trouble ticket has three elements:

1. We have been notified that a user from PILE Forensic Accounting has contacted us directly (SECHNIK Networking) and complained that from his PC (PC3) he cannot telnet into the branch router (BR). He wants this problem fixed as soon as possible.

2. Carrie, the resident network engineer at PILE, has contacted us in a panic, saying that everyone at PILE has lost Internet connectivity. She specified that from HQ1 router she can successfully ping the IP address 209.165.201.129, which is the Internet connectivity test address used at PILE.

3. Carrie mentioned a matter related to network time synchronization. She specified that the HQ1 router's time is not synchronized with the preferred Network Time Protocol (NTP) server, whose IP address is 209.165.201.193. Carrie added that there are two backup NTP servers, whose IP addresses are 209.165.201.225 and 209.165.201.129.

Troubleshooting Telnet Problem: From PC3 to BR

Based on the message left by the user of PC3 at PILE Forensic Accounting, he cannot access PILE's BR using Telnet. Example 8-19 shows that Telnet from PC3 fails.

Example 8-19   *Verifying the Problem: Telnet from PC3 to BR (Branch) Router Fails*

```
PC3# Telnet 10.0.30.7
Trying 10.0.30.7 ...
% Connection refused by remote host

PC3#
```

Gathering Information

Using the swap-the-component technique, we decided to try the Telnet session from PC1. As Example 8-20 shows, a Telnet from PC1 to the BR (Branch) router was successful. This also gave us the opportunity to examine the vty line configuration on the BR, to gather further information about the problem at hand. As you can see, access list 10 is applied to the vty lines. We then decided to display the content of access list 10. As shown in Example 8-20, access list 10 permits sessions sourced from network 10.0.10.0/24 (VLAN 10), and it explicitly denies sessions sourced from network 10.0.20.0/24 (VLAN 20), where PC3 resides. Interestingly, there is a remark within access list 10 that specifies users from VLAN 20 should not be allowed to telnet in!

Example 8-20   *Information Gathering: Telnet from PC1 to BR Succeeds*

```
PC1# telnet 10.0.30.7
Trying 10.0.30.7 ... Open


User Access Verification


Password:
BR>en
Password:
BR#
BR# show running-config | section line vty
line vty 0 4
 access-class 10 in
 password c1sc0
 login
 transport input all
BR#
BR# show running-config | section access-list 10
access-list 10 permit 10.0.10.0 0.0.0.255
access-list 10 deny   10.0.20.0 0.0.0.255
access-list 10 remark USERS from VLAN 20 should not be allowed to Telnet in
BR#
```

We can conclude that there is no problem. The BR is operating correctly, rejecting Telnet attempts sourced from VLAN 20. However, we need to notify Carrie at PILE about the request received and have her communicate with the user of PC3 about the policy in place.

Troubleshooting PILE Network's Internet Access Problem

This problem was reported by Carrie, the network engineer at PILE. She stated that PILE had lost Internet connectivity and that they urgently needed assistance.

Verifying and Defining the Problem

To verify the problem, we decided to ping the Internet reachability test IP address 209.165.200.129 from PC1 first. As shown in Example 8-21, the ping from PC1 to this address failed. However, as shown in the same example, a ping to the same address from HQ1 succeeds 100 percent of the time.

Example 8-21   *Verify the Problem: Ping the Test IP Address from PC1 and HQ1*

```
PC1# ping 209.165.200.129
Type escape sequence to abort.
Sending 5, 100-byte ICMP Echos to 209.165.200.129, timeout is 2 seconds:
.....
Success rate is 0 percent (0/5)
PC1#


HQ1# ping 209.165.200.129
Type escape sequence to abort.
Sending 5, 100-byte ICMP Echos to 209.165.200.129, timeout is 2 seconds:
!!!!!
Success rate is 100 percent (5/5), round-trip min/avg/max = 1/1/1 ms
HQ1#
```

We can conclude that from the user's perspective, the problem is verified to be accurate. The problem is defined as Internet is not reachable by user workstations within PILE's network. We can take the follow-the-path approach, starting from PC1.

Gathering Information

At PC1, we first check the status of its Ethernet interface and make sure that it is up and has an IP address. We also make sure that it has a correct gateway of last resort (default gateway) to communicate with devices outside its subnet. As shown in Example 8-22, interface Ethernet 0/0 of PC1 is up, its IP address is 10.0.10.2, and its default gateway is shown as 10.0.10.1. The IP address 10.0.10.1 belongs to DSW on VLAN 10. As shown, the ping to the default gateway is 100 percent successful.

Example 8-22   *Information Gathering: Check PC1's Ethernet Interface Status*

```
PC1# show ip int brief
Interface                  IP-Address      OK? Method Status                Protocol
Ethernet0/0                10.0.10.3       YES DHCP   up                     up
< ...output omitted... >
PC1#
PC1# show ip route
Default gateway is 10.0.10.1
```

```
Host              Gateway         Last Use    Total Uses  Interface
ICMP redirect cache is empty
PC1#
PC1# ping 10.0.10.1
Type escape sequence to abort.
Sending 5, 100-byte ICMP Echos to 10.0.10.1, timeout is 2 seconds:
!!!!!
Success rate is 100 percent (5/5), round-trip min/avg/max = 1/1/1 ms
PC1#
```

We can move on to the next device on the path, and that is the multilayer DSW. Pinging from DSW to the 209.165.200.129 fails. As shown in Example 8-23, when we examine DSW's IP routing table, we notice that it has a gateway of last resort pointing to the IP address 10.1.0.7, which is supposed to be the HQ1 router's Eth0/0 interface connected to the DSW.

Example 8-23 *Information Gathering: Check Internet Reachability from DSW*

```
DSW# ping 209.165.200.129
Type escape sequence to abort.
Sending 5, 100-byte ICMP Echos to 209.165.200.129, timeout is 2 seconds:
.....
Success rate is 0 percent (0/5)
DSW#
DSW# show ip route
< ...output omitted... >
Gateway of last resort is 10.1.0.7 to network 0.0.0.0

D*    0.0.0.0/0 [90/281600] via 10.1.0.7, 00:09:28, Ethernet1/0
< ...output omitted... >
DSW#
```

Naturally, we can now move on to the HQ1 router, which is DSW's gateway of last resort and PILE's edge router with redundant connections to the Internet. The output of the **show ip interfaces brief** command on the HQ1 router, as shown in Example 8-24, reveals that HQ1's interface Ethernet 0/0 is up and that it has the correct IP address 10.1.0.7. HQ1's other Ethernet interfaces (Eth0/1 and Eth0/2) are also up with accurate IP addresses. Finally, Example 8-24 shows that pinging from PC1 to HQ1 (10.1.0.7) is 100 percent successful.

Example 8-24 *Information Gathering: Check Internet Reachability from DSW*

```
HQ1#
HQ1# show ip interface brief
Interface             IP-Address        OK? Method Status
Protocol
Ethernet0/0           10.1.0.7          YES NVRAM  up                  up
```

```
Ethernet0/1                   209.165.200.6   YES NVRAM  up                  up
Ethernet0/2                   209.165.201.6   YES NVRAM  up                  up
< ...output omitted... >
HQ1#



PC1# ping 10.1.0.7
Type escape sequence to abort.
Sending 5, 100-byte ICMP Echos to 10.1.0.7, timeout is 2 seconds:
!!!!!
Success rate is 100 percent (5/5), round-trip min/avg/max = 1/1/1 ms
PC1#
```

Analyzing Information, Eliminating Causes, and Gathering Further Information

Based on the fact that there is no sign of internal routing and reachability problems, and that DSW correctly points to HQ1 as its gateway of last resort, we can eliminate internal routing problems as possible causes. However, to progress with our troubleshooting efforts, we need to do more information gathering.

We check the status of HQ1's BGP neighbor relationships with ISP1 and ISP2 routers. As shown in Example 8-25, both neighbor relationships show as established, with seven prefixes accepted from each of the neighbors. Next, we look for the 209.165.200.129 address in the BGP and IP routing table, and as you can see in Example 8-25, the prefix is present in both tables.

Example 8-25   *Information Gathering: Examine BGP Table and Neighbor Table*

```
HQ1# show ip bgp summary
< ...output omitted... >
Neighbor        V    AS   MsgRcvd  MsgSent  TblVer  InQ OutQ  Up/Down    State/PfxRcd
209.165.200.5   4  65111   29       22       10      0   0   00:16:47       7
209.165.201.5   4  65222   29       22       10      0   0   00:16:58       7
HQ1#
HQ1# show ip bgp  209.165.200.129
BGP routing table entry for 209.165.200.128/26, version 3
Paths: (2 available, best #1, table default)
  Not advertised to any peer
  Refresh Epoch 1
  65111 65333 78 1012 48 126
    209.165.200.5 from 209.165.200.5 (209.165.200.5)
      Origin IGP, localpref 100, valid, external, best
  Refresh Epoch 1
  65222 65333 78 1012 48 126
```

```
       209.165.201.5 from 209.165.201.5 (209.165.201.5)
          Origin IGP, localpref 100, valid, external
HQ1#
HQ1#
HQ1# show ip route 209.165.200.129
Routing entry for 209.165.200.128/26
  Known via "bgp 65000", distance 20, metric 0
  Tag 65111, type external
  Last update from 209.165.200.5 00:17:07 ago
  Routing Descriptor Blocks:
  * 209.165.200.5, from 209.165.200.5, 00:17:07 ago
      Route metric is 0, traffic share count is 1
      AS Hops 6
      Route tag 65111
      MPLS label: none
HQ1#
```

Finally, we must check whether HQ1's BGP process is advertising the inside global IP address of PILE to the ISP peers. This address is the public/registered IP address of PILE's network, which must be advertised in order for PILE's network to be reachable from outside. So, we use the **show ip bgp 209.165.200.248/29** command. As Example 8-26 shows, this prefix is present in the BGP table with the 0.0.0.0 next hop indicating that it is a local prefix. However, the prefix is "not advertised to any peer."

Example 8-26 *Information Gathering: Investigate Local Prefix Advertisement*

```
HQ1# show ip bgp 209.165.200.248
BGP routing table entry for 209.165.200.248/29, version 5
Paths: (1 available, best #1, table default)
  Not advertised to any peer
  Refresh Epoch 1
  Local
    0.0.0.0 from 0.0.0.0 (10.10.10.10)
      Origin IGP, metric 0, localpref 100, weight 32768, valid, sourced, local, best
HQ1#
```

Displaying HQ1's running-config, focused on the BGP configuration section, reveals that an outbound access list (RouteOut) is applied to both of its external BGP (eBGP) peers (see Example 8-27). We displayed the content of this access list, and as shown in Example 8-27, this access list has a single **deny** statement, effectively denying all prefixes from being advertised.

Example 8-27   *Information Gathering: Examining HQ1's BGP Configuration*

```
HQ1# show running-config | section bgp
router bgp 65000
 bgp router-id 10.10.10.10
 bgp log-neighbor-changes
 bgp redistribute-internal
 network 209.165.200.248 mask 255.255.255.248
 neighbor 209.165.200.5 remote-as 65111
 neighbor 209.165.200.5 distribute-list RouteOut out
 neighbor 209.165.201.5 remote-as 65222
 neighbor 209.165.201.5 distribute-list RouteOut out
access-list 100 permit tcp host 209.165.200.5 host 209.165.200.6 eq bgp
access-list 100 permit tcp host 209.165.200.5 eq bgp host 209.165.200.6
access-list 100 permit tcp host 209.165.201.5 eq bgp host 209.165.201.6
access-list 100 permit tcp host 209.165.201.5 host 209.165.201.6 eq bgp
HQ1#
HQ1# show access-list RouteOut
Standard IP access list RouteOut
    10 deny   209.165.200.248, wildcard bits 0.0.0.7 (1 match)
HQ1#
```

Proposing and Testing a Hypothesis

The access list RouteOut that is applied in the outbound direction to both of HQ1's eBGP peers has a single statement that denies the prefix 209.165.200.248 (with a wildcard mask of 0.0.0.7). All other prefixes are also denied by the implicit deny statement. Our proposition is that the single statement within the access list must be a **permit** statement instead of a **deny** statement. That way, HQ1 will only advertise the prefixes owned by PILE and nothing else. In Example 8-28, we modify the access list, clear HQ1's BGP sessions, and perform a reexamination using the **show ip bgp 209.165.200.248/29** command. This time the prefix is shown as advertised to two neighbors.

Example 8-28   *Proposing and Testing a Hypothesis: Correct the Outbound Filter*

```
HQ1# config term
Enter configuration commands, one per line.  End with CNTL/Z.
HQ1(config)# ip access-list standard RouteOut
HQ1(config-std-nacl)# no 10
HQ1(config-std-nacl)# permit 209.165.200.248 0.0.0.7
HQ1(config-std-nacl)# end
HQ1#
Sep  9 02:06:28.621: %SYS-5-CONFIG_I: Configured from console by console
HQ1# clear ip bgp *
< ...output emitted... >
HQ1#
HQ1# show ip bgp 209.165.200.248/29
```

```
BGP routing table entry for 209.165.200.248/29, version 5
Paths: (1 available, best #1, table default)
  Advertised to update-groups:
     2
  Refresh Epoch 1
  Local
     0.0.0.0 from 0.0.0.0 (10.10.10.10)
       Origin IGP, metric 0, localpref 100, weight 32768, valid, sourced, local, best
HQ1#
```

Solving the Problem

We must now test reachability of the Internet test address (209.165.200.129) from HQ1 (using the internal interface as the source) and from PC1. As shown in Example 8-29, both of these ping tests are 100 percent successful.

Example 8-29   *Solving the Problem: Internet Reachability Is Restored*

```
HQ1# ping 209.165.200.129 source ethernet 0/0
Type escape sequence to abort.
Sending 5, 100-byte ICMP Echos to 209.165.200.129, timeout is 2 seconds:
Packet sent with a source address of 10.1.0.7
!!!!!
Success rate is 100 percent (5/5), round-trip min/avg/max = 1/1/1 ms
HQ1#


PC1# ping 209.165.200.129
Type escape sequence to abort.
Sending 5, 100-byte ICMP Echos to 209.165.200.129, timeout is 2 seconds:
!!!!!
Success rate is 100 percent (5/5), round-trip min/avg/max = 1/1/2 ms
PC1#
```

We must now document our work and notify Carrie of the changes made to make this problem go away.

Troubleshooting BGP

BGP incoming and outgoing updates can be filtered in several ways:

1. By applying the **distribute-list** *access-list* command to a neighbor in either direction:

neighbor *ip-address* **distribute-list** *access-list-number* {**in** | **out**}

Using standard access lists, you can filter based only on the prefix itself, not the subnet mask. Using extended access lists, you can filter based on the prefix and subnet mask.

2. By applying the **distribute-list** *prefix-list* command to a neighbor in either direction:

   ```
   neighbor ip-address distribute-list prefix-list-name {in | out}
   ```

   Prefix lists are processed more efficiently by Cisco IOS, and you may find their syntax simpler than IP extended access lists.

3. By applying the **route-map** *route-map-name* command to a neighbor in either direction:

   ```
   neighbor ip-address route-map route-map-name {in | out}
   ```

   With route maps, in addition to filtering, you can modify the BGP attributes of a sent or received update.

4. By applying the **filter-list** as-path-ACL-number command to a neighbor in either direction:

   ```
   neighbor ip-address filter-list as-path-ACL-number {in | out}
   ```

   AS-Path ACLs allow you to write regular expressions that filter BGP updates based on BGP's AS-Path attribute.

Note that if a prefix list and an AS-Path ACL and a route map are all applied to a BGP neighbor, the order these tools are applied to incoming updates is prefix list first, AS-Path ACL second, and route map last. However, for outgoing updates, route maps are applied first, AS-Path ACLs are applied next, and the prefix lists are applied last.

Useful BGP diagnostic commands include the following:

- **show ip bgp:** Use this command to display the BGP table.

- **show ip bgp summary:** Use this command to display the status of the BGP neighbor relationship with each of the configured neighbors. The last column of the output displays the status of the BGP session. For established sessions, the number of prefixes received is shown, rather than the status (established).

- **show ip bgp neighbors** *neighbor-ip-address* [**routes** | **advertised-routes**]: With the **routes** option, you can see the prefixes accepted from a particular neighbor. With the **advertised-routes** option, you see which prefixes are advertised to a particular neighbor.

- **debug ip bgp updates:** You can use this command to observe sent and received updates in real time. To see significant events, use the **debug ip bgp events** command.

Troubleshooting PILE Network's NTP Problem

Carrie, the network engineer from PILE Forensic Accounting, has informed us that she configured Network Time Protocol (NTP) on the HQ1 router. There are three NTP servers: the server with the IP address 209.165.201.193 must be used as the primary NTP server, and servers 209.165.201.225 and 209.165.201.129 should serve as backup servers. However, Carrie states that the HQ1 router does not synchronize its time with the primary NTP server.

Verifying the Problem

To verify the problem, we use the **show ntp status** command, and as the output in Example 8-30 shows, HQ1's clock is synchronized, but the reference is 209.165.201.225. This is the IP address of one of the backup NTP servers. So, the problem is verified and can be defined exactly as Carrie described it.

Example 8-30   *Verifying the Problem: Check NTP Status on the HQ1 Router*

```
HQ1# show ntp status
Clock is synchronized, stratum 2, reference is 209.165.201.225
nominal freq is 250.0000 Hz, actual freq is 250.0000 Hz, precision is 2**10
ntp uptime is 88100 (1/100 of seconds), resolution is 4000
reference time is D7BA39F5.26A7F008 (18:40:17.131 PST Tue Sep 9 2014)
clock offset is 0.0000 msec, root delay is 0.00 msec
root dispersion is 7.35 msec, peer dispersion is 3.44 msec
loopfilter state is 'CTRL' (Normal Controlled Loop), drift is 0.000000004 s/s
system poll interval is 128, last update was 40 sec ago.
HQ1#
```

Gathering Information

We can start our troubleshooting effort by information gathering about HQ1's NTP configuration. We display the NTP lines of HQ1's running-config, and as shown in Example 8-31, the configuration is correct and accurate. So, we execute the **show ntp associations** command next. On the output of this command, as shown in Example 8-31, the configured NTP servers are listed, and the first column prior to the server IP addresses has flags that tell us the status of association with each server. As shown, server 209.165.201.129 has *~ beside it; ~ means configured, and * means it is a peer. Server 209.165.201.225 has +~ beside it; ~ means configured, and + means it is a candidate. Finally, server 209.165.201.193 has only ~ beside it; ~ means configured, but there is no association indicated for this server. We must find out whether the server is reachable.

Example 8-31   *Information Gathering: Check Operational Status of NTP Servers*

```
HQ1# show running-config | include ntp
ntp server 209.165.201.129
ntp server 209.165.201.225
ntp server 209.165.201.193 prefer
HQ1#
HQ1# show ntp associations
  address         ref clock       st   when   poll reach  delay  offset   disp
*~209.165.201.129 .LOCL.          1     47    64     1   1.000   0.500 189.44
+~209.165.201.225 .LOCL.          1     46    64     1   0.000   0.000 189.45
 ~209.165.201.193 .INIT.         16      -    64     0   0.000   0.000 15937.
  * sys.peer, # selected, + candidate, - outlyer, x falseticker, ~ configured
```

```
HQ1#
HQ1# ping 209.165.201.193
Type escape sequence to abort.
Sending 5, 100-byte ICMP Echos to 209.165.201.193, timeout is 2 seconds:
!!!!!
Success rate is 100 percent (5/5), round-trip min/avg/max = 1/1/1 ms
HQ1#
```

To check reachability of the primary NTP server, we ping its ip address 209.165.201.193, and as shown in Example 8-31, the ping is 100 percent successful.

Analyzing the Gathered Information and Gathering Further Information

We now know that the HQ1 is properly configured to use 209.165.201.193 as the preferred NTP server. However, even though this server is reachable, the output of the **show ntp status** command shows no association with it. We can eliminate physical, data link, and network layer reachability problems and causes. Now we should gather further information and find the problem's cause at an upper layer. The command we try next is **debug ntp packet**. As Example 8-32 shows, NTP packets are sent to the backup NTP servers, and responses from those servers are received. However, even though NTP packets are sent to the primary NTP server, no responses are received back from it. We must find out what device is blocking the NTP communication, which uses UDP and port number 123, between HQ1 and the primary NTP server.

Example 8-32 *Gathering More Information: Use NTP Packet Debugging*

```
HQ1# debug ntp packet
NTP packets debugging is on
HQ1#
Sep 10 02:37:21.155: NTP message sent to 209.165.201.193, from interface 'NULL'
  (0.0.0.0).
Sep 10 02:37:24.155: NTP message sent to 209.165.201.129, from interface
  'Ethernet0/1' (209.165.200.6).
Sep 10 02:37:24.155: NTP message received from 209.165.201.129 on interface
  'Ethernet0/1' (209.165.200.6).
HQ1#
Sep 10 02:37:26.150: NTP message sent to 209.165.201.225, from interface
  'Ethernet0/1' (209.165.200.6).
Sep 10 02:37:26.151: NTP message received from 209.165.201.225 on interface
  'Ethernet0/1' (209.165.200.6).
HQ1#
```

The HQ1 router has two interfaces, Eth0/1 and Eth0/2, facing external neighbors, ISP1 and ISP2. The next logical step in information gathering is to see whether any ACLs are applied to these interfaces. As shown in Example 8-33, HQ1's running-config reveals that access list 100 is applied to both Eth0/1 and Eth0/2 interfaces in the inbound direction. We examine the content of access control list 100, and as you can see in Example 8-33, this ACL permits UDP packets from the backup servers only.

Example 8-33 *Information Gathering: Examine Filters Applied to HQ1 Interfaces*

```
HQ1# show running-config interface eth 0/1 | include access-group
 ip access-group 100 in
HQ1# show running-config interface eth 0/2 | include access-group
 ip access-group 100 in
HQ1#
HQ1# show access-list 100
Extended IP access list 100
    10 permit tcp host 209.165.200.5 host 209.165.200.6 eq bgp
    20 permit tcp host 209.165.200.5 eq bgp host 209.165.200.6
    30 permit tcp host 209.165.201.5 eq bgp host 209.165.201.6
    40 permit tcp host 209.165.201.5 host 209.165.201.6 eq bgp
    50 permit udp host 209.165.201.129 any
    60 permit udp host 209.165.201.225 any
    70 permit icmp 209.165.0.0 0.0.255.255 any
HQ1#
```

Proposing a Hypothesis and Testing the Hypothesis

Based on the last piece of information gathered, access list 100, which is applied to HQ1's external interfaces (Eth0/1 and Eth0/2), does not have a **permit** statement for the UDP packets received from the preferred NTP server. Our proposal is to add a **permit** statement for the preferred NTP statement. In Example 8-34, we modify access list 100 as proposed. You can see that the **debug ntp packet** immediately displays the NTP responses from the preferred NTP server that used to be blocked.

Example 8-34 *Proposing a Hypothesis: Modify ACL 100 to Allow NTP Packets from the Preferred NTP Server*

```
HQ1# conf t
Enter configuration commands, one per line.  End with CNTL/Z.
HQ1(config)# ip access-list extended 100
HQ1(config-ext-nacl)# 45 permit udp host 209.165.201.193 any
HQ1(config-ext-nacl)# end
HQ1#
Sep 10 02:43:02.561: %SYS-5-CONFIG_I: Configured from console by console
HQ1# debug ntp packet
NTP packets debugging is on
HQ1#
Sep 10 02:43:58.147: NTP message sent to 209.165.201.193, from interface
 'Ethernet0/1' (209.165.200.6).
Sep 10 02:43:58.148: NTP message received from 209.165.201.193 on interface
 'Ethernet0/1' (209.165.200.6).
< ...output omitted... >
HQ1# no debug all
```

```
All possible debugging has been turned off
HQ1# wr
Building configuration...
[OK]
HQ1#
```

Solving the Problem

Now we use the **show ntp status** command on the HQ1 router once again. As Example 8-35 shows, HQ1's clock is synchronized, and the reference is 209.165.201.193. In the same example, the **show ntp associations** command shows the characters *~ beside the preferred NTP server's IP address (209.165.201.193). This means that 209.165.201.193 is a configured NTP server and that this server is the current peer for the HQ1 router. The problem is solved.

Example 8-35   *Solving the Problem: Synchronizing with the Preferred NTP Server*

```
HQ1# show ntp status
Clock is synchronized, stratum 2, reference is 209.165.201.193
nominal freq is 250.0000 Hz, actual freq is 250.0000 Hz, precision is 2**10
ntp uptime is 77100 (1/100 of seconds), resolution is 4000
reference time is D7BA39F5.26A7F008 (18:46:13.151 PST Tue Sep 9 2014)
clock offset is 0.0000 msec, root delay is 0.00 msec
root dispersion is 7.35 msec, peer dispersion is 3.44 msec
loopfilter state is 'CTRL' (Normal Controlled Loop), drift is 0.000000004 s/s
system poll interval is 128, last update was 43 sec ago.
HG1#
HQ1# show ntp associations

  address         ref clock       st   when   poll reach  delay  offset   disp
+~209.165.201.129 .LOCL.           1     42    128   377  0.000   0.000   2.868
+~209.165.201.225 .LOCL.           1    116    128   177  0.000   0.000   2.800
*~209.165.201.193 .LOCL.           1     55    128     3  0.000   0.000   3.446
 * sys.peer, # selected, + candidate, - outlyer, x falseticker, ~ configured
HQ1#
```

We must document our work and notify Carrie that the NTP problem is fixed.

Troubleshooting NTP

NTP is widely used to synchronize clocks on the network devices. NTP is a client/server protocol, where NTP servers use an accurate time source. Clients use NTP to communicate with servers to obtain correct time information. Keep the following in mind while troubleshooting NTP:

- NTP uses UDP port 123, which must be permitted by ACLs.

- It is recommended to use NTP packet authentication. NTP uses message digest 5 (MD5) authentication. Watch for possible authentication and MD5 key mismatches.

- NTP uses universal coordinated time (UTC) to synchronize clocks. To have the correct local time on the Cisco network device, you should configure the time zone with the **clock timezone** *zone hours-offset* [**minutes-offset**] command. To configure summer time, use the **clock summer-time** *zone* **recurring** command.

- If NTP server is not accessible, a network device will fail to synchronize its clock. You should configure the primary NTP server with the **ntp server** *ip-address* **prefer** command and several backup servers without the **prefer** keyword.

- If a network device is working under high CPU utilization, it may fail to process NTP packets; consequently, the clock will fail to synchronize.

- If offset is high between the client and the server, the time it takes to synchronize the clock may be very long or synchronization may fail. You should manually set the clock on the router close to the correct local time with the **clock set** *hh:mm:ss day month year* command.

- NTP uses the concept of a stratum to describe how many hops away a device is from an authoritative time source. The number is between 1 and 15. If the NTP client is synchronizing on the NTP server with stratum 15, it will fail because stratum 16 is invalid.

PILE Forensic Accounting Trouble Ticket 3

This trouble ticket stems from the fact that a flood at PILE Forensic Accounting destroyed DSW, ASW1, and ASW2 switches. Carrie, the network engineer at PILE, replaced devices and restored connectivity for critical PCs (those in VLAN 10). However, she has reported to us the following remaining problems that she needs help with:

- PC3 has lost Internet access; PC1 and PC2 from VLAN 10 can ping 209.165.201.129, but PC3 cannot.

- PC4, over at the branch office, cannot access the Internet either; the user is trying to access Cisco's web page at Cisco.com.

Troubleshooting PC3's Lack of Internet Connectivity After the Disaster Recovery

Based on what Carrie has reported to us, after she replaced switches ASW1, ASW2, and DSW and restored PILE's network operation, PC3 has no Internet connectivity and she needs help solving this problem. She indicated that PC1 and PC2 from VLAN 10 have Internet connectivity.

Verifying the Problem

As usual, we start our troubleshooting effort by verifying the problem. Example 8-36 shows that pinging to the Internet test IP address 209.165.201.129 from PC3 in VLAN 20 fails, but it succeeds 100 percent from PC1 and PC2, which reside in VLAN 10.

Example 8-36   *Verify the Problem: PC3 Cannot Ping 209.165.201.129 (Internet)*

```
PC3# ping 209.165.201.129
Type escape sequence to abort.
Sending 5, 100-byte ICMP Echos to 209.165.201.129, timeout is 2 seconds:
.....
Success rate is 0 percent (0/5)
PC3#


PC1# ping 209.165.201.129
Type escape sequence to abort.
Sending 5, 100-byte ICMP Echos to 209.165.201.129, timeout is 2 seconds:
!!!!!
Success rate is 100 percent (5/5), round-trip min/avg/max = 1/202/1006 ms
PC1#


PC2# ping 209.165.201.129
Type escape sequence to abort.
Sending 5, 100-byte ICMP Echos to 209.165.201.129, timeout is 2 seconds:
!!!!!
Success rate is 100 percent (5/5), round-trip min/avg/max = 1/202/1006 ms
PC2#
```

Now that the problem is verified, we can take the bottom-up approach and start investigating why PC3 has no Internet connectivity.

Gathering Information (First Run)

Displaying the status of PC3's Ethernet interface, by using the **show ip interface brief** command, reveals that PC3's Ethernet interface is up and that it has an adequate IP address for VLAN 20 (see Example 8-37). However, PC3's IP address is not obtained through Dynamic Host Configuration Protocol (DHCP), and based on the output of the **show ip route** command, PC3 has no default gateway!

Example 8-37   *Information Gathering: PC3 Is Not Configured as a DHCP Client*

```
PC3# show ip int brief
Interface            IP-Address      OK? Method   Status
Protocol
```

```
Ethernet0/0                    10.0.20.3          YES NVRAM  up                      up
< ...output omitted... >
PC3#
PC3# show ip route
Default gateway is not set

Host              Gateway         Last Use    Total Uses  Interface
ICMP redirect cache is empty
PC3#
```

Analyzing Information, Proposing, and Testing the First Hypothesis

PC3 must be configured as a DHCP client, but it is currently configured manually and has no default gateway configured. Clearly, without a default gateway, PC3 cannot communicate with any device outside its subnet.

We need to correct PC3's configuration to make it a DHCP client. We then have to see whether PC3 will obtain an adequate IP address, subnet mask, and default gateway through DHCP, and whether it will be able to access the Internet. This is our current hypothesis and how we will test it.

Example 8-38 shows us modifying PC3's configuration according to the plan. Subsequent to the changes made, PC3 obtains an IP address, subnet mask, and default gateway through DHCP successfully, but these addresses are not adequate for PC3, which resides in VLAN 20.

Example 8-38 *Proposing and Testing a Hypothesis: Make PC3 a DHCP Client*

```
PC3# conf t
Enter configuration commands, one per line.  End with CNTL/Z.
PC3(config)# int eth 0/0
PC3(config-if)# ip address dhcp

*Sep 11 02:38:01.359: %DHCP-6-ADDRESS_ASSIGN: Interface Ethernet0/0 assigned DHCP
  address 10.0.10.4, mask 255.255.255.0, hostname PC3

PC3(config-if)# end
PC3#
*Sep 11 02:38:21.573: %SYS-5-CONFIG_I: Configured from console by console
PC3#
PC3# show ip int brief
Interface              IP-Address       OK? Method Status            Protocol
Ethernet0/0            10.0.10.5        YES DHCP   up                up
< ...output omitted... >
```

Because PC3 obtained its address from the DHCP server (DSW) correctly, we can conclude that there are no connectivity or lower-layer problems. Our troubleshooting must take a different approach. We can now switch to the follow-the-path approach and attempt to find out why PC3 is receiving inadequate IP information through DHCP. When we connect to ASW2, as shown in Example 8-39, we notice that the prompt displays the switch name as ASW1. We also notice a message indicating a duplicate address 10.0.99.6 on VLAN 99. When we check the VLANs on this switch, we notice that VLANs 1, 10, and 99 exist, but VLAN 20 does not. Furthermore, as shown in Example 8-39, interface Ethernet 0/1 that PC3 is connected to belongs to VLAN 10! This explains why PC3 is getting inadequate IP information from the DHCP server.

Example 8-39   *Further Information Gathering: Examine PC3's Access Switch*

```
ASW1#


Sep 11 01:59:11.254: %IP-4-DUPADDR: Duplicate address 10.0.99.6 on Vlan99, sourced
  by aabb.cc80.8e00


ASW1# show vlan brief

VLAN Name                             Status    Ports
---- -------------------------------- --------- -------------------------------
1    default                          active    Et0/3, Et1/0, Et1/1, Et1/2
                                                Et1/3, Et2/0, Et2/1, Et2/2
                                                Et2/3, Et3/0, Et3/1, Et3/2
                                                Et3/3, Et4/0, Et4/1, Et4/2
                                                Et4/3, Et5/0, Et5/1, Et5/2
                                                Et5/3
10   VLAN0010                         active    Et0/1, Et0/2
99   VLAN0099                         active
< ...output omitted... >
ASW1#
```

Proposing and Testing the Second Hypothesis

Based on the observations made (after connecting to ASW2), such as the fact that the switch prompt displays ASW1 as the switch name, we can propose that after Carrie replaced switches ASW1, ASW2, and DSW, she applied ASW1's configuration to both of the new ASW1 and ASW2 switches. The hypothesis explains the duplicate address log message, why VLAN 20 does not exist, why Eth0/1 belongs to VLAN 10, and why PC3 is receiving inadequate IP information from the DHCP server.

As shown in Example 8-40, using the hardcopy backup configuration of ASW2, we enter the correct configuration commands into this switch. Next, we verify our work by using the **show vlan brief** and **show interface trunk** commands. The output of these commands looks correct, so we immediately try to renew PC3's IP information, but this time PC3 fails to receive IP information through DHCP altogether.

Example 8-40 *Proposing and Testing a Hypothesis: Correct ASW2's Config.*

```
ASW1# conf t
Enter configuration commands, one per line.  End with CNTL/Z.
ASW1(config)# hostname ASW2
ASW2(config)# vlan 20
ASW2(config-vlan)# exit
ASW2(config)# interface vlan 99
ASW2(config-if)# ip address 10.0.99.7 255.255.255.0
ASW2(config-if)# exit
ASW2(config)# int eth 0/1
ASW2(config-if)# switchport access vlan 20
ASW2(config-if)# int eth 0/2
ASW2(config-if)# switchport access vlan 20
ASW2(config-if)# end
ASW2# wr
Building configuration...
Compressed configuration from 2237 bytes to 1213 bytes[OK]
ASW2#
ASW2# show vlan brief

VLAN Name                             Status    Ports
---- -------------------------------- --------- -------------------------------
1    default                          active    Et0/3, Et1/0, Et1/1, Et1/2
                                                Et1/3, Et2/0, Et2/1, Et2/2
                                                Et2/3, Et3/0, Et3/1, Et3/2
                                                Et3/3, Et4/0, Et4/1, Et4/2
                                                Et4/3, Et5/0, Et5/1, Et5/2
                                                Et5/3
10   VLAN0010                         active
20   VLAN0020                         active    Et0/1, Et0/2
99   VLAN0099                         active
< ...output omitted... >
ASW2#
ASW2# show interfaces trunk

Port        Mode         Encapsulation Status       Native vlan
Et0/0       on           802.1q        trunking     99


Port        Vlans allowed on trunk
Et0/0       1-4094


Port        Vlans allowed and active in management domain
Et0/0       1,10,20,99
```

```
Port        Vlans in spanning tree forwarding state and not pruned
Et0/0       1,10,20,99
ASW2#


PC3# conf term
Enter configuration commands, one per line.  End with CNTL/Z.
PC3(config)# int eth 0/0
PC3(config-if)# shut
PC3(config-if)# no shut
PC3(config-if)# end
*Sep 11 02:44:44.238: %LINK-5-CHANGED: Interface Ethernet0/0, changed state to
  administratively down
*Sep 11 02:44:46.585: %LINK-3-UPDOWN: Interface Ethernet0/0, changed state to up
*Sep 11 02:44:46.808: %SYS-5-CONFIG_I: Configured from console by console
PC3# show ip int brief
Interface               IP-Address      OK? Method Status              Protocol
Ethernet0/0             unassigned      YES DHCP   up                  up
< ...output omitted... >
PC3#
```

Gathering Further Information (Second Run)

We must now go further in our follow-the-path approach and examine DSW's configuration with respect to DHCP. As shown in Example 8-41, DSW has proper address pools and other configuration adequate for both VLANs 10 and 20.

Example 8-41   *Further Information Gathering: DSW's DHCP Configuration*

```
DSW# show running-config | section dhcp
ip dhcp excluded-address 10.0.10.1
ip dhcp excluded-address 10.0.20.1
ip dhcp pool VLAN10POOL
 network 10.0.10.0 255.255.255.0
 default-router 10.0.10.1
 dns-server 209.165.201.209
ip dhcp pool VLAN20POOL
 network 10.0.20.0 255.255.255.0
 default-router 10.0.20.1
 dns-server 209.165.201.209
DSW#
```

To obtain detailed information about why the DHCP server (DSW) is not offering an IP lease to PC3, we now use the **debug ip dhcp server packet** command. As shown in Example 8-42, DSW keeps receiving the DHCP DISCOVER message, but it is not responding by sending a DHCP OFFER packet. This prompts us to determine whether DSW has an interface in VLAN 20 (subnet 10.0.39.0/24). The output of the **show ip**

interface command, also shown in Example 8-42, reveals that DSW has an SVI (VLAN 20) that is up, but its IP address has been configured incorrectly as 10.20.0.1 instead of 10.0.20.1.

Example 8-42 *Further Information Gathering: Debug DHCP on the DSW Switch*

```
DSW# debug ip dhcp server packet
DHCP server packet debugging is on.
DSW#
Sep 11 02:47:42.210: DHCPD: DHCPDISCOVER received from client 0063.6973.636f.2d61.61
  62.622e.6363.3030.2e38.3430.302d.4574.302f.30 on interface Vlan20.
Sep 11 02:47:45.706: DHCPD: DHCPDISCOVER received from client 0063.6973.636f.2d61.61
  62.622e.6363.3030.2e38.3430.302d.4574.302f.30 on interface Vlan20.
Sep 11 02:47:49.714: DHCPD: DHCPDISCOVER received from client 0063.6973.636f.2d61.61
  62.622e.6363.3030.2e38.3430.302d.4574.302f.30 on interface Vlan20.
DSW#
DSW# show ip int brief
Interface              IP-Address      OK? Method Status                 Protocol
< ...output omitted... >
Vlan1                  unassigned      YES unset  administratively down  down
Vlan10                 10.0.10.1       YES NVRAM  up                     up
Vlan20                 10.20.0.1       YES NVRAM  up                     up
Vlan99                 10.0.99.1       YES NVRAM  up                     up
DSW#
```

Proposing and Testing the Third Hypothesis

Our next hypothesis is to correct interface VLAN 20's IP address on the DSW switch. As shown in Example 8-43, after we make this correction, and in response to the received DHCP DISCOVER message, the DHCP OFFER message is sent out. Next, the DHCP REQUEST message is received, and finally, the DHCP ACK message completes the DHCP process. We disable the DHCP debugging on DSW, save its configuration, and move on to test PC3's configuration and operation.

Example 8-43 *Proposing and Testing a Hypothesis: Correct DSW's Configuration*

```
DSW# conf t
Enter configuration commands, one per line.  End with CNTL/Z.
DSW(config)# interface vlan 20
DSW(config-if)# ip address 10.0.20.1 255.255.255.0
DSW(config-if)# end
DSW# debug ip dhcp server packet
DHCP server packet debugging is on.
DSW#
Sep 11 02:52:41.928: DHCPD: DHCPDISCOVER received from client
< ...output omitted... >
```

```
Sep 11 02:52:43.944: DHCPD: Sending DHCPOFFER to client
< ...output omitted... >
Sep 11 02:52:43.945: DHCPD: DHCPREQUEST received from client
< ...output omitted... >
Sep 11 02:52:43.945: DHCPD: Sending DHCPACK to client
< ...output omitted... >
DSW# no debug all
All possible debugging has been turned off
DSW# wr
```

Solving the Problem

We now test PC3's IP configuration using the **show ip interface brief** and **show ip route** commands. As shown in Example 8-44, PC3 now has an adequate IP address, subnet mask, and default gateway, which have been obtained through DHCP. However, we can claim the problem solved only if PC3's Internet connectivity has been restored. Example 8-44 shows that our attempt to ping the Internet test IP address 209.165.201.129 is 100 percent successful.

Example 8-44   *Solving the Problem: PC3's Internet Connectivity Is Restored*

```
PC3# show ip int brief
Interface               IP-Address      OK? Method Status              Protocol
Ethernet0/0             10.0.20.3       YES DHCP   up                  up
< ...output omitted... >
PC3# show ip route
Default gateway is 10.0.20.1

Host            Gateway         Last Use    Total Uses  Interface
ICMP redirect cache is empty
PC3# ping 209.165.201.129
Type escape sequence to abort.
Sending 5, 100-byte ICMP Echos to 209.165.201.129, timeout is 2 seconds:
!!!!!
Success rate is 100 percent (5/5), round-trip min/avg/max = 1/201/1005 ms
PC3#
```

We must now document our work and notify Carrie about our work, the changes we made, and that PC3's Internet connectivity is restored.

Disaster Recovery Best Practices

Disasters are inevitable, but mostly unpredictable; they also vary in type and magnitude. Effects of disasters range from small interruptions to total operations shutdown for days or months (*catastrophe*). Every organization requires a disaster recovery plan whose goal is to restore full network functionality in a fast and efficient way. The success, speed, and efficiency of a disaster recovery depend heavily on the quality of your recovery plan/documentation and the availability of its requirements.

Disaster recovery happens in the following sequential phases:

1. **Activation phase:** The disaster effects are assessed and announced.

2. **Execution phase:** The actual procedures to recover each of the disaster-affected entities are executed.

3. **Reconstitution phase:** The original system is restored, and execution phase procedures are stopped.

In case you have to replace destroyed, damaged, or faulty devices as part of the execution phase, you should have the following items available:

- Replacement hardware

- The current software version of any device

- The current device configuration

- The tools to transfer the software and configuration to the new device, even if the network is unavailable

- Licenses (if applicable)

- Knowledge of the procedures to install software, configurations, and licenses

Missing any of these listed items can severely affect the time it takes to restore normal network conditions. To ensure that you have all the required elements available when you need them, follow these guidelines:

- During network design, build redundancy into the network at critical points and ensure that a single device or link failure can never cause your whole network to go down.

- Have a detailed and easy-to-follow disaster recovery plan.

- Make sure that you have thorough, up-to-date, accessible, and easy-to-use network documentation.

Network documentation should include the following items:

- **Network drawings:** Diagrams of the physical and logical structure of the network

- **Connection specifications:** A document, spreadsheet, or database listing all relevant physical connections, such as patches, connections to service providers, and power circuits

- **Equipment list:** A document, spreadsheet, or database listing all devices, part numbers, serial numbers, installed software versions, and (if applicable) licenses for the software

- **The IP address document:** A document, spreadsheet, or database that lists and describes the IP networks and subnets and all IP addresses that are in use

- **Configurations:** All the current device configurations (even an archive that contains all previous configurations, if possible)

- **Design document:** A document describing the reasoning for implementation choices

For certain businesses, having a backup infrastructure in place might be necessary. The backup infrastructure should be placed in geographically distant locations for recovery from catastrophe such as earthquakes, tsunamis, and so on.

Troubleshooting Inter-VLAN Routing

Inter-VLAN routing can be performed by a multilayer switch or by a router. When you connect a Layer 2 switch to a router with an 802.1Q trunk, and configure the router to perform inter-VLAN routing, you have a router-on-a-stick model.

On a multilayer switch, you can configure physical Layer 3 interfaces using the **no switchport** command. You can also configure logical Layer 3 interfaces on a switch, called virtual switch interfaces (SVIs). An SVI is considered to be up as long as at least one of the associated VLAN ports is up. To create an SVI, you use the **interface vlan** *vlan-id* command. To start routing between VLANs, you must enable routing globally using the **ip routing** command. The following commands are useful for verifying inter-VLAN routing on multilayer switches:

- **show vlan [brief]:** Enables you to examine a VLAN database

- **show vlan vlan-id:** Enables you to verify information about a particular VLAN

- **show interfaces trunk:** Enables you to verify whether trunking is configured properly and that the native VLAN matches on both sides of the trunk

- **show ip interface brief:** Enables you to verify the SVI interface status on a multilayer switch

- **ip config /all:** Enables you to verify whether the (Microsoft) host's default gateway points to the corresponding SVI interface IP address and that the subnet masks match

To provide inter-VLAN routing using the router-on-a-stick model, you must configure a router interface for trunking and connect it to a switch interface that is also configured for trunking. The router will have one subinterface per VLAN, each with a VLAN number and the proper IP address for that VLAN (IP subnet). The following commands are useful for verifying inter-VLAN routing on routers:

- **show ip** *interface.subinterface*: Enables you to verify router subinterfaces

- **show ip interface brief:** Enables you to verify status and configuration of subinterfaces

- **show vlan [brief]** and **show vlan** *vlan-id*: Enables you to verify the existence and status of VLANs

- **ip config /all:** Enables you to verify that the (Microsoft) host's default gateway points to the corresponding router subinterface and that the subnet masks match

Troubleshooting PC4's Problem Accessing Cisco.com

This case is the second problem that Carrie has contacted us at SECHNIK about, after she completed her disaster recovery tasks. She specified that the user of PC4 at PILE's branch site was complaining about Internet connectivity problems. The last website that the user was trying to access was Cisco.com. We need to investigate this issue and, if we verify that the problem is true, fix it.

Verify the Problem and Select an Approach

To verify the problem, we need to access PC4 from our location at the headquarters site. Because PC4 is configured as a DHCP client, we first need to find out its IP address. Because the branch router (BR) is the acting DHCP server at the branch site and PC4 is its only client, we can simply telnet into the BR, examine its DHCP binding table, and find out PC4's IP address. Example 8-45 shows us using the **show ip dhcp binding** command on the BR to find that PC4's address is 10.0.30.2. Next, we telnet into PC4 (we would use a Remote Desktop connection if PC4 were a real PC) and ping Cisco.com.

Example 8-45   *Verify the Problem: Ping from PC4 to Cisco.com Fails*

```
PC1# telnet 10.0.30.7
Trying 10.0.30.7 ... Open
User Access Verification
Password:
*Sep 12 01:06:46.803: %DHCP-6-ADDRESS_ASSIGN: Interface Ethernet0/0 assigned DHCP
  address 10.0.10.3, mask 255.255.255.0, hostname PC1
Password:
BR> en
Password:
BR# show ip dhcp binding
Bindings from all pools not associated with VRF:
IP address          Client-ID/                      Lease expiration         Type
                    Hardware address/
                    User name
10.0.30.2    0063.6973.636f.2d61.    Sep 12 2014 05:06 PM    Automatic
                    6162.622e.6363.3030.
                    2e37.3330.302d.4574.
                    302f.30
BR# exit
```

```
PC1# telnet 10.0.30.2

Trying 10.0.30.2 ... Open

User Access Verification

Password:

PC4> enable

Password:

PC4# ping www.cisco.com

Translating "www.cisco.com"...domain server (255.255.255.255)

% Unrecognized host or address, or protocol not running.

PC4#
```

As shown in Example 8-45, when we ping Cisco.com, PC4 tries to resolve the name to IP address using a broadcast (255.255.255.255) name-resolution attempt. When this name-resolution attempt fails, PC4 generates the "% unrecognized host or address, or protocol not running" message. We can definitely see a name-resolution problem on PC4. However, we need to do some information gathering to see whether there are any additional problems. Because we successfully accessed PC4 from our location at the headquarters site, and with confidence about the health of the lower protocol layers, we can use a top-down approach and start by focusing on the name-resolution issue first.

Gather Information and Analyze the Information

We can start our information gathering by trying to ping the Internet test IP address (209.165.201.129) from PC4. As shown in Example 8-46, the ping success rate is 100 percent, which tells us that there is no Internet connectivity problem.

Example 8-46   *Gathering Information: PC4 Can Ping the Internet Test Address*

```
XxxPC4# ping 209.165.201.129

Type escape sequence to abort.

Sending 5, 100-byte ICMP Echos to 209.165.201.129, timeout is 2 seconds:

!!!!!

Success rate is 100 percent (5/5), round-trip min/avg/max = 1/1/2 ms

PC4#
```

Based on the fact that we earlier noticed PC4's ping to Cisco.com failed after it tried to resolve Cisco.com to an IP address using IP broadcast (255.255.255.255) instead of contacting a DNS server, we now have more confidence that the problem at hand is a name-resolution problem.

We can examine the BR's DHCP server configuration to see whether it is configured to provide the DNS server's IP address (209.165.201.209) to its DHCP clients. Example 8-47 shows that PC4 can ping the DNS server; this means that the server is alive and reachable from PC4. However, in Example 8-47, you can also see that the BR's DHCP server configuration is missing a line for the DNS server.

Example 8-47 *Information Gathering: DHCP Server (BR) Configuration*

```
PC4# ping 209.165.201.209
Type escape sequence to abort.
Sending 5, 100-byte ICMP Echos to 209.165.201.209, timeout is 2 seconds:
!!!!!
Success rate is 100 percent (5/5), round-trip min/avg/max = 1/1/2 ms
PC4#


BR# show run | section dhcp
ip dhcp excluded-address 10.0.30.1
ip dhcp excluded-address 10.0.30.7
ip dhcp pool VLAN30POOL
 network 10.0.30.0 255.255.255.0
 default-router 10.0.30.7
BR#
```

Proposing and Testing a Hypothesis

Based on the concrete information gathered thus far, we propose to add the **dns-server 209.165.201.209** command line to the BR's DHCP server configuration. Example 8-48 shows us adding this line to the BR's DHCP server configuration. After the change is made, we renew PC4's DHCP lease so that it can acquire the DNS server's address.

Example 8-48 *Proposing a Hypothesis: Add a DNS Server to DHCP's Configuration*

```
BR# conf term
Enter configuration commands, one per line.  End with CNTL/Z.
BR(config)# ip dhcp pool VLAN30POOL
BR(dhcp-config)# dns-server 209.165.201.209
BR(dhcp-config)# end
BR# wr
Building configuration...
[OK]
BR#


PC4#renew dhcp ethernet 0/0
```

Solve the Problem

After renewing PC4's IP DHCP lease, we try to ping Cisco.com. As shown in Example 8-49, Cisco.com is successfully translated to the IP address 209.165.201.209 now that it has acquired the DNS address through DHCP. Finally, Example 8-49 also shows that pinging to Cisco.com is successful.

Example 8-49   *Solve the Problem: PC4 Can Now Ping Cisco.com by Name*

```
PC4# renew dhcp ethernet 0/0
PC4# ping www.cisco.com
Translating "www.cisco.com"...domain server (209.165.201.209) [OK]
Type escape sequence to abort.
Sending 5, 100-byte ICMP Echos to 209.165.201.209, timeout is 2 seconds:
!!!!!
Success rate is 100 percent (5/5), round-trip min/avg/max = 1/1/2 ms
PC4#
```

We must now document our work and notify Carrie about our work. Carrie needs to know that there was no Internet reachability problem from PC4. The problem was merely a DHCP server configuration problem on the BR, which was failing to provide a DNS server address to its DHCP client.

Troubleshooting DNS

The Domain Name System (DNS) protocol is used to resolve fully qualified domain names to IP addresses. You can configure a Cisco router as a client to a DNS server using the **ip name-server** *ip-address* command. Common DNS-related problems include the following:

- **DNS server is not configured:** The typical error message is "% Unrecognized host or address, or protocol not running." You can check the configured DNS servers on a device by using the IOS **show running-config | include name-server** command.

- **The configured DNS server IP address is incorrect:** Verify connectivity to the DNS server; make sure that the correct IP address for the DNS server is configured.

- **Verify the status of name resolution:** The **[no] IP domain-lookup** command enables and disables IP name resolution on a Cisco IOS device.

- **Verify the default domain name:** Use the **show hosts** command to display the default domain name.

- **Verify whether an IP domain list is configured:** This list defines a list of domains, each to be tried in turn to complete unqualified hostnames. If there is a domain list, the default domain name is not used. Check whether the list is overriding the domain name configured, thus excluding it from queries.

- **Only names specific to one domain are not resolved:** There might be a problem with the DNS server's database. Contact the administrator of the DNS server.

- **The DNS server is reachable, but name resolution fails:** ACLs or firewalls may be blocking DNS messages. Check outbound and inbound access lists. DNS messages are sent to UDP or TCP port 53. This port must be permitted by access lists.

Remote Device Management Notes

You can configure network devices directly using the IOS command-line interface (CLI) if you connect to the serial console or if you use a remote terminal protocol such as Secure Shell (SSH) or Telnet. Another way to configure Cisco devices, if you have a configuration file already, is by using the **copy** or **configure replace** commands. The configuration file with new commands may reside in the device flash memory, or it may be retrieved from a TFTP or FTP server. In all cases, secure storage and secure transfer protocols are preferred.

When you copy into the running-config, the **copy** command merges the source file with the current running-config. The source file, therefore, does not need to be a complete device configuration file. In contrast, the **configure replace** command uses a smart file comparison method. The source file must be a complete configuration file, because the current running-config essentially gets replaced by this file. The **configure replace** method uses the Contextual Configuration Diff utility, which works well for most of the configuration changes, but can fail in certain cases. So, use this method with caution.

In situations where your configuration changes have undesirable results, you must roll back the configuration to a previous known and working state. Assuming that you did not save the new configuration as soon as you changed it and that the working configuration is still present in the NVRAM, you have ways to undo your changes. If you still have access to the device and have documented the changes you made, you can reverse the changes as per your notes. You can also reload the device at the expense of some device downtime. However, if you have lost connection to the device after the erroneous changes, and cannot connect to it, you will have a challenge on your hands!

It is a good practice to always set an automatic fallback to the last working state. Automated fallback methods are usually based on a timer or an event/condition detection that must be set before any change is made. The timeout or some other event triggers an automatic configuration change or a reload of the device. Until then, you can apply changes to the configuration and verify the results. If everything is working as expected, you can cancel the automatic fallback. Two automated fallback configuration options are as follows:

- **reload in** [*hh:*]*mm* [*text*] command or **reload at** *hh:mm* [*month day | day month*] [*text*] command (fallback with the **reload** command): Use these commands before any configuration change is made; then, proceed to configure the device as needed. As long as no configuration changes are saved, the device will revert to its previous configuration when it reloads. If configuration changes are successful, use the **reload cancel** command to stop the pending reload. If configuration changes cause a loss of connectivity, it will be restored when the device automatically reloads.

- **configure replace** *url* **time** *seconds* command (fallback with the configure **replace** command): Enter this command before any configuration change is made; then, proceed with the configuration changes as you want. With this command, you have the option of reloading your device with a configuration other than the startup-config if you want. If your configuration changes are successful, you can stop the pending revert action by using the **configure confirm** command. You can update or speed up the revert timer with the **configure revert** {**now** | **timer** {*minutes* | *idle minutes*}} command.

PILE Forensic Accounting Trouble Ticket 4

PILE Forensic Accounting has just acquired 47 branch offices worldwide. Carrie, the network engineer at PILE, has done some research about making EIGRP more scalable and learned about the EIGRP stub configuration option. Carrie then decided to reconfigure the current sole BR to announce only connected and summary networks through the EIGRP stub configuration. Her plan was to have a proof of concept. Then when the newly acquired 47 branches needed to be connected, she would merely replicate her work on all the new BRs. However, Carrie called and left a message for us at SECHNIK asking for our help with the following items:

- After EIGRP reconfiguration, the BR lost connectivity to the Internet; please help me restore this connection.

- Carrie cannot access ASW2 via Telnet; she can, however, access all other network devices.

Troubleshooting Branch Site Internet Connectivity Problem After EIGRP Reconfiguration

After Carrie reconfigured the BR with the **eigrp stub** command that she learned about on the Internet, she left a message for us saying that the branch has lost Internet connectivity. We need to verify this problem and, if we determine that it is true, find the cause and correct it.

Verifying the Problem

To verify the problem, we need to access the BR. As shown in Example 8-50, our attempt to access (telnet) the BR from PC1 failed. However, we did manage to telnet to the BR from the HQ2 router. Next, our ping attempt to the Internet test IP address (209.165.200.129) from the BR failed, as shown in Example 8-50. The problem is verified.

Example 8-50   *Verify the Problem: Ping from Branch to the Internet Fails*

```
PC1> en
PC1# telnet 10.3.0.8
Trying 10.3.0.8 ...
% Connection timed out; remote host not responding
PC1#

HQ2# telnet 10.3.0.8
```

```
Trying 10.3.0.8 ... Open

User Access Verification
Password:
BR> en
Password:
BR# ping 209.165.200.129
Type escape sequence to abort.
Sending 5, 100-byte ICMP Echos to 209.165.200.129, timeout is 2 seconds:
.....
Success rate is 0 percent (0/5)
BR#
```

Gathering Information

To find out whether the Internet connectivity problem is limited to the branch or whether the problem is network-wide, we decided to repeat the ping test to the Internet from the HQ2 router and from PC1. As shown in Example 8-51, both pings are 100 percent successful. This first information gathering step is in line with the swap-the-component approach.

Example 8-51   *Information Gathering: Ping from HQ2 and PC1 to Internet Succeeds*

```
PC1# ping 209.165.200.129
Type escape sequence to abort.
Sending 5, 100-byte ICMP Echos to 209.165.200.129, timeout is 2 seconds:
!!!!!
Success rate is 100 percent (5/5), round-trip min/avg/max = 1/1/3 ms
PC1#

HQ2# ping 209.165.200.129
Type escape sequence to abort.
Sending 5, 100-byte ICMP Echos to 209.165.200.129, timeout is 2 seconds:
!!!!!
Success rate is 100 percent (5/5), round-trip min/avg/max = 1/1/1 ms
HQ2#
```

We now know that Internet connectivity from PILE's headquarters is working. Therefore, we can continue our troubleshooting effort with the divide-and-conquer approach and focus on the like routing problem between the branch router and the headquarters (HQ2) router.

Gathering Further Information and Analyzing Information

We start by checking the status of the neighbor relationship between the HQ2 router and the BR. We use the **show ip eigrp neighbors** command on both routers; Example 8-52 shows the results. The result for the branch router running EIGRP with ASN 1 shows no neighbors. The result for the HQ2 router running EIGRP with ASN 100 shows only one neighbor (HQ1) through the Ethernet 0/0 interface.

Example 8-52 *Gathering Information: Show IP EIGRP Neighbor on BR and HQ2*

```
BR# show ip eigrp neighbors
EIGRP-IPv4 VR(PILE_BRANCH) Address-Family Neighbors for AS(1)
BR#


HQ2# show ip eigrp neighbors
EIGRP-IPv4 Neighbors for AS(100)
H   Address            Interface            Hold Uptime    SRTT   RTO  Q   Seq
                                            (sec)          (ms)        Cnt Num
0   10.2.0.8           Et0/0                12 00:09:21      8   100  0   7
HQ2#
```

The first observation we make is that the EIGRP ASN 1 configured on the BR does not match HQ2's EIGRP ASN 100, which is PILE's documented ASN for EIGRP. We now decide to observe the EIGRP section of both routers' running-config. Example 8-53 shows the results.

Example 8-53 *Gathering Information: Show Running-Config on BR and HQ2*

```
BR# show running-config | section router eigrp
router eigrp PILE_BRANCH
 !
 address-family ipv4 unicast autonomous-system 1
  !
  topology base
  exit-af-topology
  network 0.0.0.0
 exit-address-family
BR#



HQ2# show running-config | section router eigrp
router eigrp 100
 network 10.2.0.0 0.0.0.255
 network 10.3.0.0 0.0.0.255
 eigrp stub connected summary
HQ2#
```

The running-config of the BR reveals that EIGRP on this router is configured according to the new named configuration option. Within the named configuration, the ASN is incorrectly specified as 1 for the address family IPv4 unicast. EIGRP is activated on all BR interfaces using the **network 0.0.0.0** statement within this address family. Most likely, this choice was made because Carrie wanted to be able to use this configuration on all 47 recently acquired BRs.

The running-config of the HQ2 router reveals that EIGRP on this router is configured the classic way (not named), with the correct ASN 100 and two accurate **network** statements with proper wildcard masks. Surprisingly, however, the HQ2 router's EIGRP configuration includes the EIGRP stub statement. Carrie wanted to take advantage of this EIGRP branch optimization option, but it seems that she entered this command on the wrong (HQ2) router instead of the BR.

Proposing a Hypothesis and Testing the Hypothesis

The BR's EIGRP named configuration needs to be reconfigured with the correct ASN 100.

The **network 0.0.0.0** statement can be left as is, but we need to caution Carrie that it activates EIGRP on all interfaces. Furthermore, there is a danger that if any branch has a static default route configured that points to a local interface (as opposed to a next hop), it will end up advertising the default route to the headquarters because of the **network 0.0.0.0** statement.

The **eigrp stub** statement must be removed from the HQ2's configuration and be added to BR's EIGRP configuration instead.

Example 8-54 shows us correcting the ASN for address family IPv4 on BR's configuration. As you can see, the **show ip eigrp neighbors** command output executed immediately after displays the HQ2 router (10.3.0.7) as an adjacent neighbor.

Example 8-54 *Proposing and Testing a Hypothesis: Fix the ASN on BR's Configuration*

```
BR# conf term
Enter configuration commands, one per line.  End with CNTL/Z.
BR(config)# router eigrp PILE_BRANCH
BR(config-router-af)# no address-family ipv4 unicast autonomous-system 1
BR(config-router)# address-family ipv4 unicast autonomous-system 100
BR(config-router-af)# topology base
BR(config-router-af-topology)# exit
BR(config-router-af)# network 0.0.0.0
Sep 16 06:27:33.001: %DUAL-5-NBRCHANGE: EIGRP-IPv4 100: Neighbor 10.3.0.8
  (Ethernet0/1) is up: new adjacency
BR(config-router-af)# end
BR# show ip eigrp neighbor
EIGRP-IPv4 VR(PILE_BRANCH) Address-Family Neighbors for AS(100)
H    Address                 Interface             Hold Uptime    SRTT   RTO  Q   Seq
                                                   (sec)          (ms)        Cnt Num
```

```
O    10.3.0.7                Et0/1                    14 00:00:28   11   100  0  8
BR#
BR# ping 209.165.200.129
Type escape sequence to abort.
Sending 5, 100-byte ICMP Echos to 209.165.200.129, timeout is 2 seconds:
.....
Success rate is 0 percent (0/5)
BR# show ip route
< ...output omitted... >
Gateway of last resort is not set

      10.0.0.0/8 is variably subnetted, 5 subnets, 2 masks
C        10.0.30.0/24 is directly connected, Ethernet0/0
L        10.0.30.7/32 is directly connected, Ethernet0/0
D        10.2.0.0/24 [90/1536000] via 10.3.0.7, 00:04:31, Ethernet0/1
C        10.3.0.0/24 is directly connected, Ethernet0/1
L        10.3.0.8/32 is directly connected, Ethernet0/1
BR#
```

Example 8-54 also shows that after correcting the EIGRP ASN on the BR (even though it formed adjacency with the HQ2 router), the ping from the BR to the Internet test address 209.165.200.129 still fails. Displaying BR's routing table shows that it is receiving a single network (10.2.0.0/24) from the HQ2 router and that it is not receiving a default route.

We need to remove the **eigrp stub** statement from HQ2's EIGRP configuration and add it to BR's configuration instead. Example 8-55 shows us making these changes on the HQ2 and the BR routers. Immediately after, as you can see in Example 8-55, when we display BR's routing table, we see it is now receiving routes from the HQ and a gateway of last resort (default route).

Example 8-55 *Proposing and Testing a Hypothesis: Remove the* **eigrp stub** *Command from HQ2 and Add It to BR's Configuration Instead*

```
HQ2# conf term
Enter configuration commands, one per line.  End with CNTL/Z.
HQ2(config)# router eigrp 100
HQ2(config-router)# no eigrp stub connected summary
< ...output omitted... >
HQ2(config-router)# end
HQ2# wr
Building configuration...
[OK]
Sep 16 06:36:31.998: %SYS-5-CONFIG_I: Configured from console by console
HQ2#
```

```
BR# conf term
Enter configuration commands, one per line.  End with CNTL/Z.
BR(config)# router eigrp PILE_BRANCH
BR(config-router)# !
BR(config-router)# address-family ipv4 unicast autonomous-system 100
BR(config-router-af)# !
BR(config-router-af)# eigrp stub
BR(config-router-af)#
Sep 16 06:39:36.088: %DUAL-5-NBRCHANGE: EIGRP-IPv4 100: Neighbor 10.3.0.8
  (Ethernet0/1) is down: Interface PEER-TERMINATION receivedend
BR# wr
Building configuration...
[OK]
BR# show ip route
< ...output omitted... >
Gateway of last resort is 10.3.0.7 to network 0.0.0.0

D*    0.0.0.0/0 [90/2048000] via 10.3.0.7, 00:01:18, Ethernet0/1
      10.0.0.0/8 is variably subnetted, 10 subnets, 3 masks
D        10.0.0.0/8 [90/2048000] via 10.3.0.7, 00:01:18, Ethernet0/1
D        10.0.10.0/24 [90/1541120] via 10.3.0.7, 00:01:18, Ethernet0/1
D        10.0.20.0/24 [90/1541120] via 10.3.0.7, 00:01:18, Ethernet0/1
C        10.0.30.0/24 is directly connected, Ethernet0/0
L        10.0.30.7/32 is directly connected, Ethernet0/0
D        10.0.99.0/24 [90/1541120] via 10.3.0.7, 00:01:18, Ethernet0/1
D        10.1.0.0/24 [90/2048000] via 10.3.0.7, 00:01:18, Ethernet0/1
D        10.2.0.0/24 [90/1536000] via 10.3.0.7, 00:01:18, Ethernet0/1
C        10.3.0.0/24 is directly connected, Ethernet0/1
L        10.3.0.8/32 is directly connected, Ethernet0/1
      209.165.200.0/24 is variably subnetted, 2 subnets, 2 masks
D        209.165.200.4/30 [90/2560000] via 10.3.0.7, 00:01:18, Ethernet0/1
D        209.165.200.248/29 [90/2048000] via 10.3.0.7, 00:01:18, Ethernet0/1
      209.165.201.0/30 is subnetted, 1 subnets
D        209.165.201.4 [90/2560000] via 10.3.0.7, 00:01:18, Ethernet0/1
BR#
```

Solving the Problem

We can now test Internet connectivity from the branch to see whether the problem is solved. As shown in Example 8-56, we can now telnet into the BR from PC1. Once we are at the branch router using Telnet, we ping the Internet test address using BR's Eth0/0 IP address (10.0.30.7) as the source. As shown in Example 8-56, this ping is successful, and the problem is fixed.

Example 8-56   *Solving the Problem: Ping Internet from the Branch Site Succeeds*

```
PC1# telnet 10.0.30.7
Trying 10.0.30.7 ... Open
User Access Verification
Password:
BR> en
Password:
BR# ping 209.165.200.129 source 10.0.30.7
Type escape sequence to abort.
Sending 5, 100-byte ICMP Echos to 209.165.200.129, timeout is 2 seconds:
Packet sent with a source address of 10.0.30.7
!!!!!
Success rate is 100 percent (5/5), round-trip min/avg/max = 1/1/1 ms
BR#
```

We must document our work and recommendations and notify Carrie that this problem is solved.

The EIGRP Stub Configuration

The EIGRP stub configuration option provides faster convergence in a network with stub sites; the typical topology where this feature is very beneficial is a hub-and-spoke topology. In a hub-and-spoke topology, one or more routers from the spoke site are connected to the routers at the hub site. The spoke sites may not communicate, or they may communicate through the hub site. Traffic from hub routers typically does not use the remote routers at spoke sites as transit paths.

When configured as stub EIGRP routers, the remote spokes are configured to share only a subset of routing information with their neighbors (at the hub site). When the **eigrp stub** configuration command is applied to a router at a spoke site with no optional keywords, the router advertises only its connected and summary routes. Several optional keywords can be used with the **eigrp stub** command:

- **eigrp stub connected:** The remote router advertises only its connected routes.

- **eigrp stub static:** The remote router advertises only its static routes.

- **eigrp stub redistribute:** The remote router only advertises routes redistributed from the other protocols into EIGRP.

- **eigrp stub summary:** The remote router advertises only the summary routes.

- **eigrp stub receive-only:** The remote router does not advertise any routes.

The New EIGRP Named Configuration

There are now two methods to configure EIGRP on Cisco routers. The first method is the conventional method, which is called *EIGRP autonomous system configuration*. The second method is new and it is called *EIGRP named configuration*. When using the autonomous system method, you must enter some commands in the config-router mode, and some commands in the config-interface mode, and for every address family (IPv4/IPv6), you have to configure a separate EIGRP process. When using the new named configuration method, one EIGRP process handles both IPv4 and IPv6 address families. Furthermore, interface-related commands can also be configured under the appropriate submode of each address family within the EIGRP routing process. When configuring EIGRP using the new named configuration method, you have three submodes available within the routing process:

- **Address family configuration mode:** This mode is used to configure general EIGRP parameters such as **network** statements, manually configured neighbors, and the default metric. Address family has submodes of its own.

- **Address family interface configuration mode:** This mode is used to configure interface-specific EIGRP parameters such as bandwidth, split horizon, and authentication. Interface parameters can be configured for all interfaces by configuring a default interface, or they can be configured for a particular interface. Note that the address family interface-specific configuration overrides the address family interface default configuration, which overrides the address family factory default configuration for interfaces.

- **Address family topology configuration mode:** This mode is used to provide options that operate on the EIGRP topology table, such as administrative distance, redistribution, and load balancing. The main routing table is populated from the base topology.

One of the advantages of the EIGRP named configuration method is that the verification commands are similar to the configuration commands, preceded with the **show** keyword. Useful EIGRP verification commands include the following:

- **show eigrp plugins:** Displays general information about the eigrp configuration and its address-families.

- **show ip eigrp topology:** Displays EIGRP's topology table.

- **show eigrp address-family {ipv4 | ipv6}** [*autonomous-system-number*] [**multicast**] **accounting:** Displays prefix accounting information for the appropriate address-family.

- **show eigrp address-family interfaces detail** [*interface-type interface-number*]: Displays information about interfaces that EIGRP is activated for.

- **show eigrp address-family topology route-type summary:** Displays information about all summary routes.

Troubleshooting Management Access to ASW2

Carrie (PILE's network engineer) has left us a message at SECHNIK to help her with the following problem: PC1 cannot telnet into the ASW2 switch, but telnet to all other network devices works just fine.

Verifying the Problem

To verify the problem as described by Carrie, we tried to telnet into access switch ASW2 (10.0.99.7) from PC1, and as shown in Example 8-57, the connection timed out. However, the telnet from PC1 to ASW1 (10.0.99.6) and to DSW (10.0.10.1) worked just fine.

Example 8-57   *Verify the Problem: PC1 Cannot Telnet into the ASW2 Switch*

```
PC1# telnet 10.0.99.7
Trying 10.0.99.7 ...
% Connection timed out; remote host not responding
PC1# telnet 10.0.99.6
Trying 10.0.99.6 ... Open
User Access Verification
Password:
ASW1> exit
[Connection to 10.0.99.6 closed by foreign host]
PC1# telnet 10.0.10.1
Trying 10.0.10.1 ... Open
User Access Verification
Password:
DSW> exit
[Connection to 10.0.10.1 closed by foreign host]
PC1#
```

This verifies that the problem, as explained by Carrie, is true.

Gathering Information

Knowing that PC1 cannot telnet into switch ASW2, we can take a divide-and-conquer approach and see whether it can ping it instead. As shown in Example 8-58, pinging from PC1 to the ASW2 switch fails. Ping attempts from ASW1 to ASW2, however, succeed. Keep in mind that ASW1 and ASW2 management addresses (10.0.99.7 and 10.0.99.6) are in a common IP subnet.

Example 8-58   *Information Gathering: Ping from PC1 to ASW2 Also Fails*

```
PC1# ping 10.0.99.7
Type escape sequence to abort.
Sending 5, 100-byte ICMP Echos to 10.0.99.7, timeout is 2 seconds:
```

```
.....
Success rate is 0 percent (0/5)
PC1#


ASW1# ping 10.0.99.7
Type escape sequence to abort.
Sending 5, 100-byte ICMP Echos to 10.0.99.7, timeout is 2 seconds:
.!!!!
Success rate is 80 percent (4/5), round-trip min/avg/max = 1/3/8 ms
ASW1#
```

Because the ping from ASW1 to ASW2 was successful, we can conclude that there are
no physical and data link layer connectivity problems. In addition, because PC1 can
telnet into ASW1, but not ASW2 (which is in the same subnet as ASW1), we know that
there is no routing problem either. We need to find out why ASW2 is not accessible
from outside subnet 10.0.99.0/24 but ASW1 is. We can use the compare-configurations
technique and compare ASW1's configuration with ASW2's. Example 8-59 displays output of the **show ip route** command on the ASW1 switch, and it shows that the ASW1
switch has 10.0.99.1 (interface VLAN 99 on the DSW switch) configured as its default
gateway.

Example 8-59   *Information Gathering: Output of* **show ip route** *on ASW1*

```
ASW1# show ip route
Default gateway is 10.0.99.1
Host              Gateway        Last Use    Total Uses   Interface
ICMP redirect cache is empty
ASW1#
```

We now need to access ASW2 so that we have a chance to try the **show ip route** command on the ASW2 switch. Example 8-60 shows that, unlike ASW1, the ASW2 switch
does not have a default gateway configured.

Example 8-60   *Information Gathering: Output of* **show ip route** *on ASW2*

```
ASW2# show ip route
Default gateway is not set
Host              Gateway        Last Use    Total Uses   Interface
ICMP redirect cache is empty
ASW2#
```

Proposing a Hypothesis and Testing the Hypothesis

Based on the information gathered so far, which is the lack of default gateway configuration on the ASW2 switch, we can propose a hypothesis. Our hypothesis is to configure
the ASW2 switch with the default gateway address 10.0.99.1, similar to how ASW1 is

configured. Example 8-61 shows us entering the **ip default-gateway** command on the ASW2 switch. The **show ip route** command that we tried subsequently displays the default gateway correctly shown as 10.0.99.1.

Example 8-61   *Testing a Hypothesis: Configure a Default Gateway on ASW2*

```
ASW2# conf t
Enter configuration commands, one per line.  End with CNTL/Z.
ASW2(config)# ip default-gateway 10.0.99.1
ASW2(config)# end
ASW2# sh
*Sep 17 04:11:09.539: %SYS-5-CONFIG_I: Configured from console by console
ASW2# show ip route
Default gateway is 10.0.99.1

Host              Gateway          Last Use    Total Uses   Interface
ICMP redirect cache is empty
ASW2#
```

Solving the Problem

We must now reattempt the Telnet session from PC1 to ASW2. Example 8-62 shows that a ping from PC1 to the ASW2 switch is successful; the Telnet from PC1 to ASW2 works as well.

Example 8-62   *Solving the Problem: Telnet into 10.0.99.7 (ASW2) from PC1*

```
PC1# ping 10.0.99.7
Type escape sequence to abort.
Sending 5, 100-byte ICMP Echos to 10.0.99.7, timeout is 2 seconds:
!!!!!
Success rate is 100 percent (5/5), round-trip min/avg/max = 1/202/1007 ms
PC1# telnet 10.0.99.7
Trying 10.0.99.7 ... Open
User Access Verification
Password:
ASW2> exit
[Connection to 10.0.99.7 closed by foreign host]
PC1#
```

We must now document our work and notify Carrie that this problem is solved.

Providing a Default Route on Layer 2 And Multilayer Devices

You can install a default route on a Cisco network device in a number of ways, including the following:

- **ip default-network** *network-number*: This command enables you to specify a network which will serve as a default route. It is used when routing is enabled on the device. For the command to have an effect, the network number must be present in the routing table. When this condition is satisfied, a static route entry is automatically created for the major classful network of the network number used in the command. The command **ip default-network** *network-number* is a classful command. If you use a classless network mask for the network number, the gateway of last resort will not be set, and no default route will be added to the routing table. The gateway of last resort is set only when the network number used is a classful network address. Because of its classful nature, the command is considered a legacy command and is not used any more.

- **ip route 0.0.0.0 0.0.0.0** {*ip-address* | *interface-type interface-number* [*ip-address*]}: This command is also called the static default command. This command will set the gateway of last resort. If you specify a next-hop IP address, the next-hop address must be reachable (based on the IP routing table content); otherwise, the static route is not installed in the IP routing table.

- **ip default-gateway** *ip-address*: This command is applicable only to Layer 2 switches, multilayer switches where the **ip routing** command has not been entered, or on routers with IP routing turned off by using the **no ip routing** command. On a multilayer switch or router, as soon as IP routing is enabled, this command has no effect.

Note that a Layer 3 routing device may receive a default route through a dynamic routing protocol as well.

PILE Forensic Accounting Trouble Ticket 5

Carrie, the network engineer at PILE Forensic Accounting, has contacted us at SECHNIK to explain some of the concerns she has and needs help with. She explained that because she was worried about the fact that PILE's network has been connected to the Internet using only a single edge (perimeter) router, she purchased a second edge router (HQ0) for the headquarters site. She installed the HQ0 router to connect to ISP1 and kept HQ1 connected to ISP2, as shown in Figure 8-2. Carrie specified that when she does HQ1 failure testing, Internet traffic is not properly handled and forwarded by the new HQ0 router; instead, traffic is dropped and lost. Carrie is seeking our help so that we can build a fully functional and reliable Internet connectivity solution for PILE, one that can sustain Internet connectivity when either of HQ0's or HQ1's paths fails.

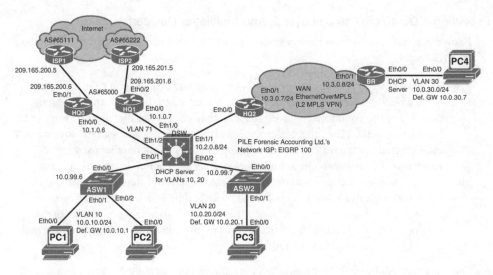

Figure 8-2 *PILE Network Diagram with the Second Edge Router*

Carrie has also expressed concern about another unrelated matter; she said that she needs to have management access to all network devices through Telnet using her personal computer (PC1). However, she has recently noticed that the user of PC3 can and has been accessing the branch router (BR) using Telnet, as well, which is unacceptable. PC3 should have Internet connectivity and should be able to ping all devices, but it should not be able to access network devices using either Telnet or SSH.

Troubleshooting the Redundant Internet Access Path Through the New HQ0 Edge Router

Based on Carrie's description of the problem, the second edge router (HQ0) that she recently installed does not maintain PILE network's Internet connectivity when the HQ1 router fails.

Verifying and Defining the Problem

Before we verify lack of redundant Internet connectivity, it is important to first verify that the primary Internet connectivity path through HQ1 router is functional. Example 8-63 shows that pinging from PC1 to the Internet reachability test IP address (209.165.200.129) is 100 percent successful.

We can now verify the reported problem by shutting down router HQ1's Eth0/0 interface (LAN/internal). This action effectively stops PILE's Internet access through the HQ1 router. As shown in Example 8-63, when we repeat the ping test from PC1 to the IP address 209.165.200.129, it is no longer successful.

Example 8-63 *Verifying the Problem: Internet Connectivity Through the New HQ0 Edge Router Is Not Functional*

```
PC1# ping 209.165.200.129
Type escape sequence to abort.
Sending 5, 100-byte ICMP Echos to 209.165.200.129, timeout is 2 seconds:
!!!!!
Success rate is 100 percent (5/5), round-trip min/avg/max = 1/1/2 ms
PC1#


HQ1# conf t
Enter configuration commands, one per line.  End with CNTL/Z.
HQ1(config)# interface ethernet 0/0
HQ1(config-if)# shut
Sep 18 05:51:38.015: %DUAL-5-NBRCHANGE: EIGRP-IPv4 100: Neighbor 10.1.0.6
  (Ethernet0/0) is down: interface down
Sep 18 05:51:38.017: %DUAL-5-NBRCHANGE: EIGRP-IPv4 100: Neighbor 10.1.0.254
  (Ethernet0/0) is down: interface down
Sep 18 05:51:40.017: %LINK-5-CHANGED: Interface Ethernet0/0, changed state to
  administratively down
Sep 18 05:51:41.021: %LINEPROTO-5-UPDOWN: Line protocol on Interface Ethernet0/0,
  changed state to down
HQ1(config-if)# end
HQ1#


PC1# ping 209.165.200.129
Type escape sequence to abort.
Sending 5, 100-byte ICMP Echos to 209.165.200.129, timeout is 2 seconds:
.....
Success rate is 0 percent (0/5)
PC1#
```

We have verified the problem as Carrie has described it. PILE's Internet connection through the newly installed router HQ0 is not functional, and it therefore does not provide a redundant alternative Internet connectivity path. Knowing that PC1 has no Internet connectivity problem while the path though HQ1 is functional, we can take a follow-the-path approach.

Gathering Information

We can now make use of a trace to see the path from PC1 toward the Internet test address until the packet gets dropped. As shown in Example 8-64, the packet makes it through two hops before it drops. The first hop is PC1's default gateway (10.0.10.1), which is the DSW switch. The second hop (10.1.0.6) is the HQ0 new edge router. We telnet to 10.1.0.6 (HQ0) to do further information gathering.

Example 8-64   *Information Gathering: Trace from PC1 to the Internet*

```
PC1# show ip route
Default gateway is 10.0.10.1
< ...output omitted... >
PC1# trace 209.165.200.129
Type escape sequence to abort.
Tracing the route to 209.165.200.129
VRF info: (vrf in name/id, vrf out name/id)
  1 10.0.10.1 1 msec 1 msec 0 msec
  2 10.1.0.6 1 msec 1 msec 1 msec
  3  *  *  *
  4  *  *  *
  5  *  *  *
PC1# telnet 10.1.0.6
Trying 10.1.0.6 ... Open
User Access Verification
Password:
HQ0>en
Password:
HQ0#
```

While at HQ0, it is best to first check this edge router's IP routing table. As shown in Example 8-65, HQ0 has plenty of Internet destinations reachable through the 209.165.200.5 next hop. We then check the status of HQ0's BGP neighbors by using the **show ip bgp summary** command. 209.165.200.5 is HQ0's external BGP neighbor, which is ISP1's BGP router (connected to HQ0). Finally, we use the **show ip bgp neighbor 209.165.200.5 advertised-routes** command to see which prefixes are advertised by the HQ0 router to the ISP. As shown in Example 8-65, HQ0 is not advertising any routes to its external BGP neighbor at all.

Example 8-65   *Information Gathering: Check HQ0 Edge Router's Routing Table*

```
HQ0# show ip route
< ...output omitted... >
      209.165.200.0/24 is variably subnetted, 5 subnets, 5 masks
C        209.165.200.4/30 is directly connected, Ethernet0/1
L        209.165.200.6/32 is directly connected, Ethernet0/1
B        209.165.200.128/26 [20/0] via 209.165.200.5, 00:22:21
B        209.165.200.192/27 [20/0] via 209.165.200.5, 00:22:21
S        209.165.200.248/29 is directly connected, Null0
      209.165.201.0/24 is variably subnetted, 4 subnets, 3 masks
B        209.165.201.128/25 [20/0] via 209.165.200.5, 00:22:21
B        209.165.201.192/28 [20/0] via 209.165.200.5, 00:22:21
B        209.165.201.208/28 [20/0] via 209.165.200.5, 00:22:21
B        209.165.201.224/27 [20/0] via 209.165.200.5, 00:22:21
```

```
HQ0# show ip bgp summary
< ...output omitted... >
Neighbor        V    AS MsgRcvd MsgSent  TblVer  InQ OutQ  Up/Down     State/PfxRcd
10.1.0.7        4    65000       0        0       1    0    0 00:13:40  Active
209.165.200.5   4    65111      38       29      12    0    0 00:23:57       7
HQ0# show ip bgp neighbor 209.165.200.5 advertised-routes
Total number of prefixes 0
HQ0#
```

We need to know or find out what public prefix of PILE Forensic Accounting must be advertised by the HQ router to the Internet (ISP). Therefore, as shown in Example 8-66, we look at the NAT section of HQ0's running-config and find out that the Network Address Translation (NAT) pool is merely 200.165.200.250. The NAT configuration seems accurate. Therefore, we must stay focused on finding out why HQ0 is not advertising the 200.165.200.250 prefix to the ISP.

Example 8-66 *Information Gathering: What Public Prefix Must Be Advertised?*

```
HQ0# show running-config | section nat
 ip nat inside
 ip nat outside
ip nat pool NAT 209.165.200.250 209.165.200.250 netmask 255.255.255.252
ip nat inside source list 1 pool NAT overload
HQ0#
HQ0# show run | begin interface Ethernet
interface Ethernet0/0
 ip address 10.1.0.6 255.255.255.0
 ip nat inside
 ip virtual-reassembly in
!
interface Ethernet0/1
 description ISP1
 ip address 209.165.200.6 255.255.255.252
 ip access-group 100 in
 ip nat outside
 ip inspect INSPECT out
 ip virtual-reassembly in
!
< ...output omitted... >
HQ0# show access-list 1
Standard IP access list 1
    10 permit 10.0.0.0, wildcard bits 0.255.255.255 (49 matches)
HQ0#
```

We now check the BGP router configuration on the HQ0 router, and as shown in Example 8-67, the HQ0 router has an accurate **network** statement attempting to advertise PILE's public 209.165.200.250/32 prefix.

Example 8-67   *Information Gathering: Examine BGP's **network** Statements*

```
HQ0# show run | section router bgp
router bgp 65000
 bgp router-id 10.10.10.9
 bgp log-neighbor-changes
 bgp redistribute-internal
 network 209.165.200.250 mask 255.255.255.255
 neighbor 10.1.0.7 remote-as 65000
 neighbor 10.1.0.7 next-hop-self
 neighbor 209.165.200.5 remote-as 65111
 neighbor 209.165.200.5 distribute-list RouteOut out
HQ0#
```

Because we confirmed that a **network** statement for the 209.165.200.250/32 prefix is indeed configured in HQ0's BGP configuration, we must now find out whether this prefix is present in HQ0's IP routing table. BGP will not advertise the prefix 209.165.200.250/32 unless it is present in the IP routing table. We now search the IP routing table looking for this prefix. As shown in Example 8-68, the 209.165.200.250/32 prefix is not present in the IP routing table; however, there is a static routing entry (via Null0) for the prefix 209.165.200.248/29. We verify this by looking in the running-config next (see the last part of Example 8-68).

Example 8-68   *Information Gathering: Check HQ0's Routing Table*

```
HQ0# show ip route 209.165.200.250
Routing entry for 209.165.200.248/29
  Known via "static", distance 1, metric 0 (connected)
  Redistributing via eigrp 100
  Advertised by eigrp 100 metric 900000 10 255 1 1500
  Routing Descriptor Blocks:
  * directly connected, via Null0
      Route metric is 0, traffic share count is 1
HQ0#
HQ0# show run | include 209.165.200.248 255.255.255.248
ip route 209.165.200.248 255.255.255.248 Null0
HQ0#
```

Proposing a Hypothesis and Testing the Hypothesis

It looks like the static route we found in HQ0's routing table was mistyped. As a result of this error, and because the prefix 209.165.200.250/32 is not present in HQ0's routing table, the BGP router will not advertise it. We therefore propose to remove the erroneous static route and replace it with an accurate one. Example 8-69 shows our work removing the erroneous static route and typing the new and accurate static route to Null0, which should now allow BGP to advertise this prefix to the ISP peer. The final section of Example 8-69 shows us verifying this advertisement. As you can see, shortly after our correction, HQ0's BGP router advertised the 209.165.200.250/32 prefix to its neighbor 209.165.200.5.

Example 8-69   *Testing the Hypothesis: Correct the Erroneous Static Route*

```
HQ0# conf term
Enter configuration commands, one per line.  End with CNTL/Z.
HQ0(config)# no ip route 209.165.200.248 255.255.255.248 Null0
HQ0(config)# ip route 209.165.200.250 255.255.255.255 Null0
HQ0(config)# end
HQ0# show ip bgp neigh 209.165.200.5 advertised-routes
BGP table version is 13, local router ID is 10.10.10.9
Status codes: s suppressed, d damped, h history, * valid, > best, i - internal,
              r RIB-failure, S Stale, m multipath, b backup-path, f RT-Filter,
              x best-external, a additional-path, c RIB-compressed,
Origin codes: i - IGP, e - EGP, ? - incomplete
RPKI validation codes: V valid, I invalid, N Not found

     Network                 Next Hop            Metric LocPrf Weight Path
 *>  209.165.200.250/32  0.0.0.0                      0         32768 i

Total number of prefixes 1
HQ0#
```

Solving the Problem

To prove that the problem is solved, we repeat the ping to the 209.165.200.129 address from PC1, and as you can see in Example 8-70, the ping is now successful. We bring up the Eth0/0 interface on the HQ1 router and repeat the ping test again. This time, the ping is successful again. Finally, we bring down the Eth0/0 interface on the HQ0 router and repeat the ping test. The ping test succeeds again. We have demonstrated that the Internet is reachable even when either HQ1 or HQ0 is unreachable.

Example 8-70   *Solving the Problem: Internet Is Reachable via HQ0 and HQ1*

```
PC1# ping 209.165.200.129
Type escape sequence to abort.
Sending 5, 100-byte ICMP Echos to 209.165.200.129, timeout is 2 seconds:
!!!!!
Success rate is 100 percent (5/5), round-trip min/avg/max = 1/1/2 ms
PC1#


HQ1# conf t
Enter configuration commands, one per line.  End with CNTL/Z.
```

```
HQ1(config)# interface eth 0/0
HQ1(config-if)# no shut
HQ1(config-if)# end
Sep 18 06:40:29.434: %LINK-3-UPDOWN: Interface Ethernet0/0, changed state to up
Sep 18 06:40:30.441: %LINEPROTO-5-UPDOWN: Line protocol on Interface Ethernet0/0,
  changed state to up
Sep 18 06:40:30.626: %DUAL-5-NBRCHANGE: EIGRP-IPv4 100: Neighbor 10.1.0.254
  (Ethernet0/0) is up: new adjacency
Sep 18 06:40:30.644: %DUAL-5-NBRCHANGE: EIGRP-IPv4 100: Neighbor 10.1.0.6
  (Ethernet0/0) is up: new adjacency
Sep 18 06:40:31.034: %SYS-5-CONFIG_I: Configured from console by console
HQ1# wr
Building configuration...
[OK]
HQ1#


PC1# ping 209.165.200.129
Type escape sequence to abort.
Sending 5, 100-byte ICMP Echos to 209.165.200.129, timeout is 2 seconds:
!!!!!
Success rate is 100 percent (5/5), round-trip min/avg/max = 1/1/1 ms
PC1#


HQ0# conf t
Enter configuration commands, one per line.  End with CNTL/Z.
HQ0(config)# inter eth0/0
HQ0(config-if)# shut
HQ0(config-if)#
Sep 18 06:45:49.697: %DUAL-5-NBRCHANGE: EIGRP-IPv4 100: Neighbor 10.1.0.7
  (Ethernet0/0) is down: interface down
Sep 18 06:45:49.699: %DUAL-5-NBRCHANGE: EIGRP-IPv4 100: Neighbor 10.1.0.254
  (Ethernet0/0) is down: interface down
Sep 18 06:45:51.695: %LINK-5-CHANGED: Interface Ethernet0/0, changed state to
  administratively down
Sep 18 06:45:52.696: %LINEPROTO-5-UPDOWN: Line protocol on Interface Ethernet0/0,
  changed state to down
HQ0(config-if)#


PC1# ping 209.165.200.129
Type escape sequence to abort.
Sending 5, 100-byte ICMP Echos to 209.165.200.129, timeout is 2 seconds:
!!!!!
Success rate is 100 percent (5/5), round-trip min/avg/max = 1/1/1 ms
PC1#
```

We must now document our work and notify Carrie that this problem is solved.

Troubleshooting BGP Route Selection

When the BGP table has several paths to the same destination, the BGP process on a Cisco device uses the following step-by-step procedure to break the tie and choose the best path:

1. A path to an IP destination may be considered for the best path selection only if it is the next hop and is reachable using the local router's routing table.

2. Prefer the path with the highest weight. Weight is a Cisco-specific attribute; it is local to the router on which it is configured, and it is not advertised to any neighbor. The default weight is 0, but local routes are given the weight of 32768.

3. Prefer the path with the highest local preference. Local preference is typically used to implement autonomous system-wide policies with regard to preferred exit points to one or more IP destinations. Local preference is advertised only to internal BGP (iBGP) neighbors. The default local preference value is 100, but it can be changed by using the **default local-preference** command.

4. Prefer the path that is locally generated. A locally originated path has a next-hop IP address value of 0.0.0.0 in the BGP table.

5. Prefer the path with the shortest AS-path attribute. This step is skipped if the command **bgp bestpath as-path ignore** is entered.

6. Prefer the path with the lowest origin code. IGP (i) is lower than EGP (e), and EGP (e) is lower than INCOMPLETE/UNKNOWN (?).

7. Prefer the path with the lowest MED value. By default, the MED values of paths are only compared if the paths are all received from the same autonomous system. If you want BGP to compare the MED values even if the paths are from different ASNs, use the **bgp always-compare-med** command.

8. Prefer the eBGP path over the iBGP path.

9. Among iBGP paths, prefer the path from the neighbor that is closer based on the IGP metric.

10. Among eBGP paths, prefer the path that has been in the BGP table longest and is therefore considered the most stable path.

11. Prefer the path from the neighbor that has the lower router ID.

12. Prefer the path from the neighbor whose IP address has the lower value. The address to be considered and compared is the address used for neighbor configuration.

Use the **show ip bgp** command to display the BGP table. In the BGP table, for each prefix path, the BGP attributes such as next hop, Multi-Exit Discriminator (MED, metric), local preference, weight, AS-Path, and origin code are shown. If a path is valid, it is marked with an asterisk at the beginning of the line. The best path is marked with the symbol right angle bracket (>). To display the details of a specific BGP prefix, you can use the **show ip bgp** *prefix* command.

The command **show ip bgp neighbors** *ip-address* **received-routes** shows all routes received from a specific neighbor. To use this command, the soft reconfiguration inbound option must be configured for the neighbor. When soft reconfiguration is enabled, the router stores all routes received by the neighbor before any policy is applied to the received routes. When you change the BGP policy, you can apply it to those stored routes. This is helpful because you do not have to restart the BGP session.

To restart the BGP session with a neighbor, you can use the **clear ip bgp** * command. When this command is issued, all BGP sessions are reset. You should avoid using this command in production networks. To reset the session with only one neighbor, you can use **clear ip bgp** *ip-address*. This command is also not recommended for use in a live production network; the route refresh (**clear ip bgp neighbor** *neighbor-ip* **in** or **clear ip bgp neighbor** *neighbor-ip* **out**) can accomplish the same tasks with much less network disturbance.

Troubleshooting Unauthorized Telnet Access

The last problem that Carrie has asked us to help her with has to do with the user of PC3 being able to telnet into the branch router (BR). Carrie says that she has put the necessary configurations in place, but that does not seem to be effective and working.

Verifying the Problem

To verify the problem, we try to telnet into the BR from PC3. As shown in Example 8-71, the Telnet attempt fails.

Example 8-71   *Verifying the Problem: Try to Telnet into the BR from PC3*

```
PC3# telnet 10.3.0.8
Trying 10.3.0.8 ...
% Connection refused by remote host
PC3#
```

We can conclude that PC3 is not directly accessing the BR through Telnet. However, PC3 may be leveraging another device to be able to access the BR indirectly.

Gathering Information

Because we cannot telnet into the branch router from PC3 directly, we should check the BR's configuration. We need to find out which addresses are, based on the branch router's configuration, allowed to telnet into the BR. Example 8-72 shows the vty line configuration on the BR. As you can see, the **access-class 10 in** command is applied to the vty lines. Access list 10 permits devices from the IP subnet 10.0.10.0/24 (VLAN 10), and it also permits devices from the IP subnet 10.3.0.0/24.

Example 8-72 *Examining the Branch Router's Configuration for the vty Lines*

```
BR# show run
< ...output omitted... >
access-list 10 permit 10.0.10.0 0.0.0.255
access-list 10 deny   10.0.20.0 0.0.0.255
access-list 10 remark USERS from VLAN 20 should not be allowed to telnet in
access-list 10 permit 10.3.0.0 0.0.0.255
!
< ...output omitted... >
!
line vty 0 4
 access-class 10 in
 password c1sc0
 login
 transport input all
BR#
```

The IP subnet 10.3.0.0/24 is implemented over the WAN link between the BR and the HQ2 router. Currently, only two addresses are allocated and assigned from this subnet. One address is assigned to the BR, and the other address is assigned to the HQ2 router. We need to find out whether PC3 can telnet into the HQ2 router (10.3.0.7). As Example 8-73 shows, PC3 can indeed telnet into the HQ2 router, and then from HQ2, PC3 can telnet into the BR (10.3.0.8).

Example 8-73 *Testing Whether PC3 Can Telnet into the HQ2 Router*

```
PC3# telnet 10.3.0.7
Trying 10.3.0.7 ... Open
User Access Verification
Password:
HQ2>en
Password:
HQ2# telnet 10.3.0.8
Trying 10.3.0.8 ... Open
User Access Verification
Password:
BR>
```

Gathering Further Information and Analysis Information

We must now find out why PC3 is able to telnet into the HQ2 router. As shown in Example 8-74, the command **access-class 10 in** that is applied to HQ2's vty lines restricts Telnet access to only the IP addresses matching access list 10. However, when we examine the contents of access list 10, we notice that its first statement permits all IP addresses with a 16-bit match to the 10.0.0.0 address. Comparing this statement to access list 10 on the BR (Example 8-61) reveals that this line is misconfigured. Telnet access must be available to only subnet 10.0.10.0/24 (VLAN 10).

Example 8-74   *Examining HQ2 Router's Configuration*

```
HQ2# show running-config | section line vty
line vty 0 4
 access-class 10 in
 password c1sc0
 login
 transport input all
HQ2# show access-list 10
Standard IP access list 10
    10 permit 10.0.0.0, wildcard bits 0.0.255.255
    20 deny   10.0.20.0, wildcard bits 0.0.0.255
HQ2#
```

Proposing a Hypothesis and Testing the Hypothesis

We can now propose that the access list 10 on the HQ2 router is misconfigured and must be corrected. The first statement of access list 10 in HQ2 must be removed and replaced with a statement that allows IP addresses with a 24-bit match to address 10.0.10.0 (VLAN 10). Example 8-75 shows our work correcting access list 10 on HQ2.

Example 8-75   *Correcting HQ2's Access List 10 Configuration*

```
HQ2# conf term
Enter configuration commands, one per line.  End with CNTL/Z.
HQ2(config)# ip access-list standard 10
HQ2(config-std-nacl)# no 10
HQ2(config-std-nacl)# 10 permit 10.0.10.0 0.0.0.255
HQ2(config-std-nacl)# end
HQ2#
*Sep 19 05:27:50.805: %SYS-5-CONFIG_I: Configured from console by console
HQ2# show access-list 10
Standard IP access list 10
    10 permit 10.0.10.0, wildcard bits 0.0.0.255
    20 deny   10.0.20.0, wildcard bits 0.0.0.255
HQ2# wr
Building configuration...
[OK]
HQ2#
```

Solving the Problem

We must now test to see whether the corrected access list will block PC3's Telnet attempt into the HQ2 router. Example 8-76 shows that the Telnet attempt from PC3 to HQ2 fails. We attempted a direct Telnet from PC3 to the BR, but that attempt also failed.

Example 8-76 *Correcting HQ2's Access List 10 Configuration*

```
PC3# telnet 10.2.0.7
Trying 10.2.0.7 ...
% Connection refused by remote host


PC3# telnet 10.2.0.8
Trying 10.2.0.8 ...
% Connection refused by remote host


PC3#
```

We must now document our work and notify Carrie that this last problem is solved.

Securing the Management Plane

Best practices to secure your networking devices' management plane include the following:

■ Use complex passwords. Passwords should be at least eight characters long; this can be enforced with the command **security password min-length.** You should use a mix of alphanumeric characters, uppercase and lowercase characters, and symbols.

■ Those who attempt management access to network devices must be authenticated. Cisco AAA (authentication, authorization, and accounting) allows credentials to be stored locally on the device or on a remote centralized server. AAA services are enabled with the **aaa new-model** command. The best practice is to use a TACACS+ or RADIUS remote server (**tacacs** or **radius server** command) and to configure authentication to use the local database as a fallback method when the remote server is not accessible (**aaa authentication login default group radius local**).

■ The goal of role-based access control (RBAC) is to define a few roles with particular privileges and assign user accounts to those roles. RBAC can be implemented with custom privilege levels or parser views. Use the command **privilege** *mode* {level *level* | reset} *command-string* to set privilege levels for the specific commands. Use parser views to implement even more sophisticated RBAC. The command to create views is **parser view** *view-name*.

■ When devices are configured remotely, you should always use encrypted management protocols. This includes SSH or HTTPS. You should use SSH Version 2. You can configure this with the command **ip ssh version 2**. To enable only SSH, use **transport input ssh** within the line vty configuration mode. When using a GUI to manage a device, use the **ip http secure-server** command to enable HTTPS.

- Event logging provides you visibility into the operation of a Cisco IOS device. Log outputs can be directed to a variety of destinations, including console, vty lines, the buffer, the SNMP server, and the syslog server. Use the **service timestamps log datetime** to include date and time in the log messages.

- Synchronize the clocks of your network devices with another device using the **ntp server** *ip-address* command. This allows you to do accurate correlation between events recorded on different system logs.

- It is recommended to use SNMPv3 for monitoring and management of network devices. SNMPv3 uses the concept of a security model and security levels. When using SNMPv2c, a complex community string is used, and you should also limit (by using ACLs) the SNMP access to hosts that need that access. Do not use community public for the read access or community private for read-write access; these are common default communities.

- To help protect a router from accidental or malicious tampering of the IOS image or startup configuration, Cisco offers a resilient configuration feature. This feature maintains a secure copy of the router IOS image and running configuration. When this feature is enabled, it cannot be disabled remotely. To protect your IOS image, use the **secure boot-image** command, and to protect your device configuration, use the **secure boot-config** command.

Summary

This chapter presented five troubleshooting tickets at PILE Forensic Accounting, a ficti-tious company, based on the topology shown in Figure 8-3.

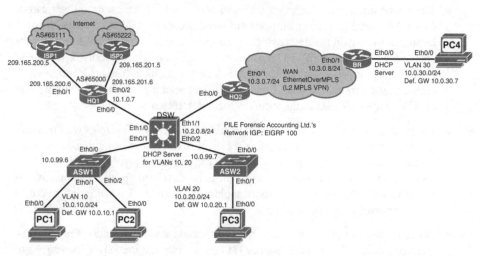

Figure 8-3 *PILE Forensic Accounting Network Diagram*

SECHNIK Networking provides technical support to PILE. As employees of SECHNIK, we solved all the following problems reported by the customer and documented them.

Trouble ticket 1: We work for SECHNIK Networking and PILE Forensic Accounting is a valuable customer. One of our staff, Peter, has made a few improvements at PILE's network over the weekend. On Monday, Carrie, who works for PILE as a resident network engineer, was made aware of two problems that she asked us to fix. The following are the problems reported and the solutions we offered:

1. The branch office at PILE has lost connectivity to the headquarters and therefore from the Internet.

   Solution: We discovered that the problem was due to an invalid network statement on the branch router's EIGRP configuration. Fixing this statement activated the branch router's EIGRP on the WAN side toward the headquarters. Consequently, the branch router's connectivity to the headquarters and the Internet was restored.

2. When ISP1's connection is lost or brought down, the connection to ISP2 does not provide Internet connectivity as backup.

   Solution: This problem, we discovered, was due to an erroneous access list applied to the HQ1 router's edge interfaces (Eth0/1 and Eth0/2), which prevented incoming BGP messages from ISP2.

Trouble ticket 2: This trouble ticket had three items. The first item was that a user from PILE Forensic Accounting contacted us directly (SECHNIK Networking) and complained that from his PC (PC3) he could not telnet into the branch router (BR), and he requested this issue to be rectified as soon as possible. The second item was that Carrie, the resident network engineer at PILE, contacted us in a panic, saying that everyone on the PILE network had lost Internet connectivity. And finally, the third item was that HQ1 router's time was not synchronized with the preferred NTP server. The following are the solutions we found for each of these items:

1. PC3 cannot telnet into the BR.

   Solution: We discovered that there was no problem; the BR is operating correctly, rejecting Telnet attempts sourced from VLAN 20 (where PC3 resides).

2. Everyone at PILE has lost Internet connectivity; however, the HQ1 router has Internet connectivity.

   Solution: We discovered that the access list applied outbound to both of HQ1 router's eBGP neighbors prevented advertisement of PILE's local networks. This was preventing PILE's networks from being reachable (from the Internet).

3. HQ1 router's time is not synchronized with the preferred NTP server.

   Solution: We discovered that this problem was due the access list applied to the edge interfaces (Eth0/1 and Eth0/2) of the HQ1 routers blocking the incoming NTP messages from the preferred NTP server.

Trouble ticket 3: This trouble ticket was a result of the flood at PILE Forensic Accounting that destroyed DSW, ASW1, and ASW2 switches. Carrie, the network engineer at PILE, replaced devices and restored connectivity for critical PCs (those in VLAN 10). However, she reported to us the following remaining problems that she needed help with:

1. After Carrie replaced switches ASW1, ASW2, and DSW, and restored PILE's network operation, PC3 lost Internet connectivity. However, Carrie indicated that PC1 and PC2 from VLAN 10 had Internet connectivity.

   Solution: We discovered that during disaster recovery the ASW1 switch backup configuration was mistakenly copied to ASW2. In addition, we found that VLAN 20's IP address on the DSW switch was incorrect.

2. Carrie has notified us that the user of PC4 at the PILE's branch site was complaining about Internet connectivity problems. Specifically, the website that the user could not access was Cisco.com.

   Solution: We discovered that the DHCP server configuration on the branch router was missing the DNS server line; hence, the end hosts (DHCP clients) had no DNS server for name resolution.

Trouble ticket 4: PILE Forensic Accounting acquired 47 branch offices worldwide. Carrie, the network engineer at PILE, after doing some research about making EIGRP more scalable, decided to reconfigure the current sole BR to announce only connected and summary networks through EIGRP stub configuration. Her plan was to have a proof of concept. Then, when the newly acquired 47 branches needed to be connected, she would merely replicate her work on all the new branch routers. However, Carrie called and left a message for us at SECHNIK asking for our help with two items. The following are the items and the solutions we found for them:

1. After EIGRP reconfiguration, the BR lost connectivity to the Internet.

   Solution: We discovered that the EIGRP ASN on the BR was misconfigured. Also, the **eigrp stub** command was mistakenly configured at the headquarters router rather than at the BR.

2. Carrie (using PC1) cannot access the ASW2 switch via Telnet; however, she can access all other network devices.

   Solution: We discovered that the ASW2 switch was configured with no default gateway.

Trouble ticket 5: Carrie, the network engineer at PILE Forensic Accounting, had purchased a second edge router (HQ0) for the headquarters site and installed the HQ0 router to connect to ISP1 and kept HQ1 connected to ISP2. Carrie specified that when she performed HQ1 failure testing, Internet traffic was not properly handled and forwarded by the new HQ0 router; traffic was dropped and lost instead. Carrie asked us to help her rectify this issue. Carrie also expressed concern about another unrelated matter; she said that she needed to have management access to all network devices through Telnet using her personal computer (PC1). However, she noticed that the user of PC3 could and had been accessing the BR using Telnet as well. She expressed that PC3 should have Internet connectivity and should be able to ping all devices, but it should not be able to access network devices using either Telnet or SSH. The solutions we found for these two problems are as follows:

1. Carrie reported that the new HQ0 router does not provide redundant Internet connectivity for the PILE network.

   Solution: We discovered that the NAT inside global address was not being advertised by BGP because the prefix was not present in the IP routing table. Hence, we corrected the static route to Null0.

2. While not "officially" allowed, PC3 could telnet into the BR by first hopping (Telnet) into other network devices.

   This, we discovered, was due to an erroneous ACL applied to the HQ2 router's vty lines.

Review Questions

1. How can you prevent forming of EIGRP adjacencies with other routers on a specific interface while still advertising that network by the EIGRP routing process?

   a. Using the proper **no network** *network* [*mask*] command
   b. Using the **no auto-summary** command
   c. Using the **passive-interface** command
   d. Using the **passive-interface default** command

2. Which of the following Layer 4 configuration errors can cause the TCP handshake for a BGP session to fail?

   a. Access lists or firewalls dropping relevant TCP packets
   b. BGP authentication misconfiguration
   c. Clocks not synchronized between BGP routers
   d. BGP neighbors not agreeing on session parameters

3. If the state of a BGP neighbor relationship between two routers is active, how should it be interpreted?

   a. The neighbor is up, and BGP is working.
   b. The router is trying to establish a TCP/BGP session with the neighbor.
   c. The local router is actively exchanging updates with the neighbor.
   d. The local router is awaiting a response from the neighbor for a query sent about a lost path.

4. For incoming BGP updates, which of the following correctly specifies the correct order of application of prefix lists, AS-Path access lists, and route maps?

   a. Prefix list, route map, AS-Path access list
   b. Route map, prefix list, AS-Path access list
   c. Prefix list, AS-Path access list, route map
   d. AS-Path access list, prefix list, route map

5. Where is the BGP outbound **distribute-list** command applied in the configuration?

    a. On the outbound interface

    b. In the global configuration

    c. Under BGP configuration, on the neighbor command

    d. None of these answers

6. Which NTP server is used for clock synchronization in the output shown here?

```
address            ref clock      st    when   poll reach  delay  offset    disp
~192.165.100.101 .INIT.           16     -     1024    0   0.000  0.000  15937.
*~192.165.100.102 .LOCL.           1    615    1024  377   0.000  0.000   2.036
+~192.165.100.103 .LOCL.           1    509    1024  377   0.000  0.000   2.016
```

    a. 192.165.100.101

    b. 192.165.100.102

    c. 192.165.100.103

    d. 127.127.0.1

7. A DNS query was sent by the 10.0.3.33 host to a DNS server at 8.8.8.8. Which access list line will be matched when the response arrives?

```
access-list 100 permit udp host 8.8.8.8 eq 53 10.0.3.33 0.0.0.255 eq 53
access-list 100 permit udp any 10.0.3.33 0.0.0.31 eq 53
access-list 100 permit udp any eq 53 10.0.3.3 0.0.0.31
access-list 100 permit udp any 10.0.3.32 0.0.0.31
```

    a. Line 1

    b. Line 2

    c. Line 3

    d. Line 4

8. You have set up a configuration archive. Its configuration is shown here. What is the purpose of the **write-memory** option?

```
R1# show running-config | section archive
archive
 path tftp://10.1.152.1/R1-config
 write-memory
 time-period 10080
```

    a. It specifies that the archive should be created in the nonvolatile memory at the remote location.

    b. It triggers an archive copy of the running configuration to be created any time the running configuration is copied to NVRAM.

    c. It specifies that the new file added to the archive should overwrite the old file added previously.

9. You have set up the configuration archive without options for automatic archiving of the configuration file. How do you add the file to the archive?

   a. You enter the **copy startup-config archive** command.
   b. You enter the **archive config** command.
   c. You enter the **copy running-config archive** command.
   d. This is done by default.

10. You access a remote router via its Serial 0/0 interface address using SSH. The first thing you do when you access the device is to check whether there is a backup of the currently running configuration. You find an archive, created automatically when issuing the **write** command. The archive is current. Two minutes after issuing a **reload in 120** command, you are cut off and cannot restore the SSH session. When you think back, you remember that you changed the IP address of the Serial 0/0 interface just a moment before the lockout. How can you restore the remote access?

   a. You cannot access the device until someone with physical access to the device helps you out.
   b. The router will reboot in 118 minutes. Then you can access the device.
   c. The router will reboot in 120 minutes. Then you can access the device.
   d. Timeout of 120 seconds expired and router rebooted. When it comes up, you can access it again.

11. You are configuring a router. After you have disabled routing with the **no ip routing** command, you enter the **ip default-gateway 10.55.47.88** command. What will you see if you enter the **show ip route** command?

   a. There will be a gateway of last resort set to 10.55.47.88, and the routing table will be empty.
   b. A new static route marked as a candidate for the default route would appear.
   c. There would be no change to the routing table, because the command used is not the appropriate one.
   d. There would be no change to the routing table because there is none on the router.

12. What is the default value for the local preference attribute on the Cisco router?

   a. 0
   b. 50
   c. 100
   d. 200

13. If the static route **ip route 10.10.0.0 255.255.0.0 Null0** is configured on a router, which of the following **network** commands will inject the route into the BGP table (to be advertised)?

   a. network 10.0.0.0
   b. network 10.10.0.0
   c. network 10.0.0.0 mask 255.0.0.0
   d. network 10.10.0.0 mask 255.255.0.0

Chapter 9

Troubleshooting Case Study: Bank of POLONA

This chapter presents four troubleshooting cases at Bank of POLONA, a fictitious company, based on the topology shown in Figure 9-1. POLONA has hired SECHNIK Networking for technical support. As employees of SECHNIK, we need to solve all problems reported by the customer and document them. Each troubleshooting case includes a few configuration errors. Configuration errors will be dealt with as real-world troubleshooting scenarios. Certain technologies are explained briefly to refresh your memory.

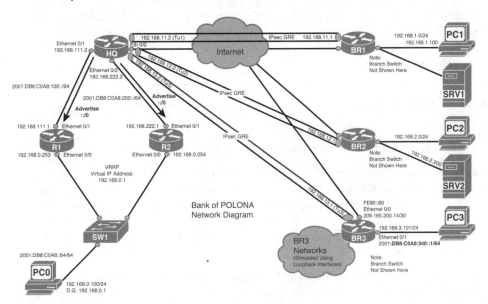

Figure 9-1   *Bank of POLONA Network Diagram*

The staff from Bank of POLONA provided us with the following notes:

- For IPv4 Internet connectivity testing, use the IP address 209.165.201.45; and for IPv6 Internet connectivity testing, use the IPv6 address 2001:DB8:D1A5:C92D::1.

- Because we perform our troubleshooting tasks during the maintenance window set by the client, we are allowed to perform intrusive and disruptive testing during our troubleshooting efforts.

- Because we operate from the headquarters, we do not have access to the branch router's console; we can use Telnet to access the branch router.

- Telnet and enable passwords on all devices are C1sc0.

Note   The networks presented in this chapter use Cisco routers to simulate the servers and personal computers (PCs); keep that in mind as you observe the output shown in the examples.

Bank of POLONA Trouble Ticket 1

We work for SECHNIK Networking, and Bank of POLONA is our company's customer. The headquarters site at Bank of POLONA connects to two branch offices; however, they just added a new branch (branch 3) through an acquisition deal. The newly acquired branch is configured with Enhanced Interior Gateway Routing Protocol (EIGRP), but the headquarters and other two branch offices are configured with Open Shortest Path First (OSPF) Protocol. Bank of POLONA is planning to reconfigure the EIGRP part of the network sometime soon.

Bank of POLONA has a resident network engineer named Tina. Tina has just called us about the following network problems at POLONA, and she has asked for help with them:

- The user of PC3 from the newly acquired branch office cannot access server SRV2.

- If R1's uplink toward the HQ fails, traffic from PC0 goes to R1 and then it is sent to R2, instead of going directly to R2. Tina wanted to implement interface tracking using Cisco's Hot Standby Routing Protocol (HSRP), but based on POLONA's policy, she is not allowed to configure HSRP. Therefore, Tina wants us to implement Virtual Router Redundancy Protocol (VRRP) and eliminate this situation of suboptimal traffic path.

- Tina is getting reports from users in headquarters that SRV2 is sometimes inaccessible. To confirm this, she configured an IP service level agreement (SLA) test on the HQ router that tests reachability of SRV2 around the clock. However, Tina complains that the IP SLA test will not start.

Troubleshooting PC3's Lack of Connectivity to SRV2

According to Tina's message, the user of PC3 at the recently acquired branch 3 site cannot access the SRV2 server. We need to investigate this issue and solve the problem.

Verifying the Problem

To verify the problem, from the HQ router we first attempt to telnet to the branch 3 (BR3) router (192.168.3.101). As you can see in Example 9-1, the Telnet is successful. This tells us that the IP Security generic routing encapsulation (IPsec-GRE) tunnel between the HQ router and the BR3 router over the Internet is operational. Then, from the BR3 router, we try a ping to the SRV2 server using BR3's LAN interface (where PC3 resides) as the source; and the ping fails, so the reported problem is verified. Next, we terminate the Telnet session, and try to ping the SRV2 server from the HQ router. As shown in Example 9-1, this time the ping is 100 percent successful. This tells us that the IPsec-GRE tunnel between the HQ router and the BR2 over the Internet is also operational.

Example 9-1 *Verify the Problem: SRV2 Is Not Reachable from the Branch 3 LAN*

```
HQ# telnet 192.168.3.101
Trying 192.168.3.101 ... Open
User Access Verification
Password:
BR3> en
Password:
BR3# ping 192.168.2.200 source 192.168.3.101
Type escape sequence to abort.
Sending 5, 100-byte ICMP Echos to 192.168.2.200, timeout is 2 seconds:
Packet sent with a source address of 192.168.3.101
U.U.U
Success rate is 0 percent (0/5)
BR3# exit
[Connection to 192.168.3.101 closed by foreign host]
HQ# ping 192.168.2.200
Type escape sequence to abort.
Sending 5, 100-byte ICMP Echos to 192.168.2.200, timeout is 2 seconds:
!!!!!
Success rate is 100 percent (5/5), round-trip min/avg/max = 5/5/6 ms
HQ#
```

Because the Internet connection and IPsec-GRE tunnels between the HQ and branch offices work as expected, the problem sounds more like an internal network problem, such as a routing problem. We can investigate the possible routing problem using the follow-the-path approach.

Gathering Information

We reconnect to the BR3 router and check its routing table. As shown in Example 9-2, the BR3 router is not learning the HQ and other branch networks through EIGRP. The output of **show ip protocols** on the BR3 router shows that the BR3 router's EIGRP configuration is adequate, and the **show ip eigrp neighbors** command output reveals HQ (192.168.13.2) as an adjacent neighbor.

Example 9-2 *Information Gathering: Examining BR3's Routing Configuration*

```
BR3# show ip route eigrp
< ...output omitted... >
Gateway of last resort is 209.165.200.13 to network 0.0.0.0


BR3# show ip protocols
*** IP Routing is NSF aware ***
Routing Protocol is "eigrp 100"
  Outgoing update filter list for all interfaces is not set
  Incoming update filter list for all interfaces is not set
< ...output omitted... >
  Routing for Networks:
    172.16.0.0
    192.168.3.0
    192.168.13.0
  Routing Information Sources:
    Gateway         Distance      Last Update
  Distance: internal 90 external 170
BR3# show ip eigrp neighbors
EIGRP-IPv4 Neighbors for AS(100)
H   Address                 Interface       Hold Uptime    SRTT   RTO  Q   Seq
                                            (sec)          (ms)        Cnt Num
0   192.168.13.2            Tu3               10 00:05:13     5   1470  0   3
BR3#
```

We can now shift our focus to the HQ router. The **show ip protocols** command on the HQ router, as shown in Example 9-3, reveals that HQ has EIGRP activated on the link to BR3 (192.168.13.0), has a neighbor relationship/adjacency with the BR3 router (192.168.13.1), and that it redistributes OSPF 1 into EIGRP.

Example 9-3 *Information Gathering: Examining HQ's Routing Configuration*

```
HQ# show ip protocols
*** IP Routing is NSF aware ***
Routing Protocol is "eigrp 100"
  Outgoing update filter list for all interfaces is not set
  Incoming update filter list for all interfaces is not set
  Default networks flagged in outgoing updates
```

```
   Default networks accepted from incoming updates
   Redistributing: ospf 1
   EIGRP-IPv4 Protocol for AS(100)
     Metric weight K1=1, K2=0, K3=1, K4=0, K5=0
     NSF-aware route hold timer is 240
     Router-ID: 192.168.10.1
     Topology : 0 (base)
       Active Timer: 3 min
       Distance: internal 90 external 170
       Maximum path: 4
       Maximum hopcount 100
       Maximum metric variance 1
   Automatic Summarization: disabled
   Maximum path: 4
   Routing for Networks:
     192.168.13.0
   Routing Information Sources:
     Gateway          Distance       Last Update
     192.168.13.1          90        00:09:06
   Distance: internal 90 external 170


Routing Protocol is "ospf 1"
  Outgoing update filter list for all interfaces is not set
  Incoming update filter list for all interfaces is not set
  Router ID 192.168.10.1
  It is an autonomous system boundary router
  Redistributing External Routes from,
    eigrp 100, includes subnets in redistribution
< ...output omitted... >
HQ#
```

Examining HQ's routing table displays the OSPF routes in HQ's routing table. Because the OSPF routes are present (see Example 9-4) in the routing table, they should redistribute into EIGRP and be advertised to BR3, as long as they have a proper seed metric. Hence, we display HQ's running-config to inspect the redistribution line.

Example 9-4 *Information Gathering: Examining HQ's Configuration*

```
HQ# show ip route
< ...output omitted... >
Gateway of last resort is 209.165.200.1 to network 0.0.0.0
< ...output omitted... >
D       172.16.19.0 [90/27008000] via 192.168.13.1, 00:12:02, Tunnel3
D       172.16.20.0 [90/27008000] via 192.168.13.1, 00:12:02, Tunnel3
O     192.168.0.0/24 [110/20] via 192.168.222.1, 00:11:56, Ethernet0/2
                     [110/20] via 192.168.111.1, 00:12:06, Ethernet0/1
```

```
     192.168.1.0/25 is subnetted, 2 subnets
O       192.168.1.0 [110/1010] via 192.168.11.1, 00:11:56, Tunnel1
O       192.168.1.128 [110/1010] via 192.168.11.1, 00:11:56, Tunnel1
     192.168.2.0/25 is subnetted, 2 subnets
O       192.168.2.0 [110/1010] via 192.168.12.1, 00:11:56, Tunnel2
O       192.168.2.128 [110/1010] via 192.168.12.1, 00:11:56, Tunnel2
< ...output omitted... >
HQ#
HQ# show running-config | section router eigrp
router eigrp 100
 network 192.168.13.0
 redistribute ospf 1
HQ#
```

Analyzing Information and Proposing a Hypothesis, and Testing the Hypothesis

The HQ router's configuration shows that even though EIGRP is configured to redistribute OSPF into EIGRP, the redistribution is ineffective because there is no configuration
of seed metric values. Therefore, we propose to modify the redistribution of OSPF into
EIGRP to include proper seed metric values. Example 9-5 shows this modification made
on the HQ router. Immediately following this change, we reconnect to the BR3 router
and examine its IP routing table. As shown in Example 9-5, BR3 is now receiving the HQ
and other branch sites' networks through EIGRP.

Example 9-5 *Testing the Hypothesis: Examine BR3's IP Routing Table*

```
HQ# conf term
Enter configuration commands, one per line.  End with CNTL/Z.
HQ(config)# router eigrp 100
HQ(config-router)# redistribute ospf 1 metric 1500 100 255 1 1500
HQ(config-router)# end
HQ# wr
Building configuration...
[OK]
HQ#
HQ# telnet 192.168.3.101
Trying 192.168.3.101 ... Open
User Access Verification
Password:
BR3> en
Password:
BR3# show ip route eigrp
< ...output omitted... >
Gateway of last resort is 209.165.200.13 to network 0.0.0.0
D EX  192.168.0.0/24 [170/26905600] via 192.168.13.2, 00:01:29, Tunnel3
```

```
      192.168.1.0/25 is subnetted, 2 subnets
D EX    192.168.1.0 [170/26905600] via 192.168.13.2, 00:01:29, Tunnel3
D EX    192.168.1.128 [170/26905600] via 192.168.13.2, 00:01:29, Tunnel3
      192.168.2.0/25 is subnetted, 2 subnets
D EX    192.168.2.0 [170/26905600] via 192.168.13.2, 00:01:29, Tunnel3
D EX    192.168.2.128 [170/26905600] via 192.168.13.2, 00:01:29, Tunnel3
D EX 192.168.11.0/24 [170/26905600] via 192.168.13.2, 00:01:29, Tunnel3
D EX 192.168.12.0/24 [170/26905600] via 192.168.13.2, 00:01:29, Tunnel3
      192.168.111.0/30 is subnetted, 1 subnets
D EX    192.168.111.0 [170/26905600] via 192.168.13.2, 00:01:29, Tunnel3
      192.168.222.0/30 is subnetted, 1 subnets
D EX    192.168.222.0 [170/26905600] via 192.168.13.2, 00:01:29, Tunnel3
BR3#
```

Solving the Problem

Finally, we repeat the ping test from the BR3 router to the SRV2 server, using BR3's LAN interface address as the source. As shown in Example 9-6, the result is successful. The branch 3 site now has adequate connectivity to the rest of POLONA's network. The problem is solved.

Example 9-6 *Solving the Problem: The Branch 3 Site Has Connectivity Now*

```
BR3# ping 192.168.2.100 source 192.168.3.101
Type escape sequence to abort.
Sending 5, 100-byte ICMP Echos to 192.168.2.100, timeout is 2 seconds:
Packet sent with a source address of 192.168.3.101
!!!!!
Success rate is 100 percent (5/5), round-trip min/avg/max = 2/6/10 ms
BR3#
```

We need to document our findings and the corrections we made. We must also notify the customer (Tina) that the problem is solved.

Troubleshooting Redistribution

When prefixes are not distributing from one process to another, you must first check whether the **redistribute** command is referencing the correct routing process with the appropriate process number. You must also check that routes are not filtered by any misconfigured distribute list or route map. Redistribution from one process to another requires that you provide a seed metric for the redistributed routes. OSPF has a default seed metric of 20, but EIGRP and RIPv2 do not have a default metric by default. You can set up a default metric for these protocols, or you can assign unique metric values on the redistribution command line. Note that prefixes are redistributed from one process into another only as long as they are present in the IP routing/forwarding table. The following protocol-specific facts relate to redistribution:

- **EIGRP:** Unlike most of the other dynamic routing protocols, EIGRP does not automatically have a default metric for any redistributed routes. If the default metric or a manual metric is not specified, EIGRP assumes a metric of 0 and does not advertise the redistributed routes. Also, EIGRP will not autosummarize external routes unless a connected or internal EIGRP route exists in the routing table from the same major network of the external routes. If an EIGRP stub router needs to redistribute routes, it has to be explicitly configured to do so using the **eigrp stub redistributed** command.

- **OSPF:** When you redistribute into OSPF, you must use the parameter **subnets** to distinguish classful and classless behavior. When any protocol is redistributed into OSPF, if the networks that are being redistributed are subnets, you must define the **subnets** keyword under the OSPF configuration. If the **subnets** keyword is not added, OSPF will ignore all the subnetted routes when generating the external link-state advertisement (LSA). The situation could also arise when connected or static routes are being redistributed into OSPF. In that case, the same rule applies: The **subnets** keyword must be entered to redistribute subnetted routes.

- **BGP:** When redistributing Interior Gateway Protocol (IGP), static, and connected routes into Border Gateway Protocol (BGP), it is important to carefully filter the redistributed routes so that invalid/private networks do not sneak into the BGP table and be announced to external BGP neighbors.

Troubleshooting VRRP with Interface Tracking

According to Tina (from Bank of POLONA), when router R1's uplink toward the HQ router fails, traffic from PC0 goes to R1, which in turn sends the traffic to R2. Tina wants to correct this suboptimal behavior. In other words, when R1's uplink toward the HQ fails, the traffic should go directly to R2. Furthermore, Tina stated that she intended to implement the solution to this problem using HSRP interface tracking, but because POLONA's policy does not allow that, she wants our help to implement the solution using VRRP.

Verifying the Problem

To verify the problem, we first use traceroute from PC0 to the Internet test IP address, while R1's uplink to the HQ router is up and working. As shown in Example 9-7, the traffic path is correct through R1 and HQ routers. However, when we shut down R1's Ethernet 0/1 interface (uplink to HQ), the traffic goes to R1 (192.168.0.253), then it is sent to R2 (192.168.0.254), and then to HQ (192.168.222.2) after. This is also shown in Example 9-7.

Example 9-7 *Verify the Problem: Traffic from PC0 to Internet Takes Suboptimal Path When R1's Uplink Is Down*

```
PC0# trace 209.165.201.45
Type escape sequence to abort.
Tracing the route to 209.165.201.45
VRF info: (vrf in name/id, vrf out name/id)
  1 192.168.0.253 1 msec 1 msec 0 msec
```

```
  2 192.168.111.2 1 msec 1 msec 1 msec
  3 209.165.200.1 1 msec 2 msec *
PC0#


R1(config)# int eth 0/1
R1(config-if)# shutdown
R1(config-if)#


PC0# trace 209.165.201.45
Type escape sequence to abort.
Tracing the route to 209.165.201.45
VRF info: (vrf in name/id, vrf out name/id)
  1 192.168.0.253 1 msec 1 msec 0 msec
  2 192.168.0.254 0 msec
    192.168.222.2 1005 msec 0 msec
  3 209.165.200.1 1 msec 2 msec *
PC0#
```

The problem as Tina explained it is present and verified. We need to investigate the VRRP configuration and object tracking on routers R1 and R2.

Gathering Information

As the first step in information gathering, we use the **show vrrp** command on the R1 router. As shown in Example 9-8, VRRP group 1 is configured on interface Ethernet 0/0, and R1 is the Master router for this group, with a priority of 110. However, there is no object tracking configuration for VRRP group 1. Furthermore, when we execute the **show track** command, we get no results; this means that no objects are being tracked at this point either.

Example 9-8 *Information Gathering: Check R1 Router's VRRP Configuration*

```
R1# show vrrp
Ethernet0/0 - Group 1
  State is Master
  Virtual IP address is 192.168.0.1
  Virtual MAC address is 0000.5e00.0101
  Advertisement interval is 1.000 sec
  Preemption enabled
  Priority is 110
  Master Router is 192.168.0.253 (local), priority is 110
  Master Advertisement interval is 1.000 sec
  Master Down interval is 3.570 sec
R1# show track
R1#
```

As the second step in information gathering, we use the **show vrrp** command on the R2 router. As shown in Example 9-9, VRRP group 1 is configured on interface Ethernet 0/0, and R2 is the backup router for this group, with a priority of 100.

Example 9-9   *Information Gathering: Check R2 Router's VRRP Configuration*

```
R2# show vrrp
Ethernet0/0 - Group 1
  State is Backup
  Virtual IP address is 192.168.0.1
  Virtual MAC address is 0000.5e00.0101
  Advertisement interval is 1.000 sec
  Preemption enabled
  Priority is 100
  Master Router is 192.168.0.253, priority is 110
  Master Advertisement interval is 1.000 sec
  Master Down interval is 3.609 sec (expires in 3.402 sec)
R2#
```

Analyzing the Information

Based on the information gathered, Ethernet 0/0 interfaces of routers R1 and R2 are configured for VRRP group 1 properly. R1 is elected as Master, with the higher priority of 110, and R2 is the designated backup, with the default priority of 100. However, because object tracking is not configured on R1, failure of R1's Ethernet 0/1 interface (uplink to HQ) does not trigger R1 to decrement its priority to allow R2 to preempt it and become the Master.

Proposing and Testing a Hypothesis

Our proposal is to log in to router R1 and create a track object 1 for interface Ethernet 0/1's line protocol. Next, we propose to configure R1's VRRP group 1 to decrement R1's priority by 20 if the created object goes down. Because "preempt" is the default behavior in VRRP (in contrast to HSRP), our expectation is that when R1 decrements its priority by 20, from 110 to 90, R2 with the priority of 100 preempts R1 and becomes the new Master for the VRRP group 1.

Example 9-10 shows our work configuring track 1 and configuring R1's VRRP group 1 to decrement R1's priority by 20 should the tracked object 1 go down. Next, Example 9-10 shows that as soon as we shut down R1's Ethernet 0/1 interface, R1's priority drops to 90 (due to "Track object 1 state Down") and 192.168.0.254 (R2) with the priority of 100 becomes the Master for VRRP group 1 (according to the output of **show vrrp**).

Example 9-10 *Testing a Hypothesis: Configure and Test Object Tracking on R1's VRRP Group 1 Configuration.*

```
R1# config term
Enter configuration commands, one per line.  End with CNTL/Z.
R1(config)# track 1 interface ethernet 0/1 line-protocol
R1(config-track)# exit
R1(config)# interface ethernet 0/0
R1(config-if)# vrrp 1 track 1 decrement 20
R1(config-if)# end
Sep 23 22:47:49.853: %SYS-5-CONFIG_I: Configured from console by console
R1#wr
Building configuration...
[OK]
R1# conf term
Enter configuration commands, one per line.  End with CNTL/Z.
R1(config)# interface ethernet 0/1
R1(config-if)# shutdown
< ...output omitted... >
R1(config-if)# end
Sep 23 22:48:40.393: %SYS-5-CONFIG_I: Configured from console by console
R1# show vrrp
Ethernet0/0 - Group 1
  State is Backup
  Virtual IP address is 192.168.0.1
  Virtual MAC address is 0000.5e00.0101
  Advertisement interval is 1.000 sec
  Preemption enabled
  Priority is 90  (cfgd 110)
    Track object 1 state Down decrement 20
  Master Router is 192.168.0.254, priority is 100
  Master Advertisement interval is 1.000 sec
  Master Down interval is 3.570 sec (expires in 3.215 sec)
R1#
```

Solving the Problem

Now that we have R1's Ethernet 0/1 (uplink to HQ) shut down, we must check whether PC0's traffic to the Internet test address will go straight to R2. Example 9-11 shows the result of a trace from PC0 to 209.165.201.45 (the Internet test IP address). As you can see, the first hop is shown as 192.168.0.254, which is R2's Ethernet 0/0 IP address. The problem is solved.

Example 9-11   *Solving the Problem: Test Traffic Path After R1 Uplink Failure*

```
PC0# trace 209.165.201.45
Type escape sequence to abort.
Tracing the route to 209.165.201.45
VRF info: (vrf in name/id, vrf out name/id)
  1 192.168.0.254 0 msec 0 msec 0 msec
  2 192.168.222.2 1 msec 1 msec 0 msec
  3 209.165.200.1 1 msec 2 msec *
PC0#
```

We must now bring R1's Ethernet 0/1 up, document our work, and notify Tina that we have solved the problem.

FHRP Tracking Options

HSRP interface tracking allows you to specify another interface on the router for the HSRP process to monitor so that you can alter the HSRP priority for a given group. If the specified interface's line protocol goes down, the HSRP priority of this router is reduced, allowing another HSRP router with a higher priority to become active (if it has preemption enabled). To configure HSRP interface tracking, use the **standby** [*group*] **track interface** [*priority*] command. When multiple tracked interfaces are down, the priority is reduced by a cumulative amount. If you explicitly set the decrement value, the value is decreased by that amount if that interface is down, and decrements are cumulative. If you do not set an explicit decrement value, the value is decreased by 10 for each interface that goes down.

The object tracking feature allows you to create a tracked object that a first-hop routing protocol (FHRP) (HSRP, Gateway Load Balancing Protocol [GLBP], or VRRP) can use to modify its behavior (lower its priority, for example) when a tracked object fails or goes down. Object tracking monitors the status of the tracked objects and communicates any changes made to the interested client (such as HSRP, GLBP, or VRRP).

Each tracked object has a unique number that is specified in the tracking command-line interface (CLI). Client processes (such as HSRP, GLBP, and VRRP) use this number to track a specific object. The tracking process periodically polls the tracked object for value changes and sends any changes (as up or down values) to interested client processes, either immediately or after a specified delay. Several clients can track the same object, and can take different actions when the object changes state. You can also track a combination of objects in a list by using either a weight threshold or a percentage threshold to measure the state of the list. You can combine objects using Boolean logic. A tracked list with a Boolean AND function requires that each object in the list be in an up state for the tracked object to be up. A tracked list with a Boolean OR function needs only one object in the list to be in the up state for the tracked object to be up.

You can track either the interface line protocol state or the interface IP routing state. When you track the IP routing state, three conditions are required for the object to be up:

1. IP routing must be enabled and active on the interface.

2. The interface line-protocol state must be up.

3. The interface IP address must be known.

If all three of these conditions are not met, the IP routing state is down.

Object tracking of IP SLA operations allows clients (such as HSRP, GLBP, and VRRP) to track the output from IP SLA objects and use this information to trigger an action (such as decrementing priority).

To display information about objects that are tracked by the tracking process, use the following command:

```
show track [object-number [brief] | interface [brief] | ip route [brief] |
   resolution | timers]
```

The following parameters are optional:

- **brief:** Displays a single line of information related to the preceding argument or keyword

- **interface:** Displays tracked interface objects

- **ip route:** Displays tracked IP route objects

- **resolution:** Displays resolution of tracked parameters

- **timers:** Displays polling interval timers

Troubleshooting IP SLA Test Not Starting

Tina, the network engineer at Bank of POLONA, has informed us that she configured an IP SLA test on the HQ router. The SLA is supposed to test reachability of server SRV2 around the clock. Tina is puzzled about why this SLA is not active; so, she has asked for our assistance to solve this problem.

Verifying the Problem

To verify the problem, we must access the HQ router and, using the **show ip sla application** command, find out how many SLAs are configured and how many SLAs are active on the HQ router. Example 9-12 shows the output of this command on the HQ router.

Example 9-12 *Verify the Problem:* **show ip sla application** *on the HQ router*

```
HQ# show ip sla application
        IP Service Level Agreements
Version: Round Trip Time MIB 2.2.0, Infrastructure Engine-III


Supported Operation Types:
```

```
        icmpEcho, path-echo, path-jitter, udpEcho, tcpConnect, http
        dns, udpJitter, dhcp, ftp, VoIP, rtp, lsp Group, icmpJitter
        lspPing, lspTrace, 802.1agEcho VLAN, Port
        802.1agJitter VLAN, Port, pseudowirePing, udpApp, wspApp
        mcast, generic

Supported Features:
        IPSLAs Event Publisher

IP SLAs low memory water mark: 26972932
Estimated system max number of entries: 19755

Estimated number of configurable operations: 19324
Number of Entries configured  : 1
Number of active Entries      : 0
Number of pending Entries     : 0
Number of inactive Entries    : 1
Time of last change in whole IP SLAs: 22:44:10.690 EDT Tue Sep 23 2014

HQ#
```

The output of the **show ip sla application** command on HQ lists 1 entry, but 0 active (1 inactive) entries. This verifies that the one and only SLA that Tina configured on the HQ router is inactive.

Gathering Information

The best initial information-gathering command for this problem is the **show ip sla configuration** command. As Example 9-13 shows, the one and only SLA configured on the HQ router is an Internet Control Message Protocol (ICMP) echo to 192.168.1.200 (SRV2). The Schedule section of the output shows "Next Scheduled Start Time: Pending Trigger." Example 9-13 also shows the output of the **show ip sla statistics** command and the output of the **show ip sla statistics aggregated** command. The former shows the configured IP SLA's operation Time To Live as 0, and the latter specifies that the operation has not started.

Example 9-13 *Information Gathering:* **show ip sla configuration** *on HQ*

```
HQ# show ip sla configuration
IP SLAs Infrastructure Engine-III
Entry number: 1
Owner:
Tag:
Operation timeout (milliseconds): 5000
Type of operation to perform: icmp-echo
Target address/Source address: 192.168.1.200/0.0.0.0
```

```
Type Of Service parameter: 0x0
Request size (ARR data portion): 28
Verify data: No
Vrf Name:
Schedule:
   Operation frequency (seconds): 30   (not considered if randomly scheduled)
   Next Scheduled Start Time: Pending trigger
   Group Scheduled : FALSE
   Randomly Scheduled : FALSE
< ...output omitted... >
HQ#
HQ# show ip sla statistics
IPSLAs Latest Operation Statistics
IPSLA operation id: 1
Number of successes: Unknown
Number of failures: Unknown
Operation time to live: 0


HQ# show ip sla statistics aggregated
IPSLAs aggregated statistics
IPSLA operation id: 1
Type of operation: icmp-echo
Operation has not started
HQ#
```

Proposing and Testing a Hypothesis

Based on the gathered information, we can propose that the reason this IP SLA has not
started is that Tina has not configured the required schedule for it. To test our hypothesis, we can display and inspect the SLA section of HQ router's running-config. Example
9-14 shows the output. As expected, there is no schedule for the configured IP SLA 1.
So, we can add the missing schedule for IP SLA 1; this is also shown in Example 9-14.

Example 9-14   *Testing a Hypothesis: See HQ's Running-Config, SLA Section*

```
HQ# show running-config | section sla
ip sla auto discovery
ip sla 1
 icmp-echo 192.168.1.200
 frequency 30
HQ#
HQ# conf term
Enter configuration commands, one per line.  End with CNTL/Z.
HQ(config)# ip sla schedule 1 life forever start-time now
HQ(config)# end
```

```
HQ# wr
Building configuration...
[OK]
HQ#
Sep 24 02:51:42.401: %SYS-5-CONFIG_I: Configured from console by console
HQ#
```

Solving the Problem

After adding a schedule for IP SLA 1 on the HQ router, we can reexecute the **show ip sla application** command on the HQ router. As shown in Example 9-15, this time the output shows one configured SLA and one active entry. Moreover, the **show ip sla statistics** command now reveals the latest start time for the IP SLA 1, and its operation Time To Live as forever. The problem is solved.

Example 9-15   *Solving the Problem: The IP SLA 1 Has Started*

```
HQ# show ip sla application
        IP Service Level Agreements
Version: Round Trip Time MIB 2.2.0, Infrastructure Engine-III


Supported Operation Types:
        icmpEcho, path-echo, path-jitter, udpEcho, tcpConnect, http
        dns, udpJitter, dhcp, ftp, VoIP, rtp, lsp Group, icmpJitter
        lspPing, lspTrace, 802.1agEcho VLAN, Port
        802.1agJitter VLAN, Port, pseudowirePing, udpApp, wspApp
        mcast, generic


Supported Features:
        IPSLAs Event Publisher

IP SLAs low memory water mark: 26972932
Estimated system max number of entries: 19755


Estimated number of configurable operations: 19121
Number of Entries configured   : 1
Number of active Entries        : 1
Number of pending Entries    : 0
Number of inactive Entries   : 0
Time of last change in whole IP SLAs: 22:51:37.325 EDT Tue Sep 23 2014


HQ# show ip sla statistics
IPSLAs Latest Operation Statistics


IPSLA operation id: 1
```

```
        Latest RTT: 2 milliseconds
Latest operation start time: 22:53:07 EDT Tue Sep 23 2014
Latest operation return code: OK
Number of successes: 3
Number of failures: 1
Operation time to live: Forever

HQ#
```

We can now save HQ's configuration, document our work, and notify Tina that the problem is solved.

Troubleshooting IP SLA

To implement Cisco IOS IP SLAs, you need to perform the following tasks:

1. Enable the Cisco IOS IP SLA's responder, if needed.

2. Configure the required Cisco IOS IP SLA's operation type.

3. Configure any options available for the specified Cisco IOS IP SLA's operation type.

4. Configure threshold conditions, if required.

5. Schedule the operation to run, and then let the operation run for a period of time to gather statistics.

Commonly used IP SLA **show** and **debug** commands include the following:

- **show ip sla application**
- **show ip sla configuration**
- **show ip sla statistics [aggregated]**

Bank of POLONA Trouble Ticket 2

We work for SECHNIK Networking, and Bank of POLONA is our company's customer. The headquarters site at Bank of POLONA connects to two branch offices; however, they just added a new branch (branch 3) through an acquisition deal. The newly acquired branch is configured with EIGRP, but the headquarters and other two branch offices are configured with OSPF. Bank of POLONA is planning to reconfigure the EIGRP part of the network sometime soon.

Bank of POLONA has a resident network engineer named Tina. Tina has just called us about the following network problems at POLONA, and she has asked for help with them:

- Although BR3 is configured to summarize branch 3's networks and only advertise the summary to the HQ router, the HQ router's routing table is still populated with all of branch 3's networks (172.16.x.x).

- PC0 does not have IPv6 Internet.

- Branch 3 devices have all lost IPv6 Internet access.

Troubleshooting Summarization Problem on BR3

As per Tina's description of this problem, although EIGRP on the BR3 router is configured to summarize branch 3's networks, the HQ router is still receiving all the individual
prefixes. Tina wants us to fix the EIGRP summarization problem in the BR3 router.

Verifying the Problem

To verify the problem, it is best to examine HQ router's IP routing table first. As
Example 9-16 shows, the subnets of the 172.16.0.0 network from branch 3 are all in
HQ's routing table, and no summarization has taken effect.

Example 9-16   *Verify the Problem: Inspect HQ Routing Table for Branch Subnets*

```
HQ# show ip route
< ...output omitted... >
Gateway of last resort is 209.165.200.1 to network 0.0.0.0
S*    0.0.0.0/0 [1/0] via 209.165.200.1
      172.16.0.0/24 is subnetted, 20 subnets
D        172.16.1.0 [90/27008000] via 192.168.13.1, 00:00:08, Tunnel3
D        172.16.2.0 [90/27008000] via 192.168.13.1, 00:00:08, Tunnel3
D        172.16.3.0 [90/27008000] via 192.168.13.1, 00:00:08, Tunnel3
< ...output omitted... >
D        172.16.18.0 [90/27008000] via 192.168.13.1, 00:00:08, Tunnel3
D        172.16.19.0 [90/27008000] via 192.168.13.1, 00:00:08, Tunnel3
D        172.16.20.0 [90/27008000] via 192.168.13.1, 00:00:08, Tunnel3
< ...output omitted... >
HQ#
```

The problem is verified.

Gathering Information

Because EIGRP summarization must be configured within interface configuration mode,
we examine BR3's configuration, searching for the phrase "ip summary-address." As
Example 9-17 shows, there is no summary address configuration on BR3's tunnel interface toward the HQ router, but a summary address configuration line can be seen on
BR3's interface Ethernet 0/0. The output of the **show ip eigrp neighbors** command on
the BR3 router confirms that the neighbor adjacency with the HQ router (192.168.13.2)
is indeed over BR3's Tunnel3 interface.

Example 9-17 *Gather Information: Examine BR3's Configuration for Summarization*

```
BR3# show running-config | include interface|summary-address
interface Tunnel3
interface Ethernet0/0
 ip summary-address eigrp 100 172.16.0.0 255.255.0.0
< ...output omitted... >
BR3#
BR3# show ip eigrp neighbor
EIGRP-IPv4 Neighbors for AS(100)
H   Address                   Interface          Hold Uptime     SRTT    RTO   Q  Seq
                                                 (sec)           (ms)        Cnt Num
0   192.168.13.2              Tu3                  11 00:06:10      5   1470   0  4
BR3#
```

Analyzing Information

We have learned that HQ and BR3 have working EIGRP adjacency and are indeed exchanging routing information. However, we have discovered that the EIGRP summarization command has been configured on BR3's Ethernet 0/0 interface rather than on BR3's Tunnel3 interface. If EIGRP is configured in the traditional way, we must remove the summarization command from Ethernet 0/0 interface and place it on the Tunnel3 interface. However, if EIGRP named configuration were intended, the **summary-address** command would have to be placed in the address family interface configuration mode. Example 9-18 shows the EIGRP section of BR3's router. The EIGRP configuration on the BR3 router is a classic (autonomous system number) configuration.

Example 9-18 *Discovering EIGRP Configuration Style on the BR3 Router*

```
BR3# show run | section eigrp 100
router eigrp 100
 network 172.16.0.0
 network 192.168.3.0
 network 192.168.13.0
BR3#
```

Proposing and Testing a Hypothesis

Based on the gathered information and the analysis performed, we propose to remove the **ip eigrp summary-address** command from BR3's Ethernet 0/0 interface configuration and place a similar command on the Tunnel3 interface instead. Note that the existing summary applied to the Ethernet 0/0 interface is the full Class B network 172.16.0.0/16. Unless all of this Class B network's subnets are planned to be at the branch 3 site, this is an inaccurate summary and can cause routing problems in the future. Example 9-19 shows us applying this summary to BR3's Tunnel3 interface for now, but we need to make a note of this and discuss it with Tina.

Example 9-19 *Proposing a Hypothesis: Replacing the Summary Command*

```
BR3# conf term
Enter configuration commands, one per line.  End with CNTL/Z.
BR3(config)# interface ethernet 0/0
BR3(config-if)# no ip summary-address eigrp 100 172.16.0.0 255.255.0.0
BR3(config-if)# exit
BR3(config)# interface tunnel 3
BR3(config-if)# ip summary-address eigrp 100 172.16.0.0 255.255.0.0
BR3(config-if)# end
BR3# wr
Sep 25 01:44:35.587: %DUAL-5-NBRCHANGE: EIGRP-IPv4 100: Neighbor 192.168.13.1
(Tunnel3) is resync: peer graceful-restart
Building configuration...
[OK]
BR3#
BR3# show ip route
< ...output omitted... >
Gateway of last resort is 209.165.200.13 to network 0.0.0.0
S*    0.0.0.0/0 [1/0] via 209.165.200.13
      172.16.0.0/16 is variably subnetted, 41 subnets, 3 masks
D        172.16.0.0/16 is a summary, 00:01:21, Null0
< ...output omitted... >
BR3#
```

Example 9-19 shows that following implementation of this change, BR3's routing table includes an entry for the 172.16.0.0/16 network pointing to Null0. This statement stops packets destined to nonexistent (or down) subnets of this network from being sent (and following a default route) to other destinations.

Solving the Problem

We can now examine HQ router's routing table to see whether subnets of 172.16.0.0/16 are suppressed and BR3 is sending only the summary address to the HQ router. Example 9-20 displays HQ router's routing table, and as you can see, the result is exactly as desired. The problem is now solved.

Example 9-20 *Solving the Problem: The HQ Router Received a Summary Only*

```
HQ# show ip route
< ...output omitted... >
Gateway of last resort is 209.165.200.1 to network 0.0.0.0
S*    0.0.0.0/0 [1/0] via 209.165.200.1
D     172.16.0.0/16 [90/27008000] via 192.168.13.1, 00:03:27, Tunnel3
O     192.168.0.0/24 [110/20] via 192.168.222.1, 00:13:21, Ethernet0/2
                     [110/20] via 192.168.111.1, 00:13:11, Ethernet0/1
< ...output omitted... >
HQ#
```

We must now document our work and notify Tina that the problem is solved. We must also remember to discuss the accuracy of the summary address configured on BR3.

Troubleshooting EIGRP Summarization

Route summarization can be used to decrease the size of the routing table. Smaller routing tables make the routing update process less bandwidth consuming; they also reduce the frequency of routing updates.

EIGRP's summarization feature is available in the form of automated summarization (limited to classful summaries) at network boundaries; EIGRP summarization can also be performed manually in classless or classful format. If the conventional (autonomous system number) EIGRP configuration method is deployed, classful autosummary is enabled by default. To disable autosummarization, use the **no auto-summary** command. To check whether autosummarization is active and which networks are included in the EIGRP process, use the **show ip protocols | section eigrp** command.

When you configure a manual summary, the summary is advertised only if at least one of its proper subnets is present in the IP routing table. The metric of the summary is taken from the subnet with the smallest metric value. The EIGRP summary address is applied within interface configuration mode when using the conventional (autonomous system number) EIGRP configuration. When configuring EIGRP named configuration, the summary address is applied to the **af-interface** *interface* section within an address family inside the EIGRP process.

If no summary route is present in the routing table, check whether the summary route and its network mask include more specific networks present in the routing table. Manually configured summary routes should not be too broad. Configure the summary route to cover only the existent networks or networks that are planned to be added in the near future.

Troubleshooting PC0's IPv6 Internet Connectivity

Tina, from Bank of POLONA, has indicated that PC0 has lost IPv6 Internet connectivity. She has asked us to investigate this issue and solve the problem if possible.

Verifying the Problem

To verify the problem, we access PC0 and ping the Internet test IPv6 address 2001:DB8:D1A5:C92D::1. As shown in Example 9-21 the ping fails, and this verifies the problem.

Example 9-21 *Verify the Problem: Ping to IPv6 Internet Test Address Fails*

```
PC0# ping 2001:DB8:D1A5:C92D::1
Type escape sequence to abort.
Sending 5, 100-byte ICMP Echos to 2001:DB8:D1A5:C92D::1, timeout is 2 seconds:
```

```
UUUUU
Success rate is 0 percent (0/5)
PC0#
```

Gathering Information

To choose an approach and start information gathering, we can first check to see whether PC0's Ethernet 0/0 interface is up, whether it has an IPv6 address and default gateway, and whether it can reach its default gateway directly. Example 9-22 shows us examining PC0 and finding that its Ethernet 0/0 interface is indeed up, has an IPv6 address (2001:DB8:C0A8::64/64) and default gateway (FE80::11), and can ping its default gateway.

Example 9-22 *Gather Information: Examine PC0's Ethernet 0/0 and IPv6 Status*

```
PC0# show ipv6 interface brief
Ethernet0/0            [up/up]
    FE80::A8BB:CCFF:FE00:A800
    2001:DB8:C0A8::64
< ...output omitted... >
PC0#
PC0# show ipv6 route
IPv6 Routing Table - default - 4 entries
< ...output omitted... >
ND  ::/0 [2/0]
    via FE80::11, Ethernet0/0
< ...output omitted... >
PC0#
PC0# ping FE80::11
Output Interface: ethernet0/0
Type escape sequence to abort.
Sending 5, 100-byte ICMP Echos to FE80::11, timeout is 2 seconds:
Packet sent with a source address of FE80::A8BB:CCFF:FE00:A800%Ethernet0/0
!!!!!
Success rate is 100 percent (5/5), round-trip min/avg/max = 1/1/1 ms
PC0#
```

Because nothing indicates physical or data link layer problems, we can focus on Layer 3 (network layer) and take the follow-the-path approach. Hence, as the next information-gathering step, we examine R1 and R2. These routers must have IPv6 Internet connectivity, and according to POLONA's documentation, they should be receiving a default route through RIPng from the HQ router. Example 9-23 shows that R1 cannot ping the IPv6 Internet test address and that it does not have an exact route or a default route to this destination. The same is true for R2; for brevity's sake, though, it is not shown in Example 9-23.

Example 9-23 *Gather Information: Examine R1's and R2's IPv6 Routing Table*

```
R1# ping 2001:DB8:D1A5:C92D::1
Type escape sequence to abort.
Sending 5, 100-byte ICMP Echos to 2001:DB8:D1A5:C92D::1, timeout is 2 seconds:
% No valid route for destination
Success rate is 0 percent (0/1)
R1# show ipv6 route 2001:DB8:D1A5:C92D::1
% Route not found
R1# show ipv6 route
IPv6 Routing Table - default - 6 entries
< ...output omitted... >
C   2001:DB8:C0A8::/64 [0/0]
     via Ethernet0/0, directly connected
L   2001:DB8:C0A8::FD/128 [0/0]
     via Ethernet0/0, receive
C   2001:DB8:C0A8:100::/64 [0/0]
     via Ethernet0/1, directly connected
L   2001:DB8:C0A8:100::1/128 [0/0]
     via Ethernet0/1, receive
R   2001:DB8:C0A8:200::/64 [120/2]
     via FE80::A8BB:CCFF:FE00:ED00, Ethernet0/0
     via FE80::10, Ethernet0/1
L   FF00::/8 [0/0]
     via Null0, receive
R1#
```

We can now proceed to the next hop in the path to the Internet, which is the HQ router. As shown in Example 9-24, pinging to the IPv6 Internet test address from the HQ router is 100 percent successful. Also, HQ's IPv6 routing table shows a static default route as the path for forwarding Internet-destined packets. When we examine the output of **show ipv6 protocols** (RIP section), we notice that RIPng is active on the appropriate interfaces. However, when we focus on RIPng's configuration by using the **show ipv6 rip ccnp** command, we notice that the HQ router is not generating default routes as expected.

Example 9-24 *Gather Information: Examine HQ Router's IPv6 Configuration*

```
HQ# ping 2001:DB8:D1A5:C92D::1
Type escape sequence to abort.
Sending 5, 100-byte ICMP Echos to 2001:DB8:D1A5:C92D::1, timeout is 2 seconds:
!!!!!
Success rate is 100 percent (5/5), round-trip min/avg/max = 1/1/1 ms
HQ# show ipv6 route
IPv6 Routing Table - default - 8 entries
< ...output omitted... >
```

```
S   ::/0 [1/0]
     via FE80::1, Ethernet0/0
< ...output omitted... >
HQ# show ipv6 protocols | section rip
IPv6 Routing Protocol is "rip ccnp"
 Interfaces:
   Ethernet0/2
   Ethernet0/1
 Redistribution:
   None
HQ# show ipv6 rip ccnp
RIP process "ccnp", port 521, multicast-group FF02::9, pid 343
     Administrative distance is 120. Maximum paths is 16
     Updates every 30 seconds, expire after 180
     Holddown lasts 0 seconds, garbage collect after 120
     Split horizon is on; poison reverse is off
     Default routes are not generated
     Periodic updates 45, trigger updates 1
     Full Advertisement 2, Delayed Events 0
 Interfaces:
   Ethernet0/2
   Ethernet0/1
 Redistribution:
   None
HQ#
```

Analyzing Information

Based on the gathered information, IPv6 addressing and RIPng routing are properly configured for routers R1, R2, and HQ. HQ has IPv6 Internet reachability using a static default route. However, routers R1 and R2 have neither exact nor default IPv6 Internet paths. What seems to be missing is HQ's default route advertisement toward routers R1 and R2.

Proposing and Testing a Hypothesis

Our proposed hypothesis is to configure interfaces Ethernet 0/1 and Ethernet 0/2 of the HQ router to generate a default route toward routers R1 and R2, respectively. Example 9-24 shows us implementing this proposal. Furthermore, this example shows that R1 is now receiving a default route through RIPng from HQ. (R2 is receiving the default route as well, but this is not shown in Example 9-25.)

Example 9-25 *Propose a Hypothesis: Configure HQ to Advertise the Default Route*

```
HQ# conf term
Enter configuration commands, one per line.  End with CNTL/Z.
HQ(config)# interface ethernet 0/1
HQ(config-if)# ipv6 rip ccnp default-information originate
HQ(config-if)# interface ethernet 0/2
HQ(config-if)# ipv6 rip ccnp default-information originate
HQ(config-if)# end
Sep 25 04:11:47.600: %SYS-5-CONFIG_I: Configured from console by console
HQ# wr
Building configuration...
[OK]
HQ#


R1# show ipv6 route
IPv6 Routing Table - default - 7 entries
< ...output omitted... >
R   ::/0 [120/2]
     via FE80::10, Ethernet0/1
< ...output omitted... >
R1#
```

Solving the Problem

We can now return to PC0 and test Internet connectivity by trying to ping the IPv6 Internet test IP address. As shown in Example 9-26, pinging is now 100 percent successful.

Example 9-26 *Solving the Problem: PC0 Can Now Reach IPv6 Internet*

```
PC0# ping 2001:DB8:D1A5:C92D::1
Type escape sequence to abort.
Sending 5, 100-byte ICMP Echos to 2001:DB8:D1A5:C92D::1, timeout is 2 seconds:
!!!!!
Success rate is 100 percent (5/5), round-trip min/avg/max = 1/1/1 ms
PC0#
```

We can now document our work and notify Tina that the problem is solved.

Troubleshooting RIPng

RIPng is a distance vector routing protocol, using hop count as a metric. It uses native IPv6 packets for routing updates exchange and a well-known multicast address (FF02::9). User Datagram Protocol (UDP) is the transport protocol and uses port number 521.

Before starting to troubleshoot IPv6 routing issues, make sure that IPv6 routing is enabled on the device and that interfaces are configured with IPv6 addresses.

If RIPng routes do not appear in the IPv6 routing table:

■ Check that RIPng is enabled on the interface. RIPng with the same process ID must be explicitly enabled on each interface that participates in the process.

■ Check that interface is operational (up).

■ Check whether the network missing the route is more than 15 hops away, because RIPng has the maximal radius of 15 hops and networks with more hops are considered unreachable.

■ Check whether the default route is propagated via RIPng. Note that routing updates for non-default-route networks can be suppressed if the command **ipv6 rip** *name* **default-route only** command was used to configure default route announcement.

■ Check whether IPv6 access control lists (ACLs) are blocking the RIPng traffic. (FF02::9 IPv6 multicast address and UDP port 521 must be permitted in the ACL.)

If the default route is not announced, check that the default route announcement is configured on the router. A RIPng default route announcement must be configured on the interface out of which it is to be announced. If RIPng is not load balancing, check the RIPng configuration for the **maximum-path** command configured value; configuring **maximum-path** to 1 turns off load balancing. Also, check that there are multiple routes to the destination received via RIPng and that they have the same metric. RIPng load balances over equal-cost paths only.

The following are some useful troubleshooting commands related to RIPng:

■ **show ipv6 route [rip]:** This command displays the RIPng entries of the IPv6 routing table.

■ **show ipv6 rip [***name***] [database]:** This command displays information about the current IPv6 RIPng process.

■ **show ipv6 protocols | section rip:** This command displays the basic RIPng information.

■ **debug ipv6 rip:** This **debug** command displays debugging messages for RIPng routing transactions.

Troubleshooting Branch 3's IPv6 Internet Connectivity

Tina, from the Bank of POLONA, has informed us that the newly acquired branch 3 has no IPv6 Internet connectivity. She has done her investigation, but she could not find the culprit. She asked us to look into this situation and solve the problem if possible.

Verifying the Problem

To verify the problem, we telnet into the branch 3 router (BR3). Because the Telnet into the BR3 router succeeds, we can rule out any physical or data link layer connectivity problems from the headquarters site to branch 3. From the BR3 router, we ping the IPv6 Internet test address using the Ethernet 0/1 (LAN) interface as the source, and as shown in Example 9-27, the ping fails. When we repeat the ping test without Ethernet 0/1 as the source interface, the ping fails again. The problem is definitely verified, but the IPv6 connectivity problem is not limited to the branch 3's LAN, because the BR3 router's ping fails regardless of the source interface.

Example 9-27 *Verify the Problem: IPv6 Ping from BR3 to the Internet Fails*

```
BR3# ping 2001:db8:d1a5:c92d::1 source ethernet 0/1
Type escape sequence to abort.
Sending 5, 100-byte ICMP Echos to 2001:DB8:D1A5:C92D::1, timeout is 2 seconds:
Packet sent with a source address of 2001:DB8:C0A8:340::1
.....
Success rate is 0 percent (0/5)
BR3#
BR3# ping 2001:db8:d1a5:c92d::1
Type escape sequence to abort.
Sending 5, 100-byte ICMP Echos to 2001:DB8:D1A5:C92D::1, timeout is 2 seconds:
.....
Success rate is 0 percent (0/5)
BR3#
```

Gathering Information

As the first step in information gathering, we check the BR3 router's IPv6 routing table (see Example 9-28) and notice that the branch router has a single path toward the Internet using the static default route (::/0), with the FE80::1 next hop, out of interface Ethernet 0/0. The output of **show ipv6 interface brief** confirms that interface Ethernet 0/0 is up, but when we ping the static default route's next hop address, FE80::1, the ping fails.

Example 9-28 *Gather Information: Inspect BR3's IPv6 Routing Table*

```
BR3# show ipv6 route
IPv6 Routing Table - default - 24 entries
< ...output omitted... >
S   ::/0 [1/0]
     via FE80::1, Ethernet0/0
< ...output omitted... >
C   2001:DB8:C0A8:340::/64 [0/0]
     via Ethernet0/1, directly connected
L   2001:DB8:C0A8:340::1/128 [0/0]
     via Ethernet0/1, receive
L   FF00::/8 [0/0]
     via Null0, receive
```

```
BR3#
BR3#
BR3# show ipv6 int brief
Ethernet0/0              [up/up]
    FE80::40
Ethernet0/1              [up/up]
    FE80::40
    2001:DB8:C0A8:340::1
< ...output omitted... >
BR3#
BR3#
BR3# ping FE80::1
Output Interface: Ethernet0/0
Type escape sequence to abort.
Sending 5, 100-byte ICMP Echos to FE80::1, timeout is 2 seconds:
Packet sent with a source address of FE80::40%Ethernet0/0
.....
Success rate is 0 percent (0/5)
BR3#
```

To gather information about why the ping to the default route next-hop address FE80::1
fails, we activate **debug ipv6 packet** and retry the ping to FE80::1 out of the Ethernet
0/0 interface. As shown in Example 9-29, the next-hop resolution (to MAC address) fails
because the incoming packet is discarded by an ACL called from_Internet.

Example 9-29 *Gather Information: Debug IPv6 Packet and Ping to FE80::1 Again*

```
BR3# terminal  monitor
BR3# debug ipv6 packet
BR3# ping FE80::1
Output Interface: Ethernet0/0
Type escape sequence to abort.
Sending 5, 100-byte ICMP Echos to FE80::1, timeout is 2 seconds:
Packet sent with a source address of FE80::40%Ethernet0/0
< ...output omitted... >
Sep 25 21:56:38.434: IPv6-Sas: SAS picked source FE80::40 for FE80::1 (Ethernet0/0)
Sep 25 21:56:38.434: IPv6-Fwd: Destination lookup for FE80::1 : i/f=Ethernet0/0,
  nexthop=FE80::1
Sep 25 21:56:38.434: IPV6: source FE80::40 (local)
Sep 25 21:56:38.434: dest FE80::1 (Ethernet0/0)
Sep 25 21:56:38.434: traffic class 0, flow 0x0, len 120+0, prot 58, hops 6
  originating
Sep 25 21:56:38.434: IPv6-Fwd: Encapsulation postponed, performing resolution
Sep 25 21:56:38.435: IPv6-ACL: Discarding incoming packet by acl from_Internet
  (admin policy)
< ...output omitted... >
BR3# no debug ipv6 packet
```

Next, we must clarify where the ACL called from_Internet is applied and find out the content of this ACL. As shown in Example 9-30, the ACL called from_Internet is applied to the Ethernet 0/0 interface in the inbound direction. Therefore, traffic coming from the Internet must be permitted by this ACL.

Example 9-30   *Gather Information: Examine the Access Control List's Content*

```
BR3# show running-config | include interface|traffic-filter
< ...output omitted... >
interface Ethernet0/0
 ipv6 traffic-filter from_Internet in
< ...output omitted... >
BR3#
BR3#
BR3# show ipv6 access-list
IPv6 access list from_Internet
    permit ipv6 any 2001:DB8:C0A8:340::/64 sequence 10
    < ...output omitted... >
    permit ipv6 any host 2001:DB8:AC10:1300::1 sequence 200
    permit ipv6 any host 2001:DB8:AC10:1400::1 sequence 210
    deny ipv6 any any (118 matches) sequence 220
BR3#
```

Analyzing Information

The IPv6 ACL called from_Internet, which is applied to BR3's Ethernet 0/0 interface in the inbound direction, has many **permit** statements for any IPv6 source (from the Internet) destined specifically to the branch router's loopback and Ethernet 0/1 interfaces. The last statement in the ACL is an explicit deny all. This explicit deny all statement is dropping the Neighbor Advertisement (NA) packets that BR3's neighbor (HQ) is sending back to BR3 in response to BR3's Neighbor Solicitation (NS) messages.

The NA and NS messages are ICMPv6 messages that perform the IPv6 address-to-MAC address resolution job, similar to the job that ARP-Request and ARP-Reply perform for IPv4 address-to-MAC address resolution. The IPv6 ACLs implicitly permit the NS and NA messages, so long as you do not enter an explicit deny all statement as the last line of an ACL. If you choose to enter an explicit deny all at the bottom of an IPv6 ACL, you must remember to enter explicit **permit** statements for NS and NA just before the explicit **deny** statement on the bottom of the IPv6 ACL.

Proposing and Testing a Hypothesis

Based on the gathered information and the analysis of the information, we propose two alternatives to solve the problem:

1. Remove the explicit **deny** statement from the bottom of the from_Internet IPv6 ACL.

2. Add two **permit icmp** statements before the explicit deny all statement for ICMP NA and NS messages.

Example 9-31 shows us removing the explicit deny 220 statement from the IPv6 ACL.

Example 9-31   *Proposing a Hypothesis: Permit ICMPv6 NS and NA in IPv6 ACL*

```
BR3# conf term
Enter configuration commands, one per line.  End with CNTL/Z.
BR3(config)# ipv6 access-list from_Internet
BR3(config-ipv6-acl)# no sequence 220
BR3(config-ipv6-acl)# end
BR3# wr
Building configuration...
[OK]
BR3#
```

Solving the Problem

We can now check whether IPv6 Internet is reachable from the branch 3 site. From the BR3 router, as shown in Example 9-32, we ping the IPv6 Internet test address using Ethernet 0/1 as the source, and the ping is now 100 percent successful. The problem is solved.

Example 9-32   *Solve the Problem: Test IPv6 Internet Reachability from BR3*

```
BR3# ping 2001:DB8:D1A5:C92D::1  source Ethernet0/1
Type escape sequence to abort.
Sending 5, 100-byte ICMP Echos to 2001:DB8:D1A5:C92D::1, timeout is 2 seconds:
Packet sent with a source address of 2001:DB8:C0A8:340::1
!!!!!
Success rate is 100 percent (5/5), round-trip min/avg/max = 1/4/10 ms
BR3#
```

We must now document our work and notify Tina that the problem is solved and explain how we solved it.

Troubleshooting Access Control Lists

When troubleshooting relates to access control lists, consider the following items:

- Determine whether the ACL exists.

- Determine where the ACL is applied.

- Determine the direction the ACL is applied (inbound versus outbound).

- Read and analyze each **access-list** statement; be aware of the wildcard mask implications and common mistakes.

- Pay special attention to the order of ACL statements; specific statements must precede general statements.

- To collect counters for denied traffic, you need to configure explicit deny statements with the log option.

- If traffic is not explicitly permitted, it is denied. (The last ACL statement is an implicit deny all.)

- IPv6 ACLs permit ICMPv6 NS and NA messages, unless an explicit deny statement is configured.

- The **log** keyword on an ACL statement instructs the router to log a message to the system log whenever a specific access list entry is matched. The logged event includes details of the packet that matched the access list entry.

- A nonexisting ACL permits all traffic, but an empty ACL denies all traffic. In IPv6, the empty ACL permits all traffic; however, if you add a comment to an empty IPv6 ACL, it will deny all traffic.

- IPv4 ACLs are applied to interfaces by using the **ip access-group** command, but IPv6 ACLs are applied to interfaces by using the **ipv6 traffic-filter** command.

Use the following IOS commands to gather information about configured ACLs:

- **show access-list:** Displays all configured access lists (IPv4 and IPv6) and their contents

- **show ip access-list:** Displays all configured IPv4 access lists and their contents, including the hit counts for each statement

- **show ipv6 access-list:** Displays all configured IPv6 access lists and their contents, including the hit counts for each statement

To determine where the ACLs are applied and in which direction they are applied, use the following commands:

- **show running-config | include line|access-class:** Displays access lines (vty, console) and the access-lists configured to control traffic to the line.

- **show running-config | include interface|access-group:** Displays all the lines form the **show running-config** command's output, if they include the word **interface** or the word **access-group**.

- **show ip interface** *interface-type interface-number*: Displays interface and IPv4 access lists applied to it. (A maximum of one ACL can be applied in each direction.)

- **show running-config | include interface|traffic-filter**

- **show ipv6 interface** *interface-type interface-number*: Displays interface and IPv6 access-list(s) applied to it. (A maximum of one ACL can be applied in each direction.)

- **show running-config | include** [*ACL-number| ACL-name* |]: Displays other applications of the access list, such as in NAT configuration lines.

Bank of POLONA Trouble Ticket 3

We work for SECHNIK Networking, and Bank of POLONA is our company's customer. The headquarters site at Bank of POLONA connects to two branch offices; however, they just added a new branch 3 through an acquisition deal. The newly acquired branch is configured with EIGRP, but the headquarters and other two branch offices are configured with OSPF. Bank of POLONA is planning to reconfigure the EIGRP part of the network sometime soon.

Bank of POLONA has a resident network engineer named Tina. Tina has just called us about the following network problems at Bank of POLONA, and she has asked for help with them:

- Branch 1 has lost IP connectivity to the headquarters site. A user of PC1 has reported that pinging from PC1 to PC0 fails; PC1 could ping PC0 before the recent upgrades.

- After the routing protocol at the new branch 3 router (BR3) has migrated to OSPF area 3, it was mandated that area 3's (branch 3's) routes must be advertised in summary format (172.16.0.0/16) to the routers (R1 and R2) in the headquarters site. However, the R1 router at headquarters is still receiving updates for the individual subnets of branch 3.

- The branch 1 router (BR1) must authenticate remote login requests (Telnet) using the local authentication method. When you attempt to telnet into BR1, you should get the prompt for username and password, but BR1 merely asks for a password.

Troubleshooting Branch 1's IP Connectivity to the Headquarters

Tina, from Bank of POLONA, has reported that branch 1 has lost connectivity to the headquarters. For example, PC1 cannot ping PC0. Branch 1 had full connectivity to the headquarters before the recent changes. The recent changes were made so that the headquarters site builds OSPF adjacency with the branch 3 router (instead of EIGRP).

Verifying the Problem

Because we cannot access PC1 (which is located at the branch 1 site) to verify the problem as stated, we can access PC0 and ping PC1 instead. As Example 9-33 shows, the ping from PC0 to PC1 fails.

Example 9-33   *Verify the Problem: Test Reachability of PC1 from PC0 (at HQ)*

```
PC0# ping 192.168.1.100
Type escape sequence to abort.
Sending 5, 100-byte ICMP Echos to 192.168.1.100, timeout is 2 seconds:
U.U.U
Success rate is 0 percent (0/5)
PC0#
```

Because this problem started immediately after the OSPF changes were made at the headquarters, we can take a divide-and-conquer approach and start our troubleshooting efforts at the network layer (Layer 3).

Gathering Information

It is best to check the HQ router's routing table first and see whether there is an OSPF path to 192.168.1.100 (PC1's address). As Example 9-34 shows, HQ has no paths to 192.168.1.100.

Example 9-34   *Gather Information: Check HQ's Routing Table*

```
HQ# show ip route 192.168.1.100
% Network not in table
HQ#
```

We must now investigate why HQ is not learning branch 1's networks through OSPF. As shown in Example 9-35, the **show ip ospf neighbor** command lists only two neighbors through Tunnel2 and Tunnel3 interfaces and none through the Tunnel1 interface. The other two OSPF neighbors are local (LAN) neighbors (R1 and R2).

Example 9-35   *Gather Information: Check HQ's OSPF Neighbor List*

```
HQ# show ip ospf neighbor
Neighbor ID      Pri   State      Dead Time   Address         Interface
192.168.222.1    1     FULL/DR    00:00:30    192.168.222.1   Ethernet0/2
192.168.111.1    1     FULL/DR    00:00:30    192.168.111.1   Ethernet0/1
209.165.200.10   0     FULL/  -   00:00:34    192.168.12.1    Tunnel2
172.16.20.1      0     FULL/  -   00:00:35    192.168.13.1    Tunnel3
HQ#
```

We must now find out why BR1 is not listed as an OSPF neighbor for the HQ router. We can start by checking the status of HQ interfaces by using the **show ip interface brief** command. As evident in Example 9-36, the Tunnel1 interface of the HQ router is listed, but it is missing its IP address.

Example 9-36   *Gather Information: Check the Status of HQ's IP Interfaces*

```
HQ# show ip interface brief
Interface              IP-Address       OK? Method Status                 Protocol
Ethernet0/0            209.165.200.2    YES NVRAM  up                     up
Ethernet0/1            192.168.111.2    YES NVRAM  up                     up
Ethernet0/2            192.168.222.2    YES NVRAM  up                     up
Ethernet0/3            unassigned       YES NVRAM  administratively down  down
Loopback0              192.168.10.1     YES NVRAM  up                     up
NVI0                   209.165.200.2    YES unset  up                     up
Tunnel1                unassigned       YES unset  up                     up
Tunnel2                192.168.12.2     YES NVRAM  up                     up
Tunnel3                192.168.13.2     YES NVRAM  up                     up
HQ#
```

Proposing and Testing a Hypothesis

Based on the gathered information, we can propose that one reason that the HQ router and the BR1 router do not have an OSPF adjacency is that the Tunnel1 interface of the HQ router is missing its IP address (192.168.11.2). Example 9-37 shows us adding the IP address to HQ's Tunnel1 interface and then pinging the tunnel end address (192.168.11.1) successfully. However, the **show ip ospf neighbor** command still does not list BR1 as a neighbor!

Example 9-37   *Propose and Test a Hypothesis: Add HQ's Tunnel1 IP Address*

```
HQ# conf t
Enter configuration commands, one per line.  End with CNTL/Z.
HQ(config)# interface tunnel 1
HQ(config-if)# ip address 192.168.11.2 255.255.255.0
HQ(config-if)# end
HQ#
Sep 30 02:02:46.303: %SYS-5-CONFIG_I: Configured from console by console
HQ# ping 192.168.11.1
Type escape sequence to abort.
Sending 5, 100-byte ICMP Echos to 192.168.11.1, timeout is 2 seconds:
!!!!!
Success rate is 100 percent (5/5), round-trip min/avg/max = 5/5/6 ms
HQ# show ip ospf neighbor
Neighbor ID     Pri   State        Dead Time   Address         Interface
192.168.222.1    1    FULL/DR      00:00:35    192.168.222.1   Ethernet0/2
192.168.111.1    1    FULL/DR      00:00:34    192.168.111.1   Ethernet0/1
209.165.200.10   0    FULL/ -      00:00:32    192.168.12.1    Tunnel2
172.16.20.1      0    FULL/ -      00:00:34    192.168.13.1    Tunnel3
HQ#
```

Gathering Further Information

Even though we added the proper IP address to HQ's Tunnel1 interface, the HQ router did not form adjacency with BR1. We must check the OSPF configuration on the HQ router and make sure that the OSPF **network** statements have OSPF activated in the Tunnel1 interface. Example 9-38 shows that the **show IP OSPF interface Tunnel1** command responds back with the message "OSPF not configured in this interface." Example 9-32 also shows that in the HQ router's configuration the OSPF **network** statement for Tunnel1 is missing.

Example 9-38 *Further Information Gathering: Check HQ's OSPF Configuration*

```
HQ# show ip ospf interface tunnel 1
%OSPF: OSPF not enabled on Tunnel1
HQ#
HQ# show run | section router ospf
router ospf 1
 redistribute static subnets
 network 192.168.12.0 0.0.0.255 area 2
 network 192.168.13.0 0.0.0.255 area 3
 network 192.168.111.0 0.0.0.255 area 0
 network 192.168.222.0 0.0.0.255 area 0
HQ#
```

Proposing and Testing Another Hypothesis

We can now propose a second hypothesis: Add an OSPF **network** statement in the HQ router's configuration to make OSPF active on the Tunnel1 interface. Example 9-39 shows us adding the 192.168.11.0 network to the HQ router's OSPF configuration. Example 9-39 also shows that immediately after this correction the HQ router gains BR1 as an OSPF neighbor over the Tunnel1 interface.

Example 9-39 *Propose and Test Another Hypothesis: Fix HQ's OSPF Configuration*

```
HQ# conf term
Enter configuration commands, one per line.  End with CNTL/Z.
HQ(config)# router ospf 1
HQ(config-router)# network 192.168.11.0 0.0.0.255 area 1
HQ(config-router)# end
Sep 30 02:06:22.555: %OSPF-5-ADJCHG: Process 1, Nbr 209.165.200.6 on Tunnel1 from
  LOADING to FULL, Loading Done
Sep 30 02:06:40.722: %SYS-5-CONFIG_I: Configured from console by console
HQ# show ip ospf neighbor
Neighbor ID     Pri   State       Dead Time   Address         Interface
192.168.222.1    1    FULL/DR      00:00:39   192.168.222.1   Ethernet0/2
192.168.111.1    1    FULL/DR      00:00:33   192.168.111.1   Ethernet0/1
209.165.200.6    0    FULL/  -     00:00:39   192.168.11.1    Tunnel1
```

```
209.165.200.10     0    FULL/ -          00:00:34     192.168.12.1    Tunnel2
172.16.20.1        0    FULL/ -          00:00:36     192.168.13.1    Tunnel3
HQ# wr
Building configuration...
[OK]
HQ#
```

Solving the Problem

After fixing the OSPF routing problems on the HQ router, we can test whether PC1 and PC0 have gained back reachability to each other. As shown in Example 9-40, PC0 can now ping PC1.

Example 9-40 *Solving the Problem: Ping PC1 from PC0*

```
PC0# ping 192.168.1.100
Type escape sequence to abort.
Sending 5, 100-byte ICMP Echos to 192.168.1.100, timeout is 2 seconds:
!!!!!
Success rate is 100 percent (5/5), round-trip min/avg/max = 1/1/2 ms
PC0#
```

The problem is solved. We must document our work. We must also notify Tina about the changes we made and let her know that the problem is now fixed.

Troubleshooting GRE Tunnels

GRE takes a network layer packet and encapsulates that packet into IP packets. A special GRE header is inserted after the transport IP header (and it identifies the payload). To configure a GRE tunnel, use the IOS command **interface Tunnel** *tunnel-id*. You also must specify tunnel source IP address or interface with the command **tunnel** *source ip-address\source-interface* and tunnel destination with the command **tunnel destination** *ip-address*. The **tunnel mode gre ip** command specifies the tunnel mode/type, but GRE is the default tunnel mode anyway.

Advantages of GRE tunnels include the following:

- Can be used to transport (tunnel) IP and non-IP, unicast, multicast, and broadcast packets

- Can be used as a workaround for networks that contain protocols with limited hop counts

- Can be used to connect discontinuous subnetworks

- Can be used to build VPNs across WAN links

Common GRE problems include the following:

- **GRE source IP address is not reachable by remote host:** Check whether the correct source IP address or interface is applied to the tunnel. You can also check routing in the backbone between the endpoint hosts.

- **GRE destination IP address is not reachable by local host:** Check whether the correct destination was configured, and also check whether hosts are reachable between them.

- **Recursive routing:** This could happen if the best route to the tunnel destination is through the tunnel itself! This will cause the tunnel interface to keep flapping. In extreme cases, your router may crash and reload.

- **GRE traffic denied by an ACL:** IP protocol number 47 identifies GRE. When using GRE, this protocol must be allowed by the access lists.

- **Further fragmentation due to the added GRE header:** The maximum transmission unit (MTU) is 1500 bytes. The GRE header is 24 bytes, which effectively decreases the MTU to 1476 bytes. Packets larger than 1476 bytes will get fragmented, and this can result in processing delays and high CPU usage.

Useful GRE troubleshooting commands include the following:

- **show interfaces Tunnel** *tunnel-id*: Displays the interface status, tunnel IP address, tunnel mode (should be GRE/IP for GRE tunnels), tunnel source and destination, and some other tunnel parameters

- **show ip interface Tunnel** *tunnel-id*: Displays the IP parameters on the tunnel interface

- **debug tunnel:** Enables you to get tunnel debugging information and see events related to the tunnel

Troubleshooting Branch 3's Route Summarization

Branch 3 at Bank of POLONA has migrated from EIGRP to OSPF (area 3). The customer's routing policy states that the individual networks of branch 3 should not be advertised to the routers (R1 and R2) at the headquarters site. However, Tina has reported that instead of 172.16.0.0/16, the R1 router is still receiving the individual subnets of this network; she wants this to be fixed as per their policy.

Verifying the Problem and Choosing an Approach

To verify the problem, we must examine the R1 router's routing table. As shown in Example 9-41, the subnets of network 172.16.0.0/16 are present in R1's routing table. The problem is verified.

Example 9-41   *Verify the Problem: Inspect R1's IP Routing Table*

```
R1# show ip route
< ...output omitted... >
Gateway of last resort is 0.0.0.0 to network 0.0.0.0

S*     0.0.0.0/0 is directly connected, Ethernet0/1
       172.16.0.0/32 is subnetted, 20 subnets
O IA      172.16.1.1 [110/1011] via 192.168.111.2, 00:01:04, Ethernet0/1
O IA      172.16.2.1 [110/1011] via 192.168.111.2, 00:01:04, Ethernet0/1
O IA      172.16.3.1 [110/1011] via 192.168.111.2, 00:01:04, Ethernet0/1
O IA      172.16.4.1 [110/1011] via 192.168.111.2, 00:01:04, Ethernet0/1
O IA      172.16.5.1 [110/1011] via 192.168.111.2, 00:01:04, Ethernet0/1
O IA      172.16.6.1 [110/1011] via 192.168.111.2, 00:01:04, Ethernet0/1
O IA      172.16.7.1 [110/1011] via 192.168.111.2, 00:01:04, Ethernet0/1
O IA      172.16.8.1 [110/1011] via 192.168.111.2, 00:01:04, Ethernet0/1
O IA      172.16.9.1 [110/1011] via 192.168.111.2, 00:01:04, Ethernet0/1
O IA      172.16.10.1 [110/1011] via 192.168.111.2, 00:01:04, Ethernet0/1
O IA      172.16.11.1 [110/1011] via 192.168.111.2, 00:01:04, Ethernet0/1
O IA      172.16.12.1 [110/1011] via 192.168.111.2, 00:01:04, Ethernet0/1
O IA      172.16.13.1 [110/1011] via 192.168.111.2, 00:01:04, Ethernet0/1
O IA      172.16.14.1 [110/1011] via 192.168.111.2, 00:01:04, Ethernet0/1
O IA      172.16.15.1 [110/1011] via 192.168.111.2, 00:01:04, Ethernet0/1
O IA      172.16.16.1 [110/1011] via 192.168.111.2, 00:01:04, Ethernet0/1
O IA      172.16.17.1 [110/1011] via 192.168.111.2, 00:01:04, Ethernet0/1
O IA      172.16.18.1 [110/1011] via 192.168.111.2, 00:01:04, Ethernet0/1
O IA      172.16.19.1 [110/1011] via 192.168.111.2, 00:01:04, Ethernet0/1
O IA      172.16.20.1 [110/1011] via 192.168.111.2, 00:01:04, Ethernet0/1
< ...output omitted... >
R1#
```

There is no evidence of any physical, data link, and network layer connectivity problems, and at this point the problem seems to be due to a routing protocol (OSPF) misconfiguration. So, we can take a shoot-from-the-hip approach and target the OSPF configurations on the routers involved. The order of our work will be based on the follow-the-path technique. Therefore, we must examine the HQ router's routing table first.

Gathering Information

To start our information gathering, we examine the HQ router's IP routing table. As shown in Example 9-42, subnets of the 172.16.0.0/16 network are present, and they all have the same next-hop address (192.168.13.1) and egress interface (Tunnel3). These subnets have all been learned from the BR3 (branch 3) router (192.168.13.1).

Example 9-42 *Gather Information: Examine HQ Router's Routing Table*

```
HQ# show ip route
< ...output omitted... >
Gateway of last resort is 209.165.200.1 to network 0.0.0.0

S*    0.0.0.0/0 [1/0] via 209.165.200.1
      172.16.0.0/32 is subnetted, 20 subnets
O        172.16.1.1 [110/1001] via 192.168.13.1, 00:04:34, Tunnel3
O        172.16.2.1 [110/1001] via 192.168.13.1, 00:04:34, Tunnel3
O        172.16.3.1 [110/1001] via 192.168.13.1, 00:04:34, Tunnel3
O        172.16.4.1 [110/1001] via 192.168.13.1, 00:04:34, Tunnel3
O        172.16.5.1 [110/1001] via 192.168.13.1, 00:04:34, Tunnel3
O        172.16.6.1 [110/1001] via 192.168.13.1, 00:04:34, Tunnel3
O        172.16.7.1 [110/1001] via 192.168.13.1, 00:04:34, Tunnel3
O        172.16.8.1 [110/1001] via 192.168.13.1, 00:04:34, Tunnel3
O        172.16.9.1 [110/1001] via 192.168.13.1, 00:04:34, Tunnel3
O        172.16.10.1 [110/1001] via 192.168.13.1, 00:04:34, Tunnel3
O        172.16.11.1 [110/1001] via 192.168.13.1, 00:04:34, Tunnel3
O        172.16.12.1 [110/1001] via 192.168.13.1, 00:04:34, Tunnel3
O        172.16.13.1 [110/1001] via 192.168.13.1, 00:04:34, Tunnel3
O        172.16.14.1 [110/1001] via 192.168.13.1, 00:04:34, Tunnel3
O        172.16.15.1 [110/1001] via 192.168.13.1, 00:04:34, Tunnel3
O        172.16.16.1 [110/1001] via 192.168.13.1, 00:04:34, Tunnel3
O        172.16.17.1 [110/1001] via 192.168.13.1, 00:04:34, Tunnel3
O        172.16.18.1 [110/1001] via 192.168.13.1, 00:04:34, Tunnel3
O        172.16.19.1 [110/1001] via 192.168.13.1, 00:04:34, Tunnel3
O        172.16.20.1 [110/1001] via 192.168.13.1, 00:04:34, Tunnel3
< ...output omitted... >
HQ#
```

The next logical step is to telnet into the BR3 router and examine its OSPF configuration. The output of the **show ip ospf** command on BR3, as shown in Example 9-43, reveals that all of BR3's interfaces are configured to be in area 3, no interfaces are active in area 0, and that an area range 172.16.0.0/16 is configured. The output of **show run | section ospf**, also in Example 9-43, reconfirms these observations: There are three **network** statements activating all of BR3's interfaces in area 3, and there is an **area 0 range** command with the address 172.16.0.0.

Example 9-43 *Gather Information: Examine BR3 Router's OSPF Configuration*

```
BR3# show ip ospf
Routing Process "ospf 1" with ID 172.16.20.1
< ...output omitted... >
 Reference bandwidth unit is 100 mbps
   Area BACKBONE(0) (Inactive)
```

```
            Number of interfaces in this area is 0
        Area has no authentication
        SPF algorithm last executed 00:07:18.208 ago
        SPF algorithm executed 1 times
        Area ranges are
            172.16.0.0/16 Passive Advertise
        Number of LSA 0. Checksum Sum 0x000000
< ...output omitted... >
        Flood list length 0
   Area 3
            Number of interfaces in this area is 22 (20 loopback)
        Area has no authentication
        SPF algorithm last executed 00:07:08.207 ago
        SPF algorithm executed 1 times
        Area ranges are
        Number of LSA 11. Checksum Sum 0x02CCAF
< ...output omitted... >
        Flood list length 0
BR3#
BR3# show run | section ospf
router ospf 1
 area 0 range 172.16.0.0 255.255.0.0
 network 172.16.0.0 0.0.255.255 area 3
 network 192.168.3.0 0.0.0.255 area 3
 network 192.168.13.0 0.0.0.255 area 3
BR3#
```

Because all of BR3 router's interfaces are configured to be in area 3, this router is not an
OSPF Area Border Router (ABR). We must check the HQ router's configuration to see
whether this router is designed to be the OSPF ABR for area 3. Example 9-44 shows the
OSPF section of HQ router's running-config. As you can see, this router is configured to
have some interfaces activated in area 0, and others in area 1, area 2, and area 3. Clearly,
the HQ router is the OSPF ABR for area 3.

Example 9-44   *Gather Information: Examine the HQ Router's OSPF Configuration*

```
HQ# show run | section ospf
router ospf 1
 redistribute static subnets
 network 192.168.11.0 0.0.0.255 area 1
 network 192.168.12.0 0.0.0.255 area 2
 network 192.168.13.0 0.0.0.255 area 3
 network 192.168.111.0 0.0.0.255 area 0
 network 192.168.222.0 0.0.0.255 area 0
HQ#
```

Analyzing the Information and Proposing a Hypothesis

Based on the information gathered, the BR3 router is an area 3 internal OSPF router. Therefore, the **area 0 range** command should not be configured on this router. However, because the HQ router is the OSPF ABR for area 3, the **area 3 range** command should be configured on this router. Therefore, we propose to remove the **area 0 range** command from BR3's OSPF configuration and add it to the HQ router's OSPF configuration.

Testing the Hypothesis and Solving the Problem

Example 9-45 shows that after we remove the **area 3 range 172.16.0.0 255.255.0.0** command from BR3's OSPF configuration and adding this command to the HQ router's OSPF configuration, the R1 router is no longer receiving the subnets of 172.16.0.0. The problem is solved.

Example 9-45 *Solve the Problem: Reexamine R1 Router's Routing Table*

```
BR3# conf term
Enter configuration commands, one per line.  End with CNTL/Z.
BR3(config)# router ospf 1
BR3(config-router)# no area 0 range 172.16.0.0 255.255.0.0
BR3(config-router)# end
BR3# wr
Building configuration...
[OK]
BR3#


HQ# conf term
Enter configuration commands, one per line.  End with CNTL/Z.
HQ(config)# router ospf 1
HQ(config-router)# area 3 range 172.16.0.0 255.255.0.0
HQ(config-router)# end
HQ# wr
Building configuration...
[OK]
HQ#
Oct  1 20:22:47.893: %SYS-5-CONFIG_I: Configured from console by console
HQ#


R1# show ip route
< ...output omitted... >
S*    0.0.0.0/0 is directly connected, Ethernet0/1
O IA  172.16.0.0/16 [110/1011] via 192.168.111.2, 00:01:37, Ethernet0/1
      192.168.0.0/24 is variably subnetted, 2 subnets, 2 masks
C        192.168.0.0/24 is directly connected, Ethernet0/0
L        192.168.0.253/32 is directly connected, Ethernet0/0
< ...output omitted... >
R1#
```

We must now document our work and notify Tina that this problem is solved.

OSPF Summarization Tips and Commands

Summarization is the consolidation of multiple routes into one single advertisement. There are two types of OSPF route summarization:

- **Interarea route summarization:** Interarea route summarization is done on ABRs, and it applies to routes from a particular connected area. This has no effect on the external routes injected into OSPF through redistribution. Summarization could be configured between any two areas, but it is better to summarize in the direction of the backbone. This way the backbone receives all the aggregate addresses. To summarize on the ABR, use **area** *area-id* **range** *ip-address mask* command, where *area-id* is the area containing networks to be summarized; the *ip-address* and *mask* is the actual summary to be advertised.

- **External route summarization:** External route summarization is specific to external routes that are injected into OSPF through redistribution. This type of summarization is done on the OSPF Autonomous System Boundary Router (ASBR). The ASBR is the actual router where redistribution of another process into OSPF is performed. The **summary-address** *ip-address mask* is used on the ASBR router to accomplish external route summarization.

OSPF summarization troubleshooting tips and commands include the following:

- Check the routing table with the command **show ip route** on the OSPF routers to check whether there are individual routes or summarized routes in the routing table. When checking the routing table on the routers that perform summarization, you should see summary routes pointing to the Null0 interface. This route is created automatically to prevent suboptimal routing or routing loops.

- You can check OSPF status with the **show ip ospf** command on the ABR router to verify which area ranges are configured for summarization.

- To check which external routes are summarized on the ASBR, use the **show ip ospf summary-address** command; all summary addresses that are configured on the router can be observed.

- To check Type 3 (or summary) LSAs, use the **show ip ospf database summary** command. You will be able to see all summary LSAs with summary network address, mask, metric, and some other parameters.

- Use **show ip ospf database external** to check Type 5 (or external) LSAs. You will see all external LSAs, with their network address, mask, metric and some other parameters.

Troubleshooting AAA Authentication on the Branch 1 Router

Tina has configured AAA authentication on the branch 1 router. Her plan was to use a RADIUS server for centralized authentication of Telnet clients, and if the RADIUS server is down or unreachable, to use local authentication. Because the RADIUS server is not available yet, she decided that for now it is best to just do local user authentication. After entering the required commands, Tina expected that when she tried to telnet into the branch 1 router, she would be prompted for username and password, but the branch 1 router prompted for a password only. Tina has asked for our assistance on this issue and provided us the username/password of admin/c1sc0 for testing purposes.

Verifying the Problem and Choosing an Approach

To verify the problem, we telnet into the BR1 router, and as shown in Example 9-46, we are merely prompted for a password rather than username and password. The problem is verified as Tina explained it.

Example 9-46   *Verify the Problem: Telnet into the BR3 Router*

```
HQ# 192.168.11.1
Trying 192.168.11.1 ... Open


User Access Verification

Password:
BR1>
```

We will take the top-down approach and start our troubleshooting effort by examining the vty line configuration on the BR1 router.

Gathering Information

To examine the vty line configuration, we use the **show running-config | section line vty** command on the BR1 router. As shown in Example 9-47, the vty lines have the **login** command and the **password c1sc0** commands configured. Therefore, when you access the vty lines, you will be prompted for a password only (and the password you need to enter to be granted access is c1sc0).

Example 9-47   *Gather Information: Check BR1's vty Line Configuration*

```
BR1# show running-config | section line vty
line vty 0 4
 password c1sc0
 login
 transport input all
BR1#
```

```
BR1# show run | include aaa
no aaa new-model
BR1#
```

Example 9-47 also shows that as we search for the keyword **aaa** in BR1's running-config, we find only one line informing us that AAA is not enabled on the BR1 router yet.

Proposing a Hypothesis

Based on the gathered information, we propose the following:

- AAA must be enabled on the BR1 user by using the **aaa new-model** command.

- The **aaa authentication login default local** command needs to be entered in BR1's global configuration mode so that the default authentication method will be based on the locally configured usernames and passwords.

When you configure AAA services with the **aaa new-model** command, local authentication is immediately applied to all the vty lines. If a new Telnet or SSH session is opened to the router after enabling this command, the user has to be authenticated using the local database of the router. Therefore, you should first check whether any local user account (and password) is configured; otherwise, you will not be able to access the router.

Before making configuration changes for access control on the remote devices, it is a good practice to use the **reload in** *[hh:]mm* command for fallback purposes. This way, the router will be reloaded and reverted to the previous configuration (in case you lock yourself out of the device). Do not forget to cancel reload if configuration is successful; you can use the command **reload cancel** to do so.

Testing the Hypothesis and Solving the Problem

As shown in Example 9-48, we first verify that the username admin is locally defined. Next, we enable AAA using the **aaa new-model** command. Finally, we configure the BR1 router to use local authentication as the default method.

Example 9-48   *Test the Hypothesis: Configure AAA on the BR1 Router*

```
BR1# conf term
Enter configuration commands, one per line.  End with CNTL/Z.
BR1(config)# aaa new-model
BR1(config)# AAA authentication login default local
BR1(config)# end
BR1# wr
Building configuration...
[OK]
BR1#
```

After making the proposed changes, we attempt to telnet into the BR1 router. As shown in Example 9-49, this time we are prompted for username and password. The problem is solved.

Example 9-49 *Solve the Problem: Telnet into the BR1 Router*

```
HQ# 192.168.11.1
Trying 192.168.11.1 ... Open

User Access Verification

Username: admin
Password:

BR1>
```

We must now document our work and notify Tina that this problem is solved.

Troubleshooting AAA

AAA services are used to control access to the management plane of the router or switch. You can use the local user database or the database on a remote server using protocols such as TACACS+ or RADIUS. TACACS+ is a Cisco proprietary protocol that runs over TCP port 49, and RADIUS is an IETF standard that runs over UDP port 1812 (or 1645) for authentication and UDP port 1813 (or 1646) for accounting. It is a common and best practice to use a centralized AAA server as the primary authentication method and use the local authentication as the backup, in cases that the AAA server is either down or unreachable. To enable AAA services on Cisco routers, use the **aaa new-model** command. Next, you can configure your preferred AAA methods using the **aaa authentication, aaa authorization,** and **aaa accounting** commands with appropriate parameters. Common problems encountered while using centralized authentication with TACACS+ and RADIUS servers include the following:

- **Server failure or server not accessible:** To prevent locking yourself out of the device when the AAA server is not accessible, use the local authentication method as the backup method for authentication. You can define up to four methods for authentication.

- **Mismatched pre-shared key:** TACACS+ and RADIUS both require a pre-shared key to be configured between the network device and the AAA server. If the keys on the AAA server and the client (network device) do not match, authentication will not be performed.

- **User credentials are rejected by the server:** You can inspect the server log to verify whether a user was correctly authenticated/authorized or whether the user was rejected because of a bad username or password.

In addition to these common problems, RADIUS port mismatch may at times become a culprit. Cisco uses UDP port 1645 and 1646 by default. UDP ports 1812 and 1813 are ports specified in the standard. Servers usually listen on both sets of ports, but you should always check whether that is the case.

To check AAA services, use the **show running-config | include aaa** command. To verify that AAA services are enabled, the output should contain the statement **aaa new-model**.

The command **debug aaa authentication** can prove very useful for troubleshooting. It displays events that are related to authentication when accessing the router. You can see the user account submitted, the method of authentication, and the access type requested by the user (console or vty). For more information about the authorization process, use the **debug aaa authorization** command, which will display services required by the user, the authorization method, and so on. To debug AAA server events, use the **debug tacacs** or **debug radius** commands.

Bank of POLONA Trouble Ticket 4

We work for SECHNIK Networking, and Bank of POLONA is our company's customer. The headquarters site at Bank of POLONA connects to three branch offices; the third branch has recently been acquired. Bank of POLONA has a resident network engineer named Tina.

Over the weekend, Tina reconfigured IPv6 routing from RIPng to OSPFv3 so that routing for both IPv4 and IPv6 within Bank of POLONA's network is done by OSPF. Tina claims that she managed to do some OSPF fine-tuning on the branch routers as well. After all of Tina's work and the effort, she still has two items that she needs help with and has contacted us at SECHNIK networking about them. Tina wants our help with the following problems:

- PC0 does not have connectivity to IPv6 Internet sites.

- Even though Tina configured the branch areas as totally stubby, all branch routers still have a lot of interarea routes in their routing tables.

Troubleshooting PC0's Connectivity to IPv6 Internet

Tina, the network engineer at the Bank of POLONA, has migrated the bank's IPv6 routing protocol from RIPng to OSPFv3. Following the migration, there are complaints about lack of Internet connectivity; for example, PC0 cannot access the IPv6 Internet at all. Tina has asked us to look into this matter and fix the problem if possible.

Verifying the Problem and Choosing an Approach

To verify the problem, we can ping the IPv6 Internet reachability test address 2001:DB8:D1A5:C92D::1 from PC0. As shown in Example 9-50, the ping fails 100 percent of the time. The problem is verified.

Example 9-50 *Verify the Problem: Ping the IPv6 Test Address from PC0*

```
PC0# ping 2001:DB8:D1A5:C92D::1
Type escape sequence to abort.
Sending 5, 100-byte ICMP Echos to 2001:DB8:D1A5:C92D::1, timeout is 2 seconds:
UUUUU
Success rate is 0 percent (0/5)
PC0#
```

Based on the fact that Tina has been making routing protocol changes over the weekend, it is natural to assume that we have an IPv6 routing problem on our hands. We can take the follow-the-path approach and move forward, hop by hop, away from PC0, starting with its default gateway, to discover the source of the routing problem.

Gathering Information

The first step in our information gathering should be to find out the default gateway for PC0. As shown in the output of Example 9-51, PC0 has a default route pointing to the IPv6 link-local address FE80::12 through its interface Ethernet 0/0.

Example 9-51 *Gather Information: Find Out PC0's Default Gateway*

```
PC0# show ipv6 route
IPv6 Routing Table - default - 4 entries
< ...output omitted... >
ND   ::/0 [2/0]
     via FE80::12, Ethernet0/0
C    2001:DB8:C0A8::/64 [0/0]
     via Ethernet0/0, directly connected
L    2001:DB8:C0A8::64/128 [0/0]
     via Ethernet0/0, receive
L    FF00::/8 [0/0]
     via Null0, receive
PC0#
```

Next, we can examine PC0's neighbor table to find the corresponding MAC address for the IPv6 address FE80::12. Example 9-52 shows the output of the **show ipv6 neighbors** command. This table, which is comparable to the ARP cache for IPv4, shows us that the FE80::12 address has the MAC address aabb.cc00.dc00.

Example 9-52 *Gather Information: Find the MAC Address for FE80::12*

```
PC0# show ipv6 neighbors
IPv6 Address                    Age Link-layer Addr State Interface
FE80::11                        4 aabb.cc00.db00     STALE Et0/0
FE80::12                        2 aabb.cc00.dc00     STALE Et0/0
2001:DB8:C0A8::FE               2 aabb.cc00.dc00     STALE Et0/0
PC0#
```

We can now examine SW1's MAC address table and see on which interface the MAC address aabb.cc00.dc00 was learned; then we can use the **show cdp neighbors** command to see which device is connected to that interface of SW1. Example 9-53 shows that the MAC address aabb.cc00.dc00 was learned through SW1's interface Eth0/2 and that R2 router (interface Eth0/0) is SW1's adjacent neighbor on this interface.

Example 9-53   *Gather Information: Examine SW1's MAC Address Table*

```
SW1# show mac address-table
        Mac Address Table
-------------------------------------------
Vlan    Mac Address      Type         Ports
----    -----------      --------     -----
   1    0000.5e00.0101   DYNAMIC      Et0/1
   1    aabb.cc00.c200   DYNAMIC      Et0/0
   1    aabb.cc00.db00   DYNAMIC      Et0/1
   1    aabb.cc00.dc00   DYNAMIC      Et0/2
Total Mac Addresses for this criterion: 4
SW1#
SW1# show cdp neighbors
Capability Codes: R - Router, T - Trans Bridge, B - Source Route Bridge
                  S - Switch, H - Host, I - IGMP, r - Repeater, P - Phone,
                  D - Remote, C - CVTA, M - Two-port Mac Relay
Device ID        Local Intrfce    Holdtme    Capability Platform  Port ID
R2               Eth 0/2          156                   R         Linux
Uni    Eth 0/0
R1               Eth 0/1          160                   R         Linux
Uni    Eth 0/0
SW1#
```

Example 9-54 shows us executing the **show ipv6 interfaces** command on R2. The output of this command confirms that the IPv6 address FE80::12 does indeed belong to R2's Eth0/0 interface. Now that we have confirmed R2 (Eth0/0) is PC0's default gateway, we can test whether this router has IPv6 Internet connectivity. Example 9-54 shows that pinging to the IPv6 Internet reachability test address from R2 fails, because R2 has no route to this destination.

Example 9-54   *Gather Information: Examine R2's IPv6 Interfaces*

```
R2# show ipv6 interface brief
Ethernet0/0              [up/up]
    FE80::12
    2001:DB8:C0A8::FE
Ethernet0/1              [up/up]
    FE80::12
    2001:DB8:C0A8:200::1
Ethernet0/2             [administratively down/down]
```

```
     unassigned
Ethernet0/3              [administratively down/down]
     unassigned
R2#

R2# ping 2001:DB8:D1A5:C92D::1
Type escape sequence to abort.
Sending 5, 100-byte ICMP Echos to 2001:DB8:D1A5:C92D::1, timeout is 2 seconds:

% No valid route for destination
Success rate is 0 percent (0/1)
R2#
```

R2 (and R1) is supposed to receive a default route from the HQ router. We must first check whether R2 and HQ have OSPF adjacency and whether HQ is configured to advertise a default route. Example 9-55 shows that the HQ router (router ID 192.168.10.1) is R2's IPv6 OSPF neighbor in Full state through R2's Eth0/1 interface; this is consistent with Bank of POLONA's network diagram. This example also shows that when we examine HQ's running-config (IPv6 Router section), IPv6 router OSPF 1 is not configured to advertise a default route.

Example 9-55 *Gather Information: Examine R2's Adjacency with the HQ Router*

```
R2# show ipv6 ospf neighbor

          OSPFv3 Router with ID (192.168.222.1) (Process ID 1)

Neighbor ID     Pri   State         Dead Time   Interface ID   Interface
192.168.10.1     1    FULL/BDR    00:00:37           5         Ethernet0/1
R2#


HQ# show running-config | section ipv6 router
ipv6 router ospf 1
HQ#
```

Analyzing the Information and Proposing and Testing a Hypothesis

Based on the gathered information, the HQ router's IPv6 OSPF (process 1) needs to be configured to advertise a default route. Example 9-56 shows us adding the **default-information originate** command in HQ's configuration. Following this change, R2 can reach the IPv6 Internet, but as shown in Example 9-56, PC0 still cannot.

Example 9-56 *Propose a Hypothesis: Configure HQ to Advertise a Default Route*

```
HQ# conf term
Enter configuration commands, one per line.  End with CNTL/Z.
HQ(config)# ipv6 router ospf 1
```

```
HQ(config-rtr)# default-information originate
HQ(config-rtr)# end
HQ# wr
Building configuration...
[OK]
Oct  2 00:27:35.340: %SYS-5-CONFIG_I: Configured from console by console
HQ#


R2#
R2# ping 2001:DB8:D1A5:C92D::1
Type escape sequence to abort.
Sending 5, 100-byte ICMP Echos to 2001:DB8:D1A5:C92D::1, timeout is 2 seconds:
!!!!!
Success rate is 100 percent (5/5), round-trip min/avg/max = 1/4/19 ms
R2#


PC0#
PC0# ping  2001:DB8:D1A5:C92D::1
Type escape sequence to abort.
Sending 5, 100-byte ICMP Echos to 2001:DB8:D1A5:C92D::1, timeout is 2 seconds:
.....
Success rate is 0 percent (0/5)
PC0#
```

We have made some progress, but we need to do further information gathering to find out why PC0 still cannot reach the IPv6 Internet.

Gathering Further Information

We should now check whether PC0 can reach the HQ router. Example 9-57 shows that pinging from PC0 to HQ's address 2001:DB8:C0A8:200::2 fails.

Example 9-57   *Gather Information: Can PC0 Reach the HQ Router?*

```
PC0# ping 2001:DB8:C0A8:200::2
Type escape sequence to abort.
Sending 5, 100-byte ICMP Echos to 2001:DB8:C0A8:200::2, timeout is 2 seconds:
.....
Success rate is 0 percent (0/5)
PC0#
```

We have confirmed that the router R2 is PC0's default gateway and that R2, using the default route it receives from the HQ router, can reach the IPv6 Internet. Based on all this information, we must now check whether HQ has a route back to the network where PC0 resides. Example 9-58 shows that the HQ router does not have an exact path to PC0's address. The default route in HQ's routing table points to FE80::1 through its Eth0/0 interface toward the Internet service provider (not toward PC0).

Example 9-58   *Gather Information: Does HQ Have an IPv6 Path Back to PC0?*

```
HQ#
HQ# show ipv6 route 2001:DB8:C0A8::6
Routing entry for ::/0
  Known via "static", distance 1, metric 0
  Route count is 1/1, share count 0
  Routing paths:
    FE80::1, Ethernet0/0
      Last updated 00:23:18 ago
HQ#
```

Analyzing Information and Proposing and Testing Another Hypothesis

Because HQ does not have an exact path to PC0's address, we propose that router R2 is not advertising this network and must be configured to do so. As shown in Example 9-59, R2's running-config confirms that IPv6 OSPF is not activated on R2's Eth0/0 interface. Therefore, we need to activate the IPv6 OSPF 1 process on R2's Eth0/0 interface. Once the IPv6 OSPF process is activated on R2's Eth0/0 interface, as shown in Example 9-59, PC0 is able to ping the IPv6 Internet reachability test IP address.

Example 9-59   *Propose a Hypothesis: Activate IPv6 OSPF on R2's Eth0/0 Interface*

```
R2# show running-config interface ethernet 0/0
Building configuration...
Current configuration : 204 bytes
!
interface Ethernet0/0
 ip address 192.168.0.254 255.255.255.0
 ipv6 address FE80::12 link-local
 ipv6 address 2001:DB8:C0A8::FE/64
 ipv6 nd prefix 2001:DB8:C0A8::/64 300 300
 vrrp 1 ip 192.168.0.1
end
R2#
R2# conf term
Enter configuration commands, one per line.  End with CNTL/Z.
R2(config)# interface ethernet 0/0
R2(config-if)# ipv6 ospf 1 area 0
R2(config-if)# end
R2# wr
Building configuration...
Oct  2 00:37:28.309: %SYS-5-CONFIG_I: Configured from console by console[OK]
```

```
R2#


PC0# ping  2001:DB8:D1A5:C92D::1
Type escape sequence to abort.
Sending 5, 100-byte ICMP Echos to 2001:DB8:D1A5:C92D::1, timeout is 2 seconds:
!!!!!
Success rate is 100 percent (5/5), round-trip min/avg/max = 1/1/1 ms
PC0#
```

Solving the Problem

Even though the problem seems to be solved, we have no choice but to wonder why, despite R2's failure to advertise its connected network to the HQ router, router R1 is not advertising this network to the HQ router. Based on Bank of POLONA's network design, both routers R1 and R2 are connected to and are supposed to advertise the network (where PC0 resides) to HQ.

We just corrected R2's configuration, but we must also check and fix R1's configuration if necessary. Example 9-60 shows that on R1, similarly to R2, the IPv6 OSPF process is not activated on its Eth0/0 interface. Therefore, we correct R1's configuration as well. Finally, we check router HQ's IPv6 routing table, and as shown in Example 9-60, HQ now has *two* paths (not just one) toward PC0's network through routers R1 and R2. The problem is now completely solved.

Example 9-60   *Solve the Problem: PC0 Has IPv6 Internet Connectivity with Redundancy*

```
R1# show running-config interface ethernet0/0
Building configuration...
Current configuration : 254 bytes
!
interface Ethernet0/0
 ip address 192.168.0.253 255.255.255.0
 ipv6 address FE80::11 link-local
 ipv6 address 2001:DB8:C0A8::FD/64
 ipv6 nd prefix 2001:DB8:C0A8::/64 300 300
 vrrp 1 ip 192.168.0.1
 vrrp 1 priority 110
 vrrp 1 track 1 decrement 20
end
R1#
R1# conf term
Enter configuration commands, one per line.  End with CNTL/Z.
R1(config)# interface ethernet 0/0
R1(config-if)# ipv6 ospf 1 area 0
*Oct  2 00:45:42.600: %OSPFv3-5-ADJCHG: Process 1, Nbr 192.168.222.1 on Ethernet0/0
```

```
from LOADING to FULL, Loading Done
R1(config-if)# end
R1# wr
Building configuration...
[OK]
R1#
*Oct  2 00:45:48.529: %SYS-5-CONFIG_I: Configured from console by console
R1#

HQ# show ipv6 route 2001:DB8:C0A8::/64
Routing entry for 2001:DB8:C0A8::/64
  Known via "ospf 1", distance 110, metric 20, type intra area
  Route count is 2/2, share count 0
  Routing paths:
    FE80::12, Ethernet0/2
      Last updated 00:01:55 ago
    FE80::11, Ethernet0/1
      Last updated 00:01:06 ago
HQ#
```

We must now document our work and notify Tina that this problem is solved.

Troubleshooting OSPF for IPv6

OSPFv3 operates in a similar way as OSPFv2. There are a few differences, though, as follows:

- **Protocol processing per link, not per subnet:** Multiple IP subnets can be configured on a single link between two routers. OSPFv3 neighbors can establish adjacency even if they do not share a common IPv6 subnet.

- **OSPFv3's router ID is a number with a dotted-decimal format:** An IPv6 address cannot be used as a router ID. If IPv6 is the only protocol enabled on a router, the router ID must be manually specified; otherwise, the OSPFv3 process will not start.

- **Support for multiple instances per link:** Multiple instances of OSPFv3 can be used on a single link. Instances are distinguished based on the instance ID (recorded in OSPFv3 packet header).

- **Use of link-local address:** An OSPFv3 router uses its link-local address as the source of its Hello packets. The next-hop addresses for the OSPFv3 routes in the IPv6 routing table are also link-local.

- **Different multicast addresses:** The multicast address FF00::5 is used to address all OSPFv3 routers, and the multicast address FF00::6 is used to address all OSPFv3 designated routers.

- **IPsec is used for authentication:** There is no OSPF-specific authentication; IPsec is used to authenticate OSPF packets.

To create an OSPFv3 process, use the global configuration mode command **ipv6 router ospf** *process-id*. If you do not specify the router ID manually, the highest IP address (loopback is preferred) of the router is used as the router ID, and if the router has no IPv4 address, the OSPFv3 process will not start. You can manually configure the router ID by using the command **router-id** *router-id* from within router configuration mode. To activate OSPFv3 on a specific interface, use the command **ipv6 ospf** *process-id* **area** *area* from within interface configuration mode.

Use the **show ipv6 ospf** *process-id* command to display the global OSPFv3 settings such as router ID, timers, areas configured on the router, and so on. To display the OSPFv3 neighbors of a router, use the command **show ipv6 ospf neighbor**. The output is similar to the neighbor table displayed for OSPFv2; it displays neighbor ID, priority, state, dead time, interface ID, and the interface that is used to establish adjacency. To display the list of interfaces where OSPFv3 is enabled, use the command **show ipv6 ospf interface**. The output not only lists all interfaces where OSPFv3 is enabled, but also reveals which area is configured on the interface, the router ID, and the OSPF network type and timers on each interface. To display the OSPFv3 database, use the command **show ipv6 ospf database**. To display details on a specific LSA, use the **show ipv6 ospf database** *lsa-type* **adv-router** *router-id* command. To see the OSPFv3 Hello packets, use the command **debug ipv6 ospf hello**, and to see all OSPF packets, use the command **debug ipv6 ospf packet**.

Troubleshooting the Dysfunctional Totally Stubby Branch Areas

Tina learned that the OSPF routers within a totally stubby area do not receive any external or interarea routes; they merely receive a default route from their area's ABRs. She then decided that this concept would suit the branch sites as well. After implementing this concept, Tina noticed that the branch routers are all still receiving many interarea routes. Tina has contacted us for help with this case so that the OSPF totally stubby areas work as they should.

Verifying the Problem and Choosing an Approach

To verify the problem, we telnet to each of the branch routers and display their routing table. Example 9-61 shows the branch 1 router's routing table with many OSPF interarea routes (O IA).

Example 9-61   *Verify the Problem: Inspect the Branch Router's Routing Table*

```
BR1# show ip route
< ...output omitted... >
Gateway of last resort is 192.168.11.2 to network 0.0.0.0

O*IA  0.0.0.0/0 [110/1001] via 192.168.11.2, 00:01:02, Tunnel1
O IA  172.16.0.0/16 [110/2001] via 192.168.11.2, 00:00:57, Tunnel1
O IA  192.168.0.0/24 [110/1020] via 192.168.11.2, 00:01:02, Tunnel1
```

```
          192.168.1.0/24 is variably subnetted, 4 subnets, 2 masks
C         192.168.1.0/25 is directly connected, Ethernet0/1
L         192.168.1.101/32 is directly connected, Ethernet0/1
C         192.168.1.128/25 is directly connected, Ethernet0/2
L         192.168.1.201/32 is directly connected, Ethernet0/2
          192.168.2.0/25 is subnetted, 2 subnets
O IA      192.168.2.0 [110/2010] via 192.168.11.2, 00:00:57, Tunnel1
O IA      192.168.2.128 [110/2010] via 192.168.11.2, 00:00:57, Tunnel1
O IA    192.168.3.0/24 [110/2010] via 192.168.11.2, 00:00:57, Tunnel1
          192.168.11.0/24 is variably subnetted, 2 subnets, 2 masks
C         192.168.11.0/24 is directly connected, Tunnel1
L         192.168.11.1/32 is directly connected, Tunnel1
O IA    192.168.12.0/24 [110/2000] via 192.168.11.2, 00:00:57, Tunnel1
O IA    192.168.13.0/24 [110/2000] via 192.168.11.2, 00:00:57, Tunnel1
          192.168.111.0/30 is subnetted, 1 subnets
O IA      192.168.111.0 [110/1010] via 192.168.11.2, 00:01:02, Tunnel1
          192.168.222.0/30 is subnetted, 1 subnets
O IA      192.168.222.0 [110/1010] via 192.168.11.2, 00:01:02, Tunnel1
          209.165.200.0/24 is variably subnetted, 3 subnets, 3 masks
S         209.165.200.0/24 [1/0] via 209.165.200.5
C         209.165.200.4/30 is directly connected, Ethernet0/0
L         209.165.200.6/32 is directly connected, Ethernet0/0
BR1#
```

The routing tables for branch 2 and branch 3 routers look similar, but are not shown here for the sake of brevity. So, we have verified the problem and now need to solve it. Unless we find other culprits, we will merely focus on the OSPF configuration of HQ and branch routers initially.

Gathering Information

Because we are investigating the OSPF totally stubby area configuration issues, the first logical step in fact gathering is to inspect the OSPF process on the ABR, which is the HQ router. Example 9-62 shows the output of the **show ip ospf** command on the HQ router. For all of the areas 1, 2, and 3, the output states that HQ has one interface active in it, and each area shows as a stub area.

Example 9-62 *Gather Information: Inspect ABR Router's (HQ) OSPF Process*

```
HQ# show ip ospf
 Routing Process "ospf 1" with ID 192.168.10.1
 < ...output omitted... >
    Area 1
        Number of interfaces in this area is 1
        It is a stub area
 < ...output omitted... >
```

```
   Area 2
       Number of interfaces in this area is 1
       It is a stub area
< ...output omitted... >
   Area 3
       Number of interfaces in this area is 1
       It is a stub area
< ...output omitted... >
HQ#
```

Because we know that these areas must be configured as totally stubby areas rather than merely stub areas, we can display the OSPF section of HQ's configuration to see what exact command is used for the configuration of areas 1, 2, and 3. Example 9-63 shows that within the OSPF section of HQ router's running-config, all three areas are configured with the **area** *area-number* **stub** command.

Example 9-63 *Gather Information: Inspect ABR Router's (HQ) Running-Config*

```
HQ# show running-config | section router ospf 1
router ospf 1
 area 1 stub
 area 2 stub
 area 3 stub
 area 3 range 172.16.0.0 255.255.0.0
 redistribute static subnets
 network 192.168.11.0 0.0.0.255 area 1
 network 192.168.12.0 0.0.0.255 area 2
 network 192.168.13.0 0.0.0.255 area 3
 network 192.168.111.0 0.0.0.255 area 0
 network 192.168.222.0 0.0.0.255 area 0
HQ#
```

We must now examine the configuration of branch routers. Example 9-64 shows branch 1 router's configuration. As you can see, branch 1 router's OSPF process is configured with the **area 1 stub no-summary** command. The configurations of branch 2 and branch 3 routers are similar, but they are not shown here for the sake of brevity.

Example 9-64 *Gather Information: Inspect Branch Router's Running-Config*

```
BR1# show run | section router ospf 1
router ospf 1
 area 1 stub no-summary
 network 192.168.1.0 0.0.0.255 area 1
 network 192.168.11.0 0.0.0.255 area 1
BR1#
```

Analyzing Information

Examining OSPF configuration of the HQ router (OSPF ABR) revealed that this router is configured with the **area** *area-number* **stub** command for all three areas 1, 2, and 3. This command must be used on all the routers within an area (except the backbone area 0), to convert that area to a stub area. Because we want these areas to be configured as totally stubby, the ABR (and only the ABR) requires the **stub** command to be used with the keyword **no-summary**. In other words, the ABR must be configured with the command **area** *area-number* **stub no-summary** for all three areas. However, branch routers 1, 2, and 3 are all configured with the **area** *area-number* **stub no-summary** command, whereas the keyword **no-summary** is not necessary on these routers, because they are not ABRs. However, the **no-summary** keyword on the non-ABR routers does not cause any harm.

Proposing and Testing a Hypothesis

To convert the OSPF areas 1, 2, and 3 to totally stubby, the ABR (HQ router) configuration must be modified. We propose to add the keyword **no-summary** to the end of the **area** *area-number* **stub** command for all three areas within HQ router's OSPF configuration.

Example 9-65 shows us modifying HQ router's configuration as proposed. Following the modification, the output of the **show ip ospf** command on the HQ router states for each area that it is a stub area and that is has no summary LSAs in this area. In other words, areas 1, 2, and 3 are now correctly configured as totally stubby areas.

Example 9-65 *Propose and Test a Hypothesis*

```
HQ# conf term
Enter configuration commands, one per line.  End with CNTL/Z.
HQ(config)# router ospf 1
HQ(config-router)# area 1 stub no-summary
HQ(config-router)# area 2 stub no-summary
HQ(config-router)# area 3 stub no-summary
HQ(config-router)# end
HQ# wr
Building configuration...
[OK]
Oct  3 01:53:45.521: %SYS-5-CONFIG_I: Configured from console by console
HQ#
HQ# show ip ospf
 Routing Process "ospf 1" with ID 192.168.10.1
< ...output omitted... >
    Area 1
        Number of interfaces in this area is 1
        It is a stub area, no summary LSA in this area
< ...output omitted... >
```

```
    Area 2
        Number of interfaces in this area is 1
        It is a stub area, no summary LSA in this area
< ...output omitted... >
    Area 3
        Number of interfaces in this area is 1
        It is a stub area, no summary LSA in this area
< ...output omitted... >
HQ#
```

Solving the Problem

We must now telnet to the branch routers and make sure that these routers no longer receive any OSPF interarea routes (summary LSAs). Example 9-66 shows the output of the **show ip route ospf** command on the branch router 1 (BR1). As you can see, the only OSPF route in BR1's routing table is the default route that it is receiving from the ABR (because the area is a stub/totally stubby). The routing tables for branch router 2 and 3 are similar, but are not shown here for the sake of brevity. This OSPF totally stubby area problem is solved.

Example 9-66 *Solve the Problem: Summary LSAs and External LSAs Do Not Penetrate into Totally Stubby Areas (ABRs Inject a Default Route Instead)*

```
BR1# show ip route ospf
Codes: L - local, C - connected, S - static, R - RIP, M - mobile, B - BGP
       D - EIGRP, EX - EIGRP external, O - OSPF, IA - OSPF inter area
       N1 - OSPF NSSA external type 1, N2 - OSPF NSSA external type 2
       E1 - OSPF external type 1, E2 - OSPF external type 2
       i - IS-IS, su - IS-IS summary, L1 - IS-IS level-1, L2 - IS-IS level-2
       ia - IS-IS inter area, * - candidate default, U - per-user static route
       o - ODR, P - periodic downloaded static route, H - NHRP, l - LISP
       + - replicated route, % - next hop override

Gateway of last resort is 192.168.11.2 to network 0.0.0.0

O*IA  0.0.0.0/0 [110/1001] via 192.168.11.2, 00:04:45, Tunnel1
BR1#
```

OSPF Stub Areas

OSPF allows certain areas to be configured as stub areas. When an area is configured as a stub area, external routes are filtered on the ABR. Instead, a default route is propagated into the area by the ABR. To configure an area as a stub area, all routers in the area must have the **area** *area-id* **stub** command configured under the router OSPF configuration mode.

A stub area can be converted to a totally stubby area. In addition to external routes, interarea routes are prevented by the ABR from penetrating into the totally stubby area. To configure a stub area as totally stubby, use the **area** *area-id* **stub no-summary** command on the ABR and **area** *area-id* **stub** on all other routers within that area.

When troubleshooting the stub feature on a router, the **show ip ospf** *process-id* command is very helpful. If stub is configured for the specific areas, you will see the "It is a stub area" note within that area section. When a totally stubby area is configured, you will see the "It is a stub area, no summary LSA in this area" note in the Area section.

The **show ip ospf database** command enables you to see the OSPF database on your router. If the stub area is configured, there should be no LSA Type 5s and Type 7s within that area, but you will see an additional LSA Type 3 with the ID 0.0.0.0. This is the default route injected by the ABR. Other summary LSAs can also be seen in the database. When the area is configured as a totally stubby area, only one summary LSA can be seen: the LSA with the ID 0.0.0.0, which is the default route injected by the ABR.

An internal router of a stub area should not have any O E1 or O E2 (OSPF external) routes in its routing table. If the area is totally stubby, no O IA (OSPF interarea) routes should be in its routing table either.

To observe your router's OSPF Hello message exchange, use the **debug ip ospf hello** command. If adjacent routers in the same area do not agree on the OSPF area type, a message similar to "OSPF: Hello from 192.168.23.2 with mismatched Stub/Transit area option bit" will appear. If you see this message, check the stub configuration on both adjacent routers.

Summary

This chapter presented four troubleshooting tickets at Bank of POLONA, a fictitious company, based on the topology shown in Figure 9-2.

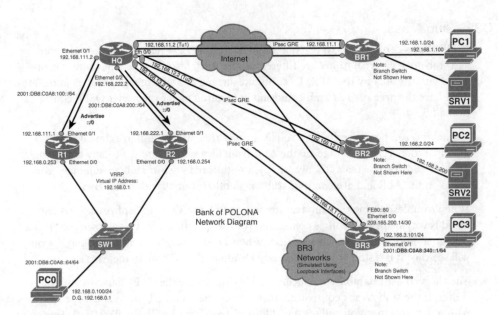

Figure 9-2 *Bank of POLONA Network Diagram*

We work for SECHNIK Networking, and Bank of POLONA is our company's customer. The headquarters site at Bank of POLONA connects to two branch offices; however, they just added a new branch 3 through an acquisition deal. The newly acquired branch is configured with EIGRP, but the headquarters and other two branch offices are configured with OSPF. Bank of POLONA is planning to reconfigure the EIGRP part of the network sometime soon. Bank of POLONA has a resident network engineer named Tina.

Trouble ticket 1: Tina called us about the following problems at Bank of POLONA's network and asked for help with them:

- The user of PC3 from the newly acquired branch office cannot access server SRV2.

  Solution: On the HQ router, we modified redistribution of OSPF into EIGRP to include proper seed metric values.

- If R1's uplink toward the HQ fails, traffic from PC0 goes to R1 and then it is sent to R2, instead of going directly to R2. Tina wanted to implement interface tracking using Cisco's HSRP protocol, but based on POLONA's policy, she is not allowed to configure HSRP. Therefore, Tina wants us to implement VRRP and eliminate this situation of suboptimal traffic path.

  Solution: On the R1 router, we created a track object 1 for interface Ethernet 0/1's line protocol. We also configured R1's VRRP group 1 to decrement R1's priority by 20 if the created object goes down. Because, contrary to HSRP, preempt is the default behavior in VRRP, when R1 decrements its priority by 20 from 110 to 90, R2 with the priority of 100 preempts R1 and becomes the new Master for the VRRP group 1.

■ Tina is getting reports from users in headquarters that SRV2 is sometimes inaccessible. To confirm this, she configured an IP SLA test on the HQ router that tests reachability of SRV2 around the clock. However, Tina complains that the IP SLA test will not start.

Solution: The reason this IP SLA would not start is that Tina has not configured the required schedule for it. We can add the missing schedule for IP SLA 1 on the HQ router.

Trouble ticket 2: Tina called us about the following network problems at Bank of POLONA and asked for help with them:

■ Although BR3 is configured to summarize branch 3's networks and only advertise the summary to the HQ router, the HQ router's routing table is still populated with all of branch 3 networks (172.16.x.x).

Solution: We removed the **ip eigrp summary-address** command from BR3's Ethernet 0/0 interface configuration and place a similar command on the Tunnel3 interface instead.

■ PC0 does not have IPv6 Internet.

Solution: We configured interfaces Ethernet 0/1 and Ethernet 0/2 of the HQ router to generate a default route toward routers R1 and R2 respectively.

■ Branch 3 devices have all lost IPv6 Internet access.

Solution: We removed the explicit deny statement from the bottom of the from_ Internet IPv6 ACL on the BR3 router. This explicit deny all statement was dropping the NA packets that BR3's neighbor (HQ) was sending back to BR3 in response to BR3's NS messages.

Trouble ticket 3: Tina called us about the following network problems at Bank of POLONA and asked for help with them:

■ Branch 1 has lost IP connectivity to the headquarters site. A user of PC1 has reported that pinging from PC1 to PC0 fails; PC1 could ping PC0 before the recent upgrades.

Solution: The first reason that the HQ router and the BR1 router did not have an OSPF adjacency was that the Tunnel1 interface of the HQ router was missing its IP address (192.168.11.2). We also had to add an OSPF **network** statement in the HQ router's configuration to make OSPF active on the Tunnel1 interface.

■ After the routing protocol at the new branch 3 router (BR3) has migrated to OSPF area 3, it was mandated that area 3's (branch 3's) routes must be advertised in summary format (172.16.0.0/16) to the routers (R1 and R2) in the headquarters site. However, the R1 router at headquarters is still receiving updates for the individual subnets of branch 3.

Solution: We removed the **area 0 range** command from BR3's OSPF configuration and added it to the HQ router's OSPF configuration. This command must be configured on the ABR.

■ The branch 1 router (BR1) must authenticate remote login requests (Telnet) using the local authentication method. When you attempt to telnet into BR1, you should get the prompt for username and password, but BR1 router merely asks for a password.

Solution: We enabled AAA on the BR1 user using the **aaa new-model** command, and entered the **aaa authentication login default local** command in BR1's global configuration mode, so that the default authentication method would be based on the locally configured usernames and passwords.

Trouble ticket 4: Over the weekend, Tina reconfigured IPv6 routing from RIPng to OSPFv3 so that routing for both IPv4 and IPv6 within Bank of POLONA's network is done by OSPF. Tina claimed that she managed to do some OSPF fine-tuning on the branch routers as well. After all of Tina's work and the effort, she still had two items that she needed help with and contacted us at SECHNIK Networking about them:

■ PC0 does not have connectivity to IPv6 Internet sites.

Solution: The HQ router's IPv6 OSPF (process 1) needed to be configured to advertise a default-route to R1 and R2. Because router R2 was not advertising its connected network (where PC0 resided), we configured it to do so. We found the same issue on R1 and corrected that, too.

■ Even though Tina configured the branch areas as totally stubby, all branch routers still had many interarea routes in their routing tables.

Solution: We added the keyword **no-summary** to the end of the **area** *area-number* **stub** command for all three areas within the HQ router's OSPF configuration.

Review Questions

1. Which CLI command should you use on an OSPF router to advertise the IP route 0.0.0.0 0.0.0.0 static default route?

   a. redistribute static subnets
   b. default-information originate
   c. redistribute default
   d. redistribute static default

2. What does the following output of the **traceroute** command mean?

```
PC0> traceroute 209.165.201.45
Type escape sequence to abort.
Tracing the route to 209.165.201.45
VRF info: (vrf in name/id, vrf out name/id)
  1 192.168.0.253 0 msec 0 msec 1 msec
  2 192.168.0.253 !H  !H  *
```

    a. !H - Host is unreachable.

    b. Router with an IP address of 192.168.0.253 has responded to the ICMP request.

    c. * - Network unreachable.

    d. !H - Host interrupted test.

3. Which **show ip sla** command displays the number of successful and failed tests?

    a. show ip sla statistics

    b. show ip sla application

    c. show ip sla configuration

    d. show ip sla results

4. You configure a router with a link-local address by using **ipv6 address fe80::123 link-local** command. When you ping another link-local address, the router prompts you to provide the source interface. Why?

    a. This is the default behavior for ping when IPv6 addresses are used. It determines which IPv6 address to use as the source address.

    b. The configured link-local address belongs to the device and not a particular interface. This is the only way for the router to determine which interface and link-local address to ping from.

    c. It uses interface information to permit the traffic returning from a link-local address in the access list, in case one is configured on the interface.

    d. The router does not know which interface leads to the link-local address you want to ping, and therefore the source interface must be manually set.

5. Which of the following IPv4 and IPv6 commands are correctly applying an ACL to an interface? (Choose two.)

    a. ipv6 traffic-filter list2 out

    b. ipv6 access-class cisco in

    c. ip access-class out

    d. ipv6 access-class 12 in

    e. ip access-group 101 out

6. Which protocol and port are used by TACACS+?

    a. TCP/47

    b. TCP/49

    c. UDP/1645

    d. UDP/1812

7. Which OSPF router is used for interarea route summarization?

    a. ASBR

    b. ABR

    c. Backbone

    d. Stub

8. Which of the following best describes the GRE protocol?

   a. GRE adds a new IP header, encapsulates the original IP packet, and adds a GRE header at the end of the IP packet.

   b. GRE adds a new IP header, inserts a GRE header, and encapsulates the original IP packet.

   c. GRE uses an original IP header and adds a GRE header at the end of the packet.

   d. GRE uses an original IP header and inserts a GRE header between IP header and payload.

9. Which IPv6 address type is used as the next-hop address when OSPFv3 installs a route in the routing table?

   a. Link-local

   b. Global

   c. Unique local

   d. Private

10. Which OSPF route types are filtered on ABR when a totally stubby area is configured? (Choose two.)

   a. Default routes

   b. Interarea routes

   c. Intra-area routes

   d. External routes

   e. Host routes

Chapter 10

Troubleshooting Case Study: RADULKO Transport

This chapter presents four troubleshooting cases at a fictitious company, RADULKO Transport, based on the topology shown in Figure 10-1. RADULKO has hired SECHNIK Networking for technical support. As employees of SECHNIK, we need to solve all problems reported by the customer and document them. Each troubleshooting case includes a few configuration errors. Configuration errors will be dealt with as real-world troubleshooting scenarios. Certain technologies are explained briefly to refresh your memory.

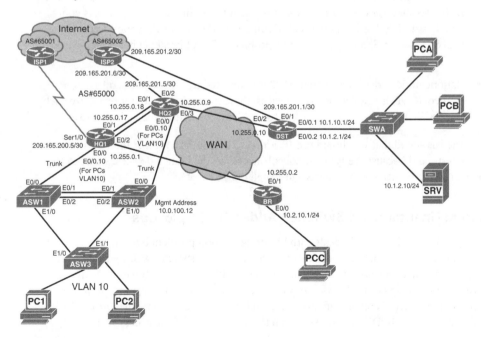

Figure 10-1 *RADULKO Transport's Network Diagram*

> **Note**   The networks presented in this and the previous chapters use Cisco routers to simulate the servers and personal computers (PCs). Keep that in mind as you observe the output shown in the examples presented.

RADULKO Transport Trouble Ticket 1

Marjorie, the network engineer at RADULKO, has contacted us about the following three network issues on her hands and needs help with them:

- RADULKO Transport's network had a Layer 2 loop problem. Marjorie isolated the problem to headquarter's SW3 switch and disconnected the offending cables. The problem was caused when an employee who wanted to have more ports at his desk connected a small switch to the SW3 switch. Marjorie wants us to provide her with a solution that does not allow this to happen again.

- At a remote location of RADULKO Transport, the distribution center, special servers regularly update their databases through the Internet. After the company bought a firewall and installed it at the corporate headquarters, the policy is to route all user traffic through the headquarters before transmitting to the Internet. However, it turned out that the only way to have functional updates for servers at the distribution center is to route server traffic directly to the Internet. As a result, Marjorie configured policy-based routing on the DST router so that all PC traffic that is destined for the Internet is sent to the headquarters and so that all server-generated traffic destined for the Internet is sent to the Internet directly. Marjorie has contacted us stating that her policy-based routing works, but PCA cannot access the local SRV server. She wants us fix this problem without breaking her policy-based routing.

- Marjorie noticed that even though SW2 is connected to SW3 and Cisco Discovery Protocol (CDP) is enabled on both devices, these two switches do not recognize each other as CDP neighbors. She wants us to look into this matter and fix it if possible.

Marjorie has stated that we should use IP address 209.165.201.133 for Internet reachability tests, and because we have no console access to the branch devices, we need to connect to the branch router using Secure Shell (SSH).

Mitigating Unauthorized Switches Added by Employees

Because Marjorie has already dealt with the bridging loop problem by finding and removing the rogue switch and the cables connecting it to switch SW3, we cannot verify the problem. Marjorie has effectively solved the problem already. However, Marjorie has asked us to help her find a way to prevent this from happening again. One way to prevent users from connecting unauthorized (rogue) switches to the network is by enabling the Cisco BPDU Guard feature on the access ports of the access switches.

Gathering Information

Before proposing a solution, it is best to examine the current configuration of the SW3 access switch. We need to find out a few critical pieces of information:

- Verify whether spanning tree is enabled, and whether it is using Cisco's Per-VLAN Spanning Tree Plus (PVST+) based on the 802.1D standard, Cisco's Rapid PVST+ based on the 802.1w standard, or Cisco's Rapid Multiple Spanning Tree (MST) based on the 802.1s standard.

- Verify which ports are configured and designated as access ports and which VLANs they belong to.

- Verify whether and where any of the spanning-tree enhancement options have been applied.

Example 10-1 shows part of SW3's running configuration, focused on interfaces and spanning-tree commands.

Example 10-1 *SW3's Running Configuration Focused on Interfaces and Spanning Tree*

```
SW3# show running-config | include interface | spanning-tree
spanning-tree mode rapid-pvst
spanning-tree extend system-id
interface Ethernet0/0
 spanning-tree portfast edge
 spanning-tree bpduguard enable
interface Ethernet0/1
 spanning-tree portfast edge
 spanning-tree bpduguard enable
interface Ethernet0/2
 spanning-tree portfast edge
 spanning-tree bpduguard enable
interface Ethernet0/3
 spanning-tree portfast edge
 spanning-tree bpduguard enable
< ...output omitted... >
interface Ethernet2/0
 spanning-tree portfast edge
 spanning-tree bpdufilter enable
 spanning-tree bpduguard enable
interface Ethernet2/1
 spanning-tree portfast edge
 spanning-tree bpdufilter enable
 spanning-tree bpduguard enable
interface Ethernet2/2
 spanning-tree portfast edge
 spanning-tree bpdufilter enable
```

```
 spanning-tree bpduguard enable
interface Ethernet2/3
 spanning-tree portfast edge
 spanning-tree bpdufilter enable
 spanning-tree bpduguard enable
< ...output omitted... >
SW3#
```

Analyzing Information

The output shown in Example 10-1 reveals that the spanning-tree mode is rapid PVST, and that all the access ports are configured with the **spanning-tree portfast edge** command. You should use this command only on ports that are connected to end-host devices that terminate VLANs and from which the port should never receive STP bridge protocol data units (BPDUs), such as workstations, servers, and router interfaces (not configured for bridging). These interfaces, however, go into Forwarding state quickly, and do not generate topology change notifications, thus causing MAC address table flushes.

The access ports are configured with the **spanning-tree bpduguard enable** command as well. This command will cause the port (interface) to shut down if a BPDU is received on that interface. This command is an effective mitigation technique used against users connecting unauthorized switches to the access ports.

Note that SW3's access ports Ethernet 2/0 through 2/3, shown in Example 10-1, are also configured with the **spanning-tree bpdufilter enable** command. When PortFast-edge BPDU filtering is explicitly configured on a port, that port does not send any BPDUs and drops all BPDUs it receives. Explicitly configuring PortFast-edge BPDU filtering on a port connected to a switch can result in bridging loops, because the port will ignore any BPDU it receives and goes into Forwarding state.

When both of the **bpduguard** and **bpdufilter** commands are applied to a switch interface, the **bpdufilter** command takes precedence. This means that if a BPDU is received, the interface does not shut down; instead, the interface ignores the BPDU and remains in Forwarding state.

Proposing a Hypothesis and Solving the Problem

Based on the gathered information and the analysis, we can conclude and propose that the **spanning-tree bpdufilter enable** command must be removed from SW3's access ports Ethernet 2/0 through Ethernet 2/3. Previously, when the user at RADULKO connected a switch to two of these SW3 interfaces, a bridging loop was created, and the only way Marjorie could stop it was by finding and removing the cables that connected the rogue switch to SW3. Example 10-2 shows us removing this unnecessary command from the corresponding interfaces.

Example 10-2   *Removing the Unnecessary Spanning-Tree* **bpdufilter** *Commands*

```
SW3# conf term
Enter configuration commands, one per line.  End with CNTL/Z.
SW3(config)# interface range ethernet 2/0-3
SW3(config-if-range)# no spanning-tree bpdufilter enable
SW3(config-if-range)# end
SW3#
*Oct 14 23:40:22.519: %SYS-5-CONFIG_I: Configured from console by console
SW3# wr
Building configuration...
[OK]
SW3#
```

We must document our analysis, conclusions, and the work done, and communicate them to Marjorie at RADULKO.

Troubleshooting Spanning Tree Protocol

The Spanning Tree Protocol (STP) is a Layer 2 protocol that runs on bridges and LAN switches, and it operates based on the IEEE 802.1D standard and specifications. The main purpose of STP is to ensure that the network is loop free but yet all devices have a communication path. Spanning tree also monitors the network for failures and changes the topology to maintain connectivity of all devices in a loop-free manner. The current spanning-tree modes supported on most Cisco LAN switches include the following:

- **PVST+:** This spanning-tree mode is based on the IEEE 802.1D standard and Cisco proprietary extensions. It is the default spanning-tree mode (in most switches) and is used on all Ethernet port-based VLANs. There is a separate instance of STP for each VLAN configured.

- **PVRST+ or Rapid PVST+:** This spanning-tree mode is based on Rapid Spanning Tree Protocol (RSTP), which is specified in the IEEE 802.1w standard. RSTP is based on the assumption that switch-to-switch connections are point-to-point full-duplex connections; therefore, interface role and state decisions are based on a proposal/ challenge/accept negotiation method rather than on timers and timeouts. This gives RSTP a much faster convergence time (subsecond).

- **MSTP:** This spanning-tree mode is based on the IEEE 802.1s standard. The current Multiple Spanning Tree Protocol (MSTP) is Rapid, but it also allows you to map multiple VLANs to the same spanning-tree instance, thus reducing the number of active STP instances.

To verify the spanning-tree mode running on a switch, check the running configuration.

Misconfiguration, hardware errors, or unexpected topology changes can result in the following STP-related issues:

- Forwarding loops

- Suboptimal traffic flow

- Excessive flooding due to the high rate of topology changes

- Convergence time-related issues

Useful spanning-tree troubleshooting commands include the following:

- **show spanning-tree:** This command enables you to check the status of the spanning-tree elements and parameters' values; it also displays the spanning-tree status for all VLANs or MST instances. To check the status of a specific VLAN or MST instance, use the **show spanning-tree vlan** *vlan-id* or the **show spanning-tree mst** *instance-id* command.

- **show spanning-tree summary:** Use this command to verify all the features that are enabled for STP; this command also displays the number of blocked, listening, learning, and forwarding interfaces.

- **show spanning-tree mst configuration:** Use this command to display which VLANs are configured for specific MST instances.

Troubleshooting STP helps to isolate and possibly find the cause for a particular failure; however, implementation of the following stability mechanisms enables us to secure the network against forwarding loops:

- **PortFast:** This feature causes a switch port to enter the spanning-tree Forwarding state immediately, bypassing the Listening and Learning states. You can enable PortFast globally with the command **spanning-tree portfast default** or per interface with the interface configuration mode command **spanning-tree portfast**. Enabling PortFast globally will enable PortFast on all nontrunking ports. To verify interface PortFast status, use the **show spanning-tree interface interface-id portfast** command.

- **PortFast BPDU Guard:** This feature prevents loops by moving a nontrunking port into an Err-Disabled state when a BPDU is received on that port. You can enable BPDU Guard globally with the **spanning-tree portfast bpduguard default** command. This will enable BPDU Guard on all PortFast ports. You can enable BPDU Guard on a single interface with the command **spanning-tree bpduguard enable** without having to enable the PortFast feature. To recover an interface from the Err-Disabled state, you can use the **shutdown** and **no shutdown** command, or use the command **errdisable recovery cause bpduguard** to enable a switch to automatically try to recover err-disabled interfaces.

- **BPDUFilter:** This feature can be enabled globally or per interface. Depending on the configuration method, there are differences in its operation. When BPDUFilter is enabled globally using the **spanning-tree portfast bpdufilter default**, it will enable BPDUFilter on PortFast interfaces. This command prevents interfaces from sending or receiving BPDUs. The interfaces still send a few BPDUs when a link comes up before the switch begins to filter outbound BPDUs. If BPDU is received on a PortFast-enabled interface, the interface loses its PortFast operational status, and BPDUFilter is disabled. You can also enable BPDUFilter per interface by using the **spanning-tree bpdufilter enable** command without also enabling the PortFast feature. This command will prevent the interface from sending or receiving BPDUs, which is functionally the same as disabling STP and can result in spanning-tree loops. Note that BPDUFilter is a very specific tool, tailored for certain occasions, such as when you need to merge two Layer 2 domains using different types of STP, and you need to filter both protocols on the connecting link.

- **Loop Guard:** You can use Loop Guard to prevent alternate or root ports from becoming designated ports because of a failure that leads to a unidirectional link. You can enable this feature by using the **spanning-tree loopguard default** global configuration mode command.

- **Root Guard:** In switched networks, any switch with the lowest bridge ID becomes the root bridge. To prevent other switches connected to specific ports on your switch from becoming the root bridge, you can use the Root Guard feature. When Root Guard is enabled on a port and spanning-tree calculation causes an interface to be selected as root port, the Root Guard places the interface in the Root Inconsistent state, which is equivalent to the port being blocked. When BPDUs with higher bridge IDs are received again, the port recovers from the Root Inconsistent state. You can enable Root Guard on an interface by using the **spanning-tree guard root** command.

> **Note**   Bridge Assurance (BA) is a feature that, if available on two adjacent switches, is a new and better feature than Loop Guard. With Bridge Assurance enabled on both sides of a point-to-point full-duplex link, both switches send out BPDUs. Both switches also expect the other party's BPDU, and upon arrival, the BPD timer is refreshed. If the BPDU is not refreshed, it expires and causes the interface to go into BKN (Broken) state because of the BA inconsistency. BA provides protection against both physical and logical link problems, including unidirectional links.

Troubleshooting Policy-Based Routing

RADULKO Transport recently purchased a firewall and installed it at the corporate headquarters site. Ever since, RADULKO policy has been that all user traffic going to the Internet must be routed through the headquarters so that it passes through the corporate firewall.

At RADULKO's distribution center, special servers regularly update their databases through the Internet. However, it turned out that the only way to have functional updates for servers at the distribution center was to route server traffic directly to the Internet.

As a result, Marjorie configured policy-based routing on the distribution center router (DST) so that all PC traffic that is destined for the Internet is sent to the headquarters and so that all server-generated traffic destined for the Internet is sent to the Internet directly.

Marjorie has contacted us stating that her policy-based routing (PBR) works, but PCA cannot access the local SRV server at the distribution center. Marjorie has asked us to fix this problem without breaking her PBR configuration.

Verifying and Defining the Problem

To verify this problem, we must access PCA at the distribution center and ping the local SRV server. Example 10-3 shows that, as stated by Marjorie, the ping attempt from PCA to SRV fails, and this verifies the problem.

Example 10-3 *Verifying the Problem: PCA Cannot Ping SRV at Distribution Center*

```
PCA# ping 10.1.2.10
Type escape sequence to abort.
Sending 5, 100-byte ICMP Echos to 10.1.2.10, timeout is 2 seconds:
.....
Success rate is 0 percent (0/5)
PCA#
```

We can now define the problem and proceed with information gathering. The problem is that ever since the PBR was implemented to force user traffic that is destined to the Internet to be routed through headquarters, PCA has not been able to contact the local SRV server.

Gathering Information

Because we have been directed to fix the DST router's undesirable routing behavior, which started after the PBR configuration was added to this router, it is best to start information gathering from the DST router itself.

It is best to first examine DST's routing table. As shown in Example 10-4, this router has a static default route sending all traffic to 10.255.0.9, which is HQ2 router's address across the WAN. As we know, PBR has been configured on this router to policy route traffic from the SRV server to the Internet. We must inspect this configuration as well. The output of **show ip policy** reveals that the policy (route map) SRV-INET-RM is applied to Ethernet 0/0.2, which is the interface that receives traffic from the SRV server.

Example 10-4 *Examine DST Router's Routing Table and PBR Configuration*

```
DST# show ip route
< ...output omitted... >
Gateway of last resort is 10.255.0.9 to network 0.0.0.0
S*    0.0.0.0/0 [1/0] via 10.255.0.9
      10.0.0.0/8 is variably subnetted, 14 subnets, 3 masks
```

```
< ...output omitted... >
     209.165.201.0/24 is variably subnetted, 2 subnets, 2 masks
C       209.165.201.0/30 is directly connected, Ethernet0/1
L       209.165.201.1/32 is directly connected, Ethernet0/1
DST#
DST# show ip policy
Interface            Route map
Ethernet0/0.2  SRV-INET-RM
DST#
DST# show route-map SRV-INET-RM
route-map SRV-INET-RM, permit, sequence 10
  Match clauses:
    ip address (access-lists): SRV-INET
  Set clauses:
    ip next-hop 209.165.201.2
  Policy routing matches: 4 packets, 472 bytes
DST# show access-list SRV-INET
Extended IP access list SRV-INET
    10 permit ip 10.1.2.0 0.0.0.255 any (8 matches)
DST#
```

The content of the SRV-INET-RM route map shows that any traffic that matches the
IP access list called SRV-INET will be sent (policy routed) to the next-hop address
209.165.201.2. The IP access list SRV-INET, also shown in Example 10-4, matches all
traffic sourced from the subnet 10.1.2.0/24, where SRV resides.

Analyzing the Information

We know that the PCs and the server SRV are in different IP subnets at the distribution
center and that they all use the DST router as their gateway. This implies that the traffic
going from PCs to the server SRV and the response all go through the DST router.

Based on the gathered information, we can conclude that if traffic from PCA is forwarded to the SRV server and the SRV server replies, the SRV server's response is policy
routed toward the IP address 209.165.201.2 (ISP2). As a result, PCA never receives any
responses back from the SRV server.

Proposing and Testing a Hypothesis

We must modify the IP access-list SRV-INET, which is used by the SRV-INET-RM route
map for PBR so that if the traffic from the SRV server is destined to internal networks
(10.0.0.0), the traffic is not policy routed. Example 10-5 shows our work inserting a **deny**
statement ahead of the existing **permit** statement in the IP access list SRV-INET. The
deny statement matches all traffic sourced from the IP subnet 10.1.2.0/24 and destined
to all of the subnets of network 10.0.0.0/8.

Example 10-5   *Proposing and Testing a Hypothesis: Modify the IP Access List*

```
DST# conf term
Enter configuration commands, one per line.  End with CNTL/Z.
DST(config)# ip access-list extended SRV-INET
DST(config-ext-nacl)# 5 deny ip 10.1.2.0 0.0.0.255 10.0.0.0 0.255.255.255
DST(config-ext-nacl)# end
DST#
DST# show access-list SRV-INET
Extended IP access list SRV-INET
    5 deny ip 10.1.2.0 0.0.0.255 10.0.0.0 0.255.255.255
    10 permit ip 10.1.2.0 0.0.0.255 any (8 matches)
DST# wr
Building configuration...
[OK]
DST#
```

The DST router's modified PBR will now send all traffic from the SRV server's subnet directly to ISP2, except the traffic destined to internal destinations.

Solving the Problem

We must now make sure that PCA can communicate with the SRV server. We must also make sure that the PCA traffic going to the Internet is sent to the HQ2 router (10.255.0.9), while the SRV server traffic going to the Internet is sent to the ISP2 router (209.165.201.2) directly. Example 10-6 shows that PCA can now ping the server successfully. This example also shows that the PCA's traffic to the Internet is sent to the headquarters (HQ2). The SRV server is successful in reaching the Internet, and its traffic is sent directly to the Internet using ISP2.

Example 10-6   *Solving the Problem*

```
PCA# ping 10.1.2.10
Type escape sequence to abort.
Sending 5, 100-byte ICMP Echos to 10.1.2.10, timeout is 2 seconds:
!!!!!
Success rate is 100 percent (5/5), round-trip min/avg/max = 1/1/1 ms
PCA#
PCA# trace 209.165.201.133
Type escape sequence to abort.
Tracing the route to 209.165.201.133
VRF info: (vrf in name/id, vrf out name/id)
  1 10.1.10.1 1 msec 1 msec 1 msec
  2 10.255.0.9 1 msec 1 msec 0 msec
< ...output omitted... >
PCA#
```

```
SRV# ping 209.165.201.133
Type escape sequence to abort.
Sending 5, 100-byte ICMP Echos to 209.165.201.133, timeout is 2 seconds:
!!!!!
Success rate is 100 percent (5/5), round-trip min/avg/max = 1/1/1 ms
SRV#
SRV# trace  209.165.201.133
Type escape sequence to abort.
Tracing the route to 209.165.201.133
VRF info: (vrf in name/id, vrf out name/id)
  1 10.1.2.1 1 msec 1 msec 1 msec
  2 209.165.201.2 1 msec 1 msec 1 msec
< ...output omitted... >
SRV#
```

Because PCA can now reach the SRV server, yet the policy-based routing is working as it should, we can consider the problem solved. We now need to document our work and communicate our findings and work to Marjorie at RADULKO Transport.

Troubleshooting PBR

The following is a short checklist helpful for troubleshooting PBR cases:

- **Check path control route-map statement:** When a packet matches a **deny route-map** statement, it is not policy routed; it is routed normally. When a packet matches a **permit route-map** statement, the statement's set commands are applied.

- **Check traffic-matching configuration:** When access control lists (ACLs) or prefix lists are used to define policy-routed traffic, verify ACLs to understand what traffic is policy routed.

- **Check actions for the matched traffic:** Understand the **set** statements applied by the PBR route map.

- **Check how the route map is applied:** Policy routing works only on inbound packets; therefore, it must be applied on the interface receiving the traffic to be policy routed.

Troubleshooting Neighbor Discovery

Marjorie, RADULKO's network engineer, has reported that even though SW2 (at RADULKO's headquarters) is connected to SW3 and CDP is enabled on both devices, these two switches do not recognize each other as CDP neighbors. She wants us to investigate and fix the problem that is causing this.

Verifying and Defining the Problem

To verify the problem, we access the SW2 and SW3 switches and type the **show cdp neighbor** command. Example 10-7 shows the output of this command on both switches.

Example 10-7   *Verifying the Problem: Show CDP Neighbor on SW2 and SW3*

```
SW2# show cdp neighbors
Capability Codes: R - Router, T - Trans Bridge, B - Source Route Bridge
                  S - Switch, H - Host, I - IGMP, r - Repeater, P - Phone,
                  D - Remote, C - CVTA, M - Two-port Mac Relay


Device ID        Local Intrfce      Holdtme    Capability  Platform  Port ID
SW1              Eth 0/2            153                R S  Linux Uni Eth 0/2
SW1              Eth 0/1            153                R S  Linux Uni Eth 0/1


SW2#


SW3# show cdp neighbors
Capability Codes: R - Router, T - Trans Bridge, B - Source Route Bridge
                  S - Switch, H - Host, I - IGMP, r - Repeater, P - Phone,
                  D - Remote, C - CVTA, M - Two-port Mac Relay
Device ID        Local Intrfce      Holdtme    Capability  Platform  Port ID
SW1              Eth 1/0            128                R S  Linux Uni Eth 1/0

SW3#
```

SW2 is supposed to see SW3 as a CDP neighbor through interface Ethernet 1/0, and SW3 is supposed to see SW2 as a CDP neighbor through interface Ethernet 1/1. However, neither switch sees the other as a CDP neighbor over those interfaces, even though CDP is running on both switches. So, the problem is verified as Marjorie has stated.

The problem is defined simply as follows: Headquarter switches SW2 and SW3 are adjacent through their interfaces Ethernet 1/0 and Ethernet 1/1, respectively, and even though they both have CDP running, neither switch sees the other through the respective interface.

Gathering Information

Because SW2's Ethernet 1/0 interface is connected to SW3, and SW3's Ethernet 1/1 interface is connected to SW2, as the first information-gathering step, we must check whether CDP is enabled on those switch interfaces. We do this because even though CDP is running on both switches, it might have been disabled on either switch's particular interface individually. Example 10-8 shows the output of **show cdp interface | include Ethernet 1/0** that we entered on SW2 and the output of **show cdp interface | include Ethernet 1/1** that we entered on SW3.

Example 10-8 *Gathering Information: Show CDP Interface on SW2 and SW3*

```
SW2# show cdp interface | include Ethernet1/0
Ethernet1/0 is up, line protocol is up
SW2#


SW3# show cdp interface | include Ethernet1/1
SW3#
```

Based on the output shown in Example 10-8, CDP is enabled on SW2's Ethernet 1/0 interface, but CDP is disabled on SW3's Ethernet 1/1 interface.

Proposing and Testing a Hypothesis

Based on the gathered information, we can propose that for SW2 and SW3 to see each other as CDP neighbors over their corresponding connection, CDP must be enabled on SW3's Ethernet 1/1 interface. Example 10-9 shows us enabling CDP on SW3's Ethernet 1/1 interface. It also shows that after we enable CDP on this interface, the **show cdp interface | include Ethernet 1/1** command displays this interface in its output.

Example 10-9 *Proposing and Testing a Hypothesis: Enable CDP on SW3 Ethernet 1/1*

```
SW3# conf term
Enter configuration commands, one per line.  End with CNTL/Z.
SW3(config)# interface ethernet 1/1
SW3(config-if)# cdp enable
SW3(config-if)# end
SW3# show cdp interface | include Ethernet1/1
Ethernet1/1 is up, line protocol is up
SW3#
```

Solving the Problem

We can now check whether SW2 and SW3 see each other as CDP neighbors. As shown in Example 10-10, we execute **show cdp neighor** on these switches once again, but this time SW2 sees SW3 through its Ethernet 1/0, and SW3 sees SW2 through its Ethernet 1/1. The problem is solved.

Example 10-10 *Solving the Problem: Show CDP Neighbor on SW2 and SW3*

```
SW2# show cdp neighbors
Capability Codes: R - Router, T - Trans Bridge, B - Source Route Bridge
                  S - Switch, H - Host, I - IGMP, r - Repeater, P - Phone,
                  D - Remote, C - CVTA, M - Two-port Mac Relay
Device ID     Local Intrfce    Holdtme    Capability    Platform     Port ID
```

```
HQ2               Eth 0/0          163           R         Linux Uni      Eth 0/0
SW1               Eth 0/2          145           R S       Linux Uni      Eth 0/2
SW1               Eth 0/1          174           R S       Linux Uni      Eth 0/1
SW3               Eth 1/0          139           R S       Linux Uni      Eth 1/1
SW2#


SW3# show cdp neighbors
Capability Codes: R - Router, T - Trans Bridge, B - Source Route Bridge
                  S - Switch, H - Host, I - IGMP, r - Repeater, P - Phone,
                  D - Remote, C - CVTA, M - Two-port Mac Relay
Device ID    Local Intrfce     Holdtme    Capability     Platform      Port ID
SW1          Eth 1/0            157         R S           Linux Uni     Eth 1/0
SW2          Eth 1/1            173         R S           Linux Uni     Eth 1/0
SW3#
SW3# wr
Building configuration...
[OK]
SW3#
```

We must now document our work and notify Marjorie that the problem is solved.

Troubleshooting CDP and LLDP

The most common issue with Cisco Discovery Protocol / Link Layer Discovery Protocol (CDP/LLDP) is that a device does not see one or more of its CDP/LLDP neighbors. To troubleshoot CDP or LLDP neighbor discovery problems, check the following items:

- Check whether all devices are Cisco devices or whether there are other vendor devices in the network as well. If the network is multivendor, use LLDP.

- Check whether CDP/LLDP is enabled globally, and check to make sure that it has not been disabled on the required interfaces. The [no] cdp run command is used to enable/disable CDP globally. The [no] cdp enable command is used to enable/disable CDP on a particular interface. The same commands are available and applicable for LLDP.

- Check the LLDP/CDP timer values. If you configure the CDP/LLDP hold time to be less than the Update timer, your device will lose its CDP/LLDP adjacencies repeatedly.

The following commands are useful for troubleshooting CDP- and LLDP-related cases:

- **show cdp, show lldp:** Display global protocol information, including timer and hold-time information and protocol version

- **show cdp entry, show lldp entry:** Display information about a specific neighboring device, including device ID, protocols and addresses, platform, interface, hold time, and version

- **show cdp interface, show lldp interface:** Display information about the interfaces on which the protocol is enabled, including status information and information about timer and hold time

- **show cdp neighbors, show lldp neighbors:** Display detailed information about neighboring devices, including the type of the device, its name, and MAC address or serial number, local interconnecting interface, remaining hold-time interval, product number, and neighbor's interconnecting interface and port number

- **show cdp neighbors detail, show lldp neighbors detail:** Display additional detail about neighbors, including network addresses, enabled protocols, and software version

- **show cdp traffic, show lldp traffic:** Display information about traffic between devices, such as the total number of packets sent and received and advertisements per version

- **debug cdp, debug lldp:** Display the protocol messages exchanged in real time

RADULKO Transport Trouble Ticket 2

Marjorie, the network engineer at RADULKO, has contacted us to help her solve some recent network problems at work. Marjorie submitted her request to us as follows:

- The switch SW2 was stolen during the weekend. I found an old switch in the storage and copied the saved configuration from the stolen switch into this switch. However, after I connected this switch to the network, PC1 and PC2 (from VLAN 10) have lost their network connectivity, VLAN 100 has disappeared, and some VLANs I don't recognize (33, 44, 87, 153) have been created.

- The branch router BR does not seem to have IPv6 connectivity to the rest of the network, and it certainly cannot reach the IPv6 Internet.

- MP-BGP is working well on the HQ1 router, but the HQ2 router has no IPv6 session with ISP2's router.

- Marjorie has stated that we should use IP address 209.165.201.133 for IPv4, and 2001:DB8:0:D::100 for IPv6 Internet reachability tests, and because we have no console access to the branch devices, we need to connect to the branch router using SSH.

Troubleshooting VLANs and PCs Connectivity Problems

Based on the note we received from Marjorie, PC1 and PC2 (VLAN 10) have lost their connectivity after she configured the new SW2 switch and connected it to the network. She also stated that VLAN 100 has disappeared and that some new VLANs (33, 44, 87, and 153) are suddenly there that she does not recognize. We need to investigate this issue, fix the problem if possible, and report back to Marjorie at RADULKO.

Verifying the Problem

To verify the problem, we ping the Internet reachability test IP address (209.165.201.133) that Marjorie gave us, from PC1. As shown in Example 10-11, the ping fails, and as you can see, PC1 does not even have an IP address on its Ethernet interface. We experienced the same result for PC2, but it is not shown here.

So, the problem is verified, and we need to start fact gathering. Because PC1 and PC2 interfaces are up, we'll take a bottom-up approach, starting at the data link layer.

Example 10-11   *Verifying the Problem: Test PC1 and PC2's Network Connectivity*

```
PC1# ping 209.165.201.133
% Unrecognized host or address, or protocol not running.


PC1# show ip interface brief
Interface              IP-Address      OK? Method Status                Protocol
Ethernet0/0            unassigned      YES DHCP   up                    up
PC1#
```

Gathering Information

We start our fact gathering on switch SW3, where PC1 and PC2 connect. As shown in Example 10-12, the output of the **show vlan** command on this switch supports Marjorie's statement about the VLANs 10 and 100 missing and the unrecognized VLANs 33, 44, 87, and 153 existing.

Example 10-12   *Gathering Information: Examine the VLAN database*

```
SW3# show vlan

VLAN Name                             Status    Ports
---- -------------------------------- --------- -------------------------------
1    default                          active    Et1/2, Et1/3, Et3/0, Et3/1
                                                Et3/2, Et3/3, Et4/0, Et4/1
                                                Et4/2, Et4/3, Et5/0, Et5/1
                                                Et5/2, Et5/3

33   VLAN0033                         active
44   VLAN0044                         active
87   VLAN0087                         active
153  VLAN0153                         active
< ...output omitted... >
SW3#
```

As the next step in fact gathering, suspecting that Virtual Trunking Protocol (VTP) might play a role in this situation, we use the **show vtp status** command on switches SW3 and SW2. The output is shown in Example 10-13. Both of these switches are in server mode and have a common VTP domain name (cisco).

Example 10-13 *Gathering Information: Examine VTP Status and Role on Both Switches*

```
SW3# show vtp status
VTP Version                  : 3 (capable)
Configuration Revision       : 7
Maximum VLANs supported locally : 1005
Number of existing VLANs     : 9
VTP Operating Mode           : Server
VTP Domain Name              : cisco
< ...output omitted...>
SW3#



SW2# show vtp status
VTP Version                  : 3 (capable)
Configuration Revision       : 7
Maximum VLANs supported locally : 1005
Number of existing VLANs     : 9
VTP Operating Mode           : Server
VTP Domain Name              : cisco
< ...output omitted... >
SW2#
```

Analyzing the Information

Based on the gathered information, we can conclude that the switch that Marjorie found in the storage room, and connected to the network to replace the stolen switch SW2, had a VTP file with a higher configuration revision number than switches SW1 and SW2. Because all of these switches have the same VTP domain name, switch SW2's VTP file (with the highest configuration revision number) was copied to SW1 and SW2. This explains why VLANs 10 and 100 disappeared and why VLANs 33, 44, 87, and 153 were added.

Proposing and Testing a Hypothesis

We can propose that VLANs 10 and 100 must be added and VLANs 33, 44, 87, and 153 must be deleted. Example 10-14 shows us deleting and adding the appropriate VLANs on the SW2 switch. This is propagated to the other switches by VTP. This is verified, as shown in Example 10-14, as we use the **show vlan** command on the SW3 switch.

Example 10-14 *Proposing a Hypothesis: Delete the Unneeded VLANs and Add the Required VLANs*

```
SW2# conf t
Enter configuration commands, one per line.  End with CNTL/Z.
SW2(config)# no vlan 33
% Applying VLAN changes may take few minutes.  Please wait...
```

```
SW2(config)# no vlan 44
% Applying VLAN changes may take few minutes.  Please wait...
SW2(config)# no vlan 87
% Applying VLAN changes may take few minutes.  Please wait...
SW2(config)# no vlan 153
% Applying VLAN changes may take few minutes.  Please wait...
SW2(config)# vlan 10
SW2(config-vlan)# exit
% Applying VLAN changes may take few minutes.  Please wait...
SW2(config)# vlan 100
SW2(config-vlan)# exit
% Applying VLAN changes may take few minutes.  Please wait...
SW2(config)# exit
SW2#



SW3# show vlan

VLAN Name                         Status     Ports
---- --------------------------   ---------  ------------------------------
1    default                      active     Et1/2, Et1/3, Et3/0, Et3/1
                                             Et3/2, Et3/3, Et4/0, Et4/1
                                             Et4/2, Et4/3, Et5/0, Et5/1
                                             Et5/2, Et5/3
10   VLAN0010                     active     Et0/0, Et0/1, Et0/2, Et0/3
                                             Et2/0, Et2/1, Et2/2, Et2/3
100  VLAN0100                     active
< ...output omitted... >
SW3#
```

Solving the Problem

Following the best practices, it is best to put all three switches in VTP transparent mode. Next, we must check whether PC1 and PC2 have IP addresses and can reach the Internet. Example 10-15 shows us changing the VTP mode to transparent on all three switches. Furthermore, this example shows that PC1 has obtained an IP address and can ping the Internet reachability test IP address. The same is true for PC2, but the results are not shown here for brevity. The problem is solved.

Example 10-15 *Solving the Problem*

```
SW3# conf term
Enter configuration commands, one per line.  End with CNTL/Z.
SW3(config)# vtp mode transparent
Setting device to VTP Transparent mode for VLANS.
```

```
SW3(config)# end
SW3# wr
Building configuration...
[OK]
SW3#


SW2(config)# vtp mode transparent
Setting device to VTP Transparent mode for VLANS.
SW2(config)# end


SW1(config)# vtp mode transparent
Setting device to VTP Transparent mode for VLANS.
SW1(config)# end


PC1# show ip interface brief
Interface                IP-Address      OK? Method Status              Protocol
Ethernet0/0              10.0.10.11      YES DHCP   up                  up

PC1# ping 209.165.201.133
Type escape sequence to abort.
Sending 5, 100-byte ICMP Echos to 209.165.201.133, timeout is 2 seconds:
!!!!!
Success rate is 100 percent (5/5), round-trip min/avg/max = 9/210/1014 ms
PC1#
```

We can now document our work and notify Marjorie that this problem is fixed.

Troubleshooting VTP

VLAN Trunking Protocol (VTP) is a Cisco proprietary LAN switch protocol that assists in VLAN management, implementing VLAN changes such as adding, deleting, naming, and mapping VLANs. Switches in a common VTP domain, as long as they have the same VTP password, copy each other's VLAN.DAT file based on this file's revision number (formally called configuration revision number). Cisco LAN switches can be in one of three modes (server, client, and transparent) in a VTP domain. Server mode is the default VTP mode. The switch in client mode does not allow you to make any changes to VLANs, but the switch in server or transparent mode does. The switch in client mode does not save the VLAN information in nonvolatile memory, and so it must learn it upon every system startup or reload. The difference between the server and transparent modes is that the switch in transparent mode keeps its revision number always at zero, and it does not generate or accept VTP advertisements. VTP advertisements from other switches are allowed to pass through the switch that is in transparent mode. The switch in server mode increments the VLAN file's configuration revision number every time a change is made, saves the file in nonvolatile memory (flash memory, often), and sends out periodic advertisements as well as change-triggered advertisements.

VTP does not prevent VLAN changes to be made on multiple switches at the same time; also, a received advertisement with a higher configuration revision number is always honored and replaces the local VLAN file. As a result, the best practice is to either put all switches in transparent mode or use VTP with caution. Being cautious with VTP means that you should have no more than two switches in server mode, should have long and uncommon domain names, and should use long and uncommon VTP passwords. Also, before connecting a switch to your network, make sure that the switch is in transparent mode. The reason is that if that switch happens to have no domain name or a similar domain name, as well as a higher configuration revision, it will impose its VLAN file to all other switches in your network, regardless of the validity of its VLAN file! It is important to know that VTP is propagated over *trunk* interfaces only and that VTP messages are not encrypted. Keep in mind that a switch with no domain name configured will adopt the domain name of the first VTP advertisement it receives. VTP Version 3 adds a new VTP mode called off. A switch in off mode acts similarly to a switch in transparent mode, but it does not forward VTP messages through.

When troubleshooting VTP, consider VTP version mismatch, authentication mismatch, and nonoperational trunk connection as possible culprits. Use the **show vlan** command to display the VLAN database and to check whether interfaces are assigned to the correct VLANs. Use the **show vtp status** command to check the status of the VTP and its settings, such as configuration revision number, VTP version supported and in use, domain name, operational mode, and so on.

Troubleshooting Branch Router's IPv6 Problems

RADULKO's branch router (BR) has no IPv6 routes to the rest of RADULKO's network, and it certainly cannot reach the IPv6 Internet. Marjorie has asked for help on this matter.

Verifying the Problem

To verify the problem, we SSH into the branch router and display its IPv6 routing table using the **show ipv6 route** command. As shown in Example 10-16, the BR router has only three connected/local entries in its IPv6 routing table. The problem is verified, and we can start our investigation.

Example 10-16 *Verifying the Problem: Display BR Router's IPv6 Routing Table*

```
BR# show ipv6 route
IPv6 Routing Table - default - 3 entries
< ...output omitted... >
C   2001:DB8:0:A210::/64 [0/0]
     via Ethernet0/0, directly connected
L   2001:DB8:0:A210::1/128 [0/0]
```

```
     via Ethernet0/0, receive
L   FF00::/8 [0/0]
     via Null0, receive
BR#
```

Gathering Information

To gather information about the IPv6 routing protocols configuration on the branch router, we can use the **show ipv6 protocols** command. As you can see in Example 10-17, EIGRP 1 is configured, and it is activated on interfaces Ethernet 0/0 and Ethernet 0/1. We must check the IPV6 routing protocols configuration on BR router's counterpart router HQ1 next.

Example 10-17   *Gathering Information: Check IPv6 Routing Protocols on BR and HQ1 Routers*

```
BR# show ipv6 protocols
< ...output omitted... >
IPv6 Routing Protocol is "eigrp 1"
  Interfaces:
    Ethernet0/0
    Ethernet0/1
  Redistribution:
    None
BR#


HQ1# show ipv6 protocols
< ...output omitted... >
IPv6 Routing Protocol is "eigrp 1"
EIGRP-IPv6 Protocol for AS(1)
< ...output omitted... >
  Metric weight K1=1, K2=0, K3=1, K4=0, K5=0
  NSF-aware route hold timer is 240
  Router-ID: 209.165.200.5
< ...output omitted... >
  Interfaces:
    Ethernet0/0.2
    Ethernet0/0.10
    Ethernet0/0.100
    Ethernet0/1
  Redistribution:
    Redistributing protocol bgp 65000 with metric 1500 2000 255 1 1500 route-map
DEFAULT6
HQ1#
```

Example 10-17 shows that even though IPv6 router EIGRP 1 is running on the HQ1 router, it is not active on the Ethernet 0/2 interface toward the BR router.

Proposing and Testing a Hypothesis

Based on the gathered information, we propose to activate IPv6 EIGRP 1 on the Ethernet 0/2 interface of the HQ1 router. As shown in Example 10-18, after we activate EIGRP 1 for IPv6 on the Ethernet 0/2 interface, HQ1 immediately forms EIGRP adjacency with the neighbor FE80::A8BB:CCFF:FE00:BB10 over the Ethernet 0/2 interface.

Example 10-18   *Proposing a Hypothesis: Activate IPv6 EIGRP 1 on Eth0/2 Int.*

```
HQ1# conf term
Enter configuration commands, one per line.  End with CNTL/Z.
HQ1(config)# interface ethernet 0/2
HQ1(config-if)# ipv6 eigrp 1
HQ1(config-if)#
*Oct 16 02:05:59.905: %DUAL-5-NBRCHANGE: EIGRP-IPv6 1: Neighbor
FE80::A8BB:CCFF:FE00:BB10 (Ethernet0/2) is up: new adjacency
HQ1(config-if)# end
HQ1# wr
Building configuration...
[OK]
HQ1#
*Oct 16 02:06:02.748: %SYS-5-CONFIG_I: Configured from console by console
HQ1#
```

Solving the Problem

After activating IPv6 EIGRP on HQ1's Ethernet 0/2 interface, we check the IPv6 routing table on the BR router. As shown in Example 10-19, the BR router is now receiving IPv6 routes through EIGRP. Furthermore, pinging to the IPv6 Internet reachability test address (2001:DB8:0:D::100) succeeds 100 percent of the time. The problem is solved.

Example 10-19   *Solving the Problem: BR Router Receives RADULKO's IPv6 Routes, and It Can Also Reach the IPv6 Internet*

```
BR# show ipv6 route
IPv6 Routing Table - default - 12 entries
< ...output omitted... >
EX   ::/0 [170/2244096]
     via FE80::A8BB:CCFF:FE00:A820, Ethernet0/1
D    2001:DB8:0:F::/64 [90/307200]
     via FE80::A8BB:CCFF:FE00:A820, Ethernet0/1
D    2001:DB8:0:11C::/64 [90/332800]
     via FE80::A8BB:CCFF:FE00:A820, Ethernet0/1
```

```
D    2001:DB8:0:A002::/64 [90/307200]
       via FE80::A8BB:CCFF:FE00:A820, Ethernet0/1
D    2001:DB8:0:A010::/64 [90/307200]
       via FE80::A8BB:CCFF:FE00:A820, Ethernet0/1
D    2001:DB8:0:A0A0::/64 [90/307200]
       via FE80::A8BB:CCFF:FE00:A820, Ethernet0/1
D    2001:DB8:0:A102::/64 [90/358400]
       via FE80::A8BB:CCFF:FE00:A820, Ethernet0/1
D    2001:DB8:0:A110::/64 [90/358400]
       via FE80::A8BB:CCFF:FE00:A820, Ethernet0/1
D    2001:DB8:0:A1A0::/64 [90/358400]
       via FE80::A8BB:CCFF:FE00:A820, Ethernet0/1
C    2001:DB8:0:A210::/64 [0/0]
       via Ethernet0/0, directly connected
L    2001:DB8:0:A210::1/128 [0/0]
       via Ethernet0/0, receive
L    FF00::/8 [0/0]
       via Null0, receive
BR#
BR# ping 2001:DB8:0:D::100
Type escape sequence to abort.
Sending 5, 100-byte ICMP Echos to 2001:DB8:0:D::100, timeout is 2 seconds:
!!!!!
Success rate is 100 percent (5/5), round-trip min/avg/max = 8/8/9 ms
BR#
```

We must now document our work and notify Marjorie that this problem is also fixed.

Troubleshooting EIGRP for IPv6

Configuring Enhanced Interior Gateway Routing Protocol (EIGRP) for IPv6 is similar to configuring EIGRP for IPv4. The main difference is that EIGRP is enabled on the interface for IPv6 with the command **ipv6 eigrp as-number**, as network statement is deprecated. Therefore, troubleshooting EIGRP for IPv6 is very similar to troubleshooting EIGRP for IPv4.

The following are a few commands you can use for troubleshooting EIGRP:

- **show ipv6 protocols:** The output of this command shows information about the locally active IPv6 routing protocols. The EIGRP section of the output displays metric weights (K parameters), router ID, EIGRP interfaces, redistribution information, and other information about EIGRP.

- **show ipv6 eigrp neighbors:** This command reveals the list of a local router's EIGRP neighbors. All EIGRP neighbors are listed, with some useful information such as interface used to connect the neighbor, timers, and so on.

- **show ipv6 eigrp interfaces:** This command displays detailed information about interfaces where EIGRP has been activated.

- **show ipv6 eigrp topology:** This command displays the EIGRP topology table. You can see all routing updates received by the router, with administrative distance (AD) and feasible distance (FD) information, next hop, and so on.

- **debug ipv6 eigrp:** This debug enables you to observe the EIGRP events observed/ processed by your local router in real time.

Troubleshooting MP-BGP Session Problem

According to Marjorie, the HQ2 router has no IPv6 session with ISP2's router. She has asked us to find the culprit and fix this issue for her.

Verifying the Problem

To verify HQ2's MP-BGP sessions with its neighbors, we can use the **show bgp all summary** command. Example 10-20 shows that for address family IPv4, HQ2 has an established session with both an interior Border Gateway Protocol (iBGP) neighbor (HQ1) and an external Border Gateway Protocol (eBGP) neighbor (ISP2). However, for IPv6 address family, HQ2 has an established session with an iBGP neighbor (HQ1) only. Therefore, for address family IPv6, the eBGP session with the ISP2 router is missing. The problem is thus verified as Marjorie has reported.

Example 10-20 *Verifying the Problem: Examine HQ2 Router's MP-BGP Sessions*

```
HQ2# show bgp all summary
For address family: IPv4 Unicast
BGP router identifier 209.165.201.5, local AS number 65000
< ...output omitted... >
Neighbor        V   AS    MsgRcvd MsgSent   TblVer   InQ  OutQ  Up/Down   State/PfxRcd
10.255.0.17     4   65000     2       2        1      0    0    00:00:11       0
209.165.201.6   4   65002     6       2        1      0    0    00:00:18       4

For address family: IPv6 Unicast
BGP router identifier 209.165.201.5, local AS number 65000
< ...output omitted... >
Neighbor        V   AS    MsgRcvd MsgSent   TblVer   InQ OutQ Up/Down   State/PfxRcd
2001:DB8:0:F::2 4   65000     2       2        1      0    0 00:00:17       0
HQ2#
```

Gathering Information

We can start our information gathering by examining the BGP configuration section of HQ2's running configuration. Example 10-21 shows the BGP section of HQ2's running configuration. You can see that neighbors 10.255.0.17 (HQ1-iBGP) and 209.165.201.6 (ISP 2-eBGP) are activated under the IPv4 address family and that neighbor 2001:DB8:0:F::2 (HQ1-iBGP) is activated under the IPv6 address family.

Example 10-21 *Gathering Information: Examine BGP Configuration on HQ2 Router*

```
HQ2# show run | section router bgp
router bgp 65000
 bgp log-neighbor-changes
 neighbor 10.255.0.17 remote-as 65000
 neighbor 2001:DB8:0:F::2 remote-as 65000
 neighbor 2001:DB8:0:11C::1 remote-as 65002
 neighbor 209.165.201.6 remote-as 65002
 !
 address-family ipv4
  network 209.165.200.18 mask 255.255.255.255
  neighbor 10.255.0.17 activate
  no neighbor 2001:DB8:0:F::2 activate
  no neighbor 2001:DB8:0:11C::1 activate
  neighbor 209.165.201.6 activate
  neighbor 209.165.201.6 prefix-list ROUTE-OUT out
 exit-address-family
 !
 address-family ipv6
  network 2001:DB8:0:A002::/64
  network 2001:DB8:0:A010::/64
  network 2001:DB8:0:A0A0::/64
  network 2001:DB8:0:A102::/64
  network 2001:DB8:0:A110::/64
  network 2001:DB8:0:A1A0::/64
  network 2001:DB8:0:A210::/64
  neighbor 2001:DB8:0:F::2 activate
 exit-address-family
HQ2#
```

Analyzing the Information and Proposing a Hypothesis

Based on the information gathered, the eBGP neighbor 2001:DB8:0:11C::1 (eBGP-ISP2) is not activated under the IPv6 address family. We therefore propose to activate this neighbor under the IPv6 address family because it seems to be the culprit. Example 10-22 shows us configuring HQ2 router's BGP and activating neighbor 2001:DB8:0:11C::1 under the address family IPv6.

Example 10-22   *Proposing a Hypothesis: Activate eBGP Neighbor (ISP2) for IPv6 Address Family*

```
HQ2# conf term
Enter configuration commands, one per line.  End with CNTL/Z.
HQ2(config)# router bgp 65000
HQ2(config-router)# address-family ipv6
HQ2(config-router-af)# neighbor 2001:DB8:0:11C::1 activate
HQ2(config-router-af)# end
HQ2# wr
*Oct 16 03:17:53.277: %SYS-5-CONFIG_I: Configured from console by console
HQ2# wr
Building configuration...
[OK]
HQ2#
*Oct 16 03:17:55.995: %BGP-5-ADJCHANGE: neighbor 2001:DB8:0:11C::1 Up
```

Solving the Problem

We can now examine the status of HQ2's BGP sessions with its neighbor for both IPv4 and IPv6 address families. Example 10-23 shows that HQ2 now has two established neighbors under the IPv4 address family and two established neighbors under the IPv6 address families. The problem is solved.

Example 10-23   *Solving the Problem: Verify That the eBGP Session with ISP2 Is Established for the IPv6 Address Family*

```
HQ2# show bgp all summary
For address family: IPv4 Unicast
BGP router identifier 209.165.201.5, local AS number 65000
< ...output omitted... >
Neighbor        V    AS     MsgRcvd  MsgSent   TblVer   InQ OutQ Up/Down  State/PfxRcd
10.255.0.17     4    65000    39       38        8       0    0  00:28:30        4
209.165.201.6   4    65002    39       35        8       0    0  00:28:37        5

For address family: IPv6 Unicast
BGP router identifier 209.165.201.5, local AS number 65000
< ...output omitted... >
Neighbor        V  AS     MsgRcvd MsgSent TblVer   InQ OutQ  Up/Down    State/
PfxRcd
2001:DB8:0:F::2    4  65000    41      38     17       0    0   00:28:36       11
2001:DB8:0:11C::1  4  65002    13      12     17       0    0   00:00:30        5
HQ2#
```

We must now document our work and notify Marjorie that this problem is solved.

Troubleshooting MP-BGP

Multiprotocol BGP extensions for IPv6 support the same features and functionality as IPv4 BGP. IPv6 enhancements to multiprotocol BGP include support for the IPv6 address family (network layer reachability information [NLRI] and next hop). To configure IPv6-specific tasks, the IPv6 address family was introduced in the router configuration mode. Use **address-family ipv6** to enter the unicast IPv6 address family. By default, neighbors that are defined using the **neighbor remote-as** command in router configuration mode exchange only IPv4 unicast address prefixes. To exchange IPv6 prefixes, neighbors must be activated using the **neighbor activate** command in address family configuration mode for IPv6 prefixes.

Configuring IPv6 multiprotocol BGP between two IPv6 routers (peers) using link-local addresses requires that the outgoing interface toward the neighbor be identified by using the **update-source** command. You also need a route map (applied to neighbor outbound) to set the next-hop attribute to a global IPv6 unicast address. Use the **debug bgp ipv6 unicast update** command to display debugging information on the updates to help determine the state of the peering.

To inject a network into an IPv6 BGP database, you must define the network using the **network** command in address family configuration mode. By default, route maps that are applied in router configuration mode using the **neighbor route-map** command are applied to only IPv4 unicast address prefixes. Route maps for IPv6 address family must be applied in IPv6 address family configuration mode using the **neighbor route-map** command. The route maps are applied either as the inbound or outbound routing policy for neighbors under the IPv6 address family.

Redistribution is the process of redistributing, or injecting, prefixes from one routing protocol (or static and connected) into another routing protocol. Prefixes that are redistributed into IPv6 multiprotocol BGP using the redistribute (router configuration mode) command are injected into the IPv6 unicast database.

Useful commands to troubleshoot IPv6 BGP include the following:

- **clear bgp ipv6 unicast *:** Use this command to reset all IPv6 BGP sessions on the router. You can use several other keywords, such as IP address of the neighbor, autonomous system number, and so on, instead of an asterisk to make some more specific clearing.

- **show bgp ipv6 unicast:** Use this command to display the IPv6 BGP table. You can see IPv6 prefixes with next-hop address, local preference, metric, autonomous system path, and other attributes.

- **show bgp ipv6 unicast summary:** Use this command to verify all IPv6 BGP peers and related information such as status of the peering, how many prefixes have been received, and so forth.

- **debug bgp ipv6 unicast updates:** This command will enable debugging for all IPv6 BGP update packets received and sent by the router.

RADULKO Transport Trouble Ticket 3

RADULKO Transport's network policy has changed, and they are no longer allowed to use proprietary protocols such as Cisco's EIGRP. Over the weekend, the network group, led by Marjorie, has reconfigured the network and migrated to Open Shortest Path First (OSPF) Protocol. They have been successful in their migration project, but Marjorie has contacted us at SECHNIK Networking about two remaining problems:

- PC1 cannot access the distribution center server (SRV) at the IP address 10.1.2.10. PC1 can only access this server if the HQ1 router at headquarters fails! HQ1 and HQ2 are the active and standby HSRP routers for the PCs in the headquarters. HQ1 tracks its serial interface, and if the line protocol on this interface goes down, HQ1 reduces its priority to allow HQ2 to preempt and becomes the active HSRP router.

- OSPF authentication between HQ1 and BR routers is not working, and their adjacency is lost. OSPF neighbor relation (adjacency) between the HQ1 and BR routers must be restored.

Troubleshooting PC1's Problem Accessing the SRV Server at the Distribution Center

This problem is a strange one. The HQ1 and HQ2 routers are redundant first hops for the PCs at RADULKO's headquarters; HQ1 is the active HSRP router and HQ2 in the standby router. When HQ1 is up and running, PC1 cannot access the SRV server at the distribution center. If HQ1 is down, PC1 can access the SRV center successfully.

Verifying and Defining the Problem

To verify the problem we try to ping the SRV server at the IP address 10.1.2.10 while HQ1 is the active HSRP server. As shown in Example 10-24, the ping from PC1 fails in this case. This is consistent with Marjorie's report. Because HQ1 tracks its serial interface, and reduces its priority if this interface goes down, we shut down its serial interface. Consequently, HQ1 reduces its priority and HQ2 preempts and becomes the active Hot Standby Routing Protocol (HSRP) router (see Example 10-24). We try the ping from PC1 to the SRV server again, and this time as Marjorie has reported correctly, the ping is 100 percent successful.

Example 10-24   *Verifying the Problem: PC1 Cannot Access SRV When HQ1 Is Up*

```
PC1# ping 10.1.2.10
Type escape sequence to abort.
Sending 5, 100-byte ICMP Echos to 10.1.2.10, timeout is 2 seconds:
...U.
Success rate is 0 percent (0/5)
PC1#
```

```
HQ1# conf term
Enter configuration commands, one per line.  End with CNTL/Z.
HQ1(config)# int serial 1/0
HQ1(config-if)# shut
HQ1(config-if)#



PC1# ping 10.1.2.10
Type escape sequence to abort.
Sending 5, 100-byte ICMP Echos to 10.1.2.10, timeout is 2 seconds:
!!!!!
Success rate is 100 percent (5/5), round-trip min/avg/max = 1/1/2 ms
PC1#
```

We have verified the problem as described by Marjorie. During the verification, we discovered/verified that the SRV server in the distribution center is up and is indeed reachable from PC1 through HQ2. If the HQ1 is the active gateway for the PCs, however, SRV becomes unreachable.

Gathering Information

Because we discovered that the SRV server is up and the connection between the headquarters and the distribution center is operational, we can start by focusing on HQ1's routing table and essentially take a shoot-from-the-hip approach. As shown in Example 10-25, HQ1 does not have a route to the SRV server's address 10.1.2.10 in its routing table, but HQ2 does. In the same example you can see the output of **show ospfv3 neighbor** command on the HQ2 router displaying 209.165.201.1 (DST router) as the only OSPF neighbor. We need to find out why HQ2 and HQ1 do not have an OSPF neighbor relationship.

Example 10-25 *Gathering Information: Inspect HQ1's Routing Table*

```
HQ1# show ip route 10.1.2.10
% Subnet not in table
HQ1#



HQ2# show ip route 10.1.2.10
Routing entry for 10.1.2.0/24
  Known via "ospfv3 1", distance 110, metric 20, type intra area
  Last update from 10.255.0.10 on Ethernet0/3, 00:07:54 ago
  Routing Descriptor Blocks:
  * 10.255.0.10, from 209.165.201.1, 00:07:54 ago, via Ethernet0/3
      Route metric is 20, traffic share count is 1
HQ2# show ospfv3 neighbor
```

```
          OSPFv3 1 address-family ipv4 (router-id 209.165.201.5)


Neighbor ID     Pri   State        Dead Time   Interface ID   Interface
209.165.201.1    1    FULL/BDR     00:00:31    5              Ethernet0/3


< ...output omitted... >
HQ2#
```

To shed some light on the lack of OSPF neighbor relation between HQ2 and HQ1 routers, we use the **debug ospfv3 ipv4 hello** command on the HQ2 router. As shown in Example 10-26, HQ2 continuously sends OSPFv3 Hello packets out of the Eth0/1 and Eth0/0.2 interfaces toward HQ1, but it is not receiving any Hello packets from the HQ1 router on those interfaces.

Example 10-26 *Gathering Information: Use **debug** to Gain Information on HQ2 and HQ1's OSPF Hello Activities*

```
HQ2# debug ospfv3 ipv4 hello
HQ2#
*Oct 22 18:41:24.898: OSPFv3-1-IPv4 HELLO Et0/0.2: Send hello to FF02::5 area 0 from
  FE80::A8BB:CCFF:FE00:EE00 interface ID 11
*Oct 22 18:41:25.157: OSPFv3-1-IPv4 HELLO Et0/1: Send hello to FF02::5 area 0 from
  FE80::A8BB:CCFF:FE00:EE10 interface ID 4
*Oct 22 18:41:25.715: OSPFv3-1-IPv4 HELLO Et0/0.100: Send hello to FF02::5 area 0
  from FE80::A8BB:CCFF:FE00:EE00 interface ID 13
HQ2#
*Oct 22 18:41:25.941: OSPFv3-1-IPv4 HELLO Et0/3: Rcv hello from 209.165.201.1 area 0
  from FE80::A8BB:CCFF:FE00:F220 interface ID 5
HQ2#
< ...output omitted... >
HQ2# no debug all
All possible debugging has been turned off
HQ2#
```

It is best to use the spot-the-differences technique and compare the OSPFv3 configuration on HQ1 and HQ2 routers. According to the output shown in Example 10-27, HQ1 does not have OSPFv3 for address family IPv4 enabled on the Eth0/0.2 and Eth0/1 interfaces; it only has OSPFv3 for address family IPv6 activated on those interfaces.

Example 10-27 *Gathering Information: Compare HQ1 and HQ2 Router's OSPFv3 Configurations (Spot-the-Differences)*

```
HQ1# show run | section interface
< ...output omitted... >
interface Ethernet0/0.2
 description HQ-SRV
```

```
 encapsulation dot1Q 2
 ip address 10.0.2.2 255.255.255.0
 ip nat inside
 ip virtual-reassembly in
 standby 2 ip 10.0.2.1
 standby 2 priority 110
 standby 2 preempt
 standby 2 track 1 decrement 20
 ipv6 address 2001:DB8:0:A002::2/64
 ipv6 enable
 ospfv3 1 ipv6 area 0
< ...output omitted... >
interface Ethernet0/1
 ip address 10.255.0.17 255.255.255.248
 ip nat inside
 ip virtual-reassembly in
 ipv6 address 2001:DB8:0:F::2/64
 ipv6 enable
 ospfv3 1 ipv6 area 0
< ...output omitted... >
HQ1#


HQ2# show run | section interface
< ...output omitted... >
interface Ethernet0/0
 no ip address
 ip nat inside
 ip virtual-reassembly in
interface Ethernet0/0.2
 description HQ-SRV
 encapsulation dot1Q 2
 ip address 10.0.2.3 255.255.255.0
 ip nat inside
 ip virtual-reassembly in
 standby 2 ip 10.0.2.1
 standby 2 priority 101
 standby 2 preempt
 ipv6 address 2001:DB8:0:A002::3/64
 ipv6 enable
 ospfv3 1 ipv6 area 0
 ospfv3 1 ipv4 area 0
< ...output omitted... >
interface Ethernet0/1
 ip address 10.255.0.18 255.255.255.248
```

```
ip nat inside
ip virtual-reassembly in
ipv6 address 2001:DB8:0:F::1/64
ipv6 enable
ospfv3 1 ipv6 area 0
ospfv3 1 ipv4 area 0
< ...output omitted... >
HQ2#
```

Analyzing Information

Based on the gathered information, we can conclude that because HQ1 does not have OSPFv3 activated for address family IPv4 on interfaces Eth0/0.2 and Eth0/1, HQ1 and HQ2 have not formed neighbor adjacency on those links for the IPv4 address family. Consequently, HQ1 has no route to the distribution center network where the SRV server resides.

Proposing and Testing a Hypothesis

We can now propose that on the HQ1 router OSPFv3 needs to be activated for address family IPv4 on the Eth0/0.2 and Eth0/1 interfaces. Example 10-28 shows us configuring the HQ1 accordingly. We also brought the serial interface up (**no shutdown**) so that HQ1 becomes the active HSRP gateway again. Example 10-28 also shows that HQ1 and HQ2 have now formed OSPFv3 adjacency for IPv4.

Example 10-28 *Testing the Hypothesis: Activate OSPFv3 for IPv4 Address Family on HQ1's Eth0/0.2 and Eth0/1 Interfaces*

```
HQ1# conf term
Enter configuration commands, one per line.  End with CNTL/Z.
HQ1(config)# int eth 0/0.2
HQ1(config-subif)# ospfv3 1 ipv4 area 0
*Oct 22 20:09:59.058: %OSPFv3-5-ADJCHG: Process 1, IPv4, Nbr 209.165.201.5 on
  Ethernet0/0.2 from LOADING to FULL, Loading Done
HQ1(config-subif)# exit
HQ1(config)# int eth 0/1
HQ1(config-if)# ospfv3 1 ipv4 area 0
*Oct 22 20:11:21.525: %OSPFv3-5-ADJCHG: Process 1, IPv4, Nbr 209.165.201.5 on
  Ethernet0/1 from LOADING to FULL, Loading Done
HQ1(config-if)# exit
HQ1(config)# int ser 1/0
HQ1(config-if)# no shut
HQ1(config-if)# end
HQ1# write
Building configuration...
[OK]
```

```
HQ1#
*Oct 22 20:11:38.340: %SYS-5-CONFIG_I: Configured from console by console
*Oct 22 20:11:38.427: %LINK-3-UPDOWN: Interface Serial1/0, changed state to up
*Oct 22 20:11:38.427: %TRACKING-5-STATE: 1 interface Se1/0 line-protocol Down->Up
*Oct 22 20:11:39.428: %LINEPROTO-5-UPDOWN: Line protocol on Interface Serial1/0,
changed state to up
*Oct 22 20:11:39.861: %HSRP-5-STATECHANGE: Ethernet0/0.100 Grp 100 state Standby ->
  Active
*Oct 22 20:11:40.391: %HSRP-5-STATECHANGE: Ethernet0/0.10 Grp 10 state Standby ->
  Active
*Oct 22 20:11:41.099: %HSRP-5-STATECHANGE: Ethernet0/0.2 Grp 2 state Standby ->
  Active
*Oct 22 20:11:53.210: %BGP-5-ADJCHANGE: neighbor 209.165.200.6 Up
HQ1# show ospfv3 neighbor


          OSPFv3 1 address-family ipv4 (router-id 209.165.200.5)


Neighbor ID     Pri    State           Dead Time   Interface ID     Interface
209.165.201.5    1     FULL/DR         00:00:38    4                Ethernet0/1
209.165.201.5    1     FULL/DR         00:00:35    11               Ethernet0/0.2
< ...output omitted... >
HQ1#
*Oct 22 20:12:01.419: %BGP-5-ADJCHANGE: neighbor 2001:DB8:0:11B::1 Up
HQ1#
```

Solving the Problem

We must now check whether PC1 can reach the SRV server at the distribution center while HQ1 is the active HSRP gateway. Example 10-29 shows that PC1's ping attempt to SRV is now 100 percent successful. The problem is solved.

Example 10-29 *Solving the Problem: PC1 Can Now Ping the SRV Server*

```
PC1>ping 10.1.2.10
Type escape sequence to abort.
Sending 5, 100-byte ICMP Echos to 10.1.2.10, timeout is 2 seconds:
!!!!!
Success rate is 100 percent (5/5), round-trip min/avg/max = 1/1/2 ms
PC1>
```

We must now document our work and inform Marjorie that this problem is solved.

Troubleshooting the OSPFv3 Address Families Feature

OSPFv3 is a link-state routing protocol originally developed for IPv6 routing only. OSPFv2 can only handle IPv4 unicast routing. With the introduction of address families within OSPFv3, this protocol now supports routing for the IPv4 unicast address family as well. The "address family" feature maps an address family to a separate OSPFv3 instance, using the Instance ID field in the packet header. Each OSPFv3 instance maintains its own adjacencies, link-state database, and shortest path computation.

OSPFv3 runs on IPv6 and it uses IPv6 link-local addresses as the source of Hello packets and next-hop calculations. To use the IPv4 unicast address family in OSPFv3, you must enable IPv6 on a link, but the link may not be participating in IPv6 unicast routing. OSPFv3 makes use of IPsec Authentication Header (AH) and therefore has a broader range of supported authentication algorithms (message digest 5 [MD5] authentication and Secure Hash [SHA]) than OSPFv2. OSPFv3 can also use IPsec Encapsulating Security Payload (ESP) for encryption purposes.

The following commands are useful for troubleshooting OSPFv3:

- **show ip route ospfv3:** Use this command to list the OSPFv3 entries in the IPv4 routing table.

- **show ipv6 route ospf:** Use this command to list the OSPFv3 entries in the IPv6 routing table.

- **show running-config | section router ospfv3:** Use this command to see the OSPFv3 configuration section of the running configuration.

- **show running-config | section interface:** Use this command to see the interface configuration section of the running configuration.

- **show ospfv3:** Use this command to display general information about the OSPFv3 routing process.

- **show ospfv3 interface:** Use this command to gather detailed information about interfaces where OSPFv3 has been activated.

- **show ospfv3 neighbor:** Use this command to gather information about OSPFv3 neighbors.

- **debug ospfv3 events:** Use this debug to gather live information about OSPFv3 events.

Troubleshooting OSPFv3 Authentication

Marjorie has informed us that there is an OSPF authentication problem between HQ1 and BR routers at RADULKO's network. She wants the OSPF neighbor relation (adjacency) between the HQ1 and BR routers restored.

Verifying the Problem

To verify this problem, we log in to the HQ1 router and use the **show ospfv3 neighbor** command to check the status of HQ1's OSPFv3 neighbors. HQ1 must have HQ2 and BR as OSPFv3 neighbors under both IPv4 and IPv6 address families. As the output shown in Example 10-30 reveals, HQ2 (209.165.201.5) is currently the only OSPFv3 neighbor for

HQ1. Because the BR router is not shown in the list of neighbors, there is definitely a culprit preventing HQ1 and BR routers to form OSPFv3 adjacency. However, we need to gather information and find out whether the root of the problem, as Marjorie has indicated, is indeed an OSPFv3 authentication error.

Example 10-30 *Verifying the Problem: Display the List of HQ1's OSPFv3 Neighbors*

```
*Oct 23 01:00:42.398: %CRYPTO-4-RECVD_PKT_MAC_ERR: decrypt: mac verify failed for
  connection id=1 spi=00000000 seqno=0000001F
HQ1# show ospfv3 neighbor


        OSPFv3 1 address-family ipv4 (router-id 209.165.200.5)


Neighbor ID     Pri   State         Dead Time    Interface ID    Interface
209.165.201.5    1    FULL/DR       00:00:34     4               Ethernet0/1
209.165.201.5    1    FULL/DR       00:00:33     11              Ethernet0/0.2
< ...output omitted... >
HQ1#
```

Gathering Information

Based on RADULKO's network diagram, the Ethernet 0/2 interface of the HQ1 router connects to the Ethernet 0/1 interface of the BR (branch) router. We can use the spot-the-differences technique and compare the OSPFv3 authentication configuration on HQ1's Ethernet 0/2 and BR's Ethernet 0/1 interfaces. Example 10-31 shows the output of **show running-config** for both of these routers.

Example 10-31 *Gathering Information: Compare OSPFv3 Authentication Configuration on HQ1 and BR Routers Adjacent Interfaces*

```
HQ1# show running-config interface eth 0/2
Building configuration...
Current configuration : 265 bytes
!
interface Ethernet0/2
 ip address 10.255.0.1 255.255.255.248
 ip nat inside
 ip virtual-reassembly in
 ipv6 enable
 ipv6 eigrp 100
 ospfv3 authentication ipsec spi 500 sha1 123456789A123456789B123456789C123456789D
 ospfv3 1 ipv4 area 0
 ospfv3 1 ipv6 area 0
end
HQ1#
```

```
BR# show run interface eth 0/1
Building configuration...

Current configuration : 199 bytes
!
interface Ethernet0/1
 ip address 10.255.0.2 255.255.255.248
 ipv6 enable
 ospfv3 authentication ipsec spi 500 md5 123456789A123456789B123456789C12
 ospfv3 1 ipv4 area 0
 ospfv3 1 ipv6 area 0
end

BR#
```

Analyzing Information

Based on the information gathered (shown in Example 10-31), HQ1's Ethernet 0/2 inter-face has OSPFv3 authentication configured using SHA1, and BR's Ethernet 0/1 interface has OSPFv3 authentication configured using MD5. This explains why authentication between these routers would fail and, consequently, why OSPFv3 adjacency between them would not form.

Proposing and Testing a Hypothesis

We propose to change the BR router's Ethernet 0/1 interface OSPFv3 authentication to use SHA1 with the same SPI (Security Parameter Index) and preshared key as its HQ1 neighbor. Example 10-32 shows our work on the BR router. The example also shows the console log messages indicating new OSPFv3 neighbor adjacency going into Full state.

Example 10-32 *Proposing a Hypothesis: Configure BR to Use SHA1 for OSPFv3 Authentication*

```
BR# conf term
Enter configuration commands, one per line.  End with CNTL/Z.
BR(config)# inter eth 0/1
BR(config-if)# $tion ipsec spi 500 md5 123456789A123456789B123456789C12
BR(config-if)# $n ipsec spi 500 sha1 123456789A123456789B123456789C123456789D
BR(config-if)# end
BR# wr
Building configuration...
[OK]
BR#
*Oct 23 01:09:07.421: %OSPFv3-5-ADJCHG: Process 1, IPv6, Nbr 10.255.0.2 on
  Ethernet0/2 from LOADING to FULL, Loading Done
BR#
```

Solving the Problem

To confirm that the neighbor relationship between the BR and HQ1 routers is restored successfully, we use the **show ospfv3 neighbor** command on the HQ1 router. As Example 10-33 shows, HQ1 now has both HQ2 (209.165.201.5) and BR (10.255.0.2) as neighbors in Full state. The problem is solved.

Example 10-33   *Solving the Problem: Display the List of HQ1's OSPFv3 Neighbors*

```
HQ1# show ospfv3 neighbor


          OSPFv3 1 address-family ipv4 (router-id 209.165.200.5)


Neighbor ID     Pri   State        Dead Time   Interface ID   Interface
10.255.0.2       1    FULL/BDR     00:00:33    4              Ethernet0/2
209.165.201.5    1    FULL/DR      00:00:35    4              Ethernet0/1
209.165.201.5    1    FULL/DR      00:00:34    11             Ethernet0/0.2


          OSPFv3 1 address-family ipv6 (router-id 209.165.200.5)


Neighbor ID     Pri   State        Dead Time   Interface ID   Interface
10.255.0.2       1    FULL/BDR     00:00:34    4              Ethernet0/2
209.165.201.5    1    FULL/DR      00:00:36    4              Ethernet0/1
209.165.201.5    1    FULL/DR      00:00:32    13             Ethernet0/0.100
209.165.201.5    1    FULL/DR      00:00:31    12             Ethernet0/0.10
209.165.201.5    1    FULL/DR      00:00:37    11             Ethernet0/0.2
HQ1#
```

We must now document our work and inform Marjorie that this problem is solved.

RADULKO Transport Trouble Ticket 4

Marjorie, the network engineer at RADULKO Transport, has contacted us with some good news. She claims that the migration projects have gone well and that the network at RADULKO is in good shape. She has just two problems left to resolve. Marjorie has given us the following problem descriptions. She wants us to solve these problems and inform her of the outcome:

- It has recently been noticed that the DST router has learned several external routes through OSPF. The learned prefixes are global/public addresses and do not belong to RADULKO Transport's address space. These routes should not be present in DST's routing table.

- PC1 and PC2 cannot access the IPv6 Internet. It has recently been decided that these PCs should be auto-configured based on stateless address auto configuration (SLAAC). However, SLAAC is not working for these PCs. There are doubts about whether this problem is related to SLAAC, HSRP, or another matter.

Troubleshooting Undesired External OSPF Routes in DST's Routing Table

Marjorie has stated that they, at RADULKO Transport, have recently noticed some external OSPF routes in the distribution center (DST) router's routing table. These routes are global/public addresses; they do not belong to RADULKO Transport, and should not be in DST router's table.

Verifying and Defining the Problem

To verify the problem, we access the DST router and display its IP routing table. Example 10-34 shows that the DST router has many prefixes with O E2 in front of them. These routes are the undesired external OSPF routes that Marjorie has reported. The problem is confirmed. We need to find out where these routes are leaking from and stop them.

Example 10-34   *Verifying the Problem: The DST Router Has Many Undesired External OSPF Routes*

```
DST# show ip route
Codes: L - local, C - connected, S - static, R - RIP, M - mobile, B - BGP
       D - EIGRP, EX - EIGRP external, O - OSPF, IA - OSPF inter area
       N1 - OSPF NSSA external type 1, N2 - OSPF NSSA external type 2
       E1 - OSPF external type 1, E2 - OSPF external type 2
       i - IS-IS, su - IS-IS summary, L1 - IS-IS level-1, L2 - IS-IS level-2
       ia - IS-IS inter area, * - candidate default, U - per-user static route
       o - ODR, P - periodic downloaded static route, H - NHRP, l - LISP
       + - replicated route, % - next hop override

Gateway of last resort is 209.165.201.2 to network 0.0.0.0

S*    0.0.0.0/0 [1/0] via 209.165.201.2
      10.0.0.0/8 is variably subnetted, 14 subnets, 3 masks
O        10.0.2.0/24 [110/20] via 10.255.0.9, 00:01:18, Ethernet0/2
O        10.0.10.0/24 [110/20] via 10.255.0.9, 00:01:18, Ethernet0/2
O        10.0.100.0/24 [110/20] via 10.255.0.9, 00:01:18, Ethernet0/2
C        10.1.2.0/24 is directly connected, Ethernet0/0.2
L        10.1.2.1/32 is directly connected, Ethernet0/0.2
C        10.1.10.0/24 is directly connected, Ethernet0/0.10
L        10.1.10.1/32 is directly connected, Ethernet0/0.10
C        10.1.100.0/24 is directly connected, Ethernet0/0.100
L        10.1.100.1/32 is directly connected, Ethernet0/0.100
O        10.2.10.0/24 [110/40] via 10.255.0.9, 00:01:18, Ethernet0/2
O        10.255.0.0/29 [110/30] via 10.255.0.9, 00:01:18, Ethernet0/2
C        10.255.0.8/29 is directly connected, Ethernet0/2
L        10.255.0.10/32 is directly connected, Ethernet0/2
```

```
O          10.255.0.16/29 [110/20] via 10.255.0.9, 00:01:18, Ethernet0/2
         209.165.200.0/32 is subnetted, 3 subnets
O E2      209.165.200.17 [110/1] via 10.255.0.9, 00:01:13, Ethernet0/2
O E2      209.165.200.18 [110/1] via 10.255.0.9, 00:01:13, Ethernet0/2
O E2      209.165.200.101 [110/1] via 10.255.0.9, 00:00:57, Ethernet0/2
         209.165.201.0/24 is variably subnetted, 5 subnets, 2 masks
C         209.165.201.0/30 is directly connected, Ethernet0/1
L         209.165.201.1/32 is directly connected, Ethernet0/1
O         209.165.201.4/30 [110/20] via 10.255.0.9, 00:01:18, Ethernet0/2
O E2      209.165.201.102/32 [110/1] via 10.255.0.9, 00:00:52, Ethernet0/2
O E2      209.165.201.133/32 [110/1] via 10.255.0.9, 00:00:57, Ethernet0/2
DST#
```

Gathering Information

As per RADULKO's network diagram, the only OSPF neighbor that the DST router must have is the HQ2 router. In Example 10-35, the output of the **show ospfv3 neighbor** command on the DST router confirms that DST has only one neighbor (209.165.201.5), the HQ2 router.

Example 10-35 *Gathering Information: Verify the List of DST's OSPF Neighbors*

```
DST# show ospfv3 neighbor

        OSPFv3 1 address-family ipv4 (router-id 209.165.201.1)

Neighbor ID     Pri   State           Dead Time   Interface ID   Interface
209.165.201.5    1    FULL/DR         00:00:39    6              Ethernet0/2

        OSPFv3 1 address-family ipv6 (router-id 209.165.201.1)

Neighbor ID     Pri   State           Dead Time   Interface ID   Interface
209.165.201.5    1    FULL/DR         00:00:38    6              Ethernet0/2
DST#
```

We can now check the content of the OSPFv3 database on the DST router to find out the advertiser router ID for the external OSPF (LSA type 5) routes. Example 10-36 shows the output of the **show ospfv3 database** command. As you can see in the "Type-5 AS External Link States" section, two router IDs, 209.165.200.5 and 209.165.201.5, are shown to be the originators (Autonomous System Border Routers [ASBRs]) of the external routes. These IDs belong to the HQ1 and HQ2 routers.

Example 10-36 *Gathering Information: Display DST Router's OSPFv3 Database*

```
DST# show ospfv3 database


          OSPFv3 1 address-family ipv4 (router-id 209.165.201.1)


              Router Link States (Area 0)


ADV Router         Age         Seq#         Fragment ID  Link count  Bits
   10.255.0.2      262         0x80000002   0             1          None
   209.165.200.5   225         0x80000003   0             2          E
   209.165.201.1   218         0x80000002   0             1          None
   209.165.201.5   219         0x80000003   0             2          E


< ...output omitted... >


              Type-5 AS External Link States


ADV Router         Age         Seq#         Prefix
   209.165.200.5   267         0x80000001   209.165.200.17/32
   209.165.200.5   195         0x80000001   0.0.0.0/0
   209.165.200.5   195         0x80000001   209.165.200.101/32
   209.165.200.5   195         0x80000001   209.165.201.133/32
   209.165.201.5   265         0x80000001   209.165.200.18/32
   209.165.201.5   194         0x80000001   0.0.0.0/0
   209.165.201.5   194         0x80000001   209.165.201.0/30
   209.165.201.5   194         0x80000001   209.165.201.102/32
   209.165.201.5   194         0x80000001   209.165.201.133/32


< ...output omitted... >


DST#
```

Analyzing Information

We can now check the OSPFv3 configuration on the HQ1 and HQ2 routers to find
the source of the external OSPF routes. Example 10-37 shows the OSPFv3 section of
the running configuration on these routers. As you can see, there is a **redistribute bgp
65000** command within the address family IPv4 unicast section. This is clearly a mistake.
The BGP table with the Internet routes can be as large as approximately 400,000 entries.
Redistributing these routes into OSPF is fatal for OSPF, unless it is controlled and filtered with a prefix list or route map. Generally speaking, BGP routes are not redistributed into the IGP (intra-autonomous system) routing protocols.

Example 10-37 *Analyzing Information: Examine the OSPFv3 Configuration on the HQ1 and HQ2 Routers*

```
HQ1# show run | section router ospfv3
router ospfv3 1
 area 0 authentication ipsec spi 500 sha1 123456789A123456789B123456789C123456789D
 !
 address-family ipv4 unicast
  redistribute bgp 65000
  default-information originate
 exit-address-family
 !
 address-family ipv6 unicast
  default-information originate
 exit-address-family
HQ1#


HQ2# show run | section router ospfv3
router ospfv3 1
 area 0 authentication ipsec spi 500 sha1 123456789A123456789B123456789C123456789D
 !
 address-family ipv4 unicast
  redistribute bgp 65000
  default-information originate
 exit-address-family
 !
 address-family ipv6 unicast
  default-information originate
 exit-address-family
HQ2#
```

Proposing and Testing a Hypothesis

We propose to remove the **redistribute bgp 65000** command from within the address family IPv4 unicast section of HQ1 and HQ2 router configurations. Next, we must check the OSPF databases of HQ1 and HQ2 routers to make sure that those undesired external OSPF routes are gone. Example 10-38 shows that after we remove the **redistribution** statements, HQ1 and HQ2 databases no longer have those external routes injected into the OSPF database. The only external link-state advertisement (LSA) routes remaining are the default (0.0.0.0/0) routes that are correctly injected into the OSPF database by the **default-information originate** command.

Example 10-38   *Proposing and Testing a Hypothesis: Remove the* **redistribute bgp** *6500 Command from HQ1 and HQ2 Router Configurations*

```
HQ1# conf term
Enter configuration commands, one per line.  End with CNTL/Z.
HQ1(config)# router ospfv3 1
HQ1(config-router)# address-family ipv4 unicast
HQ1(config-router-af)# no redistribute bgp 65000
HQ1(config-router-af)# end
HQ1# wr
Building configuration...
[OK]
HQ1#


HQ2# conf term
Enter configuration commands, one per line.  End with CNTL/Z.
HQ2(config)# router ospfv3 1
HQ2(config-router)# address-family ipv4 unicast
HQ2(config-router-af)# no redistribute bgp 65000
HQ2(config-router-af)# end
HQ2# wr
Building configuration...
[OK]
HQ2#



HQ1# show ospfv3 database
        OSPFv3 1 address-family ipv4 (router-id 209.165.200.5)
< ...output omitted... >
                  Type-5 AS External Link States
ADV Router      Age         Seq#          Prefix
 209.165.200.5  544         0x80000002    0.0.0.0/0
 209.165.201.5  570         0x80000002    0.0.0.0/0
< ...output omitted... >
HQ1#


HQ2# show ospfv3 database
        OSPFv3 1 address-family ipv4 (router-id 209.165.201.5)
< ...output omitted... >
                  Type-5 AS External Link States
ADV Router      Age         Seq#          Prefix
 209.165.200.5  792         0x80000002    0.0.0.0/0
 209.165.201.5  816         0x80000002    0.0.0.0/0
< ...output omitted... >
HQ2#
```

Solving the Problem

We can now check the routing table on the DST router to make sure the undesired external OSPF routes are no longer present. Example 10-39 displays the output of the **show ip route** command on the DST router. As you can see, the DST router's IP routing table has no OSPF external (O E2) routes left. The problem is solved.

Example 10-39 *Solving the Problem: The DST Router No Longer Receives External OSPF Routes from HQ1 and HQ2 Routers*

```
DST# show ip route
Codes: L - local, C - connected, S - static, R - RIP, M - mobile, B - BGP
       D - EIGRP, EX - EIGRP external, O - OSPF, IA - OSPF inter area
       N1 - OSPF NSSA external type 1, N2 - OSPF NSSA external type 2
       E1 - OSPF external type 1, E2 - OSPF external type 2
       i - IS-IS, su - IS-IS summary, L1 - IS-IS level-1, L2 - IS-IS level-2
       ia - IS-IS inter area, * - candidate default, U - per-user static route
       o - ODR, P - periodic downloaded static route, H - NHRP, l - LISP
       + - replicated route, % - next hop override

Gateway of last resort is 209.165.201.2 to network 0.0.0.0

S*     0.0.0.0/0 [1/0] via 209.165.201.2
       10.0.0.0/8 is variably subnetted, 14 subnets, 3 masks
O         10.0.2.0/24 [110/20] via 10.255.0.9, 00:48:47, Ethernet0/2
O         10.0.10.0/24 [110/20] via 10.255.0.9, 00:48:47, Ethernet0/2
O         10.0.100.0/24 [110/20] via 10.255.0.9, 00:48:47, Ethernet0/2
C         10.1.2.0/24 is directly connected, Ethernet0/0.2
L         10.1.2.1/32 is directly connected, Ethernet0/0.2
C         10.1.10.0/24 is directly connected, Ethernet0/0.10
L         10.1.10.1/32 is directly connected, Ethernet0/0.10
C         10.1.100.0/24 is directly connected, Ethernet0/0.100
L         10.1.100.1/32 is directly connected, Ethernet0/0.100
O         10.2.10.0/24 [110/40] via 10.255.0.9, 00:48:47, Ethernet0/2
O         10.255.0.0/29 [110/30] via 10.255.0.9, 00:48:47, Ethernet0/2
C         10.255.0.8/29 is directly connected, Ethernet0/2
L         10.255.0.10/32 is directly connected, Ethernet0/2
O         10.255.0.16/29 [110/20] via 10.255.0.9, 00:48:47, Ethernet0/2
       209.165.201.0/24 is variably subnetted, 3 subnets, 2 masks
C         209.165.201.0/30 is directly connected, Ethernet0/1
L         209.165.201.1/32 is directly connected, Ethernet0/1
O         209.165.201.4/30 [110/20] via 10.255.0.9, 00:48:47, Ethernet0/2
DST#
```

We must now document our work and notify Marjorie that this problem is solved.

Troubleshooting PCs IPv6 Internet Access

According to Marjorie, it has been decided recently that PC1 and PC2 should be getting their IPv6 address through SLAAC. PC1 and PC2 cannot connect to the IPv6 Internet. There are doubts about whether this problem is related to SLAAC, HSRP, or another matter.

Verifying the Problem

To verify the problem, we ping the IPv6 Internet reachability test address (2001:DB8:0:D::100). As shown in Example 10-40, the ping from both PC1 and PC2 fails. The problem is verified.

Example 10-40 *Verifying the Problem: PC1 and PC2 Cannot Reach the IPv6 Internet*

```
PC1# ping 2001:DB8:0:D::100
Type escape sequence to abort.
Sending 5, 100-byte ICMP Echos to 2001:DB8:0:D::100, timeout is 2 seconds:
NNNNN
Success rate is 0 percent (0/5)
PC1#


PC2# ping 2001:DB8:0:D::100
Type escape sequence to abort.
Sending 5, 100-byte ICMP Echos to 2001:DB8:0:D::100, timeout is 2 seconds:
NNNNN
Success rate is 0 percent (0/5)
PC2#
```

Gathering Information

We will now take a bottom-up troubleshooting approach and start information gathering by checking the status of the Ethernet interfaces on PC1 and PC2. Example 10-41 shows the output; this example shows that the interfaces are up, but they only have IPv6 link-local addresses.

Example 10-41 *Gathering Information: Check the Interface Status on the PCs*

```
PC1# show ipv6 interface brief
Ethernet0/0            [up/up]
    FE80::A8BB:CCFF:FE00:5700
< ...output omitted... >
PC1#



PC2# show ipv6 interface brief
```

```
Ethernet0/0              [up/up]
    FE80::A8BB:CCFF:FE00:5B00
< ...output omitted... >
PC2#
```

Because we have been told that, according to the new RADULKO policy, PC1 and PC2 are supposed to be getting their IPv6 address using SLAAC, it is best to inspect the configuration of the Ethernet interfaces on PC1 and PC2. Example 10-42 shows that PC1 and PC2 are correctly configured with the **ipv6 address autoconfig** command. This means that these PCs will accept the prefix advertised by the local routers (HQ1 and HQ2) and auto-generate the host portion of their address according to the EUI-64 format.

Example 10-42 *Gathering Information: Inspect the PCs' Interface Configuration*

```
PC1# show running-config interface ethernet 0/0
Building configuration...
Current configuration : 103 bytes
!
interface Ethernet0/0
 no ip route-cache
 ipv6 address autoconfig
 ipv6 enable
end
PC1#


PC2# show running-config interface ethernet 0/0
Building configuration...
Current configuration : 103 bytes
!
interface Ethernet0/0
no ip route-cache
 ipv6 address autoconfig
 ipv6 enable
end
PC2#
```

Now that we know the PCs are configured properly, we can check the configuration of Ethernet 0/0.10 subinterfaces on routers HQ1 and HQ2. According to RADULKO's documentation, the Ethernet 0/0.10 subinterfaces on these routers are configured for VLAN 10 where the PCs are located. Example 10-43 shows the configuration of these subinterfaces; as you can see, these subinterfaces are configured with a /69 subnet mask on both routers.

Example 10-43   *Gathering Information: Inspect the Configuration of Ethernet 0/0.10 Subinterfaces on HQ Routers*

```
HQ1# show running-config interface ethernet 0/0.10
Building configuration...
Current configuration : 267 bytes
!
interface Ethernet0/0.10
 description HQ-PC
 encapsulation dot1Q 10
 ip address 10.0.10.2 255.255.255.0
 ip nat inside
 ip virtual-reassembly in
 ipv6 address 2001:DB8:0:A010::2/69
 ipv6 enable
 ospfv3 1 ipv6 area 0
 vrrp 10 ip 10.0.10.1
 vrrp 10 priority 110
end
HQ1#


HQ2# show running-config interface ethernet 0/0.10
Building configuration...
Current configuration : 289 bytes
!
interface Ethernet0/0.10
 description HQ-PC
 encapsulation dot1Q 10
 ip address 10.0.10.3 255.255.255.0
 ip nat inside
 ip virtual-reassembly in
 ipv6 address 2001:DB8:0:A010::3/69
 ipv6 enable
 ospfv3 1 ipv6 area 0
 ospfv3 1 ipv4 area 0
 vrrp 10 ip 10.0.10.1
 vrrp 10 priority 101
end
HQ2#
```

Analyzing Information

According to the gathered information, the Ethernet 0/0.10 subinterfaces on routers HQ1 and HQ2 have IPv6 addresses with /69 subnet masks. This means that the neighbor discovery router advertisements sent by these routers announce the local prefix with a /69 subnet mask. However, the /69 subnet mask for the local prefix makes it impossible for the local PCs to do stateless address autoconfiguration, because SLAAC requires a /64 subnet-mask. The /64 subnet-mask allows the PCs to autogenerate the host portion of their address based on the EUI-64 format.

Proposing and Testing a Hypothesis

We propose to fix the subnet mask configuration error on the Ethernet 0/0.10 subinterfaces of HQ1 and HQ2 routers. Example 10-44 shows us correcting the subnet masks to /64. Following this correction, we check the status of Ethernet interfaces (PC1 and PC2), and as shown in Example 10-44, these PC interfaces were able to do SLAAC based on the new neighbor discovery router advertisements that announces a /64 subnet-mask for the local network IPv6 prefix.

Example 10-44   *Proposing a Hypothesis: Correct Subnet Masks to /64 for SLAAC*

```
HQ1# conf term
Enter configuration commands, one per line.  End with CNTL/Z.
HQ1(config)# interface Ethernet0/0.10
HQ1(config-subif)# no ipv6 address 2001:DB8:0:A010::2/69
HQ1(config-subif)# ipv6 address 2001:DB8:0:A010::2/64
HQ1(config-subif)# end
HQ1# wr
Building configuration...
[OK]
*Oct 24 01:56:53.365: %SYS-5-CONFIG_I: Configured from console by console
HQ1#


HQ2# conf term
Enter configuration commands, one per line.  End with CNTL/Z.
HQ2(config)# interface Ethernet0/0.10
HQ2(config-subif)# no ipv6 address 2001:DB8:0:A010::3/69
HQ2(config-subif)# ipv6 address 2001:DB8:0:A010::3/64
HQ2(config-subif)# end
HQ2# wr
Building configuration...
[OK]
HQ2#
*Oct 24 01:59:15.788: %SYS-5-CONFIG_I: Configured from console by console
HQ2#


PC1# show ipv6 interface brief
Ethernet0/0              [up/up]
```

```
      FE80::A8BB:CCFF:FE00:5700
      2001:DB8:0:A010:A8BB:CCFF:FE00:5700
PC1#



PC2# show ipv6 interface brief
Ethernet0/0              [up/up]
      FE80::A8BB:CCFF:FE00:5B00
      2001:DB8:0:A010:A8BB:CCFF:FE00:5B00
PC2#
```

Solving the Problem

Now we test IPv6 Internet reachability from PC1 and PC2. As shown in Example 10-45, PC1 and PC2 can both ping the IPv6 Internet reachability test address (2001:DB8:0:D::100) now. The problem is solved.

Example 10-45 *Solving the Problem: PC1 and PC2 Both Have IPv6 Internet Access*

```
PC1# ping 2001:DB8:0:D::100
Type escape sequence to abort.
Sending 5, 100-byte ICMP Echos to 2001:DB8:0:D::100, timeout is 2 seconds:
!!!!!
Success rate is 100 percent (5/5), round-trip min/avg/max = 1/4/18 ms
PC1#



PC2# ping 2001:DB8:0:D::100
Type escape sequence to abort.
Sending 5, 100-byte ICMP Echos to 2001:DB8:0:D::100, timeout is 2 seconds:
!!!!!
Success rate is 100 percent (5/5), round-trip min/avg/max = 1/4/19 ms
PC2#
```

We must now document our work and notify Marjorie that the last reported RADULKO network problem is now solved.

Summary

This chapter presented four troubleshooting tickets at RADULKO Transport, a fictitious company, based on the topology shown in Figure 10-2.

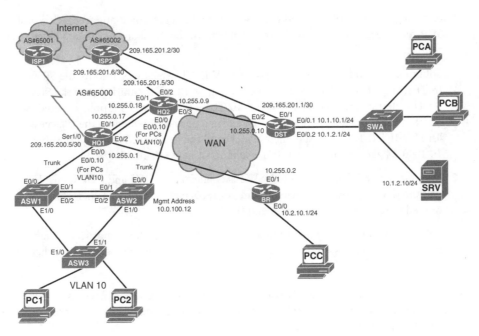

Figure 10-2 *RADULKO Transport Ltd. Network Diagram*

Trouble Ticket 1: Marjorie, the network engineer at RADULKO, contacted us about three network issues on her hands and asked us to help her solve them. The following is the list of those issues and the solutions we offered:

1. RADULKO Transport's network had a Layer 2 loop problem. Marjorie isolated the problem to headquarter's SW3 switch and disconnected the offending cabling. The problem was caused when an employee wanted to have more ports at his desk connected a small switch to the SW3 switch. Marjorie wanted us to provide her with a solution that does not allow this to happen again.

   Solution: We discovered that the **spanning-tree bpdufilter enable** command must be removed from SW3's access ports Ethernet 2/0 through Ethernet 2/3, because this command takes precedence over the BPDU Guard feature. The BPDU Guard feature is good to prevent people from connecting unauthorized switches to the network.

2. At a RADULKO remote location, the distribution center, special servers regularly update their databases through the Internet. After the company bought a firewall and installed it into the corporate headquarters, the policy was to route all user traffic through the headquarters before transmitting to the Internet. However, it turned out that the only way to have functional updates for servers at the distribution center was to route server traffic directly to the Internet. As a result, Marjorie configured policy-based routing on the DST router so that all PC traffic destined for the Internet would be sent to the headquarters and so that all server-generated traffic destined for the Internet would be sent to the Internet directly. Marjorie contacted

us stating that her policy-based routing worked, but PCA could not access the local SRV server. She wanted us to fix this problem without breaking her policy-based routing.

Solution: We modified the IP access list SRV-INET, which was used by the SRV-INET-RM route map for policy-based routing, so that if the traffic from the SRV server is destined to internal networks (10.0.0.0), the traffic is not policy routed. We inserted a **deny** statement ahead of the existing **permit** statement in the IP access list SRV-INET. The **deny** statement matches all traffic sourced from the IP subnet 10.1.2.0/24 and destined to all of the subnets of network 10.0.0.0/8.

3. Marjorie noticed that even though SW2 is connected to SW3 and CDP is enabled on both devices, these two switches did not recognize each other as neighbors. She wanted us to look into this matter and fix it if possible.

Solution: We discovered that for SW2 and SW3 to see each other as CDP neighbors over their corresponding connection, CDP must be enabled on SW3's Ethernet 1/1 interface.

Trouble Ticket 2: Marjorie, the network engineer at RADULKO, contacted us to help her solve some recent network problems at work. The following is the list of those problems and the solutions we offered:

1. RADULKO's switch SW2 was stolen during the weekend. She found an old switch in storage and copied the saved configuration from the stolen switch to this switch. However, after she connected the new switch to the network, PC1 and PC2 (from VLAN 10) lost their network connectivity, VLAN 100 disappeared, and some unrecognized VLANs (33, 44, 87, 153) were created.

Solution: The switch that replaced the stolen switch had a higher VTP configuration revision number, so it caused VLANs 10 and 100 to be deleted and the unknown VLANs 33, 44, 87, and 153 to be created. To solve the problem, all we had to do was to add VLANs 10 and 100, and delete VLANs 33, 44, 87, and 153. Before a switch is added to a network, it should be put in transparent mode.

2. The branch router BR had no IPv6 connectivity to the rest of the network, and it could not reach the IPv6 Internet.

Solution: To solve this problem, all that was needed was to activate IPv6 EIGRP 1 on the Ethernet 0/2 interface of the HQ1 router. After doing so, HQ1 immediately formed EIGRP adjacency with the neighbor FE80::A8BB:CCFF:FE00:BB10 over the Ethernet 0/2 interface.

3. MP-BGP was working well on the HQ1 router, but the HQ2 router had no IPv6 session with ISP2's router.

Solution: The eBGP neighbor 2001:DB8:0:11C::1 (eBGP-ISP2) was not activated under the IPv6 address family, so all we needed to do was to activate this neighbor under the IPv6 address family.

Trouble Ticket 3: Because of a change in RADULKO Transport's network policy, they are no longer allowed to use proprietary protocols such as Cisco's EIGRP. Over the weekend, the network group, led by Marjorie, reconfigured the network and migrated to OSPF. They were successful in their migration project, but Marjorie contacted us about two problems that remained:

1. PC1 could not access the distribution center server (SRV) at the IP address 10.1.2.10. PC1 could only access this server if the HQ1 router at headquarters failed. HQ1 and HQ2 are the active and standby HSRP routers for the PCs in the headquarters. HQ1 tracks its serial interface, and if the line protocol on this interface goes down, HQ1 reduces its priority to allow HQ2 to preempt and become the active HSRP router.

   Solution: OSPFv3 on the HQ1 router had to be activated for address family IPv4 on the Eth0/0.2 and Eth0/1 interfaces.

2. OSPF authentication between HQ1 and BR routers was not working, and their adjacency was lost. OSPF neighbor relation (adjacency) between the HQ1 and BR routers had to be restored.

   Solution: Because the OSPF authentication was not consistent between the BR and HQ1 routers, we changed the BR router's Ethernet 0/1 interface OSPFv3 authentication to use SHA1 with the same SPI and preshared key as its HQ1 neighbor.

Trouble Ticket 4: Marjorie, the network engineer at RADULKO Transport, contacted us with some good news. She claimed that the migration projects have gone well and that the network at RADULKO was in good shape. She had just two problems left to resolve. The following are the problem descriptions that Marjorie provided and the solutions we offered:

1. The DST router had learned several external routes through OSPF. The learned prefixes were global/public addresses and did not belong to RADULKO Transport's address space and had to be removed from DST's routing table.

   Solution: We removed the **redistribute bgp 65000** command from within the address family IPv4 unicast section of HQ1 and HQ2 router configurations.

2. PC1 and PC2 were not able to access the IPv6 Internet. It was decided that these PCs should be autoconfigured based on SLAAC, but SLAAC was not working for these PCs.

   Solution: We changed the subnet mask configuration on the Ethernet 0/0.10 subinterfaces of HQ1 and HQ2 routers from /69 to /64. SLAAC can only work in a network with a /64 subnet mask.

Review Questions

1. If an interface is configured for PBR using the following route map, what next-hop IP address is used when forwarding IP traffic with the source address 10.1.2.10?

```
!
route-map CONTROL-POINT permit 10
  match ip address PRB1
  set ip next-hop 209.165.201.2
!
Extended IP access list PRB1
   10 deny ip 10.1.2.0 0.0.0.0 any
!
```

   a. The 209.165.201.2 IP address.
   b. The next hop will be determined by the routing table, as the result of matching the **route-map** statement number **10**.
   c. The packet will be dropped.
   d. The next hop will be dictated by the routing table, as a result of matching the implicit **deny route-map** statement at the end of the route map.

2. SW1 and SW2 switches have the PortFast feature enabled globally. Currently, their Ethernet 0/1 interfaces are configured as access ports. In the near future, the switches will be connected using these configured as trunk. What will happen to the PortFast status of those interfaces then?

   a. They will lose PortFast status after they are connected and start sending BPDUs.
   b. They will lose PortFast status the moment they are converted to trunk.
   c. They will keep their port status until BPDU Guard or BPDUFilter features are configured.
   d. None of the these answers is correct.

3. Which two features apply to MSTP?

   a. It groups a set of instances to a single VLAN.
   b. It can group a set of VLANs to a single spanning-tree instance.
   c. A failure in one instance can cause a failure in another instance.
   d. The total number of spanning-tree instances should match the number of redundant switch paths.
   e. It is fully backward compatible with other versions of STP.

4. Which switchport mode must be used to propagate VTP information?

   a. Access
   b. Trunk
   c. EtherChannel
   d. None of the above

5. How do you configure a specific interface for EIGRP in IPv6?

   a. You configure it in global configuration mode.
   b. It is configured under EIGRP configuration with the **network** command.
   c. It is configured in interface configuration mode.
   d. None of the above

6. Which command enables you to display the IPv6 BGP table?

   a. **show ip bgp**
   b. **show ipv6 bgp**
   c. **show bgp ipv6 unicast**
   d. **show bgp ipv6 summary**

7. How can you include an interface into an OSPFv3 process for IPv4 address family?

   a. Using the global **network** command.
   b. Using the **ospfv3** *process-id* **ipv4 area** *area-id* command on the interface, after first enabling IPv6 on it.
   c. Using the **ospfv3** *process-id* **ipv4 area** *area-id* command on the interface, after first disabling IPv6 on it.
   d. Using the global OSPFv3 configuration **interface ipv4 area** *area-id* command.

8. What can you conclude from the following output?

```
HQ1# show ospfv3 interface brief

Interface   PID   Area      AF     Cost    State
Et0/1       1     0         IPv4   10      BDR
Et0/2       1     0         IPv4   10      DR
Et0/2       1     0         IPv6   10      DR
Et0/3       1     0         IPv6   10      DR
```

   a. Ethernet 0/2 interface has both IPv4 and IPv6 enabled.
   b. Ethernet 0/1 interface has IPv6 disabled.
   c. The router has only one neighbor adjacency for both address families on the Ethernet 0/2 interface.
   d. Because all neighbors are in the same area, area 0, SPF recalculation in both address families will occur for every adjacency state change.
   e. Ethernet 0/3 interface must have IPv4 enabled because OSPFv3 runs over IPv4.

9. Which CLI commands will enable OSPFv3 authentication? (Choose two.)

   a. **ospfv3 message-digest-key 1 md5 c1sc0**
   b. **ospfv3 authentication ipsec spi 500 sha1 123456789A123456789B123456789C123456789D**
   c. **area 0 authentication ipsec spi 1000 md5 1234567890ABCDEF1234567890ABCDEF**
   d. **ospfv3 ipv4 authentication ipsec spi 500 md5 123456789A123456789B123456789C12**
   e. **ospfv3 ipv6 authentication ipsec spi 501 md5 A123456789A123456789B123456789C1**

10. Which LSA type is used to advertise external routes in OSPFv3?

    a. Type 1

    b. Type 2

    c. Type 3

    d. Type 4

    e. Type 5

11. Which IP address is used as a destination IP address for Hello messages when OSPFv3 is used to transfer IPv4 routes?

    a. 224.0.0.5

    b. 224.0.0.6

    c. FF02::5

    d. FF02::56

12. Which command enables you to display IPv6 - MAC mappings on the router?

    a. show arp

    b. show ip arp

    c. show ipv6 neighbors

    d. show ipv6 mac

Appendix A

Answers to Review Questions

Chapter 1

1. a, b, and e

2. a, c, and d

3. a, b, and c

4. d

Chapter 2

1. a, b, and d

2. a and b

3. a, b, c, and e

4. a, b, and e

Chapter 3

1. a, c, and d

2. f

3. b and c

4. Risk, impact, and required resources must be balanced against urgency, necessity, and business objectives.

5. a, d, and e

6. a

7. a, b, c, e, and f

8. c

9. archive config

10. b

11. logging 10.1.1.1

12. c and d

13. c

Chapter 4

1. a

2. b and c

3. a, b, and d

4. show interfaces switchport

5. MAC address table

6. d

7. c

8. a

9. a

10. b

11. b

12. b and d

Chapter 5

1. d

2. a and b

3. b

4. c

5. c

6. d

7. a

8. d

9. a

10. a and d

11. a

12. c

13. d

14. b

Chapter 6

1. a and b

2. a

3. c

4. b

5. c

6. c

7. a

8. a

Chapter 7

1. c

2. a: Active, b: Idle, c: Connect, d: Open Confirm

3. a: No neighbor, b: Exstart/ Exchange state, c: Down state, d: Init state

4. c

5. a and d

6. b

7. a and c

8. c

Chapter 8

1. c

2. a

3. b

4. c

5. c

6. b

7. d

8. b

9. b

10. b

11. a

12. c

13. d

Chapter 9

1. b

2. a

3. a

4. d

5. a and e

6. b

7. b

8. b

9. a

10. b and d

Chapter 10

1. d

2. b

3. b and d

4. b

5. c

6. c

7. b

8. a

9. b and c

10. e

11. c

12. c

Index

Symbols

A

B

D

S

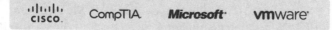